LEGAL ETHICS
and SOCIAL MEDIA

A Practitioner's Handbook

JAN L. JACOBOWITZ AND JOHN G. BROWNING

SECOND
EDITION

AMERICAN**BAR**ASSOCIATION

Center for Professional
Responsibility

Cover design by ABA Design

Printed in the United States of America.

26 25 24 23 22   5 4 3 2 1

Library of Congress Cataloging-in-Publication Data

Names: Jacobowitz, Jan L, author. | Browning, John G, author. | Center for
    Professional Responsibility (American Bar Association), sponsoring body.
Title: Legal ethics and social media : a practitioner's handbook / Jan L
    Jacobowitz and John G Browning.
Description: Second edition. | Chicago, Illinois: American Bar Association,
    [2022] | Includes bibliographical references and index. | Summary: "As
    technology impacts what we do as a profession and arguably improves how
    we do it, lawyers need to know that our existing rules of ethics still
    apply in a brave new world of status updates, tweets, Instagram
    followings, YouTube uploads, and since the first edition-Zoom and other
    video platforms. And as our book details, the tension between the
    inexorable advance of technology and the comparatively slow pace of the
    law translates to a world in which we need all the guidance we can get
    in shaping our digital communications to our ethical
    responsibilities"-- Provided by publisher.
Identifiers: LCCN 2022023104 (print) | LCCN 2022023105 (ebook) |
    ISBN 9781639051960 (paperback) | ISBN 9781639051977 (epub)
Subjects: LCSH: Legal ethics--United States. | Social media--Law and
    legislation--United States. | Electronic evidence--United States. |
    Internet in legal services--United States.
Classification: LCC KF306 .J336 2022 (print) | LCC KF306 (ebook) |
    DDC 174/.30973--dc23/eng/20220830
LC record available at https://lccn.loc.gov/2022023104
LC ebook record available at https://lccn.loc.gov/2022023105

Discounts are available for books ordered in bulk. Special consideration is given to state bars, CLE programs, and other bar-related organizations. Inquire at Book Publishing, ABA Publishing, American Bar Association, 321 N. Clark Street, Chicago, Illinois 60654-7598.

www.shopABA.org

In loving memory of my father, B. Paul Jacobowitz,
an early adopter of all things digital and forever
my touchstone. And in loving memory of my
mother, Ruth S. Jacobowitz, a wonderful
role model, an accomplished writer, and
a person who always joined the dance.
Jan L. Jacobowitz

In loving memory of my late parents,
Walter W. Browning Jr. and Claire A. Browning,
with gratitude for the many ethics lessons
they imparted to me over the
years—whether they knew it or not.
John G. Browning

··

"The only way to make sense out of change is to plunge into it, move with it, and join the dance."

—Alan Watts

··

Contents

. . . .

1

When J.D. Means "Just Don't" Know, Digital Competence Is Essential

2

The "Duty to Google": Representing Clients in the Digital Age

7

Through the Prosecutorial Looking Glass: Prosecutors, Ethics, and Social Media   133

QUESTION

8

"Friends" with No Benefits? Judges, Legal Ethics, and Social Media   147

QUESTIONS

9

Cover Your Digital Assets! Social Media's Impact on the Transactional Lawyer   195

QUESTION

5

Digital Hide-and-Seek? Preservation and Spoliation of Evidence

QUESTIONS

6

Juror, Juror on the (Social Media) Wall, Who's the Fairest of Them All?

QUESTIONS

10

Attorney Advertising in an Age of LinkedIn, Twitter, and Blogs

QUESTIONS

11

They Said *What* about Me? Ethically Filtering Your Response to a Negative Online Review

QUESTIONS

About the Authors

Jan L. Jacobowitz is the founder and owner of Legal Ethics Advisor, a full-service legal ethics consulting firm that provides risk management, training, and expert witness testimony. She is also an adjunct professor at University of Miami School of Law, where she was previously a full-time Lecturer in Law and the Director of the Professional Responsibility and Ethics Program (PREP). Under Professor Jacobowitz's direction, PREP was a 2012 recipient of the American Bar Association's E. Smythe Gambrell Award—the leading national award for a professionalism program. She is also a Fellow of the ABA Foundation.

Ms. Jacobowitz is a past president of the Association of Professional Responsibility Lawyers and also currently serves as the cochair of its Future of Lawyering Committee. She has also served as the vice chairman of the Broward Selection/Oversight Committee for the Inspector General's Office and as a commissioner on the Miami-Dade Commission on Ethics and Public Service, and she remains a member of the Anti-Defamation League Civil Rights Committee.

Ms. Jacobowitz has a J.D. from George Washington University and a B.S. in Speech from Northwestern University. She is admitted to practice in the District of Columbia, Florida, and California, and is a certified civil court mediator. Prior to devoting herself to legal education, she practiced law for more than twenty years. She began her career as a Legal Aid attorney in the District of Columbia; prosecuted Nazi war criminals at the Office of Special Investigations of the US Department of Justice; was in private practice with general practice and commercial litigation firms in Washington, D.C. and Miami; and served as in-house counsel for a large Miami-based corporation.

Ms. Jacobowitz has presented at hundreds of Ethics Continuing Legal Education Seminars throughout the country. She has written and been a featured speaker or panelist on topics such as Legal Ethics in Social Media and Advertising, Lawyers' First Amendment Rights, Cultural Awareness in the Practice of Law, Mindful Ethics, and Cybersecurity for Lawyers. She also teaches courses in Social Media and the Law and Mindful Ethics: Professional Responsibility for Lawyers in the Digital Age. Ms. Jacobowitz is often quoted in national publications, and her work is widely cited.

John G. Browning has been a partner in the Texas offices of several large national law firms, in addition to managing his own law firm. He is licensed in Texas and Oklahoma and handles civil litigation in state and federal courts, in areas ranging from employment and intellectual property to commercial cases and defense of products liability, professional liability, media law, and general negligence matters. He also served as a Justice on Texas' Fifth Court of Appeals. Justice Browning has thirty-two years of trial and appellate experience. He received his Bachelor of Arts with general and departmental honors from Rutgers University in 1986, where he was a National Merit Scholar and member of Phi Beta Kappa. He received his Juris Doctor from the University of Texas School of Law in 1989.

He is the author of two previous books on social media and the law: *The Lawyer's Guide to Social Networking: Understanding Social Media's Impact on the Law* (West 2010) and the *Social Media and Litigation Practice Guide* (West 2014). Justice Browning is also a contributing author to ten other books, the author of over forty-five published law review articles, as well as numerous articles for regional and national legal publications. His work has been cited in over 400 law review articles, in practice guides in eleven states, and by courts in New York, Texas, California, Maryland, Tennessee, Illinois, Washington D.C., Puerto Rico, and Florida. He has been quoted as a leading authority on social media and the law by such publications as *the New York Times, the Wall Street Journal, USA Today, Law 360, Time, the National Law Journal*, the *ABA Journal, WIRED*, and *Inside Counsel*. His work has been recognized with four Burton Awards for Distinguished Achievement in Legal Writing, the Texas Bar Foundation's Outstanding Law Review Article Award, the DRI's G. Duffield Smith Outstanding Publication Award, and the State Bar of Texas Presidents' Certificate of Merit, among other accolades.

Justice Browning currently serves as Distinguished Jurist in Residence and Professor of Law at Faulkner University's Thomas Goode Jones School of Law. He also serves as Chair of the Institute for Law and Technology at The Center for American and International Law. He is a past Chair of the Computer and Technology Section of the State Bar of Texas. A former member of the Professional Ethics

Committee of the State Bar of Texas, Justice Browning has received the highest honors for ethics and professionalism that a Texas lawyer can receive, the Lola Wright Foundation Award from the Texas Bar Foundation, the Jim Bowman Professionalism Award from the State Bar College, and the Luther "Luke" Soules Award from the State Bar of Texas Litigation Section. He is a frequent speaker on legal ethics at Continuing Legal Education seminars and legal symposia all over the country.

Acknowledgments

· ·

A book is a collaborative effort, and with gratitude we acknowledge those who have assisted us. We thank Sarah Forbes Orwig, Art Garwin, and Mary McDermott for the opportunity to combine our years of knowledge and for their meaningful insights and helpful guidance. And as co-authors, we each offer our own following acknowledgments.

From Jan:
Thanks to my esteemed co-author and cherished friend, John G. Browning—your unique combination of generous spirit, quick wit, and amazing intellect renders you not only a force with which to reckon, but also an amazing colleague. And to my wonderful children and grandchildren—Ryan, Jeff, Laurel, Asher, and Mackenzie—who are the wind beneath my wings and without whom neither books nor anything else in life would have meaning.

From John:
A book like this doesn't happen without the efforts of many people. First and foremost, thank you to my distinguished co-author and dear friend Jan Jacobowitz, for inviting me on this journey. You are brilliant, patient, dedicated, and humble. Finally, nothing I do would be possible—or enjoyable—without the love and support of my wife, Lisa, who has been my rock for over thirty years.

Preface

· ·

"Commit the oldest sins the newest kind of ways."
—Shakespeare, *Henry IV,*
Part 2, Act 4, Scene 5

The Bard of Avon may not have had a Facebook account or a Twitter handle, but he certainly knew that even as times changed and new inventions transformed society, mankind would still fall prey to age-old character flaws—they would simply manifest themselves in shiny new ways. And so it is with social media. These platforms enable people, including lawyers, to share all kinds of information with potentially worldwide audiences and at the speed of a search engine. Technology has truly altered the legal landscape and improved the speed and efficiency with which we can provide legal services, but it has also provided new ways for the unwary or uninformed lawyer to commit the "oldest sins," like breaching attorney-client confidentiality, making misrepresentations to third parties, or engaging in *ex parte* communications.

Why is a second edition of a book like this necessary? Because even as technology impacts what we do as a profession and arguably improves how we do it, lawyers need to know that our existing rules of ethics still apply in a brave new world of status updates, tweets, Instagram followings, YouTube uploads, and—since the first edition—Zoom and other video platforms. And as our book details, the tension between the inexorable advance of technology and the comparatively slow pace of the law translates to a world in which we need all the guidance we can get in shaping our digital communications to our ethical responsibilities.

We wrote this book to assist all lawyers, whether a millennial just embarking on practice, a somewhat tech-conversant lawyer who's comfortable enough to tap away at a keyboard but who still has uncertainty about where the ethical boundary lines are drawn, or even a legal Luddite who's being dragged kicking and screaming into the digital age. After all, we feel your pain. Neither of us came from a tech background.

As authors and attorneys, we continue to be fascinated by the evolving nature of social media, and we are particularly compelled by social media's impact on legal ethics and the practice of law. We've witnessed social media (and technology generally) go from being regarded as merely another useful tool in the attorney's toolbox to being viewed as a vital part of providing competent representation in the twenty-first century. Being a competent lawyer now requires more than what it did in "the good old days," such as keeping abreast of new case law or statutory changes. Attorneys need to understand the benefits and risks of technology in order to do their jobs competently. The COVID-19 pandemic has not only heightened that need, but also thrust the legal profession forward at warp speed. Social media is not only encompassed within the definition of technology, but also as we have seen since the publication of the first edition, social media platforms remain center stage to life and legal events.

We realize that lawyers are not only extremely busy people, but also that they occupy a broad spectrum of knowledge about social media, so we decided to share our knowledge in bite-size chunks—a question-and-answer format so that a lawyer with a particular question can zero in on our guidance. For those who may be interested in an overview of social media's impact throughout the practice of law, the chapters provide an itinerary to tour through the various aspects of legal practice.

We hope in continuing to share our interest and insights to smooth the road ahead by providing a road map that both cautions lawyers to avoid the ethical land mines lying in wait for the uninformed traveler and, also, offers inspiration for the adventurer who has been compelled in the past few years to explore and embrace the digital age.

Introduction

From Scriveners to Streaming: Technology, Legal Ethics, and the Practice of Law

A book focused on legal ethics in the digital age must inevitably begin with a look at the technological advancements that have changed the way we live and, ultimately, the way we practice law. Since the industrial revolution, technology has created dramatically different business models and produced products that have made our lives more efficient and, some would say, more hectic and complicated. As society moved from the industrial age to the information age, technology progressed at a dizzying pace.

How does technological innovation directly impact the legal profession? Just as technology alters the way we all live, so too does it change the practice of law. A look back at the legal profession of the nineteenth century reveals that the technology of the time caused law firms to shift from the use of male scriveners, who hand copied and proofread documents, to the implementation of early copy machines, vertical filing systems, and the typewriter.[1] The typewriter brought women into law firms, thereby changing law firm culture. Although typists were originally the male scriveners who were willing to adapt to the "new technology," over time female typists became the norm.

As the twentieth century began, another late nineteenth-century innovation would impact the legal profession—the telephone. Perhaps not surprisingly, the generally conservative legal profession resisted the new technology.

---

[1] M.H. Hoeflich, *From Scriveners to Typewriters: Document Production in the Nineteenth Century Law Office*, 16 GREEN BAG 2D 395, 396 (2013).

In fact, Clarence Seward, who would later become managing partner at Cravath, Swaine & Moore, opposed the use of both the typewriter and the telephone. He saw these innovations as destructive forces in American society.[2] Similarly, when John Foster Dulles joined Sullivan & Cromwell in 1911, he noted that many lawyers held fast to the belief that proper communication with clients required a hand-delivered letter.[3] Sullivan & Cromwell did not install a phone in the office until about ten years after it became available. The phone was initially installed in a separate office; employees were instructed not to use the phone, but rather only to answer the phone when it rang.[4]

Of course, the typewriter and the telephone were eventually embraced and allowed for tremendous growth in the legal profession. As this early technology was transforming the practice of law, another significant development occurred early in the twentieth century—the first Canons of Professional Ethics was adopted by the American Bar Association (ABA) on August 27, 1908.[5] The first Canons appeared the same year that Henry Ford produced his first Model T, Frenchman Henri Farman piloted the first passenger flight, and Robert Perry set sail for the North Pole—technology taking root to enhance mobility.

Viewed in this perspective, the ABA professional ethics rules emerged shortly after the invention of the typewriter and the telephone in an era of innovation and "firsts." The telephone and the communication technology that followed it brought a cultural change in communication with clients and gave rise to legal ethics questions of communication and confidentiality. The cordless phone, the telefax machine, the cellular phone, and email each caused the legal profession to pause and consider whether the technology was appropriate for client communication and confidentiality.[6] In each

---

[2] Catherine J. Lanctot, *Attorney-Client Relationships in Cyberspace: The Peril and the Promise*, 49 DUKE L.J. 147, 162 n.34 (1999).

[3] *Id.* at 164.

[4] *Id.*

[5] MODEL RULES OF PROF'L CONDUCT PREFACE (2001).

[6] *See* ABA Standing Comm. on Ethics & Prof'l Responsibility, Formal Op. 99-413 (1999), https://cryptome.org/jya/fo99-413.htm [hereinafter ABA formal Op. 99-413]; ABA Standing Comm. on Ethics & Prof'l Responsibility, Formal Op. 11-459 (2011), *Compare* St. Bar of Ariz., Formal Ethics Op. 95-11 (1995) (finding lawyer can use a cellular phone to communicate with his or her client but must take adequate

of these situations, it was necessary for a small group of lawyers to understand the technology so that the ABA and other bar associations could opine on its appropriate use.

Today, the Internet and related technology have led to the creation of cloud computing, e-filing, outsourcing, metadata, e-discovery, wearable technology, and social networking. Some of these innovations have impacted the process of practicing law, while others have infiltrated the substantive nature of legal practice. For example, a litigator does not necessarily need to understand the inner workings of cloud computing but needs to know how to appropriately use it. On the other hand, a litigator does need to understand more about social media networks because critical evidence in his case may be lying in wait.

Consequently, in August 2012, the ABA enacted an amendment to the comment to Model Rule 1.1 (Competence) to further define a competent lawyer as *one who understands the benefits and disadvantages of technology*.[7] As of the writing of the second edition of this book, approximately forty states have adopted this language, and other states are still considering the addition of it to their state bar's rule of competence.[8] The Florida Bar not only added this language, but also increased its state bar Continuing Legal Education (CLE) requirements from thirty (every three years) to thirty-three to include a three-credit technology requirement.[9]

---

precautions to avoid revealing client confidences) *with* Mass. Bar Assoc., Formal Ethics Op. 94-5 (1994) (finding that lawyer cannot discuss confidential matters with a client on a cellular telephone without client informed consent if there is any "nontrivial risk" that the confidential information may be overheard).

[7] MODEL RULES OF PROF'L CONDUCT R. 1.1 cmt. (2016) (emphasis added).

[8] Robert Ambrogi, Law Sites https://www.lawsitesblog.com/tech -competence (last visited February 7, 2022).

[9] Florida Supreme Court, No. SC16-574 In Re: Amendments to Rules Regulating the Florida Bar 4-1.1 and 6-10.3 (Sept. 29, 2016).

Florida also added the following language to its comments: "Competent representation may also involve the association or retention of a non-lawyer advisor of established technological competence in the field in question. Competent representation also involves safeguarding confidential information relating to the representation, including, but not limited to, electronic transmissions and communications." Available at http://www.abajournal.com/files/OP-SC16-574 _AMDS_FL_BAR_SEPT29_(1)_copy.pdf.

The early reluctance of the legal profession to adopt the telephone rang true in 2017 during the publication of this book as many lawyers had continued to shun technology and resisted adopting new methods of practice. The adoption of the ABA language, along with the use of new technology by both clients and a millennial generation of lawyers, had begun to catapult the profession forward as evidenced by increasing numbers of ethics advisory opinions, disciplinary cases, court opinions, CLE seminars, articles, and books focused on various aspects of technology and social media.

Then, what some have referred to as a black swan event—the COVID-19 pandemic—changed the world and the legal profession with it.[10] Confined to our homes and disconnected physically from our colleagues, clients, opposing counsel, and courtrooms, the legal profession had to suddenly embrace technology to survive.

Remarkably to some, resilience carried the day and the legal profession not only survived, but also in many ways thrived. Silver linings abound: work from home can be productive; traveling may no longer be necessary for short hearings and distant depositions; and lawyers understand the need for technology. Unfortunately, however, ethical land mines remain, and perhaps the ensuing uncertainty and stress of the pandemic contributed to lawyers' continuing missteps on social media.[11]

Bottom line: The use of technology, including social media, is no longer an option; it is a matter of both professional competence and survival.

---

[10] Jan L. Jacobowitz, *Chaos or Continuity? The Legal Profession: From Antiquity to the Digital Age, the Pandemic, and Beyond,* 23 VANDERBILT JOURNAL OF ENTERTAINMENT AND TECHNOLOGY LAW 279 (2021).

[11] Jan L. Jacobowitz, *Negative Commentary—Negative Consequences: Legal Ethics, Social Media, and the Impact of Explosive Commentary,* 11 ST. MARY'S JOURNAL ON LEGAL MALPRACTICE & ETHICS 312 (2021).

CHAPTER 1

When J.D. Means "Just Don't" Know, Digital Competence Is Essential

. . . .

Because today's social media networking could not exist without the Internet and other innovations, we spend some time addressing a few digital-age questions about technology that impacts the process of practicing law. While there are entire books written on some of these subjects, our goal here is to raise awareness and provide some basic information. In the next chapter, we address technology as it impacts the substantive practice of law.

QUESTIONS

1. What is the cloud, and how may it be used?

The "cloud" or cloud computing is today's updated document filing and retention system. While vertical filing systems and file cabinets offered the nineteenth-century lawyer a more efficient manner to store documents in the office, today's technology offers the practitioner a virtual file cabinet, thereby potentially eliminating the need for both office file cabinets and large computer servers.[1]

Simply stated, the cloud is software that is delivered to your computer via the Internet rather than installed directly on your computer. It allows lawyers to store client files and other work product on the software provider's remote servers, thereby increasing a law practice's storage space without

---

[1] M.H. Hoeflich, *From Scriveners to Typewriters: Document Production in the Nineteenth Century Law Office*, 16 GREEN BAG 2D 395, 396 (2013).

the need to increase the law practice's office space, increase computer capacity, or have the law practice purchase its own server. Whether cloud computing is advisable from an economic standpoint is a business decision. If deemed economically advisable, then there are ethical considerations.

The advent of cloud computing has given rise to at least thirty states issuing ethics advisory opinions that provide guidance for appropriate use.[2] The underlying concern is generally a combination of the ethical requirements of competence, diligence, and the confidentiality of client information.

The opinions overall caution the practitioner to carefully investigate the vendor, ensure confidentiality, consult with clients and obtain consent when highly sensitive information is involved, stay abreast of changes in technology, and ensure that the practitioner can retrieve his or her data if the vendor goes out of business or the practitioner changes vendors. The basic standard applied is "reasonable care"—the same standard that has been used throughout the years when evaluating the permissible use of cordless phones, cellular phones, and email communication.[3]

2. What is outsourcing, and under what conditions is it acceptable?

Outsourcing is a term of art that became popular in the past decade as offshore companies began offering legal services, such as legal research and document preparation, at low costs to US law firms. The use of the term has expanded to connote any outsourcing of administrative or legal services, whether to a local company or to one located abroad. (Indeed, cloud computing is a form of outsourcing.)

Just as hiring typists in the nineteenth century provided efficiency and economies of scale, today many law firms have concluded that outsourcing document review, legal research, or administrative functions is a more efficient and economic way to conduct the business of law. Large firms require fewer full-time employees. Smaller firms can take on larger matters without hiring additional employees and increasing overhead.

Outsourcing is another industry, fueled by the Internet and technology, that has caused several state and city bar associations to issue ethics advisory

---

[2] Joshua Lenon, A List of All Ethics Opinions on Cloud Computing for Lawyers, Clio, July, 20 2021 https://www.clio.com/blog/cloud-computing -lawyers-ethics-opinions/ (last visited July 26, 2022).

[3] *Id.* (The Clio chart provides links to each of the state opinions.)

opinions to highlight many of the legal ethics rules that are implicated.[4] The ABA captured the gist of these opinions in August 2012 when it enacted amendments to the comments to Rule 1.1 (Competence) and Rule 5.3 (Responsibilities Regarding Nonlawyer Assistants).[5]

The comments to Rule 1.1 and Rule 5.3, along with the ethics opinions, caution that outsourcing should ordinarily be done after receiving client consent.[6] The outsourcing company should be fully vetted as to qualifications of its employees, where the work will be performed, what procedures

---

[4] *See* ABA Standing Comm. on Ethics & Prof'l Responsibility, Formal Op. 08-451 (2008); St. Bar of Cal., Standing Comm. on Prof'l Responsibility & Conduct, Formal Op. 2004-165 (2004); Colo. Bar Ass'n, Formal Op. 121 (2009), http://www.cobar.org/Portals/COBAR /repository/ethicsOpinions/FormalEthicsOpinion_121_2011.pdf; Fla. St. Bar Prof'l Ethics Comm., Ethics Op. 07-2 (2008); N.C. St. Bar, Formal Op. 2007-12 (2008), https://www.ncbar.gov/for-lawyers/ethics /adopted-opinions/2007-formal-ethics-opinion-12/; N.Y. St, Bar Ass'n. Comm. on Prof'l Ethics, Ethics Op. 762 (2003); The Ass'n of the Bar of the City of New York Comm. on Prof'l & Jud. Ethics, Formal Op. 2006-3 (2006), http://www.nycbar.org/member-and-career-services /committees/reports-listing/reports/detail/formal-opinion-2006-3 -outsourcing-legal-support-services-overseas-avoiding-aiding-a -non-lawyer-in-the-unauthorized-practice-of-law-supervision-of -non-lawyers-competent-representation-preserving-client-confidences -and-secrets-conflicts-checking-appropriate-billing-client-consent; Ohio Sup. Ct. Bd. of Comm'rs on Grievances & Discipline, Advisory Op. 2009-06 (2009); Ass'n of the Bar of the City of New York Comm. on Prof'l Responsibility, Report on the Outsourcing of Legal Services Overseas (2009), http://www.nycbar.org/member-and-career-services /committees/reports-listing/reports/detail/the-outsourcing-of-legal -services-overseas-november-2009; San Diego Cty. Bar Ass'n, Ethics Opinion 2007-1 (2007), https://www.sdcba.org/index.cfm?Pg=ethics opinion07-1; L.A. Cty. Bar Ass'n Prof'l Responsibility & Ethics Comm., Opinion No. 518 (2006), http://www.lacba.org/docs/default-source /ethics-opinions/archived-ethics-opinions/ethics-opinion-518.pdf; D.C. Bar, Ethics Opinion 362 (2012). (All sources in this footnote hereinafter "Outsourcing Opinions").

[5] Model Rules of Prof'l Conduct R. 1.1 comment 6 (Am. Bar Ass'n, 2016); Model Rules of Prof'l Conduct R. 5.3 comments 3 & 4 (Am. Bar Ass'n, 2016).

[6] Outsourcing Opinions, *supra* note 16; Model Rules of Prof'l Conduct R. 1.2 (Am. Bar Ass'n, 2016) (Scope of Representation); Model Rules of Prof'l Conduct R. 1.4 (Am. Bar Ass'n, 2016) (Communication).

and physical security are employed to protect data, and the relevant privacy laws in the company's jurisdiction.[7] The client should only be billed the net costs of outsourcing, with possibly a small attorney fee for supervision and review depending on the circumstance.[8] The outsourcing company and its employees should be bound by confidentiality agreements.[9] A conflict check should be conducted so that the outsourcing company is not working for opposing parties in a case.[10] A lawyer should supervise to ensure that the outsourcing company's conduct conforms to the legal ethics rules.[11] A lawyer should also make sure that he or she is not delegating legal service tasks to an outsourcing company that may be interpreted as encouraging the unauthorized practice of law.[12]

3. **What about using my laptop at the airport or at a coffee shop on the free Wi-Fi?**

California's ethics opinion 2010-179 warns that an attorney's use of a public Wi-Fi system places the lawyer at risk of violating his or her ethical duties of competence and confidentiality, unless he or she takes appropriate precautions such as using a personal firewall, file encryption, and encryption of wireless transmissions.[13] Depending on the sensitivity of the matter, the attorney may need to avoid the use of a public Wi-Fi or notify the client of the inherent dangers of a potential disclosure of confidential information and obtain the client's consent.

The Florida Bar Best Practices for Effective Electronic Communication cautions attorneys to avoid public Wi-Fi; turn off the sharing files feature on

---

[7] Outsourcing Opinions, *supra* note 4; MODEL RULES OF PROF'L CONDUCT R. 1.3 (AM. BAR ASS'N, 2016) (Diligence).

[8] Outsourcing Opinions, *supra* note 4; MODEL RULES OF PROF'L CONDUCT R. 1.5 (AM. BAR ASS'N, 2016) (Fees).

[9] Outsourcing Opinions, *supra* note 4; MODEL RULES OF PROF'L CONDUCT R. 1.6 (AM. BAR ASS'N, 2016) (Confidentiality).

[10] Outsourcing Opinions, *supra* note 4; MODEL RULES OF PROF'L CONDUCT R. 1.7 (AM. BAR ASS'N, 2016) (Conflicts).

[11] Outsourcing Opinions, *supra* note 4; MODEL RULES OF PROF'L CONDUCT R. 5.3 (AM. BAR ASS'N, 2016) (Responsibilities Regarding Nonlawyer Assistants).

[12] Outsourcing Opinions, *supra* note 4; MODEL RULES OF PROF'L CONDUCT R. 5.3 (AM. BAR ASS'N, 2016) (Unauthorized Practice of Law).

[13] St. Bar of Cal. Standing Comm. On Prof'l Responsibility & Conduct, Formal Op. No. 2010-179 (2010).

a laptop; and beware of other threats, including someone looking over your shoulder or theft of a device that is not encrypted and password protected.[14]

There have been many articles written on the basics—encryption (a process that transforms language into a code so that it may not be read while in transit) and password selection and protection. ("Password" and "123456" are reportedly two of the most common passwords being used and clearly not the most competent choices.)[15] Unencrypted emails have been analogized to the mailing of a postcard where everyone may see what the sender has written.[16] While ethics opinions have required reasonable care and have not deemed email encryption mandatory, the topic provides an ongoing source of debate.[17]

A complete exploration of this topic is beyond the scope of this book, but as mentioned above, it is included to raise awareness. The old saying that

---

[14] THE FLA. BAR, BEST PRACTICES FOR EFFECTIVE ELECTRONIC COMMUNICATION (2015).

[15] Jamie Condliffe, *The 25 Most Popular Passwords of 2015: We're All Such Idiots*, GIZMODO (Jan. 19, 2016, 12:01 AM) http://gizmodo.com/the-25-most-popular-passwords-of-2015-were-all-such-id-1753591514.

[16] David G. Ries & John W. Simek, *Encryption Made Simple for Lawyers*, 29 ABA: GPSOLO (Nov./Dec. 2012). (Parts of the paper are adapted from prior materials prepared by the author, including David G. Ries, *Safeguarding Confidential Data: Your Ethical and Legal Obligations*, 36 L. PRAC. 49 (2010) and David G. Ries, *Cybersecurity for Attorneys: Understanding the Ethical Obligations*, L. PRAC. TODAY (2012).

[17] *E.g.*, ABA Standing Comm. on Ethics & Prof'l Responsibility, Formal Op. 99-413 (1999), https://cryptome.org/jya/fo99-413.htm [hereinafter ABA formal Op. 99-413] ("based upon current technology and law as we are informed of it . . . a lawyer sending confidential client information by unencrypted e-mail does not violate Model Rule 1.6(a) . . . this opinion does not, however, diminish a lawyer's obligation to consider with her client the sensitivity of the communication, the costs of its disclosure, and the relative security of the contemplated medium of communication. Particularly strong protective measures are warranted to guard against the disclosure of highly sensitive matters."); *see also* D.C. Bar, Ethics Op. 281 (1998), (Transmission of Confidential Information by Electronic Mail) ("In most circumstances, transmission of confidential information by unencrypted electronic mail does not per se violate the confidentiality rules of the legal profession. However, individual circumstances may require greater means of security."). *But see* Peter Geraghty & Susan Michmerhuizen, *Encryption Conniption*, ABA: YOUR ABA-EYE ON ETHICS (July 2015).

"a wise person knows what he does not know"[18] is applicable—attorneys must realize that there are both technical and ethical issues at play in the appropriate use of laptops, tablets, and smartphones in a public setting. They need to either become educated as to proper use or avoid working in public spaces.

4. Do I need to be concerned about cybersecurity when I am working in my office or in my home?

The short answer is a resounding YES! The duties of competence and confidentiality compel lawyers to understand and take precautions to protect the confidentiality of client documents.[19] Moreover, savvy clients are beginning to ask about cybersecurity, and some corporate clients are requiring cybersecurity audits before selecting or continuing with a law firm.[20]

The ABA has taken several steps to encourage lawyers and law firms to move forward and to embrace the need to attend to cybersecurity. In fact, in 2012, in addition to the general proviso to understand the benefits and disadvantages of technology added to the comment to Rule 1.1, the ABA enacted amendments to Rule 1.6 (Confidentiality) and to the comment to Rule 1.6.[21]

The section that was added to Rule 1.6 requires "a lawyer to make reasonable efforts to prevent the inadvertent or unauthorized disclosure of, or unauthorized access to, information relating to the representation of a client."[22] Comment 18 to the rule, Acting Competently to Preserve Confidentiality, explains that a lawyer will not be in violation of the rule if he or she has

---

[18] The adage perhaps originates with Socrates: "I am the wisest man alive, for I know one thing, and that is that I know nothing." *Socrates Quotes*, BRAINYQUOTE, http://www.brainyquote.com/quotes/quotes/s/socrates125872.html (last visited Sept. 20, 2016).

[19] MODEL RULES OF PROF'L CONDUCT r. 1.1 (Am. Bar Ass'n, 2016); MODEL RULES OF PROF'L CONDUCT R. 1.6 (AM. BAR ASS'N, 2016).

[20] *See* Kenneth N. Rashbaum, et al., *Cybersecurity: Business Imperative for Law Firms*, N.Y. L. J. (Dec. 10, 2014), http://www.newyorklawjournal.com/id=1202678493487/Cybersecurity-Business-Imperative-for-Law-Firms?slreturn=20141127155939; *see also* Sharon D. Nelson & John W. Simek, Clients Demand Law Firm Cyber Audits, 39(6) L. PRAC. 22 (2013).

[21] MODEL RULES OF PROF'L CONDUCT R. 1.6 & comment 18 (Am. Bar Ass'n, 2016).

[22] *Id.*

made reasonable efforts to protect client confidentiality. Reasonable efforts are defined by considering such factors as the sensitivity of the information, the likelihood of disclosure if additional safeguards are not employed, the cost of additional safeguards, the difficulty of implementing these safeguards, and the adverse impact on the lawyer's ability to represent clients. The comment also notes that a lawyer may be subject to other privacy laws that fall outside of the ethics rules.[23]

The amendments to Rules 1.1 and 1.6 mirror the advice provided in many state ethics opinions with regard to outsourcing, cloud computing, emailing, using public Wi-Fi, and using office copiers and other technological devices. For example, Florida's 2010 opinion focused on the use of modern copy machines, which contain hard drives.[24] The opinion cautions lawyers that if they choose to use devices that contain storage media, then they must identify and address potential threats to confidentiality, maintain an inventory of all of these devices, supervise nonlawyers' use of the devices, and ensure that the device is sanitized when it is returned to the vendor or sold.[25]

Additionally, in 2014, the ABA passed the following resolution:

RESOLVED, That The American Bar Association encourages all private and public sector organizations to develop, implement, and maintain an appropriate cybersecurity program that complies with applicable ethical and legal obligations and is tailored to the nature and scope of the organization and the data and systems to be protected.[26]

The message here is to be aware and obtain assistance.

The message applies to both the traditional law office and the home office on which there was less focus prior to the pandemic. While many law offices already had onsite or readily available IT assistance prior to the pandemic, cybersecurity became more challenging when almost everyone began working from home.

Lawyers found themselves sharing office space with family members, smart devices, and sometimes even a shared family computer. The devices

---

[23] *Id.*

[24] The Fla. Bar, Opinion 10-2 (2010).

[25] *Id.*

[26] ABA RES. 109 (2014).

should be using a network that meets cybersecure standards to protect client confidentiality, and lawyers also need to be cognizant of the shared spaces. Whether a client communication takes place on the phone or through an Internet platform, the client's conversation should remain private. Similarly, client files, whether electronic or paper, should be out of reach of others. Whether the other is a child logging on to do homework or a roommate in need of the dining room table that is covered with client documents, lawyers need to ensure that safeguards are in place.

Moreover, as work from home became the pandemic norm, so did video platforms such as Zoom, Blue Jeans, and Go to Meeting, to name a few. These platforms gave rise to both the concerns inherent in outsourcing your information and client confidentiality—the details of the technology and the humans using (or misusing them) became a focus of discussion.

In fact, there is an entire cottage industry that developed to assist lawyers and other businesses in developing strategies that comport with the reasonable efforts standard to achieve a more cyber-secure environment—the industry has grown by geometric proportion since the pandemic. You may want to start by taking a look at another book published by the ABA, *Locked Down—Information Security for Lawyers*, by Sharon Nelson, John Simek, and David Ries.[27] The authors have an incredible amount of knowledge about both the legal ethics rules and cybersecurity, which they communicate in an easily understandable manner both in their book and on their website. Regardless of where you begin . . . just begin!

---

[27] SHARON D. NELSON, ET AL., LOCKED DOWN: INFORMATION SECURITY FOR LAWYERS (ABA 2016).

CHAPTER 2

The "Duty to Google": Representing Clients in the Digital Age

The previous chapter discussed how technology has impacted the process by which we practice law; in other words, the systems through which we communicate with clients, store documents, delegate work, and otherwise employ a business model that is ethical, efficient, and profitable. The options have become vast, and the technology has become sophisticated to such a degree that competent lawyers now need to understand its advantages and disadvantages.

While technological innovations, such as the telephone and copy machine, have long impacted the business aspects of a law firm, the Internet and the resulting innovations of the digital age have uniquely invaded the substantive process of practicing law. The competent lawyer today needs to understand how to employ technology to investigate a case and effectively represent a client.

A lawyer who fails to "Google" a potential client and review that client's online presence may find himself or herself representing a client who is claiming a severe injury and disability, while simultaneously posting vacation pictures on Facebook that reveal her ability to waterski and zip line. Or assume that your client's claims are legitimate and that she is entitled to a default judgment. After attempting to locate the defendant through traditional methods, you are unsuccessful; however, the judge refuses to enter a default judgment on behalf of your client because you failed to search on Google for the defendant—a so-called "duty to Google" is emerging in the practice of law.[1]

The *Cannedy* case highlights another unfortunate failure to embrace technology and social media. A criminal defense lawyer failed to honor his client's request to speak to a witness who had seen the victim's online message to her friends.[2] The defendant was accused and convicted of molesting his stepdaughter. On appeal, the defendant prevailed on his ineffective assistance of counsel claim based on the fact that the stepdaughter had admitted in her message that the allegations against the defendant were not true; she had alleged false allegations in an attempt to be permitted to live with her biological father.[3]

The duty to Google may also apply to substituted service of process. Several courts in the United States have recognized service of process through Facebook.[4] Initially, Facebook service was approved in cases in which the defendant was located abroad; more recently two New York judges allowed service through Facebook in domestic family law cases, finding that it was the best alternative for providing the defendants with adequate notice.[5] In fact, Utah's rules for substitute service specifically mention that if a claimant can locate the defendant on social media, such as Facebook, the court may approve social media substitute service.[6]

---

[1] *See, e.g.*, Munster v. Groce, 829 N.E.2d 52 (Ind. Ct. App. 2005); Dubois v. Butler, 901 So.2d. 1029, 1031 (Fla. 4th DCA 2005) (Attorney who used directory assistance as the sole means to locate a defendant was admonished by the court for using a method that was the equivalent of relying on "the horse and buggy and the eight track stereo.").

[2] Cannedy v. Adams, EDCV 08-1230-CJC (E), 2009 WL 3711958, at *1 (C.D. Cal. 2009), aff'd 706 F.3d 1148 (9th Cir. 2013), amended on denial of reh'g, 733 F.3d 794 (9th Cir. 2013).

[3] *Id.*

[4] *See, e.g.*, Mpafe v. Mpafe, No. 27-FA-11-3453 (D. Minn. May 10, 2011), available at http://www.scribd.com/doc/70014426/Mpafe-v-Mpafe-order; F.T.C. v PCCare247 Inc., No. 12 Civ. 7189(PAE), 2013 WL 841037, at *4 (S.D.N.Y. Mar. 7, 2013).

[5] *See* Matter of a Support Proceeding Noel B v. Anna Maria A, 2014 N.Y. Misc. LEXIS 4708 (N.Y. Fam. Ct. Sept. 12, 2014); Baidoo v. Blood-Dzraku, 48 Misc. 3d 309, 311 (N.Y. Sup. Ct. 2015).

[6] *Motion for Alternative Service*, UTAH COURTS, https://www.utcourts .gov/howto/service/alternate_service.html (last visited Sept. 4, 2016, 12:45 PM) [hereinafter Utah Alternative Service].

A duty to Google also pertains to jury selection. One Missouri court granted a new trial after it was presented with evidence of a juror lying during voir dire but admonished the attorneys. The court suggested that the digital age imbues attorneys with a responsibility to investigate jurors' online presence so that the court may avoid mistrials based on juror bias or misconduct that could have been discovered during voir dire.[7]

Of course, between the service of the complaint and selection of the jury resides the discovery process, which has been dramatically impacted by technology and social media. The failure to properly advise a client about social media evidence cost one attorney over $500,000 and a suspension of his license.[8] Other attorneys have been handicapped by adverse inference instructions.[9] And in a Delaware case, a lawyer explained, "I have to confess to this Court, I am not computer literate. I have not found presence in the cybernetic revolution. I need a secretary to help me turn on the computer. This was out of my bailiwick." The court was not sympathetic and held that "[p]rofessed technological incompetence is not an excuse for discovery misconduct."[10]

The need to be competent when dealing with e-discovery is further reinforced by California's 2015-193 ethics opinion that provides lawyers who lack competence in e-discovery with three options: (1) acquire the expertise before it is needed, (2) associate

---

[7] Johnson v. McCullough, 306 S.W.3d 551, 558–59 (Mo. 2010) (en banc). After Johnson, the Missouri Supreme Court Rules were changed to affirmatively require attorneys to conduct a review of "Case.net" before the jury is sworn. Missouri Supreme Court Rule 69.025 was added to the Rules in January 2011. Section (a) reads: "A party seeking to inquire as to the litigation history of potential jurors shall make a record of the proposed initial questions before voir dire. Failure to follow this procedure shall result in waiver of the right to inquire as to litigation history." MO. SUP. CT. R. 69.025(a) (2011). Section (b) reads: "For purposes of this Rule 69.025, a 'reasonable investigation' means review of Case.net before the jury is sworn." MO. SUP. CT. R. 69.025(b) (2011).

[8] Allied Concrete Co. v. Lester, 736 S.E.2d 699 (Va. 2013); *see* Lester v. Allied Concrete Co., Nos. CL08-150, CL09-223, Final Order (Va. Cir. Ct. Oct. 21, 2011).

[9] Gatto v. United Air Lines, Inc., 10-CV-1090-ES-SCM, 2013 WL 1285285, at *3 (D.N.J. 2013).

[10] James v. Nat'l Fin. LLC, CA No. 8931-VCL, 2014 WL 6845560, at *12 (Del. Ch. 2014).

with competent counsel or a technical consultant, or (3) decline the representation.[11] It is important to note that if an attorney associates or retains an e-discovery vendor or technical consultant, the attorney must still fulfill his or her duty to supervise—judges have issued sanctions against attorneys whose "laid-back" approach contributes to e-discovery violations.[12]

Other discovery issues newly on the horizon are the significance of Fitbit and Apple Watch data and the use of emoticons. Fitbit data caused one law enforcement agency to dismiss a victim's alleged rape report and instead charge her with filing a false report.[13] A federal court found the thumbs-up "like" symbol on Facebook to constitute protected speech,[14] and several courts have found emoticons to be relevant evidence that are entitled to contextual interpretation.[15]

Thus, as technology and social media evolve at a frenetic pace, lawyers must discover a way to walk in lockstep on the constantly changing terrain in order to remain effective advocates for their clients. The questions and answers that follow define and provide information about some of the most popular social media networks and how some of these networks have impacted the early stages of a case, such as jurisdiction and service of process.

The chapters that follow explore in more detail some of the other aspects of the practice of law that are in flux due to digital-age developments. The authors pose the questions that are being asked in the legal profession, and they provide answers based on the current state of the law and technology.

---

[11] State Bar of Cal., Standing Committee on Prof. Resp. and Conduct, Formal Op. No. 2015-193 (2015).

[12] See HM Elecs., Inc. v. R.F. Techs., Inc., 12CV2884-BAS-MDD, 2015 WL 4714908, at *24 (S.D. Cal. 2015), vacated in part, 12-CV-2884-BAS-MDD, 2016 WL 1267385 (S.D. Cal. 2016).

[13] Jacob Gershman, *Prosecutors Say Fitbit Device Exposed Fibbing in Rape Case*, WALL STREET J. (Apr. 21, 2016, 1:53 PM), http://blogs.wsj.com/law/2016/04/21/prosecutors-say-fitbit-device-exposed-fibbing-in-rape-case/.

[14] Bland v. Roberts, 730 F.3d 368, 386 (4th Cir. 2013), as amended (Sept. 23, 2013).

[15] Amanda Hess, *Exhibit A:;-): Courts Are Evaluating Emoticons as Evidence—but Nobody Really Knows What They Mean*, SLATE (Oct. 26, 2015, 4:34 PM), http://www.slate.com/articles/technology/users/2015/10/emoticons_and_emojis_as_evidence_in_court.html.

QUESTIONS

1. What is a social media network?

A social media network is a website where users may create online identities, which may exist as public or private profiles. Users may establish
relationships with other users and join various communities of users who
share connections and communicate via different types of posts or messaging services.[16]

Social media networks encompass blogs, social networking sites, forums,
wikis, and photo-sharing sites, all of which provide users with platforms to
share information, content, interests, opinions, and experiences.[17]

Most forms of social media share the same characteristics: (1) active
participation, (2) connections and sense of community, and (3) interaction
where contributions and feedback are encouraged.[18]

2. How many people participate in social media networks?

In 2021, there were 295 million social media users in the United States—
roughly three quarters of the population. The number is projected to increase
to over 302 million in 2022.[19] Globally, in 2020, 3.6 billion people participated in social media networks, and that number is expected to increase to
almost 4.41. billion by 2025.[20] On average, users access social media for
approximately almost 144 minutes per day.[21]

According to a Pew Research Center 2021 report on social media usage,
age is an indication of usage.[22] Among nineteen- to twenty-nine-year-olds,

---

[16] *Id.*

[17] Charles P. Kindregan Jr., et al., *What Is Social Media?*, 2 Mass. Prac.,
Family Law and Practice § 39:1 (2015).

[18] *Id.*

[19] Statistica, Number of Social Media Users in the United States from
2017–2026 https://www.statista.com/statistics/278409/number-of-social
-network-users-in-the-united-states/ (Last visited on February 7, 2022).

[20] Statistica, Number of Social Media Users Worldwide 2017–2025
https://www.statista.com/statistics/278414/number-of-worldwide
-social-network-users/.

[21] *Id.* https://www.statista.com/statistics/278414/number-of-worldwide
-social-network-users/.

[22] Pew Research Center Social Media Fact Sheet https://www.pew
research.org/internet/fact-sheet/social-media/ (Last visited February 7,
2022).

84 percent have at least one social media profile.[23] For those sixty-five and older, 45 percent are using social media—a substantial increase from only 2 percent in 2005.[24]

3. What are some examples of popular social media networks of which lawyers should be aware?

Facebook, Twitter, LinkedIn, Instagram, and TikTok are the most popular social media networks of which lawyers should be aware.

Facebook, currently being rebranded as Meta, is the market leader in social media platforms. There were 2.9 billion daily active users as of January 2022.[25] Facebook provides people with the opportunity to share information about themselves through vehicles such as status updates, photos, links, and videos.[26] A Facebook participant can post on other users' pages, "friend" users to become a part of their networks, send private messages through Facebook's instant messaging feature, create events, create business profile pages, and be "tagged" in other users' posts or pictures.[27] A user can also select various privacy settings, thereby controlling who may see the user's information.[28]

Twitter is a "real-time information network" that connects people with the latest news, ideas, opinions, and stories about various topics.[29] On Twitter, users share short messages known as "tweets" with other users, where they can include pictures or links as well.[30] A user can choose to share tweets with the public or designate tweets as private, where only individuals whom the user has accepted as a "follower" will be able to view the tweets.[31] Users may select various individuals, companies, public figures, or organizations to follow and see those individuals' or entities' tweets on the user's own Twitter

---

[23] *Id.*

[24] *Id.*

[25] https://www.statista.com/statistics/268136/top-15-countries-based-on-number-of-facebook-users/

[26] Mark Allen Chen, *Interactive Contracting in Social Networks*, 97 CORNELL L. REV. 1533, 1540–41 (2012).

[27] *Id.*

[28] *Id.*

[29] *Id.*

[30] *Id.*

[31] *Id.*

homepage.[32] Tweets can also be "retweeted" by other users, disseminating those tweets to whoever follows the user who retweeted the original posts.[33] Twitter has approximately 400 million users.[34]

LinkedIn is a social networking site for businesses and professionals and is primarily employment and career focused.[35] LinkedIn is similar to other sites because users can update their status, add connections, join groups, and network. Users can post their education, job history, and awards, supply information about publications and specialties, and request testimonials from their connections.[36] LinkedIn is essentially an online, interactive resume and business networking site.[37] Employers can search for candidates and advertise prospective employment opportunities.[38] As of February 2022 LinkedIn listed 800 million people as registered on LinkedIn in more than 200 countries and territories throughout the world.[39]

Instagram is a photo-sharing website that is affiliated with Facebook. On Instagram, users can "follow" other users and automatically see all the photos posted by those users on the Instagram homepage.[40] Instagram features filters and editing software for users to apply to their photos to enhance them. The pictures uploaded on Instagram are more like "day-in-the-life" images and, sometimes, artistic statements.[41] As of October 2021, Instagram had 1 billion monthly active users, up from 500 million in June 2016.[42] Instagram is more popular with young adults—31 percent of young

---

[32] *Id.*

[33] *Id.*

[34] Brian Dean, How Many People Use Twitter in 2022? January 5, 2022, https://backlinko.com/twitter-users#twitter-statistics

[35] Andrew B. Delaney and Darren A. Heitner, *Made for Each Other: Social Media and Litigation*, 85 N.Y. St. B. J. 10, 12 (2013).

[36] *Id.*

[37] *Id.*

[38] *Numbers of LinkedIn Members 2009–2016*, STATISTA (last visited Sept. 3, 2016, 10:30 AM), http://www.statista.com/statistics/274050/quarterly-numbers-of-linkedin-members/.

[39] https://about.linkedin.com

[40] Neil Merkl, *Social Media: Some Principal Sites*, 4E N.Y. PRAC., COM. LITIG. IN N.Y. ST. COURTS § 113:3 (2015).

[41] *Id.*

[42] *Instagram: Number of Monthly Active Users*, STATISTA (last visited Sept. 4, 2016, 12:20 PM), http://www.statista.com/statistics/253577/number-of-monthly-active-instagram-users/; S. Dixon, Instagram Users

adults age eighteen to twenty-nine use Instagram, whereas only 2.2 percent of adults 65 or older who are online use the site.[43]

TikTok is a short-form video sharing application that allows users to create and post fifteen-second videos on any topic. It holds the record for the fastest growing social media application to hit the planet. It penetrated 30 percent of all social media users within four years and as of January 2022 has over a billion users.[44]

4. What are some of the ways in which social media has impacted the practice of law?

Social media has had a significant impact on the practice of law—one that continues to evolve as lawyers, bar associations, and the courts define both the required and permissible use of social media in a legal practice. Required? Yes, competence mandates the use of social media in some areas of law and various aspects of a case.[45] Permissible? Yes, there are areas, such as advertising, where competence does not compel the use of social media. Nonetheless, state bar associations and lawyers are struggling (and litigating) to determine the permissible use of social media for attorney advertising and how to apply the traditional attorney advertising rules to Internet advertising.[46]

In fact, both social media's nascent stage and the rapidly evolving technology that constantly fuels new iterations of social media give rise to the ethical issues that compel the inquiries explored in this book. You will find entire chapters dedicated to areas such as advising clients, informal

---

World Wide, Statistica (last visited July 26, 2022), https://www.statista .com/statistics/183585/instagram-number-of-global-users/.

[43] https://www.statista.com/statistics/325587/instagram-global-age-group/

[44] Brian Dean, TikTok User Statistics, January 6, 2022, https://backlinko .com/tiktok-users#monthly-active-tiktok-users.

[45] See Jan L. Jacobowitz and Danielle Singer, *The Social Media Frontier: Exploring a New Mandate for Competence in the Practice of Law*, 68 U. Miami. L. Rev. 2 (2014); *see also* Penn. Bar Ass'n Formal Op. 2014-300, https://www.pabar.org/members/catalogs/Ethics%20Opinions/formal /F2014-300.pdf; competence is more fully discussed in Chapter 5 of this book.

[46] See Jacobowitz and Singer, *supra* note 45; Ass'n of Prof. Resp. Lawyers, 2015 Report of the Regulation of Lawyer Advertising Committee 5 (2015), https://aprl.net/wp-content/uploads/2016/07/APRL _2016_Lawyer-Advertising-Supplemental-Report_04-26-16_w-Attach .pdf; *see* Chapter 12 of this book for a deeper discussion of these issues.

and formal discovery, investigating jurors, and attorney advertising. Other related areas in which competence and diligence mandate that an attorney develop an awareness of the need to explore social media's appropriate use, such as the admissibility of social media evidence during trial or the consideration of social media restrictions during the due diligence stage in mergers and acquisitions, have been incorporated into related chapters.[47]

In the next couple of questions in this chapter, we provide examples that serve as an introduction as to how social media has crept into the practice of law in less obvious ways than the Facebook evidence that may undermine a plaintiff's personal injury claim or demonstrate a juror's bias. Determining appropriate jurisdiction and service of process are preliminary matters in the filing of a lawsuit. Lawyers are sometimes surprised to learn that social media has already generated a growing body of jurisprudence in both of these areas. The competence and diligence rules of professional conduct arguably include an evaluation of social media's role in determining jurisdiction and achieving service on the opposing party.

5. How has social media impacted the establishment of appropriate jurisdiction in the litigation of a matter?

Generally, courts are guided by due process and the standards established by US Supreme Court precedent when determining the jurisdiction of a state over an individual residing in another state. The court analyzes whether the defendant could reasonably foresee being sued in a particular state,[48] whether the defendant maintains continuous and systematic minimum contacts with the state,[49] whether the claim arose out of those contacts,[50] and whether the exercise of jurisdiction comports with "traditional notions of fair play and substantial justice."[51] All of the cases that originated these standards predate the Internet and social media, so there is a new growing body of jurisprudence that is attempting to apply "traditional notions of fair play" to jurisdiction in the digital age.

---

[47] *See, e.g.,* Chapter 5 (discovery chapter) for a brief discussion of admissibility of evidence and Chapter 9 for insights into the significance of social media when considering the viability of an acquisition.

[48] World-Wide Volkswagen Corp. v. Woodson, 444 U.S. 286, 295 (1980).

[49] Helicopteros Nacionales de Colombia, S.A. v. Hall, 466 U.S. 408, 416 (1984).

[50] Burger King Corp. v. Rudzewicz, 471 U.S. 462, 472 (1985).

[51] International Shoe Co. v. State of Wash., Office of Unemployment Compensation and Placement, 326 U.S. 310, 316 (1945).

Today, an effective, ethical lawyer must consider placing social media on the list of jurisdictional considerations when evaluating a case. An early Internet case, *Zippo Manufacturing C. v. Dot Com, Inc.*,[52] provides a foundation for considering social media presence as a basis for jurisdiction. The *Zippo* case provides a sliding scale with which to weigh the significance of a defendant's Internet presence: passive, somewhat interactive, and highly interactive. A passive Internet presence is a site that merely provides information—there is no interaction or transaction of business with the public—thus jurisdiction is generally not proper.[53] The somewhat interactive site allows information to be exchanged, and the court must look to the degree of interactivity and the commercial nature of the interaction.[54] The highly interactive site is one from which the defendants are unquestionably conducting business by entering into contracts with individuals from other states and transferring computer files, thereby rendering personal jurisdiction to be appropriate.

Courts that have found jurisdiction based on a social media presence include a Florida court that found jurisdiction to be appropriate over an Indiana company that used social media sites and video to allege that the plaintiff, a Florida company, sold defective products.[55] A California court accepted jurisdiction over a Florida company in a trademark infringement case where the Florida company had established a LinkedIn page that listed Los Angeles as its headquarters and a Twitter account with its feed originating in Los Angeles. The defendant claimed that it had not directed any of its activities toward California, but the court was not persuaded.

"Defendant's semantics lack substance. A finding of personal jurisdiction does not require defendant's having actually posted to Twitter from Los Angeles, or maintained a physical headquarters in California—only that defendant represented itself as having done so for its own commercial gain."

In another case, the defendant was a Delaware corporation whose tweets in Houston significantly contributed to a Texas court's finding of jurisdiction in a maritime case where plaintiff's claims involved crewmen who

---

[52] Zippo Mfg. v. Zippo Dot Com, Inc., 952 F. Supp. 1119, 1124 (W.D. Pa. 1997).

[53] *See, e.g.*, McGill v. Gourmet Technologies, Inc., 300 F. Supp. 2d 501, 507 (E.D. Mich. 2004).

[54] *Zippo*, 952 F. Supp. at 1124.

[55] Spectra Chrome, LLC v. Happy Jack's Reflections in Chrome, Inc., 8:11-CV-23-T-23MAP, 2011 WL 1337508, at *2 (M.D. Fla. 2011).

were injured when Somali pirates hijacked their ship.[56] The defendant regularly used Twitter from the dock in Houston's port to announce its arrival and advertise its capability and capacity in order to solicit additional cargo.

While there have been other courts that have not been persuaded by jurisdictional arguments based on an assertion of the defendant's social media presence, the goal in including this issue in the chapter is to raise awareness: the competent lawyer should consider the social media presence of a defendant when analyzing the most advantageous jurisdiction in which to file a client's case or defend a client who objects to jurisdiction outside his or her home state. Primary factors to consider are whether the defendant is actively engaged on social media accounts and whether the defendant's social media statements, tweets, or posts may be considered directed to particular individuals or to a specific jurisdiction. While a thorough examination of social media as a basis for jurisdiction is beyond the scope of this book, a robust analysis of recent case law may be found in John Browning's chapter on jurisdiction in his book, *Social Media and Litigation Practice Guide.*[57]

6. Have any courts approved substituted service of process via a social media network?

The simple answer is yes! Today's competent lawyer should include social media on his or her list of potential methods to achieve substituted service. Service via social media is a natural evolution in the use of technology for service of process.[58]

Service of process informs the opposing party that a complaint has been filed and provides the opportunity to respond to the allegations against him or her. Thus, a court must analyze due process concerns before approving a request for substituted service.[59] Service must be "reasonably calculated to reach the defendant and allow the opportunity to object and respond to the litigation."[60]

---

[56] Waterman Steamship Corp. v. Ruiz, 355 S.W.3d 387, 424 (Tex. App. 2011).

[57] *See* JOHN G. BROWNING, SOCIAL MEDIA AND LITIGATION PRACTICE GUIDE 11–27 (Thomson Reuters, 2014).

[58] See *Id.* at 25–35. (Service of process has evolved since 1878 when the US Supreme Court required personal service in the forum state to permissible substituted service by mail, publication, the use of telex, email, and social media.)

[59] *See* International Shoe Co., 326 U.S. at 310.

[60] In Re Heckman Corp., CA 10-378-LPS-MPT, 2011 WL 5855333, at *4 (D. Del. 2011) (approving service of process by email).

Australia is the first of eight countries in which service of process by social media has been approved in various cases.[61] In the United States, some of the first cases in which courts approved the use of social media involved substituted service of process on defendants in foreign countries.[62] However, more recently, two state courts in New York approved service of process where both parties resided in New York.[63] Courts that have approved service by social media have often done so with the additional requirement that notice also be mailed or emailed to the defendant.[64]

An increasing number of states have warmed to the idea of substituted service via social media. Some have recognized this in cases of first impression, such as New Jersey.[65] Others, such as Texas in 2020, have passed statutes specifically permitting such service and setting forth rules to govern the practice.[66]

In another New York case, Facebook service was approved as the only means of service after the court determined that the plaintiff could not locate the defendant's address or email, and the plaintiff's affidavit provided the court with the assurance that the Facebook page to be served belonged to the defendant who regularly checked his Facebook page.[67] The court also found that the statutorily permissible alternative of publication would be less likely to provide notice to the defendant than Facebook service.[68]

7. What do I need to demonstrate to the court to obtain permission to use substitute service via social media?

Generally, a lawyer needs to demonstrate that he or she has made a credible but unsuccessful attempt to accomplish personal service, and that service

---

[61] MKM Capital Property Ltd. v. Corbo & Poyser, ACT Sup. Ct., 12 Dec. 2008 (No. SC 608 of 2008); see BROWNING, *supra* note 56, at 80.

[62] *See, e.g.,* Mpafe, No. 27-FA-11-3453 at 1; *see also* F.T.C., 2013 WL 841037, at *4.

[63] In Noel B., 2014 NY Misc LEXIS 4708, at *4; Baidoo, 48 Misc. 3d at 311; *see also* Utah Alternative Service, *supra* note 6 (Utah's service rules which include court-approved social media service as an option).

[64] F.T.C., 2013 WL 841037, at *5; WhosHere, Inc. v. Orun, 1:13-CV-00526-AJT, 2014 WL 670817, at *4; In Noel B., 2014 NY Misc LEXIS 4708, at *4.

[65] K.A. v. J.L., 450 N.J. Super. Ct. 247 (Ch. Div. 2016).

[66] TEX. CIV. PRAC. & REM. CODE § 17.033 (Vernon 2021).

[67] Baidoo, 48 Misc. 3d at 311-312.

[68] *Id.*

by social media is a reliable, effective method for contacting the defendant. The courts generally evaluate whether social media substituted service is appropriate by considering the following factors: (1) personal service is not possible, (2) the statutory methods of substituted service would be an exercise in futility, and (3) the method of service being proposed is "one that the court can endorse as being reasonably calculated to apprise defendant that he is being sued."[69]

It is the third requirement that may pose an additional burden on the plaintiff. A lawyer must be prepared to demonstrate that the social media account that the plaintiff is seeking approval to serve is authentic and belongs to the defendant who regularly accesses his account. The court may be assured by evidence such as a printout of an exchange on the social media account between the plaintiff and the defendant, pictures and biographical data about the defendant that are reinforced by information on the account, and a sworn affidavit signed by the plaintiff.[70]

The bottom line is that if personal service is not possible and other statutory methods of substituted service are not as likely to provide the defendant with notice of the lawsuit as service via social media, then a plaintiff's lawyer should seek court approval for service on social media.

Courts might be hesitant at first about this practice. But as one federal court observed about the "relatively novel concept" of service by Facebook, "history teaches that, as technology advances and modes of communication progress, courts must be open to considering requests to authorize service via technological means of then-recent vintage, rather than dismissing them out of hand as novel."[71]

Conclusion

As this book goes to press, courts continue to explore the boundaries of how technology can impact service of process. On June 2, 2022, the Supreme Court of New York granted an order permitting service via the transfer of a non-fungible token ("NFT") on the Ethereum cryptocurrency blockchain. In LCX, *AG v. John Does* 1-25, this innovative use of 'Web 3.0' enabled an anonymous defendant to be served by having the service NFT airdropped into

---

[69] *Id.* at 312.

[70] *See, e.g., Id.* at 314-315.

[71] FTC v. PCCare247, Inc., 2013 WL 841037 (S.D.N.Y. Mar. 7, 2013).

a digital wallet controlled by that defendant. The token contained a "service hyperlink" to a website created by the plaintiff's attorney where the court's order and other papers were displayed. This hyperlink featured an alert notifying counsel when it's been clicked on, thus verifying that the defendant has been given notice of the proceedings.

CHAPTER 3

You Posted *What*? Advising Your Client about Social Media

Sooner or later, virtually every lawyer practicing in the digital age will have to confront two related questions: (1) Just how aware or involved must I be in what my clients are doing on social media platforms like Facebook or Twitter? and (2) What are my ethical boundaries in advising clients to "clean up" their social media profiles?

As to the first question, the short answer is "very." Regardless of your area of practice, the ubiquitous nature of social media, combined with the dizzying array of personal information that is shared every day via social media and the increasing extent to which lawyers are mining this digital treasure trove of information, make it a critical aspect of the attorney-client relationship in the twenty-first century. Not only have entire cases been undermined by revelations from a party's Facebook page or Twitter account, but the social media missteps by attorneys and clients alike have resulted in spoliation findings and sanctions rulings in cases throughout the country, as we discuss later. As the duties of "attorney and counselor at law" expand in the digital age to include counseling clients on what is posted in the first place on a site like Facebook, whether to post anything at all, what privacy settings or restrictions to adopt, and—perhaps most importantly—what content can be taken down and what must be preserved, it has become vital for lawyers to know where the ethical lines are drawn.

This chapter provides guidance to attorneys on how the ethical landscape has shifted by discussing the entire spectrum of attorney involvement from the relatively benign (advising clients on adopting privacy settings) to the more problematic issues of removing social media content and risking spoliation of evidence.

In doing so, this chapter examines the "new normal" for twenty-first-century lawyers by analyzing the various ethics opinions and guidelines nationwide that address the limits on how far lawyers can go in this regard. In the following chapter, we explore the inter-relationship among legal ethics rules, ethics advisory opinions, and the law of spoliation by examining how courts throughout the US have treated parties who have removed content from their social networking pages, deactivated their Facebook accounts, or taken other measures to keep potentially incriminating posts or photos from prying eyes.

QUESTIONS

1. How did social media savvy become a component of attorney competence?

Being at least "socially aware" (if not quite social media savvy) is now considered part of the most fundamental responsibility for attorneys: the duty to provide competent representation to clients. Social media is a relatively new phenomenon, so how did social media expertise find its way into the definition of attorney competence?

The answer begins with the recommendations of the ABA Commission on Ethics 20/20 (which was created in 2009 to study how the Model Rules of Professional Conduct should be updated in light of globalization and technology's impact on the legal profession) that resulted in the ABA adopting certain changes to the Model Rules in August 2012.[1] One of these changes was to Model Rule 1.1 (Duty of Competence). As the revised comment 8 reflects, to maintain the requisite knowledge and skill, "a lawyer should keep abreast of changes in the law and its practice, including the benefits and risks associated with relevant technology."[2]

This change reflects the belated recognition of how technology affects "nearly every aspect of legal work, including how we store confidential information, communicate with clients, conduct discovery, engage in research,

---

[1] ABA COMM'N ON ETHICS 20/20, REPORT TO THE HOUSE OF DELEGATES RESOLUTION 105A (2012), http://www.americanbar.org/content/dam/aba /administrative/ethics_2020/2012_hod_annual_meeting_105a_filed _may_2012.authcheckdam.pdf [hereinafter ABA Res. 105A].

[2] *Id.*

and provide legal services."[3] As the revision to Rule 1.1 indicates, competence means more than just keeping current with statutory developments or common law changes in one's particular field of practice. It also requires having sufficient familiarity with, and proficiency in, technology—both insofar as to its impact on a substantive area of law itself and as to how the lawyer delivers his or her services. Regarding the latter, the ABA Commission noted, for example, that "a lawyer would have difficulty providing competent legal services in today's environment without knowing how to use email or create an electronic document."[4] And as to the former, an understanding of social networking sites such as Facebook is critical to accomplishing lawyerly tasks in the digital age.

In fact, ethics opinions in New York, Pennsylvania, North Carolina, Florida, West Virginia, and the District of Columbia (D.C.) have specifically noted that competence requires a lawyer to understand social media so that he or she may properly advise clients.[5] Moreover, given the vast wealth of information about individuals just a few mouse clicks away, and with "digital digging" becoming the norm for attorneys, it becomes harder for an attorney to credibly maintain that he or she has met the standard of competence when he or she has ignored social media avenues.

This certainly includes the searching side. For example, in a 2010 survey of its members by the American Academy of Matrimonial Lawyers, 81 percent reported using evidence from social networking sites in their cases.[6] In a 2013 criminal case, the Ninth Circuit held that a lawyer's failure to locate and use a purported sexual abuse victim's recantation on her social

---

[3] Diane Karpman, *ABA Model Rules Reflect Technology, Globalization*, CAL. BAR J: ETHICS BYTE (Sept. 2012), http://www.calbarjournal.com /September2012/EthicsByte.aspx.

[4] ABA Res. 105A at 3. It is important to note that the Comment to Rule 1.1 also says that "Competent representation can also be provided through the association of a lawyer of established competence in the field in question."

[5] Pa. Bar Ass'n, Formal Op. 2014-300 (2014), https://www.pabar.org /members/catalogs/Ethics%20Opinions/formal/F2014-300.pdf [hereinafter Pa. Op. 300]; *see also* Prof'l Ethics of The Fla. Bar, Op. 14-1 (2015); W. Va. Office of Disciplinary Couns., L.E.O. No. 2015-02 (2015), http://www.wvodc.org/pdf/LEO%202015%20-%2002.pdf; D.C. Bar Ethics Opinion 371 (2016). An analysis of each opinion is provided in the appendix at the end of this chapter.

[6] JOHN BROWNING, THE LAWYER'S GUIDE TO SOCIAL NETWORKING: UNDERSTANDING SOCIAL MEDIA'S IMPACT ON THE LAW (Thomson Reuters 2010).

networking profile constituted ineffective assistance of counsel.[7] In addition, a number of state courts nationwide considering due diligence issues have held that lawyers have a duty to make use of online resources. One Florida appellate court compared a lawyer's failure to go beyond checking directory assistance to find an address for a missing defendant to the equivalent of using "the horse and buggy and the eight-track stereo" in an age of Google and social media.[8]

But just as being competent in the digital age encompasses being able to do the searching and vetting online, it also includes advising one's clients that the other side will be actively engaged in such investigation as well, and that such online digging will likely include the client's social media activities, too.

2. How much do I really need to know about my clients' social media activity?

The short answer is that you have to know what's out there. Lawyers uncomfortable with technology cannot afford to take a "head in the sand" approach when it comes to their clients' activities on Facebook and other social media sites. One of the main reasons is the fact that social media has become the rule, rather than the exception. As of 2021, approximately 4.48 billion people throughout the world use social media.[9] Moreover, social media users maintain and monthly access an average of 6.6 social media platforms.[10]

---

[7] Cannedy v. Adams, 706 F.3d 1148 (9th Cir. 2013).

[8] Dubois v. Butler ex. rel. Butler, 901 So.2d 1029 (Fla. 4th DCA 2005). As we discuss in chapter 6, the expectations for a lawyer to be technologically proficient also extend to jury selection. The ABA, in its Formal Opinion 466, has upheld the practice of researching the social media profiles of prospective jurors, as have the ethics bodies of every jurisdiction to examine this issue. *See* John Browning, *Should Voir Dire Become Voir Google? Ethical Implications of Researching Jurors on Social Media*, 17 SMU Sci. & Tech. L. Rev 603, 604 (2014); In one state, Missouri, the Supreme Court has even created an affirmative duty for lawyers to conduct online research of jurors during the voir dire process. Johnson v. McCullough, 306 S.W.3d 551 (Mo. 2010) (en banc).

[9] Brian Dean, *Social Network Usage & Growth Statistics: How Many People Use Social Media in 2022?* (October 21, 2021) https://backlinko .com/social-media-users (Last visited February 15, 2022)

[10] *Id.*

In fact over one half of the world's population is active on social media; the percentage increases to 82 percent in North America.[11] In the United States in 2020 there were 240 million on social media platforms and active monthly use was at 72.3 percent.[12] And in the United States the breakdown by age results in the following: 84 percent aged 18–29; 81 percent aged 30–49; 73 percent aged 50–64; 45 percent aged 65+.[13] In other words, clients, opposing counsel, witnesses, jurors, and judges of all ages are potential social media users.

The fact that so many people are active social media users assumes tremendous significance for attorneys. What a client has posted or decides to post can have significant consequences for his or her case. Incriminating statements found in a status update or photos and videos that contradict a key claim or defense can damage and even completely undermine a case. Consider the power attributed to photos posted on Facebook by a Florida appellate court reviewing their relevance and discoverability in a premises liability lawsuit, as follows:

> In a personal injury case where the plaintiff is seeking intangible damages, the fact-finder is required to examine the quality of the plaintiff's life before and after the accident to determine the extent of the loss. From testimony alone, it is often difficult for the fact-finder to grasp what a plaintiff's life was like prior to an accident. It would take a great novelist, a Tolstoy, a Dickens, or a Hemingway, to use words to summarize the totality of a prior life. If a photograph is worth a thousand words, there is no better portrayal of what an individual's life was like than those photographs the individual has chosen to share through social media before the occurrence of an accident causing injury. Such photographs are the equivalent of a "day in the life" slide show produced by the plaintiff before the existence of any motive to manipulate reality. The photographs sought here are thus powerfully relevant to the damage issues in the lawsuit.[14]

---

[11] *Id.*

[12] *Id.*

[13] *Id.*

[14] Nucci v. Target Corp., 162 So.3d 146 (Fla. 4th DCA 2015).

Moreover, a "day in the life" of a prospective client may reveal the tenuous nature of a claim. Model Rule 3.1[15] requires that lawyers have a reasonable basis in fact and in law to support a claim. If a lawyer reviews a client's social media at the initial client meeting, then there is an opportunity for the lawyer to either obtain a reasonable explanation for social media that appears to be inconsistent with the client's claim or to decline the representation. In fact, the D.C. opinion provides that a lawyer *must* address any inconsistencies between a client's social media presence and a client's legal claims before submitting any court or agency filings.[16] The D.C. opinion also notes social media risks for lawyers representing clients in transactions and in a regulatory practice. The opinion explains,

> [f]or example, review of client social media for their consistency with representations, warranties, covenants, conditions, restrictions, and other terms or proposed terms of agreements could be important because inconsistency could create rights or remedies for counterparties. Similarly, competent and zealous representation under Rules 1.1 and 1.3 in regulatory matters may require ensuring that representations to agencies are consistent with social media postings and that advice to clients takes such postings into account.[17]

If the inconsistent social media evidence is discovered during the course of a lawsuit, one of the two New York opinions advised, "if a client's social media posting reveals to an attorney that the client's lawsuit involves the assertion of materially false factual statements, and if proper inquiry of the client does not negate that conclusion, the attorney is ethically prohibited from proffering, supporting or using these false statements."[18] Similarly, an attorney should take "prompt remedial action" if a client fails to answer truthfully when asked whether changes were ever made to a social media profile.[19] Finally, a lawyer who finds fundamentally inconsistent evidence may need to withdraw. For example, a plaintiff's attorney with access to her client's private Facebook page who views Facebook comments by the client making it clear in a personal injury case that the client was hurt as

---

[15] MODEL RULES OF PROF'L CONDUCT r. 3.1 (Am. Bar Ass'n, 2016).

[16] D.C. Bar Ethics Opinion 371 (2016).

[17] *Id.*

[18] New York Cty. Law. Ass'n, Ethics Op. 745 (2013), https://www.nycla .org/siteFiles/Publications/Publications1630_0.pdf.

[19] *Id.*

a result of his own horseplay and not by the negligence of the defendant should make plans to withdraw as counsel rather than continue to pursue a frivolous claim.

Thus, best practice mandates an early discussion and review of a client's social media. Some attorneys have suggested using a flash drive to download the client's social media content prior to filing suit, thereby protecting both the lawyer and the client from claims of frivolous pleading and spoliation. However, the very real prospect of social media posts coming back to haunt a client, damage a case, or create ethical exposure for the lawyer are the overarching reasons for attorneys to be aware of the potential impact of social media. Perhaps the more fundamental question to explore is this: what are the limits in counseling clients about policing their online selves, in making their Facebook accounts private, or in removing potentially harmful content from a profile?

3. May I advise my client to use or change her privacy settings?

Yes! The states that have addressed this question are in accord.[20] The Philadelphia opinion explains that changing privacy settings only renders the information more difficult to obtain, but access to the other party remains possible through formal discovery channels.[21] In fact, many individuals are unaware of privacy settings,[22] and it is probably good advice, regardless of the content, to advise clients to limit the exposure of their personal lives by electing an appropriate privacy setting. However, the D.C. opinion cautions that "[t]o provide competent advice, a lawyer should understand that privacy settings do not create any expectation of confidentiality to establish privilege or work-product protection against discovery and subpoenas."[23]

---

[20] Pa. Bar Ass'n, Formal Op. 2014-300 (2014), https://www.pabar.org/members/catalogs/Ethics%20Opinions/formal/F2014-300.pdf [hereinafter Pa. Op. 300]; see also Prof'l Ethics of The Fla. Bar, Op. 14-1 (2015); W. Va. Office of Disciplinary Couns., L.E.O. No. 2015 -02 (2015), http://www.wvodc.org/pdf/LEO%202015%20-%2002.pdf.; D.C. Bar Ethics Opinion 371 (2016), [hereinafter known as State Examples]. An analysis of each opinion is provided in the appendix at the end of this chapter.

[21] Phila. Bar Ass'n, Op. 2014-5 (2014).

[22] New York Cty. Law. Ass'n, Ethics Op. 745 (2013), https://www.nycla.org/siteFiles/Publications/Publications1630_0.pdf.

[23] D.C. Bar Ethics Opinion 371 (2016).

4. May I advise my client as to what to post on social media?

The North Carolina opinion concludes that advising a client as to social media posting, both before and after the filing of a lawsuit, is tantamount to providing competent and diligent representation to clients.[24] In fact, North Carolina explained that if a client's social media postings might impact that client's legal matter, then "the lawyer must advise the client of the legal ramifications of existing postings, future postings, and third party comments."[25]

The New York opinion agrees, "it is permissible for an attorney to review what a client plans to publish on a social media page in advance of publication . . . [and] . . . to guide the client appropriately, including formulating a corporate policy on social media usage."[26] The New York opinion further explains that guidance could involve the following attorney tasks: counseling the client to publish truthful, favorable information; discussing the content and advisability of social media posts; advising the client how social media posts might be perceived; advising the client about how legal adversaries might obtain access to even "private" social media pages; reviewing both posts not yet published and those that have been published; and discussing potential lines of questioning that might result.[27]

Consider, for example, a lawyer defending a chemical plant operator in a wrongful death suit brought by the surviving family members of workers killed in an explosion at the plant. Pursuant to North Carolina and New York's guidance, the lawyer may advise the company that it is fine, and even advantageous, to post on its Facebook page about the operator being cleared of wrongdoing in a subsequent Occupational Safety and Health Administration (OSHA) investigation. The lawyer might also discuss the timing of a post about the plant's longtime safety manager's retirement, due to how it might appear in close temporal proximity to the underlying accident. Defense counsel might even approve of Facebook posts touting the company's upcoming sponsorship of a community event or a charitable donation, given the anticipated spike in goodwill and burnishing of his client's public image. However, the same lawyer adhering to his ethical obligations should counsel against

---

[24] N.C. St. Bar, Formal Ethics Op. 2014-5 (2015), https://www.ncbar.gov/for-lawyers/ethics/adopted-opinions/2014-formal-ethics-opinion-5/ [hereinafter N.C. Op. 2014-5].

[25] *Id.*

[26] New York Cty. Law. Ass'n, Ethics Op. 745 (2013), https://www.nycla.org/siteFiles/Publications/Publications1630_0.pdf.

[27] *Id.*

company employees tweeting gossip about one of the surviving children not having standing to sue due to not being the decedent's biological child—especially if the lawyer knows such a statement to be false.

Of course, the commonsense caveat here is one that runs through most of the ethics opinions: a lawyer may not advise a client to post any false or misleading information on a social media website.

5. My client has some Facebook posts that could really hurt our case. May I ethically tell her to take them down or delete them? And may I tell her to refrain from using social media during the case?

Generally, the states that have opined on this issue have concluded that an attorney may advise a client to remove social media posts as long as relevant information is otherwise preserved so that it may be produced in discovery.[28] (Consider the use of a flash drive discussed above.) A failure to preserve and produce the evidence when appropriately requested not only implicates competence, but also the ethical obligations of fairness to opposing counsel and candor to the tribunal.[29]

Of course, the New York State Bar opinion notes that if litigation is not pending or reasonably anticipated, then removing social media content is fair game[30]; however, carefully query as to whether "reasonably anticipated" applies to the client's situation. By way of illustration, a lawyer whose client wants to delete some embarrassing photos from the office Halloween costume party that were posted to the company Facebook page would normally have no problem advising the client to go ahead and do so. However, if the client had received a letter from an attorney representing a recently terminated employee and asserting claims of sexual harassment and hostile workplace (including actionable comments or conduct at that office Halloween party), then these photos are potentially relevant, and the attorney should take steps to preserve them electronically (although they may still be taken down).

---

[28] State Examples, *supra* note 18.

[29] For a comprehensive discussion of the ethical implications that may arise during discovery, see chapter 4.

[30] THE SOCIAL MEDIA COMM. OF THE COMMERCIAL & FED. LITIG. SECTION, N.Y. ST. BAR ASS'N SOCIAL MEDIA GUIDELINES OF THE COMMERCIAL AND FEDERAL LITIGATION SECTION OF THE NEW YORK STATE BAR ASSOCIATION 15. (2015), http://www.nysba.org/socialmediaguidelines/ [hereinafter N.Y. St. Bar Social Media Guidelines].

The Florida opinion noted that determining relevance may require "a factual case-by-case determination,"[31] because social media evidence that may not be "related directly" to the incident for which damages are being sought may nevertheless be deemed relevant to a case.[32] For example, social media comments on a personal injury plaintiff's Facebook page about her "personal best" times in local running events may on the surface not relate directly to her subsequent accident. However, if she asserts a claim that she is unable to enjoy the same kind of success in post-accident competitive running, then such content is certainly relevant to her damages claims.

Additionally, attorneys may also advise clients to refrain from using social media during the case—much like the old-school advice to a client not to talk about his or her case. The Pennsylvania opinion notes, "[i]t has become common practice for lawyers to advise clients to refrain from posting any information relevant to a case on any website, and to refrain from using these websites until the case concludes."[33]

6. Should I monitor my client's use of social media during the case?

Since it has become reasonable to expect that opposing counsel will monitor a client's social media account, the Pennsylvania opinion reasoned, "[t]racking a client's activity on social media may be appropriate for an attorney to remain informed about developments bearing on the client's legal dispute."[34]

While monitoring is a judgment call that depends on assessing both your client and his or her case, consider the following real-world examples of the importance of knowing what your client is up to on social media. In a recent Florida employment discrimination case, *Gulliver Schools, Inc. v. Snay*, the former headmaster of a private academy sued for discrimination.[35] The case resulted in a $150,000 settlement ($70,000 of which was attorney's fees and back wages), which contained a standard confidentiality provision calling for any settlement monies paid to be forfeited if the plaintiff disclosed the amount or terms of the settlement to any third parties. When the defendants learned of a Facebook post by the settling plaintiff's daughter that breached this confidentiality clause (reading "Mama and Papa Snay won the case

---

[31] Prof'l Ethics of The Fla. Bar, Op. 14-1 (2015).

[32] *Id.*

[33] Pa. Bar Ass'n, Formal Op. 2014-300 (2014), https://www.pabar.org/members/catalogs/Ethics%20Opinions/formal/F2014-300.pdf.

[34] *Id.*

[35] Gulliver Sch., Inc. v. Snay, 137 So.3d 1045, 1046 (Fla. 3d DCA 2014).

against Gulliver. Gulliver is now officially paying for my vacation to Europe this summer. SUCK IT."), they sued. The court found that the disclosure by Snay to his teenage daughter leading to the Facebook post was a breach of the settlement agreement; it ordered a disgorgement of Snay's $80,000 settlement.

And in West Virginia, Kanawha County public defender Sara Whitaker found herself before a judge accused of contempt in December 2015 after allegedly giving her client a copy of a packet containing the identity of a confidential informant.[36] The informant's name and address were posted on Facebook by the former roommate of client Tracie Jones, complete with captions like "exposed" and "cheap whore." Although Whitaker ultimately received only a fine, this case illustrates how quickly a client's social media posts could lead to witness intimidation charges as well as potential ethical violations for the lawyer.

Another cautionary tale about the importance of monitoring a client's social media activities comes straight from the headlines. Famed rapper 50 Cent filed for bankruptcy in 2015 in the wake of a $7 million jury verdict against him. But evidently, 50 Cent (real name: Curtis Jackson, III) didn't quite grasp the underlying concept of Chapter 11 bankruptcy, because he proceeded to post numerous photos to his social media accounts, including Instagram, depicting him holding, pointing to, or surrounded by stacks and stacks of cash. One photo showed stacks of cash stashed in his refrigerator. Another featured the rapper with money strewn across his bed (along with a caption referencing 50 Cent's song "I'm Too Rich"), and yet another showed the singer with stacks of cash carefully arranged to spell the word "BROKE."[37]

His creditors, including headphone company Sleek Audio and SunTrust Bank, were not amused and filed pleadings bringing the photos to the court's attention, and implying that 50 Cent was hiding assets. The rapper's lawyers insisted that the photos were being publicized in an attempt to "smear" 50 Cent, said that his social media postings were simply part of maintaining "his brand and image," and even maintained that the stacks of cash were from a Hollywood prop company and were not actual currency.

---

[36] Erin Beck, *Lawyer Will Have to Explain Informant ID Release*, CHARLESTON GAZETTE-MAIL (Dec. 17, 2015), http://www.wvgazettemail .com/news/20151217/lawyer-will-have-to-explain-informant-id-release.

[37] Katy Stech, *Bankruptcy Judge Scolds Fifty Cent for Courthouse Photo*, WALL STREET J.: BANKRUPTCY BEAT (Apr. 7, 2016, 4:26 PM), http://blogs .wsj.com/bankruptcy/2016/04/07/bankruptcy-judge-scolds-50-cent-for -courthouse-photo/.

Concerned about "allegations of nondisclosure and a lack of transparency in the case," Connecticut bankruptcy Judge Ann Nevin ordered 50 Cent to appear and explain the photographs at a hearing. Despite the gravity of his situation, 50 Cent continued to post on Twitter and Instagram, including one photo depicting the rapper with stacks of cash stuck in his waistband that was apparently taken inside the federal courthouse in Hartford. Judge Nevin was clearly not amused and scolded the rapper, saying: "There's nothing funny going on here. This is very serious stuff." Ultimately, though, the court stopped short of banning him from posting to social media accounts.[38]

Final Thoughts on the "Clean Up" Issue

Pragmatic questions continue to plague lawyers when it comes to counseling clients on their postings on social media and the presentation of social networking content. For example, in what form should social media content be preserved? Is a paper "print-out" or screenshot of information enough, or does information need to be saved in a way that preserves all metadata? No ethics regulatory bodies have tackled the question of whether a paper print-out of a Facebook post or Twitter tweet violates Rule 3.4. In the e-discovery arena, a number of courts have mandated that electronically stored information (ESI) must be preserved and produced in its native format. Given the dynamic nature of social media content, an argument can certainly be made that such data should be produced in its "original" format.

Another practical issue that is likely to present ethical concerns in this area for the foreseeable future is the explosive growth in self-deleting applications that delete data shortly after it is shared. The wildly popular Snapchat, as well as similar apps like Telegram, Confide, and Wickr, actively erase text or pictures once the recipient has viewed them. Instagram has a story feature that similarly disappears. If a party uses such applications, the question shifts from whether such erased or disintegrated content can be retrieved to whether, for evidence preservation purposes, it was ever evidence that "existed" in the first place. And is it spoliation if a user didn't have control over the evidence and a duty to preserve it at the time of its loss?

As a matter of providing competent representation in a world of seemingly endless amounts of data being shared and ever-changing

---

[38] *Id.*

mechanisms for that data to be shared, lawyers must embrace new responsibilities insofar as counseling clients on their social media activities is concerned. An attorney must be aware of what his or her client has done, is doing and plans to do in terms of the client's online presence. Lawyers should address this issue in the very first client interview as well as in the initial written communication or engagement agreement (a sample of such a first letter appears in the Appendix). In other words, when it comes to advising clients on "cleaning up" their Facebook profiles and other social media musings, a lawyer must serve as a kind of "client's keeper."

Appendix of State Ethics Advisory Opinions

This appendix provides a chronological state-by-state discussion of the advisory opinions that address advising a client on social media. It includes some of the examples provided above but offers the reader a more detailed look at the specifics and nuances of the individual opinions and provides insight as to how the opinions connect and build on one another.

New York

The first ethics governing body to address the question of just how far a lawyer may go in advising a client regarding his or her social media presence was the New York County Lawyers Association Committee on Professional Ethics in July 2013, with its Formal Opinion 745.

In this opinion, the committee began by noting not only the prevalence of social media use (with an estimated 20 percent of Americans' online time being spent on social networking sites), but also the highly personal nature of the information being posted on these platforms.[39] With so many people posting information that could be viewed and used by everyone from potential employers to admissions officers to romantic contacts, and so many social media users ignorant of or oblivious to privacy settings, the Committee noted—with a nod to ethics opinions from around the country that have concluded that attorneys may ethically access publicly viewable social media pages—that attorneys have to be cognizant of what their clients are risking. Because serious privacy concerns may be implicated, the committee concluded, "it is permissible for an attorney to review what a client plans to publish on a social media page in advance of publication." It advised lawyers "to guide the client appropriately, including formulating a corporate policy on social media usage."[40] Such guidance, according to the committee, could involve the following attorney tasks: counseling the client to publish truthful, favorable information; discussing the content

---

[39] New York Cty. Law. Ass'n, Ethics Op. 745 (2013), https://www.nycla .org/siteFiles/Publications/Publications1630_0.pdf.

[40] *Id.*

and advisability of social media posts; advising the client how social media posts might be perceived; advising the client about how legal adversaries might obtain access to even "private" social media pages; reviewing both posts not yet published and those that have been published; and discussing potential lines of questioning that might result.[41]

However, in addition to such proactive rules, the committee cautioned that the attorney's advice regarding social media use by clients must still abide by other overarching ethical responsibilities. These include refraining from bringing or defending a frivolous proceeding; accordingly, the committee reasoned, "if a client's social media posting reveals to an attorney that the client's lawsuit involves the assertion of materially false factual statements, and if proper inquiry of the client does not negate that conclusion, the attorney is ethically prohibited from proffering, supporting or using these false statements."[42] Similarly, an attorney should take "prompt remedial action" if a client fails to answer truthfully when asked whether changes were ever made to a social media profile.[43]

But after reaffirming that an attorney may proactively counsel a client about keeping his social media privacy settings maximized, or counseling against posting certain content, the committee dropped its biggest bombshell with only a fleeting reference. An attorney, the committee stated, may offer advice as to what content may be "taken down" or removed, "[p]rovided that there [are] no violations of the rules or substantive law pertaining to the preservation and/or spoliation of evidence."[44] This bit of advice is provided with no further discussion or elaboration as a kind of afterthought in the opinion's brief conclusion—and yet it is arguably the most important subject mentioned by the committee. Many questions are left unanswered: for example, what kind of conduct might constitute spoliation in the digital age? Would deactivating an account suffice? And about deleting content—would it matter if content of questionable relevance were deleted, or if the "taking down" of content occurred prior to suit actually being filed? These questions, and others, were left unanswered. It would be up to later ethics opinions and to courts to fill in some of the blanks.

---

[41] *Id.*

[42] *Id.*

[43] *Id.*

[44] *Id.*

New York would return to this issue and re-affirm Formal Opinion 745 in March 2014, when the New York State Bar Association's Commercial and Federal Litigation Section issued a sweeping set of "Social Media Ethics Guidelines."[45] These guidelines address a broad array of attorney tasks when using social media, including lawyer advertising, communicating with clients via social networking platforms, furnishing legal advice on social media, case investigation using social media, and researching the social media profiles of prospective and actual jurors. In its section on "Ethically Communicating with Clients," the New York Committee includes some advice on counseling clients about their social media activities. Guideline No. 4.A makes it clear that advising a client on what privacy settings should be used is within the lawyer's purview, noting that "[a] lawyer may advise a client as to what content may be maintained or make private on her social media account."[46] Later on, as part of Guideline No. 4.B on "Adding New Social Media Content," the committee also indicates there is no problem in advising a client on posting new content on a social media profile.[47] In its comment, the committee points to the scenario of pre-publication review by a lawyer on what the client plans to post, as well as providing appropriate guidance to that client (including formulating a policy on social media usage for business clients). The only caveat is that the proposed content must not be something the lawyer knows to be "false or misleading information that may be relevant to a claim."[48]

As the comment to this guideline discusses, a lawyer may "counsel the client to publish truthful information favorable to the client; discuss the significance and implications of social media posts (including their content and advisability); review how the factual content of a post may affect a person's perception of the post; and how such posts might be used in litigation, including cross-examination."[49] As to the last item, this guideline points out

---

[45] THE SOCIAL MEDIA COMM. OF THE COMMERCIAL & FED. LITIG. SECTION, N.Y. ST. BAR ASS'N SOCIAL MEDIA GUIDELINES OF THE COMMERCIAL AND FEDERAL LITIGATION SECTION OF THE NEW YORK STATE BAR ASSOCIATION 15. (2015), http://www.nysba.org/socialmediaguidelines/ [hereinafter N.Y. St. Bar Social Media Guidelines].

[46] *Id.*

[47] *Id.*

[48] *Id.*

[49] *Id.*

that the lawyer's proactive role in this regard may include advising a client "to consider the possibility that someone may be able to view a private social media profile through court order, compulsory process, or unethical conduct."[50]

To reinforce the lawyer's ethical obligation to avoid being complicit in offering false statements or testimony, the committee added Guideline No. 4.C on "False Social Media Statements." In this guideline, the committee reminds lawyers of their ethical duties not to bring a frivolous claim or assert a baseless defense, including asserting materially factual statements that are false. No. 4.C cautions a lawyer against "proffering, supporting, or using false statements if she learns from a client's social media posting that a client's lawsuit involves the assertions of materially false factual statements or evidence that supports such a conclusion."[51]

In an age in which one of the most persistent criticisms of the Internet has been its potential for the dissemination of false or inaccurate information, this is a timely warning. And while some of these guidelines' directions may seem to place the lawyer in the role of "public relations flak" more than that of "attorney at law," there are valid and pragmatic reasons for doing so.

Consider the example on page 32, in which a lawyer is defending a chemical plant operator in a wrongful death suit brought by the surviving family members of workers killed in an explosion at the plant. Pursuant to these guidelines, the lawyer may advise the company that it is fine, and even advantageous, to post on its Facebook page about the operator being cleared of wrongdoing in a subsequent Occupational Safety and Health Administration (OSHA) investigation. The lawyer might also discuss the timing of a post about the plant's longtime safety manager's retirement, due to how it might appear in close temporal proximity to the underlying accident. Defense counsel might even approve of Facebook posts touting the company's upcoming sponsorship of a community event or a charitable donation, given the anticipated spike in goodwill and burnishing of his client's public image. However, the same lawyer adhering to his ethical obligations and these guidelines should counsel against company employees tweeting gossip about one of the surviving children not having standing to sue due to not being the decedent's biological child—especially if the lawyer knows such a statement to be false.

---

[50] *Id.*

[51] *Id.*

On the flip side, a plaintiff's attorney may be alerted that it is time to withdraw rather than file a frivolous claim after a review of a client's social media presence reveals that the client's mishap was caused by the client's own carelessness rather than the defendant's alleged negligence.

But what about removing or deleting social media content? Guideline No. 4.A states that a lawyer may advise a client "as to what content may be 'taken down' or removed, whether posted by the client or someone else, as long as there is no violation of common law or any statute, rule, or regulation relating to the preservation of information."[52] The guideline goes on to reinforce this obligation to preserve evidence, stating that "Unless an appropriate record of the social media information or data is preserved, a party or non-party may not delete information from a social media profile that is subject to a duty to preserve."[53]

Just what kind of content must be preserved, and when? The Comment to Guideline No. 4.A points out that this preservation obligation extends to "potentially relevant information," and that it begins "once a party reasonably anticipates litigation."[54] It follows and even quotes from NYCLA Formal Opinion 745, observing that as long as the removal of content does not constitute spoliation of evidence, "there is no ethical bar to 'taking down' such material from social media publications."[55] In a situation when litigation is neither pending nor reasonably anticipated, the guideline notes, "a lawyer may more freely advise a client on what to maintain or remove from her social media profile."[56] And, like Formal Opinion 745, Guideline No. 4.A also reminds lawyers that in the digital age, "delete" doesn't necessarily translate to "gone forever." It cautions lawyers "to be aware that the act of deleting electronically stored information does not mean that such information cannot be

---

[52] The Social Media Comm. of the Commercial & Fed. Litig. Section, N.Y. St. Bar Ass'n Social Media Guidelines of the Commercial and Federal Litigation Section of the New York State Bar Association 15. (2015), http://www.nysba.org/socialmediaguidelines/ [hereinafter N.Y. St. Bar Social Media Guidelines].

[53] *Id.*

[54] *Id.*

[55] *Id.*

[56] *Id.*

recovered through the use of forensic technology," particularly if a "live" posting is "simply made 'unlive.'"[57]

For example, as discussed above, a client who wants to remove embarrassing office party photos from the company's Facebook page may be advised to do so; however, if there is a pending sexual harassment claim against the company by a terminated employee (that includes actionable comments or conduct at the office party) then the client must be advised to electronically preserve the removed photos.

Philadelphia

The next ethics body to consider this issue was the Philadelphia Bar Association Professional Guidance Committee. In its Opinion 2014-5, issued in July 2014, the committee considered the following questions:

1. Whether a lawyer may advise a client to change the privacy settings on a Facebook page so that only the client or the client's "friends" may access the content
2. Whether a lawyer may instruct a client to remove a photo, link, or other content that the lawyer believes is damaging to the client's case from the client's Facebook page
3. Whether a lawyer who receives a Request for Production of Documents must obtain and produce a copy of a photograph posted by the client, which the lawyer previously saw on the client's Facebook page, but which the lawyer did not previously print or download
4. Whether a lawyer who receives a Request for Production of Documents must obtain and produce a copy of a photograph posted by someone other than the client on the client's Facebook page, which the lawyer previously saw on the client's Facebook page, but which the lawyer did not previously print or download[58]

As to the first question, Philadelphia's Committee held that a lawyer can certainly counsel a client to restrict access to his or her social media information, reasoning that changing privacy settings only made it more cumbersome for an opposing party to obtain the

---

[57] *Id.*

[58] Phila. Bar Ass'n, Op. 2014-5 (2014).

information, not impossible, thanks to formal discovery channels.[59] Helping a client manage the content of her account, the committee opined, was simply part of a lawyer's responsibilities, especially in light of the changing standard of attorney competence. Providing competent representation, according to the committee, necessarily entailed having a basic knowledge of how social media sites work as well as advising clients about issues that might arise due to their use of such platforms.[60]

For the remaining questions posed, the committee held that a lawyer may not instruct or knowingly allow a client to delete or destroy a relevant photo, link, text, or other content.[61] Citing to and adopting the New York Bar's Social Media Guidelines, the committee reasoned that a lawyer could only instruct her client to "delete" damaging information if she also took care to "take appropriate action to preserve the information in the event it should prove to be relevant and discoverable."[62] The committee, citing the now-infamous Virginia social media spoliation case of *Allied Concrete Co. v. Lester*, also reminded lawyers of their duties under Rule 3.3(b) of the Pennsylvania Rules of Professional Conduct to take reasonable remedial measures, "including if necessary, disclosure to the tribunal,"[63] if the lawyer learns that her client has destroyed evidence.

As to the remaining issues presented, Philadelphia's Committee ruled that in order to comply with a Request for Production (or any other discovery request), a lawyer "must produce any social media content, such as photos and links, posted by the client, including posts that may be unfavorable to the client."[64] Reminding lawyers of their obligations under the Rules of Professional Conduct not to engage in conduct "involving dishonesty, fraud, deceit, or misrepresentation," the committee held that a "lawyer must produce all of the requested photographs and other information from Facebook, regardless of whether it was favorable to the client."[65] Furthermore, if a lawyer knows or reasonably believes that extant social media content has not been produced by the client (and the social media

---

[59] *Id.*

[60] *Id.*

[61] *Id.*

[62] *Id.*

[63] *Id.*

[64] *Id.*

[65] *Id.*

content is in the client's or lawyer's possession), then the lawyer "must make reasonable efforts to obtain" the "photograph, link or other content about which the lawyer is aware."[66]

The Philadelphia Committee's opinion is significant not only because it adopts and builds upon the New York Bar's Social Media Guidelines, but because it elaborates and lends context to the discussion surrounding the issue that NYCLA Ethics Opinion 745 only mentioned in passing—advising a client on "taking down" damaging social media content. Equally important, the Philadelphia Committee's insights are set against the backdrop of the attorney's duty of competence in the digital age. Being able to provide both proactive and reactive counseling to clients regarding their online presence is an expected part of the attorney-client relationship in the twenty-first century, not an added value or special distinguishing trait for a lawyer.

Pennsylvania

Soon after the Philadelphia Committee's opinion, the Pennsylvania Bar Association handed down its Formal Opinion 2014-300, an eighteen-page opinion that provided comprehensive guidance on a whole host of issues related to an attorney's use of social media.[67] These issues ranged from using social media for marketing purposes to mining social media for evidence on witnesses and even researching jurors on social media.[68]

A significant portion of Formal Opinion 2014-300 is devoted to the subject of advising clients on the content of their social media accounts. Referencing cases like the Gulliver Schools opinion from Florida, the Pennsylvania Bar reminded lawyers that "a competent lawyer should advise clients about the content that they post publicly online and how it can affect a case or other legal dispute."[69] Since it has become reasonable to expect that opposing counsel will monitor a client's social media account, the committee reasoned, "[t]racking a client's activity on social media may be appropriate for an attorney to remain informed about developments bearing on the client's legal dispute."[70]

---

[66] *Id.*

[67] Pa. Op. 300, *supra* note 5.

[68] *Id.*

[69] *Id.*

[70] *Id.*

Lawyers, according to the Pennsylvania Bar, "should be certain that their clients are aware of the ramifications of their social media actions," and "should also be aware of the consequences of their own actions and instructions when dealing with a client's social media account."[71] The Pennsylvania Bar Committee agreed with and followed both the Philadelphia Bar's advice as well as the New York Bar's Social Media Guidelines, stating that a lawyer "may not instruct a client to alter, destroy, or conceal any relevant information regardless of whether that information is in paper or digital form."[72] However, consistent with its predecessors, the Pennsylvania Bar concluded that a lawyer may "instruct a client to delete information that may be damaging from the client's page, provided the conduct does not constitute spoliation or is otherwise illegal, but must take appropriate action to preserve the information in the event it is discoverable or becomes relevant to the client's matter."[73]

In addition, citing the same Rules of Professional Conduct as its Philadelphia and New York counterparts, the Pennsylvania Bar Committee stated that attorneys may neither advise clients to post false or misleading information on a social networking page nor offer evidence that the lawyer knows to be false from a social media site.[74] The Pennsylvania Bar pointed out that, while it may be newly articulated, the reasoning underlying this advice is itself not exactly novel. As the opinion noted, "[i]t has become common practice for lawyers to advise clients to refrain from posting any information relevant to a case on any website, and to refrain from using these websites until the case concludes."[75]

North Carolina

In April 2014, the North Carolina Bar Association's Ethics Committee weighed in with its 2014 Formal Ethics Opinion 5, on "Advising a Civil Litigation Client about Social Media."[76] This opinion posed

---

[71] Id.

[72] Id.

[73] Id.

[74] Id.

[75] Id.

[76] N.C. St. Bar, Formal Ethics Op. 2014-5 (2015), https://www.ncbar.gov/for-lawyers/ethics/adopted-opinions/2014-formal-ethics-opinion-5/ [hereinafter N.C. Op. 2014-5].

three questions. First, both prior to and after the filing of a lawsuit, may a lawyer give a client advice about the legal implications of posting on social media sites and coach the client on what should and should not be shared via social media? Second, may a lawyer instruct a client to remove existing social media postings—either before or after litigation commences? Third, may a lawyer instruct the client to change her security and privacy settings on a social media page, either before or after litigation?[77]

As to the first question, the North Carolina Committee answered in the affirmative, pointing out that providing such advice, both before and after the filing of a lawsuit, is part of the lawyer's duty to provide competent and diligent representation to clients.[78] As the opinion states, if a client's social media postings might impact that client's legal matter, then "the lawyer must advise the client of the legal ramifications of existing postings, future postings, and third party comments."[79] This last observation about third-party postings is interesting, and apparently unique to the North Carolina Ethics Committee's opinion. In an age where public reaction occurs not only in response to the postings by the user himself, but also to the "likes," "shares," "comments," "retweets," and "tags" by those reading such a post, it is timely and valuable advice to remind a client about the sort of comments his post might generate. In a small but growing number of cases, individuals have experienced legal fallout not from their own social media post, but from the comments and reactions by other parties.[80]

In responding to the second question, the committee (citing NYCLA Ethics Opinion 745) answered that as long as the removal of postings "does not constitute spoliation and is not otherwise illegal or a violation of a court order," then a lawyer may instruct a client to take down existing social media posts.[81] The committee did add the caveat that if there is the potential that removing such

---

[77] *Id.*

[78] *Id.*

[79] *Id.*

[80] *See, e.g.,* Jake New, *Suspended for Spouse's Comments?,* INSIDE HIGHER ED (Feb. 13, 2015), https://www.insidehighered.com/news/2015/02/13/u-tulsa-student-banned-campus-over-facebook-comments-posted-his-husband (discussing the case of University of Tulsa student George Barnett, who was suspended by the school over allegedly offensive Facebook posts on his page made by his spouse).

[81] N.C. Op. 2014-5, *supra* note 74.

content might constitute spoliation, the lawyer "must also advise the client to preserve the postings by printing the material, or saving the material to a memory stick, compact disc, DVD, or other technology (including web-based technology) used to save documents, audio, and video."[82] In addition, according to the committee, a lawyer "may also take possession of the material for purposes of preserving the same."[83]

For the North Carolina Committee, the third question presented was the easiest to answer. Devoting no discussion to the issue, the committee stated simply that a lawyer may indeed advise his or her client to implement heightened privacy settings, whether before or after suit is filed, as long as such counseling "is not a violation of law or a court order."[84]

Florida

One of the more recent ethics bodies to consider whether lawyers may advise clients to "clean up" their social media profiles was the Florida Bar's Professional Ethics Committee with its Proposed Advisory Opinion 14-1, issued January 23, 2015.[85] In this opinion, limiting itself to a pre-litigation time frame, the committee considered the following questions:

- May a lawyer advise a client to remove posts, photos, videos, and information from social media pages/accounts "that are related directly to the incident for which the lawyer is retained"? How about social media content that is not directly related to the incident for which the lawyer is retained?
- May a lawyer advise a client to change her social media privacy settings in order to remove the profile or account from public view?
- If the lawyer has advised the client to implement more restrictive privacy settings, must a lawyer advise a client not to remove social media content whether or not directly related to the litigation?

---

[82] *Id.*

[83] *Id.*

[84] *Id.*

[85] Prof'l Ethics of The Fla. Bar, Proposed Advisory Op. 14-1 (Jan. 23, 2015).

Not surprisingly, the Florida Bar's opinion cited and agreed with the conclusions of the ethics opinions that had preceded it from the New York, Philadelphia, Pennsylvania, and North Carolina bars. Florida's Committee also agreed that "the general obligation of competence" mandates that lawyers must advise clients "regarding removal of relevant information from the client's social media pages, including whether removal would violate any legal duties regarding preservation of evidence, regardless of the privacy settings."[86] With respect to the most benign level of involvement with a client's social media activities, the Florida Bar's Ethics Committee stated that "a lawyer may advise that a client change privacy settings on the client's social media pages so that they are not publicly accessible."[87]

As far as actual removal of content is concerned, Florida's Committee held that, "[p]rovided that there is no violation of the rules or substantive law pertaining to the preservation and/or spoliation of evidence, a lawyer also may advise that a client remove information relevant to the foreseeable proceeding from social media pages as long as an appropriate record of the social media information or data is preserved."[88] But just what did Florida's Committee mean by "relevant" to the reasonably foreseeable proceeding?

The committee acknowledged that relevance may certainly lie in the eyes of the beholder, or at least require "a factual case-by-case determination."[89] The committee noted that social media content that may not be "related directly" to the incident that made the basis for a lawsuit may nevertheless be deemed relevant to a case.[90] For example, social media mentions on a personal injury plaintiff's Facebook page about her weight training accomplishments and goal to become a personal trainer may not directly relate to the alleged accident, but may be relevant to her damages claim if she is alleging that her injuries are life altering.

Like earlier ethics opinions, Proposed Advisory Opinion 14-1 makes reference to the emerging body of case law on social media spoliation including the *Lester* and *Gatto* decisions discussed later on. And interestingly, prior to issuing this proposed opinion, Florida considered an alternative approach that would have prohibited

---

[86] *Id.*

[87] *Id.*

[88] *Id.*

[89] *Id.*

[90] *Id.*

removal of social media content completely, regardless of steps taken to preserve that content.

West Virginia

West Virginia issued one of the most recent opinions addressing social media advice to clients.[91] The opinion echoes the views of the other states regarding both privacy settings and the removal and preservation of social media. The opinion advises lawyers that they should advise their clients about social media use and must also be mindful of the consequences of their own conduct in providing such advice. It also cautions lawyers about the impermissible use of social media evidence that lawyers know to be false. Notably, the West Virginia opinion acknowledges that "social media is a rapidly and constantly evolving entity" and observes that there is no way certain to anticipate such changes.[92] Therefore, West Virginia "instructs attorneys to adhere to the spirit of the . . . Rules when using social media and not simply the language" of the opinion.[93]

District of Columbia

In November 2016, the District of Columbia issued a comprehensive social media opinion geared to the general provision of legal services. As discussed above, the D.C. opinion is notable in its acknowledgment of the impact of social media in litigation, transactional, and regulatory practice areas.[94] In all three practice areas, D.C. joins the state opinions in advising that competence requires lawyers to understand social media and "at least consider whether and how social media may benefit or harm client matters in a variety of circumstances."[95]

In considering advice to clients about social media, the D.C. opinion notes that competence may require that lawyers review all of their clients' relevant social media postings and advise clients to change privacy settings. The D.C. opinion adds that lawyers should understand and advise clients that a privacy setting does

---

[91] W. Va. Office of Disciplinary Couns., L.E.O. No. 2015-02 (2015), http://www.wvodc.org/pdf/LEO%202015%20-%2002.pdf.

[92] *Id.* at 2.

[93] *Id.*

[94] D.C. Bar Ethics Opinion 371 (2016).

[95] *Id.*

not create an expectation of confidentiality that will establish privilege or work product protection.[96]

Regarding the removal of social media postings, D.C. advises that lawyers may "need to include social media in advice and instructions to clients about litigation holds, document preservation, and document collection."[97] The opinion addresses whether clients may remove social media once litigation or regulatory proceedings are anticipated by directing lawyers to consider not only the legal ethics rules, but also the other statutes, regulations, and case law relevant to the specific legal matter—so there is no clear answer here.[98] The only clear direction is that if anything is removed, an accurate copy must be retained.[99] The opinion does suggest that "in the absence of unlawful activity or anticipation of litigation or adversary proceedings" a lawyer advising a client in a transactional or regulatory matter may be able to advise a client to adjust his social media content so long as the client does not make "fraudulent or unlawful adjustments."[100]

Given the murkiness and lingering uncertainty for attorneys surrounding the "clean up your Facebook page" issue, it is likely that the District of Columbia will not be the last jurisdiction that will address this subject.

---

[96] *Id.*

[97] *Id.*

[98] *Id.*

[99] *Id.*

[100] *Id.*

CHAPTER 4

Social Sleuthing
and Discovery

. . . .

A discussion about social media discovery and legal ethics often parses the distinction between *informal* and *formal* discovery. While formal discovery rules have long been part of both state and federal rules of civil procedure, a sense of codified informal discovery rules has recently emerged in light of digital options.[1] Prior to the Internet, attorneys were required to sufficiently investigate a case in accordance with both statutory rules and the legal ethics rules[2]; however, the options for investigation were more finite.

The Internet has provided a window into the daily activities and thoughts of a vast number of individuals. With more than 1.96 billion[3] people engaged in social media networking, it is likely that an Internet search will reveal relevant information in a vast number of litigious situations.

In fact, a lawyer's social media investigation of a potential case may be determinative in the lawyer's analysis of whether to accept the case. For example, a potential client claiming debilitating injuries from a car accident who is demonstrating yoga prowess on his public Facebook page may not provide the lawyer with the

---

[1] *See* Agnieszka McPeak, *Avoiding Misrepresentation in Informal Social Media Discovery,* 17 SMU SCI. & TECH. L. REV. 449, 582 (2014).

[2] Agnieszka McPeak, *Social Media Snooping and Its Ethical Bounds,* 46 ARIZ. ST. L.J. 845, 853 (2014).

[3] *Percentage of U.S. Population with a Social Media Profile from 2008 to 2016,* STATISTA (last visited Sept. 1, 2016, 04:05 PM), http://www.statista.com/statistics/273476/percentage-of-us-population-with-a-social-network-profile/.

"reasonable basis in fact and law" that warrants the filing of a meritorious case.[4] Moreover, informal discovery on social media may prove critical in determining case strategy.

Let's assume that there is a reasonable explanation for the apparent Facebook contradiction (e.g., yoga's therapeutic value) and the case is filed. Defense counsel must be aware of the possibility that damaging Facebook photos exist and should be ready to further "informally" investigate the credibility of the plaintiff's claim, especially in relation to "yoga therapy." After scouring the Internet and various social media sites to gather any additional information, defense counsel is much better prepared to serve formal discovery that is designed to gain access to information that may be hidden behind privacy walls or that may have been removed but preserved on a flash drive.

The formal discovery process implicates several ethical obligations, including digital competency, fairness to opposing counsel, candor to the tribunal, the duty not to engage in conduct that is intended to burden or embarrass the opposing party, and counseling clients about their social media activities. While it may seem fairly basic, "competence" also encompasses being timely and accurate in one's discovery (or, if you opt for doing keyword searches of documents, anticipating the use of variations on or incorrect versions of a party's name).

Consider, for example, a recent 10th Circuit case, *Pahoua Xiong v. Knight Transportation, Inc.*[5] Pahoua Xiong had a collision with a Knight Transportation truck in May 2009; a little over a year later, in September 2010, she was injured in a second car wreck. After a plaintiff's jury verdict, Knight Transportation moved for a new trial, alleging that it should have been allowed to present more evidence of the second collision as well as evidence that Xiong had committed fraud upon the court.

It seems that after the trial, a Knight Transportation paralegal discovered a photo of Xiong on her cousin's Facebook page. That led to the discovery of more photos that contradicted Xiong's trial testimony of a life characterized by painkillers and void of the activities she had enjoyed prior to the accident. The "Facebook version" of Xiong's life displayed a very different Xiong—there were photos of her clubbing, taking Las Vegas vacations, and enjoying outings to restaurants, weddings, and friends' homes. Based on

---

[4] MODEL RULES OF PROF'L CONDUCT r. 3.1 (Am. Bar Ass'n, 2016).

[5] Pahoua Xiong v. Knight Transp., Inc., No. 14-1390, 2016 WL 4056115, at *1 (10th Cir. 2016).

the social media content that contradicted Xiong's trial testimony, defense counsel hired a private investigator, and obtained even more incriminating evidence from surveillance.

Yet despite the Facebook evidence, the trial court denied Knight's motion for a new trial, and the 10th Circuit affirmed. Why? Under part of the court's multipart test for granting a new trial based on newly discovered evidence, the evidence in question not only had to be newly discovered and material, but the moving party must also have been diligent in discovering it. Here, the trucking company failed to find the Facebook content until after trial (and did not retain a private investigator until after that), and the fact that Xiong had her own name misspelled on her Facebook page did not matter in the eyes of the appellate court. The 10th Circuit pronounced Knight's efforts "hardly diligent."[6]

Here, adhering to the ethical duty of competence would have meant making a much earlier and more diligent search for Xiong's social media postings, including through written discovery requests and independent keyword searches that included variations on the names being searched.

Counseling clients about their discovery obligations in a pending lawsuit necessarily includes a frank discussion of what potentially responsive material is out there and of how to respond. Honesty is key here, and if a lawyer has a client brush off such an inquiry with a response like "I don't have a Facebook account," she should consider following Ronald Reagan's approach to dealing with the former Soviet Union: "Trust but verify."

For example, in the trucking accident case of *Rhone v. Schneider Nat'l Carriers, Inc.*, personal injury plaintiff Alecia Rhone received formal discovery requests for any relevant postings on Facebook and Twitter, including a fairly broad request for a "Download Your Info" report of her Facebook account.[7] Through her counsel, Rhone objected on relevance grounds and failed to disclose the existence of a Facebook account.

Schneider's lawyers conducted their own independent investigation that revealed Rhone's Facebook account and potentially other social media profiles as well. The court was not happy that "Plaintiff did not initially disclose the existence of any social media accounts," and ordered her to comply with the "Download Your Info" request and to provide the defense with a complete list of all

---

[6] *Id.*

[7] Rhone v. Schneider Nat'l Carriers, Inc., No. 4:15-CV-01096-NCC, 2016 WL 1594453 (E.D. Mo. 2016).

of her social media accounts.[8] The moral of the story: when your client says she's one of the dwindling number of people on the planet who doesn't have a social media profile, trust—but verify.

Thus, although social media savvy as a standard of competence and diligence is becoming the norm, there remains a wide discrepancy in knowledge among members of the legal profession. A lack of savvy may have dire consequences for lawyers and their clients, as seen in the cases above. Additionally, the possible outcomes in the simple informal yoga example above range from a lawyer filing a frivolous lawsuit (assume plaintiff's counsel does not ask about social media and there is no plausible explanation) to a defense counsel who fails to competently defend his or her client by impeaching the plaintiff's credibility because the defense counsel failed to investigate the plaintiff's social media presence informally or formally. It is this range of possibilities that the questions in this chapter are designed to explore and thereby provide guidance for how to competently employ social media in both the informal and formal stages of discovery.

QUESTIONS

1. What is informal social media discovery?

As discussed above, informal social media discovery refers to the Internet investigation of a case that commences prior to or simultaneously with the meeting of a potential client at the beginning of litigation. Informal discovery lays the foundation for formal social media discovery and may continue throughout the case. As evidenced by a growing body of ethics advisory opinions, informal social media discovery is subject to the legal ethics rules—wandering in social media terrain without a roadmap may subject a lawyer to stumbling on ethical land mines.[9]

---

[8] *Id.*

[9] *See* John G. Browning, *Digging for the Digital Dirt: Discovery and Use of Evidence from Social Media Sites*, 14 SMU Sci. & Tech. L. Rev. 465, 466-68 (2011); *See generally* Hope A. Comisky & William M. Taylor, *Don't Be a Twit: Avoiding the Ethical Pitfalls Facing Lawyers Utilizing Social Media in Three Important Areas—Discovery, Communications with Judges and Jurors, and Marketing*, 20 Temp. Pol. & Civ. Rts. L. Rev. 297 (2011); *see also* Jan L. Jacobowitz & Danielle Singer, *The Social Media Frontier: Exploring a New Mandate for Competence in the Practice of Law*, 68 U. Miami L. Rev. 445, 457 (2014).

2. What are the primary legal ethics rules that pertain to informal social media discovery?

A brief overview of the most common legal ethics rules that have been applied to the use of social media in the discovery process provides context for the specific questions that will follow. Some of the related rules have been grouped together for efficiency.

The following Model Rules of Professional Conduct are the most frequently cited rules when providing guidance as to how to ethically engage in social media informal discovery:

Rule 1.1 Competence[10]

Rule 1.3 Diligence[11]

The competence rule has long required lawyers to stay abreast of changes in the law; however, the 2012 amendment to the comments of the rule also explains that lawyers need to understand both the benefits and disadvantages of technology.

The diligence rule requires that a lawyer act with "reasonable diligence and promptness in representing a client." The comment to the rule highlights the need for zeal and warns about the pitfalls of procrastination. These admonitions evoke a higher sense of urgency when dealing with the Internet, where information that is readily available today may be taken down or hidden behind a privacy wall tomorrow. Thus, diligence is often linked with competence in ethics opinions that address social media.[12]

Rule 1.6 Confidentiality[13]

Confidentiality is a broad protection afforded to clients and generally pertains to all the information that a lawyer learns in the course of the representation of a client. Historically, it has been viewed as the fundamental underpinning of the attorney-client relationship that promotes the trust and loyalty necessary for effective representation.[14]

---

[10] MODEL RULES OF PROF'L CONDUCT r. 1.1 (Am. Bar Ass'n, 2016).

[11] MODEL RULES OF PROF'L CONDUCT r. 1.3 (Am. Bar Ass'n, 2016).

[12] *See, e.g.*, N.Y.C. Bar Ass'n, Formal Op. 2012-2 (2012), http://www .nycbar.org/member-and-career-services/committees/reports-listing /reports/detail/formal-opinion-2012-2-jury-research-and-social-media.

[13] MODEL RULES OF PROF'L CONDUCT r. 1.6 (Am. Bar Ass'n, 2016).

[14] *See* Jan L. Jacobowitz & Kelly Rains Jesson, *Fidelity Diluted: Client Confidentiality Gives Way to the First Amendment & Social Media in Virginia State Bar, ex rel. Third District Committee v. Horace Frazier Hunter*, 36 CAMPBELL L. REV. 75, 80 (2014).

As discussed in chapter 12, a lack of understanding about the application of the client confidentiality rule to social media posting has caused problems for lawyers; however, in the discovery context it is more of a red herring. Clients often assert a right to confidentiality or privacy regarding their social media posts, which the courts have largely disregarded.

As one judge explained, "If you post a tweet, just like if you scream it out of the window, there is no reasonable expectation of privacy. There is no proprietary interest in your tweets, which you have now gifted to the world."[15]

Thus, Rule 1.6 is mentioned here not only because it is a fundamental rule, but also to clarify that lawyers need to ensure their clients are aware of the limitations of the confidentiality rule regarding social media and discovery.

Rule 3.1 Meritorious Claims and Contentions[16]

Rule 3.3 Candor to the Tribunal[17]

Both Rule 3.1 and Rule 3.3 remind lawyers that social media is a tool to assist them in meeting not only their obligations to file actions that are based in fact and law, but also the obligation to not offer any false evidence. While these rules are not generally the focal point of the ethics advisory opinions, they are important as they underlie the ethical, effective practice of law, and the failure to investigate or properly advise a client about social media may ultimately result in a violation of one of these rules.[18]

Rule 3.4 Fairness to Opposing Party and Counsel[19]

Unlike Rules 3.1 and 3.3, Rule 3.4 regarding Fairness to Opposing Party and Counsel has been a focal point of social media discovery. As

---

[15] People v. Harris, 949 N.Y.S.2d 590, 591-92 (N.Y. Crim. Ct. 2012)

[16] MODEL RULES OF PROF'L CONDUCT r. 3.1 (Am. Bar Ass'n, 2016).

[17] MODEL RULES OF PROF'L CONDUCT r. 3.3 (Am. Bar Ass'n, 2016).

[18] See N.Y. Cnty. Lawyers' Ass'n, Formal Op. 745 (2013) ("[I]f a client's social media posting reveals to an attorney that the client's lawsuit involves the assertion of material false factual statements, and if proper inquiry of the client does not negate that conclusion, the attorney is ethically prohibited from proffering, supporting or using those false statements.").

[19] MODEL RULES OF PROF'L CONDUCT r. 3.4 (Am. Bar Ass'n, 2016).

discussed below, the mishandling of social media discovery has led to sanctions, fees, and in one case contributed to a five-year suspension of a lawyer's license.[20]

Rule 4.1 Truthfulness in Statements to Others[21]

Rule 4.2 Communication with Person Represented by Counsel[22]

Rule 4.3 Dealing with Unrepresented Person[23]

Rule 4.4 Respect for Rights of Third Persons[24]

The Model Rules categorizes these rules as pertaining to "transactions with persons other than clients." Not surprisingly, these rules are often the subject of ethics advisory opinions that offer guidance on the propriety of contacting witnesses and opposing parties on social media as well as obtaining information from their social media accounts.[25] Essentially the rules require transparency and honesty when communicating with others. Of course, in the case of a represented party, no direct contact via Internet or otherwise is permissible without consent of the party's counsel.[26]

---

[20] Allied Concrete Co. v. Lester, 736 S.E.2d 699 (Va. 2013). *See* Final Order, Lester v. Allied Concrete Co., Nos. CL08-150, CL09-223 (Va. Cir. Ct. Oct. 21, 2011).

[21] MODEL RULES OF PROF'L CONDUCT r. 4.1 (Am. Bar Ass'n, 2016).

[22] MODEL RULES OF PROF'L CONDUCT r. 4.2 (Am. Bar Ass'n, 2016).

[23] MODEL RULES OF PROF'L CONDUCT r. 4.3 (Am. Bar Ass'n, 2016).

[24] MODEL RULES OF PROF'L CONDUCT r. 4.4 (Am. Bar Ass'n, 2016).

[25] *See* Phila. Bar Ass'n Prof'l Guidance Comm., Formal Op. 2009-02 (2009), http://www.philadelphiabar.org/WebObjects/PBAReadOnly.woa /Contents/WebServerResources/CMSResources/Opinion_2009-2.pdf [hereinafter Phila. Formal Op. 2009-02]; N.Y. St. Bar Ass'n, Formal Op. 843 (2010); N.Y.C. Bar Ass'n, Formal Op. 2010-2 (2010), http://www .nycbar.org/ethics/ethics-opinions-local/2010-opinions/786-obtaining -evidence-from-social-networking-websites ("There are boundaries to allowing a lawyer to 'friend' an unrepresented party, but they are not crossed when the lawyer uses 'only truthful information.'"); N.H. Bar Ass'n Ethics Comm., Advisory Op. 2012-13/05 (2013), [hereinafter N.H. Op.].

[26] *See* San Diego Cnty. Bar Ass'n, Formal Op. 2011-2 (2011), https:// www.sdcba.org/index.cfm?pg=LEC2011-2.

<u>Rule 5.1 Responsibilities of a Partner or Supervisory Lawyer[27]</u>

<u>Rule 5.2 Responsibilities of a Subordinate Lawyer[28]</u>

<u>Rule 5.3 Responsibilities Regarding Nonlawyer Assistance[29]</u>

The supervisory rules have also come into play in social media scenarios. The degree of social media savvy among lawyers varies wildly from lawyers with almost no knowledge to lawyers and paralegals to whom social media is second nature. The problem arises when a partner or supervisory lawyer has little or no knowledge about social media and the subordinate lawyer or paralegal has little or no knowledge about the application of the legal ethics rules to discovery. Lawyers cannot expect to avoid disciplinary action by asserting the "cave man defense" (i.e., I don't understand because it's not my era) when a subordinate's social media discovery conduct crosses an ethical line.[30]

<u>Rule 8.4 Misconduct[31]</u>

Finally, the misconduct rule serves as an umbrella under which all of the rules reside. Rule 8.4 (a) provides that it is misconduct to violate or attempt to violate any of the rules. However, when social media discovery is involved, Rule 8.4 (c) is often invoked because of its specific prohibition against engaging in conduct "involving dishonesty, fraud, deceit or misrepresentation." Thus, Rule 8.4 (c) is often paired with the rules discussed above that govern transactions with persons other than the client.[32]

With the primary rules in mind, let's take a look at the questions that are frequently posed during the informal discovery process.

3. May I review an opposing party's social media accounts?

If an opposing party maintains social media accounts that are available for public viewing, then the answer is a resounding "yes."[33] Public Internet posts

[27] MODEL RULES OF PROF'L CONDUCT r. 5.1 (Am. Bar Ass'n, 2016).

[28] MODEL RULES OF PROF'L CONDUCT r. 5.2 (Am. Bar Ass'n, 2016).

[29] MODEL RULES OF PROF'L CONDUCT r. 5.3 (Am. Bar Ass'n, 2016).

[30] *See* **Robertelli v. New Jersey Office of Atty. Ethics**, 224 N.J. 470 (N.J. 2016).

[31] MODEL RULES OF PROF'L CONDUCT r. 8.4 (Am. Bar Ass'n, 2016).

[32] *See, e.g.*, Phila. Formal Op. 2009-02, *supra* note 25.

[33] *See* THE FLORIDA BAR, THE FLORIDA BAR BEST PRACTICES FOR EFFECTIVE ELECTRONIC COMMUNICATION 21 (2015); THE SOCIAL MEDIA COMM. OF

and pages have been compared to the newspaper searches "back in the day" before the Internet. In fact, if you fail to do so then arguably you are not competently or diligently investigating a client's case. Moreover, if relevant evidence is found on a social media account, a lawyer should not only review it, but should also download or otherwise preserve it, because it might not be visible as the case progresses. A printout of what was there on a certain day may go a long way toward successfully obtaining additional social media evidence during formal discovery, as discussed below.[34]

4. May I contact an opposing party by connecting or friending him on social media? If the answer is yes, what is the proper procedure for doing so?

The answer to this question lands in the "it depends" column. What does it depend upon? First, is the opposing party represented? If the answer is yes, then you may not connect with him on social media because sending a request to connect is tantamount to directly speaking to an opposing party without the consent of his lawyer.[35] And it is important to note that if you cannot connect, then you may not ask a secretary or paralegal to do what you are not permitted to do.[36] Moreover, claiming ignorance about technology in

---

THE COMMERCIAL & FED. LITIG. SECTION, N.Y. ST. BAR ASS'N SOCIAL MEDIA GUIDELINES OF THE COMMERCIAL AND FEDERAL LITIGATION SECTION OF THE NEW YORK STATE BAR ASSOCIATION 15. (2015), http://www .nysba.org/socialmediaguidelines/ [hereinafter N.Y. St. Bar Social Media Guidelines]; Colo. St. Bar, Formal Opinion 127—Use of Social Media for Investigative Purposes (2015), [hereinafter Colo. Op 127]; D.C. Bar Ethics Opinion 371 (2016).

[34] Christopher B. Hopkins, *Ten Steps to Obtain Facebook Discovery in Florida*, TRIAL ADVOC. Q. 11, 15 (2015).

[35] *See* Phila. Formal Op. 2009-02, *supra* note 25.

[36] *Id. See also* JOHN BROWNING, FROM DINOSAUR TO AVATAR—ETHICAL USE OF SOCIAL MEDIA FROM INVESTIGATION THROUGH DISCOVERY AND TRIAL, 2013 MIDYEAR MEETING: INT'L ASS'N OF DEFENSE COUNS. (2013), ("A May 2012 state court lawsuit in Cleveland, Ohio alleged that an Ohio insurance defense firm hired an investigator to gain access to the privacy-restricted Facebook page of a 12-year-old girl who was the plaintiff in a dog bite lawsuit. According to the plaintiff's complaint, the investigator posted as one of the girl's Facebook friends, enabling him to view her private information and access over 1,000 posted messages and 221 photos between the minor plaintiff and her friends. This pretexting or 'false friending' has resulted in claims of invasion of privacy as

this regard is no excuse, as two New Jersey attorneys learned when they allegedly instructed their paralegal to friend the plaintiff during the trial of a personal injury case.[37] The attorneys claimed that they did not understand Facebook and the meaning of sending a friend request. The personal injury case ultimately settled, but the matter of the friend request took on a life of its own when plaintiff's counsel assisted his client in filing ethics complaints against the two defense lawyers.[38]

The New Jersey State Bar prosecuted the attorneys for violating New Jersey Rule of Professional Conduct (RPC) 4.2 (communications with represented parties); RPC 8.4(c) (conduct involving dishonesty and violation of ethics rules through someone else's actions or inducing such violations); RPC 8.4(d) (conduct prejudicial to the administration of justice); and RPC 5.3(a), (b), and (c) (failure to supervise a nonlawyer assistant). The senior attorney was also charged with violating RPC 5.1(b) and (c), which govern the ethical obligations incumbent upon lawyers for the actions of the attorneys they supervise.[39]

On the other hand, if a party is not represented, then several advisory opinions have indicated that you may contact the opposing party as long as you clearly identify yourself. It is important to learn whether your jurisdiction

---

well as violations of applicable wiretapping statutes interception of communications"). For a discussion on the propriety of searching the private pages of a social media account when access is gained via an employee or other third party that was a Facebook friend of the represented opposing party or witness prior to the lawsuit, *see* the answer to question 8 *infra*.

[37] *See* Robertelli v. New Jersey Office of Atty. Ethics, 134 A.3d 963, 965 (N.J. 2016).

[38] *See* CHRISTOPHER S. PORRINO & MARGARET A. COTOIA, THE LEGAL ETHICS OF SOCIAL MEDIA, N.J. ATTY. GENERAL'S ADVOCACY INSTITUTE (2016); *see also* Robertelli, 134 A.3d at 965; *see also* Debra Cassens Weiss, *Lawyers Accused of Using Paralegal to Friend Litigant on Facebook Are Facing Ethics Probe*, ABA J. (Apr. 20, 2016, 7:45 AM), http://www.abajournal .com/news/article/lawyers_accused_of_using_paralegal_to_friend _litigant_face_ethics_probe_aft.

[39] *See* Jason C. Gavejian, *"Friend" Request Lands Attorneys in Hot Water*, JACKSON LEWIS P.C. (Sept. 7, 2012), http://www.workplace privacyreport.com/2012/09/articles/social-networking/friend -request-lands-attorneys-in-hot-water/.

has opined on this question because the bar associations that have provided guidance have differed as to the degree of transparency that is required.

For example, the New York City Bar Association Committee on Professional Ethics and the Commercial and Federal Litigation Section of the New York State Bar Association have advised that a request to an unrepresented party that includes only the lawyer's name is sufficient.[40] Oregon agreed, but added the caveat that if the unrepresented party asks for additional information, then the requesting lawyer must be forthcoming.[41]

New Hampshire, Colorado, and the District of Columbia adopted much stricter standards, opining that a lawyer who merely provides his name is implicitly signaling that he is disinterested in violation of Rule 4.2.[42] The Colorado opinion explains

> [L]awyers and their agents must provide sufficient disclosure to allow the unrepresented person to make an informed decision concerning whether to grant access to restricted portions of a social media profile. This means (1) providing the name of the lawyer requesting access or for whom the requesting person is acting as an agent, (2) disclosing that the lawyer is acting on behalf of a client, and (3) disclosing the general nature of the matter in connection with which the lawyer is seeking information. The lawyer also must identify the client if disclosure is necessary to avoid a misunderstanding regarding the lawyer's role.[43]

---

[40] N.Y.C. Bar Ass'n, Op. 2010-2 (2010), http://www.nycbar.org/pdf /report/uploads/20071997-FormalOpinion2010-2.pdf; *see also* N.Y. St. Bar Social Media Guidelines, *supra* note 33.

[41] Or. St. Bar, Formal Op. 2013-189 (2013), https://www.osbar.org /_docs/ethics/2013-189.pdf (Accessing Information About Third Parties Through a Social Networking Website).

[42] N.H. Op., *supra* note 25.

[43] Colo. Op 127, *supra* note 33; *see also* James Carlson and Amy DeVan, *New Tools, Same Rules*, 1 OARC UPDATE (2013), (advising lawyers who make a "friend" request seeking nonpublic information of an **unrepresented** party to "truthfully identify yourself and your purpose") (bolded text in original).

5. I'm suing this company for employment discrimination, and I'm sure many of my client's former co-workers who are still there have some good dirt on the employment practices at their firm. A number of them are on Facebook. May I ethically reach out to them via social media?

The short answer is likely "No," at least not without further investigation. The defendant company is represented by counsel, and therefore its current employees may be represented as well. As questions like this illustrate, while there may be uncertainty among practitioners about where the ethical boundary lines are drawn when it comes to social media use, a handy rule of thumb to remember is that the existing rules of professional conduct still apply to newer forms of communication like social media—if you wouldn't say it in person, over the phone, or in a letter, then you shouldn't post it or tweet it either. The Model Rules of Professional Conduct provide guidance in Comment [7] to Rule 4.2, which explains

> In the case of a represented organization, this Rule prohibits communications with a constituent of the organization who supervises, directs or regularly consults with the organization's lawyer concerning the matter or has authority to obligate the organization with respect to the matter or whose act or omission in connection with the matter may be imputed to the organization for purposes of civil or criminal liability. Consent of the organization's lawyer is not required for communication with a former constituent. If a constituent of the organization is represented in the matter by his or her own counsel, the consent by that counsel to a communication will be sufficient for purposes of this Rule . . . In communicating with a current or former constituent of an organization, a lawyer must not use methods of obtaining evidence that violate the legal rights of the organization.

The San Diego County Bar Association's Legal Ethics Committee considered a situation much like the one posed in this question in a May 2011 opinion on the dangers of communicating via social media with a represented party. The opinion concerned permissibility of sending friend requests to two of the defendant employer's high-ranking staff, hoping to access disparaging Facebook posts about the company. The ethics committee advised that such requests would violate both the rule against contacting a represented party and the attorney's duty not to deceive third parties. Thus, lawyers seeking access to the social media of a represented party in a corporate setting must adhere to formal discovery channels or obtain consent from the party's counsel.[44]

6. May I review a witness's social media accounts?

Yes, you may review any social media that is accessible to the public.

7. May I contact a witness through social media? If the answer is yes, what is the proper procedure for doing so?

The guidelines for contacting an opposing party on social media also apply to connecting to a witness on social media. In fact, most of the opinions discussed in the answer to question 4 primarily distinguish between a represented and unrepresented individual rather than between an opposing party and a witness. Thus, if a witness is represented then the no contact rule applies. If a witness is unrepresented, the conservative approach (and arguably the best practice "Colorado" approach) is for a lawyer to identify himself, the fact that he is representing a client, and the general nature of the matter about which he is inquiring.

8. Do the contact rules for the opposing party or witness differ if I have a law clerk or paralegal engage in the contact?

The rules remain the same—what a lawyer is not permitted to do, he may not ask a law clerk or paralegal to do on his behalf.[45] The 5.1–5.3 supervisory rules discussed above require supervisory lawyers to supervise subordinate lawyers, nonlawyer staff, and any independent contractors that may be retained in a case so as to avoid a violation of the rules of professional contact. A lawyer is not permitted to contact a represented witness on social media and is not allowed to contact an unrepresented witness in a deceptive manner; therefore, it is impermissible for a lawyer to ask another to engage in such conduct.

---

[44] San Diego Cty. Bar Ass'n, Legal Ethics Op. 2011-2 (2011), https://www.sdcba.org/?pg=LEC2011-2.

[45] Phil Bar Ass'n Prof'l Guidance Comm., Op. 2009-02 (2009), http://www.philadelphiabar.org/WebObjects/PBAReadOnly.woa/Contents/WebServerResources/CMSResources/Opinion_2009-2.pdf.

9. Is it permissible to review an opposing party or witness's social media postings that are behind a privacy wall if my client, a witness, or an employee at my firm has been connected on social media to the opposing party or witness prior to the incidents that are the subject of the current lawsuit?

This debatable question is most often answered in the affirmative.[46] The analysis involves a parsing of the concepts of both public information and deceptive conduct. For example, the New Hampshire Bar's ethics opinion states that where "a person, not acting as an agent or at the behest of the lawyer, has obtained information from the witness's social media account . . . the lawyer may receive the information and use it in litigation as any other information."[47] While the ethics opinions may seem to draw a bright line distinction between public and private, the reality of social media accounts is more nuanced.

In other words, on Facebook, information that is not available to the general public may be available to an individual's group of Facebook friends. Additionally, the same individual may belong to various Facebook groups on which the members' posts are public. So while the information is not readily available to a member of the public, it is easily accessible to Facebook friends and group members who do not owe an inherent (or contractual) duty of confidentiality to their Facebook friends.

The New York State Bar Association's (NYSBA) guidelines on social media note that most bar associations have not directly addressed this question: whether a lawyer may nondeceptively view a social media account that may technically be private, but that a lawyer has the ability to view through an alumni network or by being a "friend of a friend" of that person.[48] However, the NYSBA definition of restricted content provides some guidance:

> Information that is not available to a person viewing a social media account because an existing on-line relationship between the account holder and the person seeking to view it is lacking (whether

---

[46] N.H. Op., *supra* note 25; *see also* DANIEL BLAU, SOCIAL NETWORKING AS AN INVESTIGATIVE TOOL, UNC SCHOOL OF GOVERNMENT 2014 SPRING PUBLIC DEFENDER ATTORNEY & INVESTIGATOR CONFERENCE 3 (2014) ("Although bar organizations have offered minimal guidance in this area, this type of investigative tactic is probably permissible").

[47] N.H. Op., *supra* note 25.

[48] N.Y. St. Bar Social Media Guidelines, *supra* note 33, at 33.

directly, e.g., a direct Facebook "friend," or indirectly, e.g., a Facebook "friend of a friend"). Note that content intended to be 'restricted' may be 'public' through user error in seeking to protect such content, through re-posting by another member of that social media network, or as a result of how the content is made available by the social media network or due to technological change.[49]

Although bar organizations have offered minimal guidance in this area, the literature indicates viewing private information through another person's account with that person's assistance is "probably permissible."[50] For example, a lawyer's paralegal has been Facebook friends with another individual for two years. The individual has just become the defendant in one of the lawyer's new cases. The lawyer is able to view the private Facebook information on the opposing party's account via the use of his paralegal's Facebook account.

The lawyer's viewing of the information is likely permissible, because the original friend request between the paralegal and the opposing party occurred before the litigation, was not made for any purpose related to the subject matter of the litigation and did not involve any deceit or misrepresentation. Thus, there is arguably no deception by the lawyer because "the witness chose to reveal information to someone who was not acting on behalf of the lawyer. The witness took the risk that the third party might repeat the information to others."[51]

Moreover, courts in several jurisdictions have found, in the context of motions to compel social media discovery, that there is no right to privacy on social media accounts, which reinforces the notion that obtaining information that is not generally available to the public, but that is obtained by a lawyer without resort to deception should be ethically permissible.[52] However, since this scenario remains largely unexplored by the ethics advisory opinions and case law to date, a cautious approach is recommended.

---

[49] *Id.*

[50] Blau, *supra* note 46, at 5.

[51] *Id*; *see also* N.H. Op., *supra* note 25.

[52] *See* Robert Keeling, et al., *Neither Friend Nor Follower: Ethical Boundaries on the Lawyer's Use of Social Media,* 24 Cornell J. L. & Pub. Pol'y 145, 162-64 (2014).

10. **In the event that I permissibly view and locate potential evidence on any aspect of the social media accounts of the opposing parties or any of the witnesses in a case, what, if any, other steps should I take to preserve the evidence?**

If potential evidence is located, it should be preserved so that it may be used not only during depositions and in the trial, but also to obtain additional social media discovery as is explained in the answer to question 15. Additionally, a lawyer should notify the opposing party or counsel to preserve the party's social media information.[53] The Illinois Bar, for example, suggests sending out a preservation-of-evidence letter immediately to the opposing counsel, or to an unrepresented party if the sender makes sure the letter is very clear. The D.C. Bar advises that competent representation may require that a lawyer include social media in a litigation hold letter to an adversary.[54] Preservation letters remind opponents to preserve evidence but also serve to lay the foundation for a subsequent claim for spoliation by "helping to establish bad faith and conscious disregard of the duty to preserve relevant evidence."[55]

Following a preservation letter, the next steps are to use the standard methods of discovery such as informal requests, written interrogatories, and document production requests to parties, and subpoenas to nonparties.[56] These types of formal discovery are discussed in further detail in the questions below.

It is important to note that when preserving social media information, a screenshot may not suffice if the information becomes evidence.[57] Evidence ultimately must be authenticated to be admissible. Screenshots or printouts of a picture or post do not contain the recorded metadata. Metadata includes important information such as when something was posted, who authored it, or whether it has been edited.[58] As an alternative, there are several programs that can electronically capture and authenticate social

---

[53] Gary L. Beaver, et al., *Social Media Evidence—How to Find It and How to Use It*, A.B.A. Section of Litigation: 2013 A.B.A. Annual Meeting 14 (2013).

[54] Ed Finkel, *Evidence/Social Media; Building Your Case with Social Media Evidence*, 102(6) Ill. B. J. 276 (2014), https://www.isba.org /ibj/2014/06/buildingyourcasewithsocialmediaevid; D.C. Bar Ethics Opinion 371 (2016).

[55] *Id.*

[56] Beaver, *supra* note 53, at 14.

[57] Finkel, *supra* note 54.

[58] *Id.*

media; the Illinois Bar suggested Snagit or Camtasia, for example.[59] Another tool found on a quick Google search is Social Media Information, a site that offers an "export" service.[60]

11. What is formal discovery as it relates to social media?

Formal discovery as it relates to social media is traditional discovery that is conducted in accordance with the state or federal rules of civil procedure, which govern interrogatories, requests for production of documents, requests for admissions, and notices of deposition. From a legal ethics standpoint, competence, diligence, communication, fairness to opposing counsel, and candor to the tribunal all apply and contribute to the necessity of not only understanding social media, but also to knowing when and how to incorporate social media into formal discovery. In fact, the D.C. opinion advises that "in litigation, discovery requests should expressly include social media as sources, and discovery responses should not overlook them."[61] The final questions in this chapter are offered to provide some insight into the appropriate incorporation of social media into formal discovery.[62]

12. What types of questions should I be asking in interrogatories?

The specific interrogatories that are propounded vary by the facts and issues at play in a specific case; however, interrogatories should include questions geared to ascertaining whether the other party has or has ever had a social media presence and if so, on what networks the party has accounts.[63] Depending on the jurisdiction, you may want to include follow-up questions or plan to send follow-up interrogatories. If the party has accounts, then

---

[59] *Id.* (The authors of this book have no knowledge as to the quality of these programs, but just assert that the Illinois Bar included them as examples.)

[60] JoEllen Marsh, *Exports: When to Save Social Media Profiles*, SOCIAL MEDIA INFORMATION (Sept. 8, 2015), https://smiaware.com/export/use-cases/ ("Just last week, SMI Exported a 1,200-page Facebook profile only a day before all content was made private").

[61] D.C. Bar Ethics Opinion 371 (2016).

[62] The answers to questions eleven to fifteen are meant to introduce practical considerations for the ethical and effective use of social media in discovery but are not designed to offer specific discovery strategy, which may vary with the area of law and facts at issue in a specific case.

[63] *See* Hopkins, *supra* note 34. *See* JOHN G. BROWNING, SOCIAL MEDIA AND LITIGATION PRACTICE GUIDE (Thomson Reuters, 2014).

the follow-up questions may become more specific as to duration of the accounts, types of posts, password requests, and so on.

13. What questions should I include in a request for production of documents?

There are different strategies currently being employed by attorneys who routinely request social media production. Some attorneys indicate that they start with an extremely broad request. Their experience has been that often the opposing attorney willingly produces vast amounts of information and sometimes shares his client's passwords. While a broad request may be a successful method, if opposing counsel has any social media savvy, he will object to the request as overly broad. Then the requesting attorney must regroup and redraft the questions or file a motion to compel. As discussed below, courts across the country have inconsistently ruled on whether a broad request is enforceable.[64]

Moreover, a broad formal discovery request may implicate the ethical duty to refrain from conduct involving third parties that is calculated primarily for purposes of delay, embarrassment, or burden. Discovery of a party's social media postings often elicits objections based on privacy grounds—an argument that has been resoundingly rejected by nearly all courts to consider the objection. Certainly, narrowly tailored discovery requests that seek all relevant or potentially relevant social media content are the preferred way to go. Casting a much wider net and simply seeking "all of [opposing party's] social media posts—ever" or demanding passwords and login credentials is likely to not only draw objections from opposing counsel, but also a rebuke from the trial judge. The general trend nationwide in reported cases involving discovery disputes over social media content is to reject such overly broad requests and "fishing expeditions" in favor of more narrowly driven searches for relevant evidence. As one beleaguered federal judge in Louisiana put it:

> The Court suspects that even a casual reader would view these requests as intrusive particularly given the fact that the combination of requests for log-in and password information and an accompanying request for an authorization that Facebook turn over all the sought-after information would eventually render moot any exercise

---

[64] *Id.* at 80. *See* Agnieszka A. McPeak, *The Facebook Digital Footprint: Paving Fair and Consistent Pathways to Civil Discovery of Social Media Data*, 48 WAKE FOREST L. REV. 887, 910 (2013).

of discretion by Farley or his counsel in determining what, if any, information was actually discoverable . . . No doubt the proliferation of activity on social networking sites ("SNS") is affecting what have been fairly well-established conventions when it comes to formal discovery in federal-court litigation. Smart, opportunistic lawyers are now routinely seeking to exploit the 'brave new world' feel of this ever-evolving aspect of how many average Americans go about their daily lives to gain an advantage in litigation. This Court's recent experience and research confirms this observation, evident not only in the cascade of motions like the one now before this Court that seek surprisingly broad disclosure of "private" online disclosure, but in the relative paucity of on-all-fours precedent that might otherwise guide us as to how a litigant's social media activity and conduct fit into what lawyers and judges already understand about the breadth and limits of discovery under the Federal Rules of Civil Procedure.[65]

Making blanket requests for everything under the sun in terms of the other side's social media won't just risk an objection from opposing counsel or the ire of the presiding judge. It also risks violating ethical prohibitions against engaging in conduct calculated solely to embarrass or burden a third party. Sure, the Facebook photos of your personal injury plaintiff boasting about her personal best in the local 10k two weeks after the "devastating" accident are highly relevant to her claims and your client's defenses, but do you need all those embarrassing photos from her best friend's bachelorette party? And while the job-related postings of your employment client's immediate supervisor may strengthen your discrimination and hostile work environment claims, do you really need his vacation photos with the family? ABA Model Rule 4.4 cautions lawyers not to use means "that have no substantial purpose other than to embarrass, delay, or burden a third person, or use methods of obtaining evidence that violate the legal rights of such a person." Lawyers should keep in mind pragmatic concerns about limiting discovery to what they need, but they should also remember Rule 4.4.

　　Best practice dictates the application of the traditional rules—a request for documents that are relevant or reasonably calculated to lead to admissible evidence in connection with the claims in the case.[66] For example, in a personal injury case, a request for the opposing party's entire Facebook

---

[65] Farley v. Callais & Sons LLC, No. 14-2550, 2015 WL 4730729, at *1 (E.D. La. 2015).

[66] BROWNING, *supra* note 63, at 76.

account with no limitation on dates or type of material being requested would be difficult to justify to the court in a motion to compel (see answer to question 14 below). In other words, analyze what types of information may be relevant to the case without regard to social media and then draft a request that includes social media.

14. What questions should I pose in opposing party or witness depositions?

Depositions provide another opportunity to ask the deponent about his or her social media presence. South Florida attorney Christopher Hopkins suggests the following questions as an example of what defense counsel may ask at plaintiff's deposition. Moreover, he suggests that even if these questions are not asked at a deposition, they should be considered in the defense's overall discovery strategy:

a. Confirm the plaintiff's social media accounts listed in the answer to interrogatory.

b. What is the plaintiff's frequency of use? What does the plaintiff typically do on Facebook?

c. Number of friends? Privacy settings?

d. Does plaintiff acknowledge that Facebook itself can see his or her content? And that friends might share what the plaintiff has posted?

e. On Facebook, does plaintiff discuss his or her activities, physical condition, or emotional/mental condition?

f. On Facebook, has the plaintiff or anyone else discussed or made statements about this case?

g. Does plaintiff post pictures/video? Do "friends" typically tag the plaintiff in posted images?

h. Are there pictures/video on Facebook of the plaintiff that relate to any claim or defense in this case?

i. Are there "before and after" photos/video on Facebook? Are there captions or comments to those images?

j. Does the plaintiff typically insert comments or captions along with images uploaded to Facebook? Do plaintiff's friends typically comment/reply to plaintiff's posts?

k. Has the plaintiff altered, removed, or deleted any content since the incident that is the subject of this lawsuit? What, when, and why?[67]

---

[67] Hopkins, *supra* note 34, at 16.

Additionally, a lawyer should investigate a party's social media presence both prior to and after the deposition. The *Nucci* case demonstrates the importance of the pre-deposition investigation.[68]

In the *Nucci* case, the plaintiff was alleging injuries as a result of an accident in a Target store. Defense counsel checked the plaintiff's public Facebook page before the deposition and saw a large number of photos. During the deposition, plaintiff was asked about her social media presence. When the Facebook page was examined shortly after the deposition, the number of photos had significantly decreased. This quick strategy eventually became a key component in the defense counsel's ability to prevail on a motion to compel that was ultimately decided by Florida's Fourth District Court of Appeals after an interlocutory appeal.[69] The photos contradicted the plaintiff's claim and the case settled.[70]

The *Nucci* result and the questions above are offered as examples of the use of social media in discovery with the goal of creating awareness that the fundamental legal ethics requirements of competence and diligence mandate attorneys to explore the possible significance of social media in any case.

15. If I receive discovery that requests social media information or production of documents from my client, what are appropriate objections to the requests?

Objections to social media requests track the traditional objections—not relevant, not likely to lead to admissible evidence, unduly burdensome. Essentially, the jurisprudence in this area, while somewhat inconsistent throughout the country, looks at whether a request is narrowly tailored and relevant to the claims in the case.[71] Moreover, the courts have rejected privacy claims and concluded that once information is posted on the Internet, an individual no longer has an expectation of privacy regardless of various privacy walls that may be in place.[72] However, there must be a predicate

---

[68] Nucci v. Target Corp., 162 So.3d 146, 148 (Fla. 4th DCA 2015).

[69] *Id.*

[70] *Id.* (also supported by conversation with Nucci counsel).

[71] *Id.* at 5; Levine v. Culligan of Florida, Inc., 2013 WL 1100404 (Fla. 15th Cir. Ct. 2013).

[72] *See* U.S. v. Meregildo, 883 F. Supp.2d 523, 526 (S.D.N.Y. 2012); *see also* Patterson v. Turner Construction Co., 931 N.Y.S.2d 311, 312 (N.Y. App. Div. 2011) ("... not shielded from discovery merely because plaintiff used the service's privacy settings to restrict access"); Romano v.

advanced to support a request to access social media information that is posted behind a privacy wall.[73]

For example, the assertions that evidence on a public page suggests that there will be additional relevant information on the private page have been successful.[74] But, the sole argument that there might be relevant information behind privacy walls because of the nature of social media has been denied and characterized as an impermissible fishing expedition.[75]

16. If the other party is refusing to respond or objecting to interrogatories or a request for production of documents, what is the likelihood that I will succeed in obtaining the information if I file a motion to compel?

There is a growing body of jurisprudence that addresses motions to compel and mirrors the answer to question 15 concerning the appropriate objections to social media discovery requests. Generally, the courts have compelled production of social media evidence when the party who is seeking the evidence adequately demonstrates the relevance to the case and the narrowly tailored nature of the request.[76] Fishing expeditions are frowned upon, so it is often better to seek to compel information based on a request framed in a reasonable finite time period and in which the information itself was narrowly defined. In other words, if you can demonstrate that photographs are relevant and will assist the prosecution or defense of a case, then perhaps seeking only photographs as opposed to an entire Facebook account is the way to prevail.[77]

From a legal ethics standpoint, the important takeaway is that in order to be competent, a lawyer must be aware that social media discovery may be a significant part of a case and must understand when and how to incorporate social media discovery. Failure to explore social media discovery may cost a

---

Steelcase, Inc., 907 N.Y. 650, 655 (N.Y. Sup. Ct. 2010) ("To permit a party claiming very substantial damage . . . to hide behind self-set privacy controls on a website . . . risks depriving the opposite party of access to material. . . ."); Levine v. Culligan of Florida, Inc., 2013 WL 1100404 (Fla. 15th Cir. Ct. 2013).

[73] *See Id.*; Hogwood v. HCA Holdings Inc. et al., Case No. 2011CA013010 (Fla. 15th Cir. Ct. 2015).

[74] *See* Romano, 907 N.Y. at 650.

[75] *See* Levine, 2013 WL 1100404 at *1.

[76] *See* Nucci, 162 So.3d at 146; Romano, 907 N.Y. at 650; Hogwood, Case No. 2011CA013010 at *1.

[77] *Id.*

client a case and the lawyer his reputation or worse—he may be subjected to a bar complaint or a malpractice claim.[78]

17. Assuming that I obtain useful social media discovery, what issues arise if I choose to use social media evidence at trial?

Using social media evidence at trial raises the traditional issues of relevance, authentication, and exclusionary rules, but once again the challenge is to apply these standards to the digital age.[79] Relevance considerations are essentially the same ones that are discussed above in connection with succeeding on a motion to compel.

Authentication issues have courts throughout the country creating a new body of law and the court opinions have been inconsistent. For example, for several years the inconsistency was reflected in the disagreement between Maryland and Texas decisions on the requisite proof for authentication; the decisions were often cited and used for guidance.[80] Maryland originally required direct authentication while Texas accepted circumstantial authentication. However, recently the Maryland Supreme Court essentially reversed its position and adopted the Texas view in an opinion that decided three cases at once that concerned social media evidentiary issues.[81]

The Maryland Supreme Court concluded that social media evidence may be authenticated by circumstantial evidence if that evidence is sufficient to allow a reasonable juror to conclude that the social media evidence is what it purports to be. (The Maryland decision involved three cases in which there were screenshots of social media messages sent through Facebook and Twitter accounts.) The Maryland court also noted that social media authentication issues are case and context specific. Thus, it is important for a lawyer not only to know the case law in his jurisdiction, but also to understand

---

[78] *See* Jan L. Jacobowitz & Danielle Singer, *The Social Media Frontier: Exploring a New Mandate for Competence in the Practice of Law*, 68 U. Miami L. Rev. 445, 469-76 (2014).

[79] *See* Jeffrey Cole, *The Brave New World of Internet Evidence—It's Not as Brave or New as It Seems,* 42(4) A.B.A. Litigation J. (2014); Michael R. Holt & Victoria San Pedro, *Social Media Evidence: What You Can't Use Won't Help You—Practical Considerations for Using Evidence Gathered on the Internet,* 88 Fla. Bar J. 8 (2014).

[80] Griffin v. State, 192 Md. App. 518 (2010), judgment rev's, 419 Md. 343 (2011); Tienda v. State, 358 S.W.3d 633 (Tex. Crim. App. 2012).

[81] Sublet v. State, 442 Md. 632, 636 (Md. 2015) (opinion addresses Sublet v. State, Harris v. State, and Monge-Martinez v. State).

the opinions from other jurisdictions in order to frame the most compelling argument for authentication.[82]

If relevance and authentication standards are both met, then the evidence may be admitted unless it is subject to an applicable exclusionary rule. Generally, where social media is involved, it is often the hearsay rule objections that must be confronted. A person's Facebook post or tweet is an out-of-court statement, but it is being offered to prove the truth of the matter asserted therein. In demonstrating the purpose for which the statement is being offered, the most common exceptions to the hearsay rule that come into play are admission against interest and admission by a party opponent. Among other exceptions that should be considered are present sense impressions and excited utterances—the speed at which individuals are recording their impressions and reactions is such that these exceptions may become more common. Of course, the court may still find that the prejudicial impact of a social media post may outweigh its probative value. Regardless, today's competent trial lawyer must be aware of the possible arguments and defenses when the admission of social media evidence is at stake.[83]

---

[82] *See* Cole, *supra* note 79; BROWNING, *supra* note 63, at 130.

[83] For a more detailed analysis and practice pointers, see, generally, BROWNING, *supra* note 63.

CHAPTER 5

Digital Hide-and-Seek?
Preservation and
Spoliation of Evidence

··

There is a growing body of case law interpreting not only the discoverability of social media content and its impact on all kinds of cases, but also the importance of taking care to preserve evidence as required by the previously discussed ethics opinions. The opinions grant permission to change privacy settings and remove social media posts as long as there is no spoliation or other violation of the law. However, it is beyond the scope of the advisory opinions to define the law, explain the various nuances that may be involved in the definition of the appropriate preservation of social media, or discuss the repercussions of a failure to preserve.

Moreover, there are additional ethical issues raised by the failure (however well intentioned) to *properly* preserve and produce social media discovery. For example, the South Carolina case of *Wellin v. Wellin* provides an illustration of how *not* to preserve and produce evidence.[1] In this case, the defense had to move to compel the production of certain electronically stored information, including emails, text messages, and Facebook posts, in their native format.

The motion was granted in part because plaintiffs' earlier attempts at production had been somewhat, shall we say, Stone Age. It seems the plaintiffs had "printed out responsive emails and provided photocopies of certain portions of these emails to

---

[1] Wellin v. Wellin, No. 2:13-CV-1831-DCN, 2014 WL 3496514, at *1 (D.S.C. 2014).

Defendants. Additionally, [one plaintiff] provided the context of several text message exchanges and Facebook posts by transcribing these messages on loose-leaf paper."[2] Yes, that's right—loose-leaf paper!

Another ill-fated and ethically deficient effort at social media preservation illustrates the practical consequences of the failure to properly preserve evidence. In an employment case out of Indiana, the court weighed the manner in which the plaintiff had "preserved" social media comments that she was now seeking to admit.[3] The court observed

> These exhibits purport to be Facebook conversations between plaintiff and [the defendant's former] employees in support of her reduction in force allegation. She appears to have re-typed the conversations on clean sheets of paper and submitted them as her evidence. There is no documentation from Facebook detailing these conversations or any other indicia of reliability; consequently, the exhibits are unreliable and will not be considered.[4]

Thus, a lawyer must not only be aware that he or she must preserve social media evidence, but also must understand how to do so. The law of spoliation dovetails with a lawyer's ethical responsibilities. Establishing the relationship between the rules of professional conduct and spoliation lays the foundation for exploring questions that arise regarding social media evidence and for looking to case law for some of the answers.

QUESTIONS

1. **What is the relationship between the Model Rules of Professional Conduct and spoliation?**

   The law of spoliation predates the Model Rules of Professional Conduct and is designed to prevent the destruction of information by an individual who knows that the information is likely to become evidence in a pending lawsuit

---

[2] *Id.*

[3] Maddox v. Meridian Sec. Ins. Co., No. 1:13-cv-01551-RLY-DML (S.D. Ind. June 30, 2015).

[4] *Id.*

or in a future one that can be reasonably anticipated.[5] The legal obligation to preserve evidence may originate in common law, a statute, a contract, or a discovery order.[6] A party's destruction of evidence may result in court-ordered sanctions such as dismissal of a claim, exclusion of expert witness testimony, or adverse jury instructions.[7]

The Model Rules of Professional Conduct that require fairness in dealing with opposing counsel[8] and candor to the tribunal,[9] and that prohibit both misrepresentation and any other conduct that impinges upon the fair administration of justice,[10] dovetail with the law of spoliation.

Model Rule 3.4 (a) specifically reinforces the legal prohibition against spoliation and provides that a lawyer shall not

> unlawfully obstruct another party's access to evidence or unlawfully alter, destroy or conceal a document or other material having potential evidentiary value. A lawyer shall not counsel or assist another person to do any such act;

The comments to the rule explain that the requisite fairness in the adversary process is hindered when there is not ready access to relevant evidence in a case. Thus, as discussed above, when dealing with social media evidence, it is imperative that a lawyer ensure that his or her client's social media evidence is preserved, especially if the client plans to change his or her privacy settings or remove social media evidence from his or her social media account.

---

[5] *See* John G. Browning, Social Media and Litigation Practice Guide 94 (Thomson Reuters 2014) (In eighteenth-century England a jeweler suffered spoliation sanctions for keeping the stone from a ring that was brought to him for an appraisal. The jury was instructed to "presume the strongest against the jeweler and the make the value of the best jewels the measure of damages." Internal citations omitted.).

[6] *See, e.g.*, Gayer v. Fine Line Constr. & Elec., Inc., 970 So.2d 424, 426 (Fla. 4th DCA 2007).

[7] *See* Point Blank Sols., Inc. v. Toyobo Am., Inc., No. 09-61166-CIV, 2011 WL 1456029, at *27-28 (S.D. Fla. 2011).

[8] Model Rules of Prof'l Conduct r. 3.4 (Am. Bar Ass'n, 2016) (Fairness to Opposing Counsel).

[9] Model Rules of Prof'l Conduct r. 3.3 (Am. Bar Ass'n, 2016) (Candor to the Tribunal).

[10] Model Rules of Prof'l Conduct r. 8.4 (Am. Bar Ass'n, 2016) (Misconduct).

Interestingly, as mentioned above, the ethics advisory opinions previously discussed generally allow parties to remove social media evidence as long as the removal does not violate the law of spoliation. The ethics opinions neither attempt to define the law of spoliation nor suggest the appropriate method for preserving social media evidence, which remains the subject of some debate and may impact not only the ethics rules and the law of spoliation, but also the ability to authenticate the evidence for use at trial.[11]

2. What if a client has changed his privacy setting prior to the lawsuit, but after the incident that gives rise to the legal claim?

In re Platt demonstrates the potential fallout from changing one's social media privacy settings immediately after the incident that gives rise to a legal claim.[12] The case concerns an adversary proceeding in bankruptcy court, following a state court personal injury suit arising out of a physical altercation at a bar between plaintiff Will Rhodes and defendant Justin Platt.[13] Platt filed bankruptcy, and Rhodes sought to have any debt from the civil suit classified as nondischargeable due to "willful and malicious" conduct by Platt.[14] To determine if his conduct met this standard, the court had to examine Platt's behavior and credibility, including his conduct after the incident, to see if Platt had the intent to injure Rhodes.[15]

The court observed that although immediately after the incident the bar staff members "were initially able to identify Defendant by finding his Facebook account, Defendant made his Facebook account private soon after the incident occurred."[16] The court noted that this act in which "Defendant's account was 'made private' such that an unknown third party searching for Defendant would no longer be able to find him on Facebook," supported an inference that the defendant acted with the specific intent to injure the plaintiff, and therefore the debt was not dischargeable.[17]

While a case like Platt appears to be an outlier in its condemnation of the act of adopting a heightened privacy setting for a Facebook profile,

---

[11] See discussion in Chapter 4 on discovery, question 17.

[12] In re Pratt, No. 11-12367-CAG, 2012 WL 5337197 (Bankr. W.D. Tex. 2012).

[13] Id.

[14] Id.

[15] Id.

[16] Id.

[17] Id.

there are those who raise the concern that lawyers advising clients to make their privacy settings more restrictive could be exposed to accusations of "obstructing access to evidence." After all, under ABA Model Rule of Professional Conduct 3.4, a lawyer may not "obstruct" another party's access to evidence or alter, destroy, or "conceal" any material that may be of evidentiary value.

Commentators have suggested that "moving material behind a privacy wall could be considered improper concealment."[18] Such concerns overlook the fact that a client may have perfectly legitimate, non-litigation related reasons to make his or her social media profiles nonpublic. Individuals may wish to change privacy settings to shield information from prospective employers. (In fact, a growing number of states have passed employee/applicant privacy legislation that prevents employers from demanding access to privacy-protected social media accounts.)

A student who is being cyberbullied or an individual being harassed or stalked online may also choose to change his or her privacy settings. Lawyers give clients advice on maintaining privacy all the time, from placing the designation "confidential" on correspondence to simply advising a client to close his or her window blinds, to telling an individual not to publicly discuss a pending case. Advising a client to adopt more stringent privacy settings on his or her Facebook profile has no legal distinction from such counsel. As long as the relevant social media content is preserved, no ethical rule has been violated.[19] A party is well within its rights to change privacy settings to limit future exposure of statements or photos—including those posted by others—that might be embarrassing, irrelevant, or even harmful.

---

[18] Matt Fair, *Pa. Bar's Facebook Advice May Spur Obstruction Claims*, Law360 (Nov. 24, 2014, 5:51 PM), http://www.law360.com/articles /594261/pa-bar-s-facebook-advice-may-spur-obstruction-claims.

[19] Perhaps another reason for not imposing ethical prohibitions on a lawyer advising a client about her privacy settings is to protect the ignorant client. A number of studies have looked at attitudes toward and user utilization of privacy settings on social networking profiles. According to one *Consumer Reports* study in 2012, only about 37 percent of Facebook users had used the site's privacy tools to customize how much information could be shared with third parties. The same study revealed that nearly 13 million Facebook users had never set or were ignorant of these privacy settings themselves. For a number of clients, therefore, a lawyer's advice on privacy settings may not only be timely but may save the client from him- or herself.

3. Is there any problem with a client changing privacy settings during a pending case?

Lawyers need to consider whether a client's alteration of privacy settings during a pending case would risk violating a court order. In a 2016 case surrounding Fair Housing Act claims in the Western District of New York, the defense counsel sought discovery of the plaintiff Thurmond's social media postings in the case.[20] After the defense counsel—who had been able to view and print off screenshots from the plaintiff's publicly viewable Facebook and Instagram accounts—complained of posts "disappearing," a motion to compel and accusations of spoliation followed.

Although the court rejected the defense's request for relief (noting that plaintiff Thurmond had produced "hundreds of postings" over an extended period of time), the judge also stated that "an apparent modification of Thurmond's security settings" made her posts "hidden from defendant's view."[21] The court found it "troubling" that the posts were removed from public view "after the Court issued a consent order designed to preserve the status quo of her social media accounts." It concluded that "[b]y altering her Facebook account, Thurmond violated the Court's May 21 order."[22]

Although the judge didn't consider it spoliation, he observed that Thurmond's conduct would be "a fair subject for cross-examination and could result in the impeachment of her credibility."[23] Thus, in the spirit of there being exceptions to every rule, a judge's order to maintain the social media status quo trumps the ethics advisory opinions' permission to advise a client to change privacy settings.

4. Does deactivating a social media account constitute spoliation?

An area that poses considerable concern for lawyers advising clients about their social media presence involves deactivating social networking accounts. Clients and lawyers alike may be unaware of not only the consequences of account deactivation, but also the fact that sites vary in terms of their deactivation policies; consequently, content may still be viewable for a period of time after deactivation.

---

[20] Thurmond v. Bowman, No. 14-CV-6465W, 2016 WL 1295957 (W.D.N.Y. 2016).

[21] *Id.*

[22] *Id.*

[23] *Id.*

For example, after deactivating one's Twitter account, some content may be viewable for at least several days afterward. And while Twitter purportedly retains data for 30 days from the date of deactivation, Twitter retains its license to use content that was posted, and a Twitter profile may still appear in public search engine results.[24] Facebook accounts disappear 30 days after deactivation, although some information may remain on backup copies for as long as 90 days. In addition, certain content not stored in a Facebook account (such as messages, or postings to a group) will remain even after deactivation.[25] With a site like LinkedIn, on the other hand, while information is generally removed within 24 hours, LinkedIn doesn't delete a closed account for up to 30 days, and termination requires an official notification letter to the site. Moreover, terminating a LinkedIn account may bar the user from future use of the site.[26]

Because information will become irretrievable after some period of time, an attorney concerned about evidence preservation obligations should never counsel a client to deactivate his or her social networking account, because it is likely to result in a spoliation finding. In *Chapman v. Hiland Operating, LLC*, Plaintiff Tracy Chapman had to respond to a motion to compel the production of, among other things, Facebook postings relevant to the allegations in the lawsuit.[27] Chapman responded that she had a Facebook account until spring of 2013, when it was deactivated; during her deposition, she testified that she deactivated it at that time "on the advice of her attorney."[28]

As a result, when she attempted to reactivate her account to respond to discovery requests, she could not remember her password and was unable to do so. She and her attorney also claimed that the account was not likely to include relevant information, since "she rarely used the account, and when she did it was primarily to communicate with her nieces and nephews."[29]

In addition to compelling the reactivation of the account, defense counsel sought to "be present when the account is reactivated and to examine the

---

[24] Marlisse Silver Sweeney, *How to Purge Social Media from the Web*, LAW TECHNOLOGY NEWS, June 19, 2014.

[25] *Id.*

[26] *Id.*

[27] Chapman v. Hiland Operating, LLC, 1:13-CV-052, 2014 WL 2434775, at *1 (D.N.D. 2014).

[28] *Id.*

[29] *Id.*

entire contents of the account to prevent spoliation of relevant evidence."[30] The court, while skeptical that the Facebook account would yield any relevant noncumulative information, did order Chapman and her attorney to "make a reasonably good faith attempt to reactivate Tracy Chapman's Facebook account." But it declined to order that defense counsel be allowed to be present.[31] And to the considerable relief of the plaintiffs and their counsel, no spoliation sanctions were imposed.

Another Facebook deactivation case resulted in less lenient treatment by the presiding judge. In *Crowe v. Marquette Transportation Company Gulf-Inland, LLC*, plaintiff Brandon Crowe allegedly injured his knee at work, and sued his employer.[32] Based on a Facebook message Crowe supposedly sent a friend, the employer believed the injury had occurred on a personal fishing trip and thus denied the claim. Marquette, acting on its suspicions, sought "an unredacted, unedited digital copy of [Crowe's] entire Facebook page from the onset of [his] employment with Marquette until present."[33]

Crowe disingenuously replied that he "does not presently have a Facebook account"—an answer that was technically correct only because Crowe had deactivated his account four days after Marquette's document request.[34] Soon thereafter, pursuant to a court order, Crowe reactivated his Facebook account and submitted over 4,000 pages of content to the court for an *in camera* review.

The court responded to Crowe's *in camera* request and Facebook flooding by ordering the production of all of the documents to the employer and directing Crowe to permit Marquette access to Crowe's Facebook account. The court also found that Marquette was entitled to explore the timing of the deactivation, investigate Crowe's claim of his iPhone being "hacked," and have Crowe execute an authorization for his employer to obtain records from Facebook independent of what was already produced.[35]

Noting that "Crowe's efforts to avoid producing this material have unnecessarily delayed these proceedings and have wasted the time of his opponent and this Court," the court made it clear that Crowe's credibility was shot. The judge was "troubled by Crowe's refusal to produce any

---

[30] *Id.*

[31] *Id.*

[32] Crowe v. Marquette Transp. Co. Gulf-Inland, LLC, No. 2:14-cv-01130 (E.D. La. 2015).

[33] *Id.*

[34] *Id.*

[35] *Id.*

responsive documents on the basis of the statement that he did not presently have a Facebook account. The records indicate that Crowe did not delete his account but deactivated it. It is readily apparent to any user who visits the page instructing how to reactivate an account that the two actions are different and have different consequences."[36]

While the record is silent as to any role played by Crowe's counsel, one would hope that the client solely instigated the deactivation. Even so, the case serves as a cautionary tale for lawyers who should visit with their clients and verify that independent "clean-up" actions or account deactivation have not occurred.

5. Does an inadvertent deactivation constitute spoliation?

In at least one instance, Facebook account deactivation has resulted in a spoliation finding.[37] *Gatto v. United Airlines, Inc.* also serves as a cautionary tale for lawyers to communicate with their clients about their social media activities and to counsel them appropriately. In fact, the *Gatto* case is referenced in several of the ethics opinions addressing the topic of advising a client on "cleaning up" a social media profile. In *Gatto*, airport baggage handler Frank Gatto brought a personal injury suit after being struck by a set of stairs used for aircraft refueling on January 21, 2008.[38] He sued Allied Aviation Services (which owned the stairs) and United Airlines (which owned the plane), claiming to be permanently disabled.[39]

In July 2011, the defendants sought discovery pertaining to Gatto's social media activities, asking for Facebook "posts, comments, status updates, and other information posted [by the defendant before the accident]."[40] Other discovery requests inquired more specifically into Gatto's mentions of the accident on social media and, also, any eBay business operated by Gatto.[41] Gatto agreed to change his Facebook password to "alliedunited" for the purpose of defense counsel accessing documents and information from his Facebook account.[42]

---

[36] *Id.*

[37] Gatto v. United Air Lines, Inc., No. 10-CV-1090-ES-SCM, 2013 WL 1285285 (D.N.J. 2013).

[38] *Id.*

[39] *Id.*

[40] *Id.* at 3.

[41] *Id.*

[42] *Id.*

From this point, the parties' recountings of the Facebook episode sharply diverge. Gatto claimed that he thought there would not be "unauthorized access to the Facebook account online." He said his attorney claimed he understood that defense counsel would use the changed password to obtain information from Facebook's corporate offices rather than through online access.[43] In any event, as of December 5, 2011, Gatto had not yet changed the password, prompting United's attorney to contact plaintiff's counsel and request that it be done that day.[44] It was, and defense counsel was able to access Gatto's Facebook account and print off certain materials that day.[45]

On December 6, Facebook notified Gatto that his account had been accessed by an unknown IP address in New Jersey. Gatto, claiming that he had been through contentious divorce proceedings and was worried about his account being "hacked into," deactivated his Facebook account on December 16, 2011, because "unknown people were apparently accessing my account without my permission."[46] Facebook automatically deleted the data on December 30, 2011.[47] Gatto maintained that he was unaware that United's counsel was the one accessing his account until later.[48]

Meanwhile, the attorneys were oblivious to these developments. Facebook advised United's counsel that it would not disclose Gatto's data, but Gatto himself could download the account contents through a "download my profile" button. It was agreed that Gatto would download the contents of his Facebook profile and then provide a copy to the defense along with a certification that he had not made any changes to it.[49] Two weeks later, Plaintiff's counsel had to inform the defense of Gatto's account deactivation and the sad fact that once an account has been deactivated for a period of two weeks, it is permanently deleted and cannot be reactivated.[50]

---

[43] *Id.*

[44] *Id.* at *2.

[45] *Id.*

[46] *Id.*

[47] Gatto, 2013 WL 1285285, at *1.

[48] *Id.* at *2.

[49] *Id.*

[50] *Id.* It is important to note that social media networks, such as Facebook, have various and changing policies regarding deactivating and deleting material. For example, when the *Gatto* case occurred, if an account was deactivated then after two weeks Facebook would permanently delete the account. As of the writing of this book, Facebook's stated policy is that a deactivated account may be reactivated at any

As one would expect, the defendants moved for sanctions based on spoliation, claiming not only that the deactivation was intentional, but also that if all the lost postings had been recovered, they would have refuted Gatto's damages claims.[51] Gatto maintained that there was no intentional destruction or suppression of evidence.[52]

The court disagreed with Gatto, pointing out that

> Even if plaintiff did not intend to permanently deprive the defendants of the information associated with his Facebook account, there is no dispute that Plaintiff intentionally deactivated the account. In doing so, and then failing to reactivate the account within the necessary time period, plaintiff effectively caused the account to be permanently deleted. Neither defense counsel's allegedly inappropriate access of the Facebook account, nor Plaintiff's belated efforts to reactivate the account, negate the fact that plaintiff failed to preserve the relevant evidence.[53]

In weighing the appropriate sanction, US District Court Judge Mannion ultimately declined to assess monetary sanctions. However, he did grant the defense's request for an adverse inference instruction for Gatto's failing to preserve his Facebook account.

6. What happens when my client has already deleted posts?

For attorneys counseling clients who have already deleted potentially damaging posts, it is important to remember that, thanks to cyberforensic tools, "deleted" doesn't necessarily mean "destroyed," and even deleted social media content is discoverable.

For example, in the case of *Romano v. Steelcase, Inc.*, a personal injury plaintiff tried unsuccessfully to resist a defense motion to compel access

---

time; however, a deleted account renders it permanently inaccessible. *See* https://www.facebook.com/help/224562897555674?helpref=related. Additionally, deleted material from an active account may or may not remain on Facebook's servers. *See* https://www.facebook.com/help/356107851084108?helpref=uf_permalink.

[51] *Id.* at *4. The limited materials printed out by defense counsel purportedly showed Gatto taking vacations, participating in social activities, and running an eBay business.

[52] *Id.*

[53] Gatto, 2013 WL 1285285, at *24.

not only to her privacy-restricted Facebook photos and posts, but also to those that she had already deleted.[54] The court granted a motion providing the defendant "access to Plaintiff's current and historical Facebook and MySpace pages and accounts, including all deleted pages and related information."[55]

Lawyers must also be cognizant of the fact that even advice at the most benign end of the spectrum when it comes to a client's social networking activities—such as advising a client on adapting more restrictive privacy settings—is not without its legal risks. Consider, for example, the 2013 trucking accident lawsuit against driver Jerry O'Reilly, his employer, Try Hours, and National Interstate Insurance Company in DeKalb County, Georgia.[56] Among the allegations made by Plaintiff Kristin Meredith was that the accident involving her sedan and the defendants' tractor-trailer was caused by truck driver O'Reilly's inattention.

Although during his deposition O'Reilly initially denied using a camera, phone, or computer while driving, plaintiffs' counsel then confronted him with dozens of Facebook posts that helped establish a pattern of distracted and even aggressive driving.[57] One post consisted of a photo of his truck cab along with a caption that read, "[m]y new bumper. Now pull your ass out in front of me."[58] Significantly, O'Reilly also admitted to changing his Facebook profile to "private" during the deposition and just before plaintiff's counsel began his questioning—a fact that the attorney gleefully pointed out to portray O'Reilly as untrustworthy. The case resulted in a $1 million settlement shortly thereafter.[59]

7. When deletion of relevant evidence occurs after counsel is retained, will it constitute spoliation that may result in severe sanctions? And what may happen if the court finds that counsel participated in or ratified the deletion?

The short answer to the first question: Yes! In fact, beyond adopting heightened privacy settings and the deactivation—temporary or otherwise—of a social

---

[54] Romano v. Steelcare, Inc., 907 N.Y.S.2d 650 (N.Y. Sup. Ct. 2010).

[55] *Id.*

[56] Kathleen Baydala Joyner, *Trucker's Facebook Habit Settles Case for Injured Driver*, DAILY REPORT (Sept. 25, 2014), http://www.daily reportonline.com/id=1202671247938/Truckers-Facebook-Habit -Settles-Case-for-Injured-Driver-.

[57] *Id.*

[58] *Id.*

[59] *Id.*

networking account, few actions arouse as much ire as deleting social media content from a profile. While there have been a number of cases involving spoliation of social media content, two in particular stand out because of the role played by the spoliating party's counsel.

In one recent sexual harassment case, the defendant employer (a dentist named Aaron Atwood) maintained that his relationship with the plaintiff Heather Painter was consensual.[60] Specifically, Atwood argued that Painter had posted comments and pictures on Facebook detailing how much she enjoyed her job, what a great boss Atwood was, and how Urgent Dental was a great place to work.[61]

After discovery closed, Atwood filed a motion for sanctions, alleging that Painter and two of her witnesses intentionally destroyed Facebook posts, as well as text messages, that supported the defense's claims and contradicted the plaintiff's allegations and deposition testimony.[62] Defendants were aware of these posts because Dr. Atwood's wife Kelly was a Facebook "friend" of the plaintiff for an extended period of time before being "unfriended."

Painter's explanation was that she removed the social media content— even after she retained counsel—because it was her habit to routinely delete comments and photos from her Facebook page.[63] Her attorney argued that Painter was just "a 22-year-old girl who would not have known better than to delete her Facebook comments."[64]

The court was not sympathetic. The court observed, "it is of no consequence that Plaintiff is young or that she is female and, therefore, according to her counsel, would not have known better than to delete her Facebook comments."[65] Nor did the federal judge spare Painter's lawyer for his failure to affirmatively advise Painter regarding her social media activities. The judge noted, "once Plaintiff retained counsel, her counsel should have informed her of her duty to preserve evidence and, further, explained to Plaintiff the full extent of that obligation."[66] Since the plaintiff knew or should have known that the Facebook comments at issue were relevant to the defendant's case at the time she deleted them, the court held that the requisite culpability

---

[60] Painter v. Atwood, No. 2:12-CV-01215-JCM, 2014 WL 1089694, at *1 (D. Nev. 2014).

[61] *Id.* at *2.

[62] *Id.* at *4.

[63] *Id.* at *2.

[64] *Id.* at *6.

[65] *Id.*

[66] *Id.*

standard for spoliation was satisfied and "an adverse inference regarding Plaintiff's deleted Facebook comments . . . is appropriate."[67]

A lawyer's failure to properly and in a timely manner counsel a client about her social media activities and her evidence preservation obligations is a serious ethical concern. However, of even greater concern is an attorney who takes an active role in advising his or her client to delete damaging social media content. That is the focal point of probably the best-known case of social media spoliation, *Allied Concrete Co. v. Lester*.[68] In this Virginia wrongful death case, the defense learned of a number of photos on plaintiff Isaiah Lester's Facebook page that could be damaging to the surviving widower's case.

On March 25, 2009, the defense counsel issued a discovery request to the plaintiff, seeking "screen print copies on the day this request is signed of all pages from Isaiah Lester's Facebook page including, but not limited to, all pictures, his profile, his message board, status updates, and all messages sent or received."[69] Attached to the discovery request was a copy of one of the photographs the defense lawyer had downloaded off of Lester's Facebook page.[70] It depicted Lester surrounded by women, holding a beer can, and wearing a T-shirt with the slogan, "I [heart] hot moms"—not quite the portrait of a grieving widower![71] That evening, Mr. Murray sent an email to his client about the discovery request and the attached photo.[72]

The following day, Murray instructed his paralegal to have Lester "clean up" his Facebook page because "[w]e do not want any blow-ups of this stuff at trial."[73] The paralegal emailed Lester (as part of a thread that would later be referred to as "the stink bomb email") directing him to "clean up" his Facebook page because "[w]e do NOT want blow ups of other pics at trial so please, please clean up your [F]acebook and [M]yspace!"[74]

On April 14, 2009, Lester informed the paralegal that he had deleted his Facebook page.[75] The next day, plaintiff's counsel served an answer to the

---

[67] *Id.* at *9.

[68] **Allied Concrete Co. v. Lester**, 285 Va. 295, 301 (Va. 2013).

[69] *Id.*

[70] *Id.* at 302.

[71] *Id.*

[72] *Id.*

[73] *Id.*

[74] *Id.*

[75] *Id.*

discovery request, with Lester's statement that "I do not have a Facebook page on the date this is signed, April 15, 2009."[76]

Allied Concrete's lawyers filed a motion to compel, and plaintiff's counsel contacted Lester.[77] He reactivated his Facebook page, and his lawyers were able to print off copies of what was then on the profile. However, consistent with the advice to "clean up" his Facebook page, Lester had already deleted at least sixteen photos from his profile."[78] According to David Tafuri (a member of the defense team), there was evidence to suggest that considerably more than sixteen photos had been deleted, but the defense forensics expert was only able to definitively show spoliation of sixteen photos.[79]

In May and October 2009, plaintiff's counsel provided additional, "updated" copies of Lester's Facebook page.[80] At a December 2009 deposition, Lester denied deactivating his Facebook page, but Allied Concrete would later subpoena Facebook and obtain testimony that contradicted Lester.[81]

As a sanction for the spoliation, the trial court gave two adverse inference instructions to the jury (one while Lester was testifying, the other before closing arguments), instructing them to presume "that the photograph or photographs [Lester] deleted from his Facebook account were harmful to his case."[82] The court also sanctioned Lester and his attorney $722,000 for their misconduct ($542,000 against Murray and $180,000 against Lester) and also to cover Allied Concrete's attorney's fees and costs in addressing the Facebook spoliation.[83]

In response to a motion for a new trial, the court also sharply reduced the plaintiff's $8.58 million verdict by $4.127 million, but ostensibly for reasons unrelated to the spoliation. In his order, Charlottesville Circuit Court Judge Edward Hogshire was appalled at the spoliation and misconduct by plaintiff and his counsel. Judge Hogshire referred to "the extensive pattern

---

[76] *Id.*

[77] *Id.*

[78] *Id.*

[79] *Id.* at 302-3.

[80] Author's interview with David Tafuri.

[81] *Lester*, 285 Va. at 303. The Virginia Supreme Court would later note that Lester made a number of false statements during discovery, including lying about supposed volunteer work, his use of antidepressants, and his history of depression.

[82] *Id.* at 304.

[83] *Id.*

of deceptive and obstructionist conduct of Murray and Lester," but he denied the request for a new trial.[84]

In January 2013, the Virginia Supreme Court vacated the remittitur and reinstated the original verdict; it did, however, let the sanctions levied against Murray and Lester stand.[85] Later that year, facing disciplinary action from the Virginia State Bar, Murray entered into an agreed disposition of the charges against him for engaging in "dishonesty, fraud, deceit, or misrepresentation," and his law license was suspended for five years—effectively ending his legal career.[86]

Although almost a decade has passed since the *Allied Concrete* case, it remains the "poster child" for all that can go extremely wrong when social media is not understood, investigated, and properly handled in a litigation matter.

8. What are the potential repercussions of a client removing social media evidence in a criminal case?

Criminal law is replete with examples of social media investigations and evidence, but the analysis for obtaining and removing social media implicates significantly different legal issues. For example, on the one hand the government may be constrained by the Fourth Amendment in conducting a search for social media.[87] On the other hand, unlike a private citizen, the government has the ability to subpoena social media information from an entity, such as Facebook, that hosts a social media network.[88]

Today's criminal defense lawyer may have a client who posted his criminal conduct on Facebook.[89] Unlike the civil litigator who may decide to instruct a client to remove and preserve social media so that it may be

---

[84] *Id.*

[85] *Id.*

[86] Disciplinary System Actions, VA. ST. BAR, http://www.vsb.org/disciplinary .html (last visited Nov. 4, 2013).

[87] United States v. Meregildo, 883 F. Supp. 2d 523, 525 (S.D.N.Y. 2012) (Police obtained search warrant to obtain additional Facebook evidence after a Facebook friend of the defendant cooperated with the government by sharing some of defendant's private Facebook posts.).

[88] Stored Communications Act 18 U.S.C. §§ 2701–11 (enacted in 1986 as part of the Electronic Communications Privacy Act (Pub.L. No. 99–508)); People v. Harris, 949 N.Y.S.2d 590, 597 (N.Y. Crim. Ct. 2012).

[89] *See, e.g.,* THADDEUS A. HOFFMEISTER, SOCIAL MEDIA IN THE COURTROOM: A NEW ERA FOR CRIMINAL JUSTICE? 65 N. 4 & 5 (2014).

produced in discovery, the criminal defense lawyer must consider whether removal constitutes criminal conduct in accordance with any tampering with evidence statute. The 2014 Florida opinion in the *Constanzo* case provides relevant analysis.[90]

Constanzo was convicted of evidence tampering after he deleted a video from his phone that was relevant to a pending investigation in an unrelated criminal case concerning two of Constanzo's fellow officers at the Broward County Sheriff's office.[91] On appeal, the court reversed his conviction based on the fact that Constanzo had texted the video to one of the defendants, played the video for his supervisor, and emailed the video to the president of the police benevolent association. The court found that although Constanzo had knowledge of the pending investigation (meeting one prong of the tampering statute), his conduct did not evidence the intent to destroy the evidence and thereby impede the investigation.[92]

The court analogized Constanzo's deletion of the video to a defendant's tossing of drugs into the street or onto a sandy surface during a police chase in a drug possession case. Both the video and the drugs are recoverable regardless of whether the police happen to locate them.[93] The court noted, "the statute does not criminalize deleting evidence existing in the memory of a particular electronic device, particularly where such evidence resides elsewhere in the electronic ether."[94]

Thus, although issues of authentication and admission of social media evidence are similar for criminal and civil litigators, the initial handling of social media evidence implicates both statutory and constitutional issues in criminal law. Competence mandates that the criminal lawyer understand both social media's import and the unique considerations arising in the criminal law arena.

---

[90] Costanzo v. State, 152 So.3d 737, 738 (Fla. 4th DCA 2014), reh'g denied (Dec. 29, 2014).

[91] *Id.*

[92] *Id.* at 739.

[93] *Id.* at 738. The drug-tossing scenario is distinguished from the situation in which the drugs are incapable of recovery because they have been swallowed or flushed down the toilet.

[94] *Id.* at 739.

CHAPTER 6

Juror, Juror on the (Social Media) Wall, Who's the Fairest of Them All?

Unfortunately, given the variable of human nature, prospective jurors are not always inclined toward complete honesty. In some instances, the prospective juror may be a "stealth juror," someone with an agenda to serve who desires to be on a particular jury due to the issues or individuals involved or simply its high-profile nature. Such was the case with a juror dismissed from the murder trial of New England Patriots player Aaron Hernandez after it was revealed that the juror had previously expressed interest in serving on that jury and had lied during voir dire about how many Patriots games she had attended.[1]

In other situations, the lying juror may be covering up past run-ins with the law, including ones that could impact that juror's consideration of issues in the case. For example, in the recent New Jersey trial of Travis Hartsfield Jr.—who was accused (and later convicted) of murdering his twenty-month-old daughter—juror Wacoa Stanford was indicted for perjury for allegedly lying during jury selection about her criminal history and experience with New Jersey's Division of Youth and Family Services.[2] Stanford allegedly

---

[1] Lindsey Adler, *Aaron Hernandez Juror Released for Lying About How Many Patriots Games She's Attended*, BUZZFEED (Feb. 3, 2015), http://www.buzzfeed.com/lindseyadler/aaron-hernandez-juror-released-for-lying-about-how-many-patr#.hoDRlGnAo (last visited Mar. 2, 2015).

[2] Bill Wichert, *Former Juror Indicted for Lying during Trial of Man Convicted of Murdering Baby Daughter, Prosecutor Says*, N.J.COM

lied about a disorderly conduct conviction, and had not only been investigated by New Jersey's Division of Youth and Family Services for child abuse but also had discussed it with other jurors.[3]

And given the pervasive nature of social networking communications in an era in which 78 percent of adult Americans have at least one social media profile, it is hardly surprising that some of the misconduct by jurors occurs via social media platforms, and that social media profiles continue to yield information important to lawyers' jury selection considerations.

In the Akron, Ohio, murder trial of Shaun Ford Jr. in October 2014, one juror was dismissed ten hours into deliberations over concerns about her Facebook "friends" list.[4] The juror, a paralegal, had a list of Facebook friends that included the county prosecutor and other high-level members of the prosecutor's office. Interestingly, it was the prosecution that brought this to light, having researched her profile in detail during jury deliberations over concerns that she might be the lone holdout.[5]

While the juror acknowledged being Facebook friends with many legal professionals due to the nature of her job, she stated that her online friendships had not impacted her judgment in the trial. Although the court denied a defense motion for a mistrial, it did dismiss her and seated an alternate in her place.[6]

Jurors' online misconduct has been a persistent problem in courtrooms nationwide.[7] And despite revised jury instructions that specifically warn against online investigation or communications about a case through social media, instances of tweets and Facebook posts causing mistrials are common. Moreover, judges are granting mistrials and issuing increasingly stiff punishments for errant jurors.

(Feb. 26, 2015), http://www.nj.com/essex/index.ssf/2015/02/former_juror _indicted_on_perjury_charges_related_t.html.

[3] *Id.*

[4] Dave Nethers, *Juror in Murder Trial Sent Home Because of Facebook Friends List*, Fox8.Com (Oct. 21, 2014), http://fox8.com/2014/10/21 /juror-in-murder-trial-sent-home-because-of-facebook-friends-list/.

[5] *Id.*

[6] *Id.*

[7] *See, e.g.*, John G. Browning, The Lawyer's Guide to Social Networking: Understanding Social Media's Impact on the Legal System (2010); Thaddeus H. Hoffmeister, Social Media in the Courtroom: A New Era for Criminal Justice? 49–54 (2014).

For example, Memphis, Tennessee, juror Renita Scott was found in contempt of court in February 2015 and sentenced to ten days in jail after she communicated with defendant Markelvious Moore during his aggravated robbery trial.[8] Scott acknowledged that she and Moore were already Facebook friends before trial and that she had communicated with him during deliberations before joining her fellow jurors in returning a guilty verdict.

And there are other cases in which jurors' social media misconduct has provided the grounds for a motion for a new trial or appeal, albeit unsuccessfully. Regardless of the outcome, the juror's misconduct occupied the post-trial time and expense of the parties; it may also leave the parties wondering whether the outcome might have been different had the jurors been social media vetted before and during the trial.

For example, in *United States v. Liu, et al.*, a federal district court upheld the conviction of three defendants (two of whom were lawyers) for immigration fraud, even though two different jurors tweeted about the trial.[9] One of the jurors, identified as "Juror 10," acknowledged tweeting daily during trial, including the tweet "Add in just one song & dance number, and this federal case would rival anything I've seen on #broadway, #jurydutyrocks."[10] She was dismissed, with the court's observation that "her tweeting had been improper."[11]

Another juror (Juror 2), who had admitted to being an aspiring crime fiction writer during voir dire, also acknowledged that she tweeted throughout the trial. Her tweets centered on either frustration with the commitment of serving on a long jury trial or gaining potential ideas for future writing projects.

The court rejected the defense's argument that Juror 2 had failed to answer questions honestly about her social media activity, noting that she "was never asked specifically whether she had discussed the case with anyone on Twitter or other social media."[12]

---

[8] *Juror in Memphis Communicated with Defendant on Facebook*, ASSOCIATED PRESS (Feb. 6, 2015), http://archive.commercialappeal.com /news/crime/juror-who-communicated-via-facebook-sentenced-ep -917447826-324468401.html.

[9] U.S. v. Liu, et al., No. 1:12:CV-00934-RA (E.D.N.Y. Nov. 14, 2014).

[10] *Id.*

[11] *Id.*

[12] *Id.*

As to the defense's argument that this juror had ignored the court's instructions, the court noted that

> When the embrace of social media is ubiquitous, it cannot be surprising that examples of jurors using platforms like Facebook and Twitter 'are legion'. . . . Juror 2 was an attentive juror who, while engaging in banter with fellow Twitter users about her experience, was nonetheless careful never to discuss the substance of the case, as instructed by the Court.[13]

And in a true case of irony, former Cameron County, Texas, District Attorney Armando Villalobos—who himself had been an early proponent of "Facebooking the jury," even issuing iPads to his prosecutors for the very purpose of juror social media research—challenged his own criminal racketeering and extortion conviction on grounds of juror online misconduct.[14] The Fifth Circuit affirmed his conviction, finding that the pre-trial and trial Facebook posts by the juror in question failed to show that the juror lied during voir dire, betrayed a bias toward law enforcement, or engaged in juror misconduct.[15]

Thus, researching the social media activity of prospective jurors, and continuing to monitor social media activity during trial, can be vital to seating an honest, unbiased jury, and to ensuring that any online misconduct is promptly brought to the court's attention. The practice of such investigation has not only become a key part of the role played by modern jury consultants,[16] it has also been immortalized in pop culture in television courtroom dramas like *The Good Wife* and *How to Get Away with Murder*. In September 2016, one of the major networks premiered *Bull*, a series highlighting the role of the jury consultant and the significance of researching the jury.[17]

---

[13] *Id.* (quoting U.S. v. Fumo, 655 F.3d 288, 332 (3d Cir. 2011)).

[14] U.S. v. Villalobos, Case No. 14-40147 (5th Cir., Feb. 11, 2015).

[15] *Id.*

[16] Marc Davis & Kevin Davis, *Jury Consultants Are Changing with the Times 20 Years After the OJ Verdict*, ABA J. (Jan. 1, 2015, 6:00 AM), http://www.abajournal.com/magazine/article/pretrial_pros.

[17] Rick Folbaum, *New CBS Show "Bull" Takes On the Jury*, CBS Miami (Sept. 20, 2016), http://miami.cbslocal.com/2016/09/20/new-cbs-show -bull-takes-on-the-jury/ ("Dr. Bull is a character modeled after the early

No doubt, digital research has become a critical tool in documenting juror misconduct.[18] The ready availability of juror research applications and affordable, user-friendly software has leveled the playing field for solos and small-firm attorneys who may not be able to afford trial consultants.[19]

In fact, lawyers and jury consultants frequently define social media research as a part of digital competence. A lawyer who fails to engage in online juror research while his opposing counsel is Googling the jury panel is conducting voir dire with less insight and less information—akin to bringing a knife to the proverbial gunfight, or worse, showing up unarmed. And while lawyers and judges who are uncomfortable with this practice, calling it "creepy" or "voyeuristic," often cite juror privacy and juror uneasiness as reasons for not "Facebooking the jury," today's juror may be less guarded than we think.

A 2016 study by trial consulting firm Vinson & Company surveyed jurors about this practice, and it revealed that 82 percent of respondents expected the lawyers to conduct Internet researches and background checks on prospective jurors.[20] Only 18 percent were surprised to hear that it is done, and only 21 percent said they would consider it an invasion of privacy.[21] The jurors responding to this survey also demonstrated a fairly sophisticated take on the advisability of performing online juror research when the stakes were high; for example, 76 percent of them felt that given the amounts and issues in controversy, corporate defense attorneys representing big companies would "always" conduct social media investigations of potential jurors. Sixty-three percent indicated

---

career of Dr. Phil McGraw, when he was a jury consultant. Dr. Bull is in demand, helping his clients pick a jury that will deliver the verdict they want.").

[18] Richard Raysman & Peter Brown, *Social Media Use as Evidence of Juror Misconduct*, N.Y.L.J. (Apr 11, 2013).

[19] Robert D. Gibson & Jesse D. Capell, *Social Media and Jury Trials: Where Do We Stand?*, N.Y.L.J. (Dec. 1, 2014), http://www.newyorklaw journal.com/id=1202677394659/Social-Media-and-Jury-Trials-Where -Do-We-Stand?slreturn=20160829132614.

[20] Stephen Paterson, *Using Social Media and Other Background Research in Voir Dire: Why Jurors Don't Care, But You Should*, Vinson & Company (2016), http://vinsoncompany.com/wp-content/uploads/2015/09 /Using-Social-Media-Other-Background-Research-in-Voir-Dire.pdf.

[21] *Id.*

they not only considered the lawyers to be just "doing their job," but they also respected them for doing the job discreetly.[22]

In this chapter we examine the ethical considerations for lawyers pondering whether to "Facebook the jury," and will discuss not only ethics opinions, but also cases from around the country where courts have weighed in on this issue. We also explore some of the leading reasons why attorneys may want to conduct online juror research, as well as the potential dangers for attorneys in doing so.

QUESTIONS

1. **I have a big trial coming up, and I want to gather as much "intel" on the jury panel as I can before I make my strikes. May I research the social media profiles and online postings of the venire members?**

The answer to this question is generally "yes," but with some qualifiers and caveats (that are outlined in the following questions and answers). It's certainly understandable why lawyers routinely engage in this practice. After all, in civil and criminal cases, attorneys on both sides probe using questions during voir dire that seek to learn more about the prospective jurors and whether they might be likely to align with that lawyer's side of the case, or whether the jurors might have a pre-existing bias on a particular issue.

Everything from a panelist's body language during questioning to her television viewing habits translates into more data to be factored into the jury selection process.[23] And while most cases don't feature the lengthy, detailed questionnaires used in high-profile or complex litigation, the importance of weeding out the "wrong" jurors and seating the "right" jurors has spawned an effort to find out as much about potential jurors as possible and has driven the growth of fields like jury consulting.[24] And thanks to the Internet and the explosive growth of social networking sites like Facebook and Twitter, lawyers and litigants now have a digital treasure trove of information right at their fingertips accessible with the speed of a research engine.[25]

---

[22] *Id.*

[23] Stephanie Clifford, *TV Habits? Medical History? Tests for Jury Duty Get Personal*, N.Y. TIMES (Aug. 20, 2014), http://www.nytimes.com/2014/08/21/nyregion/for-service-on-some-juries-expect-a-lengthy-written-test.html.

[24] *See Id.*

[25] WSJ Staff, *LinkedIn Search in Spotlight at Bank of America Trial*, WALL ST. J. (Sept. 27, 2013, 4:48 PM), http://blogs.wsj.com/law/2013/09/27/linkedin-search-in-spotlight-at-bank-of-america-trial/.

2. Can I get in trouble for "Facebooking" the jury? What are the potential impediments or dangers involved?

Alienation of a Juror

The most obvious reason that online investigation of jurors can be dangerous is that no trial lawyer wants to alienate a juror or prospective juror by appearing invasive or disrespectful. While this is a strategic reason, it is also a matter of competence in the digital age. Lack of understanding of the potential disadvantages of using technology in certain ways no doubt contributes to effective representation of a client. For example, one New York law firm suffered through what must have been an extremely awkward moment when the judge received a complaint from a juror who had received an automatic notification from LinkedIn that a junior lawyer on its trial team had viewed the juror's LinkedIn profile.[26] It seems that the judge had neither instructed the jurors that the lawyers might be conducting online research nor instructed the lawyers as to whether an automatic notification from a social media site to a juror was impermissible contact. Regardless, alienating or upsetting a juror is far from optimal. Moreover, as discussed below, it remains subject to debate as to whether a LinkedIn message to a juror is tantamount to a violation of Rule 3.5, which prohibits ex parte contact with a juror.

Use of Juror Information

Beyond juror alienation and potentially impermissible contact, attorneys must consider how to use any social media information that is legitimately obtained. Information that leads an attorney to inappropriately strike a juror may cause problems. For example, an assistant district attorney in Texas decided to use a peremptory strike to remove an African American woman from the jury panel after learning about her National Association for the Advancement of Colored People (NAACP) membership on Facebook and also observing a comment and a link to the *Negro Motorist Green Book* (a travel guide for African Americans during the Jim Crow era). The strike resulted in a Batson proceeding.[27] The assistant district attorney asserted that the woman "appeared to be an activist."[28] The court concluded that the peremptory strike was not based on race-neutral reasoning and sustained

---

[26] *Id.*

[27] Jasmine Ulloa & Tony Plohetski, *District Attorney Lehmberg Fires Key Lawyer in Her Office*, Austin Am.-Statesman, June 12, 2014, at A1.

[28] *Id.*

the challenge.[29] The woman remained on the jury panel, but the assistant district attorney lost his job.[30]

The Judicial and Legislative Concerns about Privacy of the Jurors

Another potential impediment to investigating jurors online is the fact that some courts and legislators also have concerns about the privacy of a juror's social networking profile. A Michigan judge rejected the social media monitoring concerns raised by lawyers regarding the empanelling of an anonymous jury. He noted that lawyers do not have a right to monitor the jury's use of social media. Moreover, he was concerned about a chilling effect on jurors' willingness to serve if they feel harassed and believe that their privacy is threatened.[31]

And, in February 2014, California became the first state in the country to introduce legislation that would safeguard a juror's social media username and password.[32] A.B. 2070, introduced by State Representative Nora Campos, would prohibit a court from revealing or requesting a juror or prospective juror to disclose a username or password "for the purpose of accessing personal social media," or requiring the juror or prospective juror to access personal social media "in the presence of the judge, counsel for either party, or any other officer of the court."[33] Although ultimately the social media provisions were not enacted, the proposed legislation remains as another reflection of the judicial and legislative concerns with juror privacy.

---

[29] *Id.*

[30] *Id.*

[31] United States v. Kilpatrick, No. 10-20403, 2012 WL 3237147, at *3 (E.D. Mich. Aug. 7, 2012) (rejecting the arguments made against the empanelling of an anonymous jury, since an anonymous jury would prevent the lawyers from monitoring the jurors' use of social media during the trial in order to determine if the jurors were engaging in online misconduct). *See also* Steve Stout, *Judge Denies Arias Motion for Change of Venue, Jurors' Twitter Names,* CBS 5 KPHO (Dec. 23, 2013, 6:40 AM), (Judge denied defense counsel's motion to order jurors to reveal Twitter account information during the penalty phase of the trial, finding that juror privacy trumped the defense request to monitor juror conduct.).

[32] A.B. 2070, 2013-14 Cal. Leg., Reg. Sess. (Cal. 2014).

[33] *Id.*

3. Are there risks involved in not "Facebooking" the jury?

The short answer is absolutely yes. While the dangers of alienating jurors, inadvertently contacting jurors, violating juror privacy, and risking revelations of an improper basis for peremptory strikes are genuine, they are outweighed by the dangers of not conducting online research.[34]

Risk of a Mistrial or Overturned Verdict

Jurors' social media misconduct has already wreaked havoc in courtrooms throughout the country.[35] And that's just jurors behaving badly in cases in which they were "caught." A lawyer who fails to research and monitor jurors risks never learning of juror misconduct that may be significantly impacting his or her case.

Some jurors have been less than honest about their online conduct[36] and have been discovered to be posting or tweeting about jury duty and their deliberations as well as sending "friend requests" or otherwise attempting to communicate with witnesses or parties to the case.[37] In fact, one juror's tweets from the jury box resulted in a capital murder conviction being overturned by the Arkansas Supreme Court.[38] Thus, a lawyer who fails to investigate jurors on social media may be doing a disservice both to his client and the legal system.

Seating the Lying Juror and Suffering the Consequences

While uncovering a juror's dishonesty after the commencement of a trial has resulted in removal of the juror or cause for a new trial, the courts appear to be moving toward being less receptive to appeals based on a juror's social media posts when counsel could have learned the damaging information prior to opening statements.

---

[34] *See, e.g.,* State v. Abdi, 191 Vt. 162, 174-75 (Vt. 2012).

[35] *See, e.g., Id.*

[36] For example, in one recent Florida case, juror Andrew Sutton made comments on his Facebook page that reflected disdain for jury service and arguably demonstrated bias, and then compounded the wrongdoing by lying to the judge about it, resulting in contempt charges. *See* Jane Musgrave, *Palm Beach County Juror Removed in Handcuffs, Faces Contempt Charge Over Facebook Posting,* THE PALM BEACH POST (June 2, 2014), https://www.palmbeachpost.com/story/news/crime/2014/06/01/palm-beach-county-juror-removed/6791315007/.

[37] *See, e.g.,* State v. Dellinger, 696 S.E.2d 38, 40, 44 (W. Va. 2010).

[38] Dimas-Martinez v. State, 385 S.W.3d 238, 248-49 (Ark. 2011).

A 2011 case that illustrates the benefit of the early removal of a lying juror involves a prospective Oklahoma juror. She was questioned during voir dire in the murder trial of Jerome Ersland, a pharmacist who allegedly shot a would-be robber five times while the thief lay wounded and motionless on the floor.[39]

During voir dire she indicated that she had not expressed a prior opinion about the case.[40] However, the defense team's online research revealed that the prospective juror had, six months earlier, posted her thoughts about the trial. Her Facebook post declared: "First hell yeah he needs to do sometime (sic)!! The young fella (sic) was already dead from the gunshot wound to the head, then he came back with a different (sic) gun and shot him 5 more times. Come on let's be for real it didn't make no (sic) sense!"[41] When asked about the post, the woman claimed that she had forgotten about her post. Nonetheless, the judge dismissed the woman from the jury pool, but not before finding her in contempt and sentencing her to 100 hours of community service.[42]

The judicial system's growing impatience with the disruption created by social media and the lying juror is reflected in a Florida judge's recent proposal: to require online searches of jurors' backgrounds so that trial lawyers can bring any withheld information to the court's attention before the start of actual trial.[43] The comments were prompted by post-trial online research that

---

[39] Jeffrey T. Frederick, *Did I Say That? Another Reason to Do Online Checks on Potential (and Trial) Jurors*, JURY RESEARCH BLOG (Oct. 13, 2011).

[40] *Id.*

[41] *Id.*

[42] *Id.* Indeed, juror dishonesty during voir dire, and its consequences for all involved in the justice system, are an issue commanding increasing attention. In 2015, the US Supreme Court decided the case of *Warger v. Shauers*, in which the central issue was whether Federal Rule of Evidence 606(b) (the juror anti-impeachment rule) permits a party moving for a new trial based on juror dishonesty during voir dire to introduce juror testimony about statements made during deliberations that tend to show the alleged dishonesty. The court held that a party seeking a new trial cannot use a federal juror's comments during deliberations to demonstrate that she lied about her ability to be fair during voir dire. Warger v. Shauers, 721 F.3d 606, 610 (8th Cir. 2013) *cert. granted*, 134 S. Ct. 1491 (2014).

[43] Stephen Nohlgren, *Pinellas Judge: New Process May Be Needed to Screen Jurors*, TAMPA BAY TIMES (July 8, 2014), http://www.tampabay.com/news/courts/civil/pinellas-judge-new-process-may-be-needed-to-screen-jurors/2187689.

revealed that all six jurors in a civil trial had failed to disclose their personal civil litigation histories.[44] Among all of the jurors, the lawyers discovered that there had been three bankruptcies, two foreclosures, an eviction, a child support action, a paternity suit, a declaratory judgment, an appeal, and a contract lawsuit.[45]

A requirement that lawyers research jurors and raise objections after jury selection, but prior to trial, would not only assist the trial process but also "would avoid handing lawyers a 'gotcha card' in which they could wait and see how the verdict turned out before choosing to come forward with the results of online research."[46]

Sluss v. Commonwealth of Kentucky is a prime example of the potential risks for lawyers who do not investigate the jury and some of the courts' still uncertain position regarding online investigation of jurors.[47] The case involved an appeal by the defendant Sluss who had been convicted of murder and driving under the influence. Sluss hit an SUV, killing an eleven-year-old girl.[48] The case was highly publicized, which resulted in the court employing extensive voir dire procedures.[49]

Nonetheless, Sluss alleged juror misconduct as grounds for overturning his conviction. He asserted that two of the jurors, Virginia Matthews and jury foreperson Amy Sparkman-Haney, were Facebook "friends" of the victim's mother, April Brewer.[50] During voir dire, the jurors had been asked if they knew the victim or any of the victim's family; Matthews and Sparkman-Haney had been silent.[51] Additionally, Matthews had unequivocally indicated that she did not have a Facebook account.[52] Sparkman-Haney had revealed that

---

[44] *Id.*

[45] Stephen Nohlgren, *Jurors Who Didn't Reveal Personal Legal History Could Cause New Trial in Pinellas Assisted Living Facility Death*, TAMPA BAY TIMES (Jan. 12, 2014), http://www.tampabay.com/news/courts /civil/jurors-who-didnt-reveal-personal-legal-history-could-cause-new -trial-in/2160715 (There were also five domestic violence cases.).

[46] John G. Browning, *Voir Dire Becomes Voir Google: Ethical Concerns of 21st Century Jury Selection*, 45 THE BRIEF 2 (2016).

[47] Sluss v. Commonwealth, 381 S.W.3d 215 (Ky. 2012).

[48] *Id.* at 217.

[49] *Id.*

[50] *Id.* at 222.

[51] *Sluss*, 381 S.W.3d at 221.

[52] *Id.*

she had a Facebook account, but acknowledged only a vague notion of some reference that had been made about the victim on Facebook.[53]

Although the court was disturbed by the jurors' misstatements during trial, it ultimately concluded that the nature of the Facebook "friend" status between the jurors and the victim's mother alone did not establish grounds to support a new trial.[54] The record did not reflect "to what extent the victim's mother and the jurors had actually communicated, or the scope of any actual relationship they may have had."[55]

Thus, the Supreme Court of Kentucky, acknowledging that the social media issue was one of first impression, ordered the lower court to conduct a hearing to determine the nature and extent of the Facebook conduct, and whether that conduct warranted a new trial.[56] Although the court excused the attorneys' failure to discover the Facebook relationship prior to the trial based on the circumstances of the case,[57] the court did discuss the value of attorneys appropriately investigating jurors on social media sites. The court also noted that "a reasonable attorney without guidance may not think this investigatory tactic appropriate, and it is still such a new line of inquiry that many attorneys who themselves are not yet savvy about social media may never even have thought of such inquiry."[58]

The following year, the Supreme Court of Kentucky had the opportunity to revisit the issue of jurors being less than forthcoming during voir dire about Facebook relationships and the consequences of an attorney's belated discovery of such connections.[59] In *McGaha v. Commonwealth of Kentucky*, Jeffrey McGaha appealed his conviction for murder, citing, among other grounds, the fact that a juror had failed to disclose during voir dire that she was Facebook "friends" with the victim's wife.[60]

"Juror 234," as the opinion refers to her, was directly asked if she was related to anyone involved in the case.[61] She acknowledged knowing some of the victim's family, "not close, but I do know them," and described any

---

[53] *Id.* at 222.

[54] *Id.* at 223.

[55] *Id.* at 223-24.

[56] *Id.* at 228-29.

[57] *Sluss*, 381 S.W.3d at 226.

[58] *Id.*

[59] McGaha v. Commonwealth, 414 S.W.3d 1 (Ky. 2013).

[60] *Id.* at 4.

[61] *Id.*

relationship as "casual."[62] As the court pointed out, "[n]o one asked Juror 234 about any social media relationship she may have with any of the participants in the case," she was "not challenged for cause by either side, and she was eventually seated on the jury to try the case."[63] It was only after trial that McGaha learned that the victim's wife, Charlene Cowan, was one of Juror 234's 629 Facebook "friends."[64]

In denying McGaha's appeal, the Supreme Court of Kentucky harkened back to its earlier opinion in *Sluss*, saying that Facebook "friendships" do not carry the same weight as live friendships or relationships in the community.[65] Moreover, the fact that this juror had 629 "friends" made it even less likely that she could have had a "disqualifying relationship with each one of them."[66] Importantly, the court found Juror 234's answers to questions during voir dire to be both responsive and truthful, saying that there was no indication that she was attempting to be deceptive or attempting to conceal the social media relationship.[67]

The court pointed out that counsel could have delved deeper "to discover the depth and scope of her acquaintances within the Cowan family," but declined to do so.[68] While it stopped short of requiring lawyers to research the jury's social media presence in *Sluss*, the Kentucky Supreme Court in *McGaha* seems to say that while it may behoove an attorney to do so, it won't necessarily result in game-changing findings.[69]

4. If a judge asks me to justify my "Facebooking the jury," or orders the parties to brief the issue, is there any case support that I may cite?

While not every jurisdiction has addressed this, there is a growing body of case law from around the country that supports a lawyer's right to research jurors online. The cases generally have found that not only do lawyers have a right to bring a laptop to court to research potential jurors, but also that attorneys have an obligation to conduct online research of jurors at least to the extent that they intend to use online evidence to contest the seating of

---

[62] *Id.*

[63] *Id.* at 5.

[64] *Id.*

[65] *McGaha*, 414 S.W.3d at 6.

[66] *Id.*

[67] *Id.*

[68] *Id.*

[69] *See Id.*

a juror or the ultimate decision in the case. In other words, if social media evidence is available prior to the commencement of a trial, it may be too late to successfully use it in support of a motion for a mistrial or in an appeal, but perhaps not too late to question the attorney's competence in handling the case.

Here are snapshots of some of the most important cases.

Carino v. Muenzen

In this New Jersey medical malpractice case, the appellate court considered the plaintiff attorney's request for a new trial after the lawyer had been prevented by the trial judge from conducting online research on the venire panel.[70] As jury selection began on May 14, 2009, defense counsel objected when he noticed his adversary accessing the Internet on his laptop.[71] After acknowledging to the court that he was Googling the potential jurors, and pointing out "we've done it all the time, everyone does it. It's not unusual," the plaintiff's attorney was stunned when the court refused to allow it.[72] The trial judge felt that allowing such juror research would jeopardize maintaining "a fair and even playing field."[73]

Although the appellate court affirmed the defense verdict on other grounds, it explicitly recognized the right to use the Internet to investigate potential jurors during voir dire, and concluded that the trial judge had acted unreasonably in preventing use of the Internet by plaintiff's counsel.[74] The court held:

> There was no suggestion that counsel's use of the computer was in any way disruptive. That he had the foresight to bring his lap-top computer to court, and defense counsel did not, simply cannot serve as a basis for judicial intervention in the name of "fairness" or maintaining "a level playing field." The "playing field" was, in fact, already "level" because Internet access was open to both counsel, even if only one of them chose to utilize it.[75]

---

[70] Carino v. Muenzen, No. L-0028-07, 2010 WL 3448071, at *7, *9 (N.J. Super. Ct. App. Div. 2010).

[71] *Id.* at *4.

[72] *Id.*

[73] *Id.*

[74] *Id.* at *10.

[75] *Id.*

Burden v. CSX Transportation, Inc.

In this federal court personal injury case, the defense appealed the unfavorable verdict on the grounds of post-trial Internet research into two jurors. The research revealed that the jurors had failed to disclose material injuries and lawsuits involving themselves and relatives in response to questions posed in a juror questionnaire and voir dire.[76] The online research was performed using public records databases to get information that included lawsuits filed.[77]

The court rejected the defense's argument that there was recently discovered evidence of juror bias, finding instead that "defendant waived its present objections because the basis of the objections might have been known or discovered through the exercise of reasonable diligence."[78] In other words, no new trial was warranted because online resources were widely available to the defense long before the actual verdict, and the defense had an obligation to explore them.[79]

Johnson v. McCullough

After a defense verdict in a medical malpractice trial, plaintiff's counsel discovered that one of the jurors had lied when asked about whether she had ever been a party to litigation.[80] The information was discovered by searching an online database available in the courthouse.[81] The trial court granted the plaintiff's motion for a new trial.[82] On appeal, the Missouri Supreme Court reversed and noted that:

> [I]n light of advances in technology allowing greater access to information that can inform a trial court about the past litigation history of venire members, it is appropriate to place a greater burden on the parties to bring such matters to the court's attention at an earlier stage. Litigants should not be allowed to wait until a verdict has been rendered to perform a Case.net search . . . when, in many instances, the search could have been done in the final stages of

---

[76] Burden v. CSX Transp., Inc., No. 08-cv-04-DRH, 2011 WL 3793664, at *1 (S.D. Ill. 2011).

[77] *Id.* at *6-8.

[78] *Id.* at *10.

[79] *See Id.*

[80] *Id.* at 554.

[81] *Id.*

[82] *Id.*

jury selection or after the jury was selected but prior to the jury being empanelled.[83]

The court found that "a party must use reasonable efforts to examine the litigation history of a prospective juror on Case.net of those jurors selected but not empanelled and present to the trial court any relevant information prior to trial."[84] The *Johnson* Court's mandate was codified in Missouri Supreme Court Rule 69.025,[85] which requires lawyers to conduct online (Case.net) searches of a potential juror's litigation history.[86]

Khoury v. ConAgra Foods

Khoury followed the *Johnson* case and the Missouri Supreme Court's new rule. The case involved Elaine Khoury's allegations that the cause of her lung disease was exposure to chemical vapors from preparing ConAgra's microwave popcorn.[87] The parties conducted a search of the potential jurors' litigation history in accordance with the *Johnson* case and Missouri Supreme Court Rule 69.025.[88] The jury was empanelled, and prior to opening arguments ConAgra's counsel researched the jurors' social media presence and discovered Facebook posts by one of the jurors that indicated a bias against corporations and a failure to disclose information during voir dire.[89]

ConAgra lawyers informed the court that the juror was "a prolific poster for anti-corporation, organic foods" and moved for a mistrial[90] or, alternatively, to strike the juror from the jury.[91] The court removed the juror and proceeded to trial with one less alternate juror.[92]

The plaintiff lost at trial and appealed based on the fact that the juror should not have been removed because the defense's Internet search and Facebook findings were not timely. The plaintiff's assertion was unsuccessful as the appellate court found that the Johnson case and Supreme Court

---

[83] *Id.* at 558-59.

[84] *Id.* at 559.

[85] Khoury v. Conagra Foods, Inc., 368 S.W.3d 189, 202 (Mo. Ct. App. 2012).

[86] *Id.* at 192-93.

[87] *Id.* at 193.

[88] *Id.*

[89] *Id.*

[90] *Khoury*, 368 S.W.3d at 193.

[91] *Id.*

[92] *Id.* at 199.

Rule 69.025 require only Case.net searches of potential juror's litigation history.[93] The court explained:

> The rule could have similarly required "reasonable investigation" into other areas of "possible bias" and could have required such "reasonable investigation" to include a search of Internet social and business networking sites such as *Facebook, MySpace*, or *LinkedIn*, to name a few. And, the rule could have similarly required "reasonable investigation" of potential jurors via Internet search engines such as *Google* or *Yahoo!*, to name a few. Or, the rule could have simply required a blanket "Internet search" on "any and all issues of prospective juror bias." But, clearly, it does not.[94]

Although the appellate court limited itself to the plain text of the rule, it did acknowledge the potential in the digital age for a revisiting of Rule 69.025, stating that "the day may come that technological advances may compel our Supreme Court to rethink the scope of required 'reasonable investigation' into the background of jurors that may impact challenges to the veracity of responses given in voir dire before the jury is empanelled."[95]

5. **My upcoming trial is in front of a judge who doesn't seem to be the type to embrace technology. Is this typical, and what are some of the judicial concerns about online research on prospective jurors that I should anticipate?**

Judges Concerned with Juror Privacy and Juror Intimidation

The trial judge in *Carino v. Muenzen* is by no means alone in his reservations about attorneys performing online research on prospective jurors. In a 2013 state court criminal trial of a man accused of child sexual abuse, Montgomery County (Maryland) Judge Richard Jordan banned online research during voir dire, explaining that it would discourage people from performing their civil duty of reporting for jury duty.[96] "There's a real potential for a chilling effect on jury service, by jurors, to know 'I'm going to go out

---

[93] *Id.* at 202-3.

[94] *Id.* at 203 n.12.

[95] *Khoury*, 368 S.W.3d at 203.

[96] St. John Barned-Smith, *Montgomery Judge Denies Internet Searches for Jury Selection*, GAZETTE.NET (MAY 15, 2013).

to the courthouse . . . I'm going to be Googled. They're going to find all kinds of stuff on me,' and it feels kind of uneasy, at least," said Judge Jordan.[97]

Federal judges have displayed similar reticence. The Federal Judicial Center's May 2014 survey of judges revealed that 25.8 percent of the judges responding ban social media use during voir dire; however, almost 70 percent responded that they have never addressed this issue with lawyers.[98] Those who do not allow social media indicated reasons such as juror privacy and logistical considerations.[99] Judges also noted other concerns, which included juror intimidation, prolonged voir dire, and unnecessary distraction caused by online research.[100] A small fraction of the judges responding pointed to concerns with creating an unfair advantage for one side, while an even smaller fraction cited the inability to verify the accuracy of the online information gathered.[101]

With regard to the potential ethical dangers of attorneys engaging in inappropriate use of such networking information gathering, only 5 percent of the responding judges reported experiencing a problem with a lawyer's conduct.[102] According to the survey, this was limited to attorneys following prospective jurors on Twitter.[103] There were no reports of improper "friending," pretexting, or other efforts to get past a would-be juror's privacy settings.[104]

Of course, some judges' concerns may be specific to a particular social networking platform. In one New York federal case, the judge, responding to a motion *in limine*, forbade attorneys from searching jurors on LinkedIn and other sites in which the account holder could receive a notification as to who looked at his page, but allowed searches on other sites.[105]

---

[97] *Id.*

[98] MEGHAN DUNN, FED. JUDICIAL CTR., JURORS' AND ATTORNEYS' USE OF SOCIAL MEDIA DURING VOIR DIRE, TRIALS AND DELIBERATIONS: A REPORT TO THE JUDICIAL CONFERENCE COMMITTEE ON COURT ADMINISTRATION CASE MANAGEMENT 13 (2014).

[99] *Id.*

[100] *Id.* at 13-14.

[101] *Id.* at 14.

[102] DUNN, *supra* note 98.

[103] *Id.*

[104] *Id.*

[105] United States v. Watts, 934 F. Supp.2d 451, 494–95 (E.D.N.Y. 2013).

On the Other Hand . . . A Judicial Lack of Awareness

While some judges have expressed concerns about juror privacy and intimidation, many judges appear to be unaware of how many lawyers are routinely using the Internet to investigate prospective jurors. Additionally, some of the judges who may be aware of juror research have not addressed the issue with lawyers appearing before them. Notably, the 2014 survey by the Federal Judicial Center reported that about 90 percent of the judges responding have no idea whether attorneys are accessing potential jurors' social media profiles during voir dire.[106]

6. **Should I notify the judge if I plan to conduct online research of the jurors?**

Regardless of the statistics concerning judicial awareness of juror online research, the better practice is to make sure in advance that the judge is aware of your intention to perform such research, and to determine whether the judge plans to set any parameters for doing so. After all, judges in both state and federal courts typically enjoy broad discretion in overseeing courtroom behavior, including conducting examination of jurors. Being upfront with the judge is a good idea.

In one recent Florida case, the appellate court vacated a $74,000 sanction levied against a lawyer who had allegedly given "evasive" and "dishonest" answers when she was asked how she discovered a Facebook connection between a juror and a litigant in the trial.[107] The wife of attorney Petia Tenev's client found the jury list in her husband's jacket pocket, researched the jurors online, discovered that one juror was a Facebook friend of a witness, and asked Tenev to strike the juror. When the trial judge inquired how Tenev learned of this connection, she allegedly gave three different answers. Concerned about what he considered "dishonesty" and an attempt "to make improper contact with the juror," the trial judge sanctioned Tenev and granted a mistrial.[108]

But the appellate court disagreed, pointing out there actually was no finding of any contact with the juror and that Tenev—while not being candid with the tribunal—was fulfilling her duty as an officer of the court to "notify

---

[106] Dunn, *supra* note 98.

[107] Tenev v. Thurston, No. 2D14-4566, 2016 WL 886280, at *3 (Fla. 2d DCA 2016).

[108] *Id.*

the court of a potentially biased juror."[109] Moreover, the appellate court noted, "[t]here is no prohibition in Florida against an attorney researching jurors before, during, and throughout a trial so long as the research does not lead to contact with a juror."[110] Regardless of the eventual outcome, the time and effort of the appeal with the consequent delay for the client might have been avoided with an upfront discussion about online juror investigation.

7. Do judges restrict online research of jurors?

Some judges will restrict lawyers from researching prospective jurors online. Consequently, attorneys who choose to disregard such bans risk sanctions, including contempt of court. In an August 2016 healthcare antitrust trial involving hundreds of millions of dollars, the lead plaintiffs' lawyer used Internet research during jury selection despite US District Judge Roy Dalton Jr.'s pre-trial order banning the practice.[111] The lawyer was found in contempt and fined $500.[112]

Perhaps the most high-profile example of such a ban came in the recent patent infringement trial between tech giants Oracle and Google. Judge William Alsup of the US District Court for the Northern District of California had serious doubts before trial about whether the lawyers should be allowed to use social media to research perspective jurors.[113] After denying the parties' joint request to collect questionnaires from potential jurors before voir dire, and suspecting that both sides wanted "to conduct extended Internet investigations on the venire," Judge Alsup indicated that he was considering imposing a ban on both sides "on any and all internet research on the jury prior to verdict."[114]

The reasons for his concern included (1) worries about dragging out the voir dire procedure; (2) the possibility of the lawyers sitting on what they discover and using it strategically as post-verdict challenges to jurors' answers to voir dire questions; and (3) the concern that jurors admonished

---

[109] *Id.*

[110] *Id.*

[111] Nathan Hale, *Atty Fined for Using Internet During Health First Antitrust Trial*, Law360 (Aug. 19, 2016, 9:23 PM), http://www.law360.com/articles/830741/atty-fined-for-using-internet-during-health-first-antitrust-trial.

[112] *Id.*

[113] Order, Oracle Am., Inc. v. Google, Inc., No. 3:10-cv-03561 (N.D. Cal. March 14, 2016).

[114] *Id.*

by the court when told not to conduct their own Internet research might be tempted to disregard this instruction if they find out the lawyers are allowed to do it. So Judge Alsup asked both sides to brief the issue of "how far" the parties and their counsel could go.

Predictably, both Oracle and Google pointed Judge Alsup to many of the same cases and ethics opinions discussed in this chapter, arguing that passive review of publicly viewable social media profiles was ethically permissible. However, this didn't satisfy Judge Alsup, who issued a series of follow-up orders seeking more details. In one, for example, he asked how both sides' attorneys planned to use information about potential jurors' relationship status, as well as their political or religious ties. He also demanded that each side provide "three concrete examples of information you expect to find" that "would lead to a for-cause challenge that would be unlikely to surface during normal voir dire."[115]

In other orders, Judge Alsup directed the parties to address the extent to which their investigation would involve accessing Twitter accounts of prospective jurors or asking a potential juror's Facebook friends or LinkedIn connections to access more private levels of postings. He even inquired into how each party would handle a scenario in which an investigator happened to have a "friend" or "friend of a friend" connection to a prospective juror, enabling that investigator to have access to information not disclosed to the public.

Clearly, from the detailed questions posed and information sought, Judge Alsup was troubled by the practice of online juror investigation. Even after the reassurances from both Oracle and Google about the ethical permissibility of "Facebooking the jury," Judge Alsup ordered that if the parties wanted to conduct any such Internet research of the panel, they would be required to disclose that they did so and be prepared to share with each juror the results of their investigations. Not surprisingly, when faced with such a Hobson's choice, both Oracle and Google decided that they could somehow live without online investigations of potential jurors.

8. Do some courts have identifiable rules for researching jurors?

There is another good reason to check with a court in advance. Given the prevalence of the practice of researching prospective jurors online, courts are just beginning to articulate and implement specific rules governing this process. For example, the Local Rules of the US District Court for the

---

[115] *Id.*

Northern District of New York were recently amended to add Civil Rule 47.6, providing guidance on using social media to investigate prospective jurors. The rule specifically permits attorneys to use "websites available to the public" (including social networking sites) to research jurors or prospective jurors, as long as they adhere to certain conditions:

- The website or information must be available and accessible to the public.
- The attorney may not send an access or "friend" request to a juror's social media profile.
- No direct communications or contact between the attorney and juror/prospective juror may occur, including any "friend" requests, "follow" requests, or "connection" requests.
- The attorney must do the social media research anonymously, seeking only publicly accessible information and not disclosing to the juror who is conducting the inquiry.
- Deception must not be used to gain access to a profile or to information.
- Any third parties (like paralegals or investigators) working for an attorney in doing such research are subject to the same restrictions as attorneys.
- If the lawyer becomes aware of a juror's posting online about the case in which he or she is serving, the lawyer must report it to the court.[116]

The US District Court for the District of Idaho, Civil Rule 47.2 on "Social Media Juror Inquiries," is nearly identical. It adds a requirement that if an attorney through his or her online research learns of a juror's conduct that is criminal or fraudulent, the lawyer must take remedial measures, including reporting such conduct to the court if necessary.[117] In short, lawyers would be well advised to check with the court first, including consulting any case management or pre-trial orders, before embarking on a "voir Google" campaign.

9. Have any ethics opinions addressed online juror research, and what kind of guidance has been provided?

A growing number of ethics opinions nationwide are confronting the subject of researching prospective jurors online. Generally, the opinions advise that researching jurors online is ethically permissible so long as the juror's

---

[116] N.D.N.Y. L.R. 47.6.

[117] D. Idaho, Civ. R. 47.2 ("Social Media Juror Inquiries").

information is publicly available and there is no direct online contact with the juror.

As discussed in more detail below, the ABA delineated three types of online juror research: passive, active, and passive with electronic notification to the juror. The ABA concluded that passive review, meaning viewing what is available to the public, is permissible. On the other hand, active review, meaning sending a request to connect with the juror, is impermissible as it amounts to ex parte contact with a juror. The ABA parted company with New York by finding that the third category, in which the juror receives a message from the social media site that his profile has been viewed, is also permissible. The ABA opinion reasoned that the juror is not being contacted directly by the lawyer, but rather receiving an electronic notice from the online site. Because the electronic notice category resides in the proverbial gray area of the juror investigation analysis, best practice is to avoid logging on to a site that will notify a juror of your review of his profile. However, most sites allow for anonymous searches—once again it becomes the lawyer's responsibility to understand the options for conducting an online search.

What follows is a chronological compendium of the ethics advisory opinions in this area with a discussion of the analysis applied by the various ethics committees that have opined on the permissibility of juror research.

New York County

On May 18, 2011, the New York County Lawyers Association Committee on Professional Ethics issued Formal Opinion 743, which considered not only lawyer research online into prospective jurors, but also the ramifications of New York Rule of Professional Conduct 3.5 and the investigation of jurors during an ongoing trial.[118] It divided its discussion into two distinct phases: (1) the pre-trial phase in which there are only prospective, not actual, jurors; and 2) the evidentiary or deliberation phases of a trial.[119] There are common ethical concerns in both phases, including avoiding communications with the jurors and taking care not to engage in any misrepresentations or act with deceit.[120] However, as to the later phases, there is the additional ethical concern regarding how a lawyer must react if he or she learns of jury misconduct.[121]

---

[118] N.Y. Cty. Law. Ass'n. Comm. on Prof'l Ethics, Formal Op. 743, 1 (2011), https://www.nycla.org/siteFiles/Publications/Publications1450_0.pdf [hereinafter NYCLA Op. 743].

[119] *Id.* at 2.

[120] *Id* at 3.

[121] *Id.*

The Committee advised that "passive monitoring of jurors such as viewing a publicly available blog or Facebook page" is permissible so long as the lawyer has no direct or indirect contact with jurors.[122] However, the Committee somewhat muddies the water when it warns lawyers to "not act in any way by which the juror becomes aware of the monitoring."[123] As the Committee opined, "[i]f a juror becomes aware of an attorney's efforts to see the juror's profiles on websites, the contact may well consist of an impermissible communication, as it might tend to influence the juror's conduct with respect to the trial."[124] Clearly, this would include actual substantive communications, such as an attorney sending a Facebook message to the juror. And, according to the committee, other "communications" typical of the digital age would be similarly proscribed:

> Significant ethical concerns would be raised by sending a "friend request," attempting to connect via LinkedIn.com, signing up for an RSS feed for a juror's blog or "following" a juror's Twitter account. We believe that such contact would be impermissible communications with a juror.[125]

This approach is consistent with courts around the country that have held that even such relatively minimal contacts, such as friend requests or "pokes," constitute communications sufficient to constitute a violation of a court's "no contact" order or restraining order.[126] However, the committee carries the analysis further and concludes that an indirect (and impermissible) communication may include an automatic notification sent by a site to its user to inform the user that a third party has viewed his or her profile.[127]

Whether the committee's logic in defining impermissible contact to include indirect notification is workable as technology is rapidly evolving remains to be seen. The opinion refers specifically to Twitter's practice of messaging the account holder that someone is now "following" him, as well as LinkedIn's auto-communication feature that one's profile has been recently viewed. But the opinion also states that it "is intended to apply to whatever

---

[122] *Id.* at 2-3.

[123] NYCLA Op. 743, *supra* note 118, at 2-3.

[124] *Id.* at 3.

[125] *Id.* at 3.

[126] JOHN BROWNING, THE LAWYER'S GUIDE TO SOCIAL NETWORKING: UNDERSTANDING SOCIAL MEDIA'S IMPACT ON THE LAW 46–47 (2010).

[127] NYCLA Op. 743, *supra* note 118, at 2-3.

technologies now exist or may be developed that enable the account holder to learn the identity of a visitor."[128] Nonetheless, is an auto-notification truly a "communication"? And even if it is, the site itself generates it automatically. A terse, automatically generated notification lacking any substantive content does not seem to be reasonably considered a "communication." Perhaps as jury venire instructions evolve there will be a standard instruction that informs jurors that online research is a part of the process and auto-notifications are not sent by the lawyers. Alternatively, social media sites may provide anonymous methods for conducting searches. LinkedIn has an anonymous search function and often an individual's social media presence may be accessed through an indirect, anonymous Google search rather than through a specific social media site.

The second aspect of the committee's ruling that merits further consideration is its analysis of the obligation to report juror misconduct under Rule 3.5 (of the New York Rules of Professional Conduct as well as the ABA's Model Rules). This rule provides that "[a] lawyer shall reveal promptly to the court improper conduct by a member of a venire or a juror, or by another toward a member of the venire or a juror or member of his or her family of which the lawyer has knowledge."[129] Taking note of the prevalence of online misconduct by jurors, despite instructions prohibiting this behavior, the committee held that:

> Any lawyer who learns of juror misconduct, such as substantial violations of the court's instructions, is ethically bound to report such misconduct to the court under RPC 3.5, and the lawyer would violate RPC 3.5 if he or she learned of such misconduct yet failed to notify the court. This is so even should the client notify the lawyer that she does not wish the lawyer to comply with the requirements of RPC 3.5.[130]

While the committee acknowledged that a lawyer "has no ethical duty to routinely monitor the web posting or Twitter musings of jurors," if he does elect to do so he will be under a duty to "promptly notify the court of any impropriety of which the lawyer becomes aware."[131] This duty takes

---

[128] NYCLA Op. 743, *supra* note 118, at 3 n.2.
[129] N.Y. RULES OF PROF'L CONDUCT r. 3.5(d) (2009).
[130] NYCLA Op. 743, *supra* note 118, at 4.
[131] *Id.*

precedence over the lawyer's own duties to his or her client. As the opinion goes on to point out, a lawyer who learns of a juror's improper conduct "may not use this information to benefit the lawyer's client in settlement negotiations, or even to inform the lawyer's settlement negotiations."[132]

So, a lawyer who, while monitoring a juror's online presence, learns of a juror venturing online in violation of the court's instructions must bring this to the court's attention, regardless of whether that online foray revealed something favorable to his client's case. This is consistent with other courts' approaches to the primacy of the attorney's duty of candor to the tribunal.[133]

New York City Bar Association

New York City agreed with New York County and advised that appropriate online juror investigation is permissible. New York City also focused on the definition of communication and whether the juror would become aware of the lawyer's actions. "The central question an attorney must answer before engaging in jury research on a particular site or using a particular service is whether her actions will cause the juror to learn of the research."[134]

The committee went on to state:

> [I]f a juror were to (i) receive a "friend" request (or similar invitation to share information on a social network site) as a result of an attorney's research, or (ii) otherwise to learn of the attorney's viewing or attempted viewing of the juror's pages, posts, or comments, that would constitute a prohibited communication if the attorney was aware that her actions would cause the juror to receive such message or notification. We further conclude that the same attempts to research the juror might constitute a prohibited communication even if inadvertent or unintended.[135]

---

[132] *Id.*

[133] *See* United States v. Daugerdas, 867 F. Supp.2d 445, 484 (S.D.N.Y. 2012) (stating, "[a]n attorney's duty to inform the court about suspected juror misconduct trumps all other professional obligations, including those owed a client. Any reluctance to disclose this information—even if it might jeopardize a client's position—cannot be squared with the duty of candor owed to the tribunal.").

[134] *Id.* at *4.

[135] *Id.* at *2.

New York's position, which prohibits a direct request to connect from a lawyer to a juror, is consistent with the trend in cases around the country, as well as the relatively recent requirement under the Rule 1.1 of the Model Rule of Professional Conduct to be technologically conversant as part of providing competent representation. It holds attorneys to a higher standard as far as technology is concerned. New York is currently an outlier as to its suggestion that automatic messages from an online site to a juror constitute communication; however, as discussed above, regardless of a lawyer's position on the issue, it is not advisable to risk alienating the juror who receives a message that a lawyer is viewing the juror's online profile.

The New York City Bar opinion reminds lawyers that "communication" will be understood in its broadest sense, and urges them to be mindful of the fact that a communication is "the process of bringing an idea, information or knowledge to another's perception."[136] And, like its New York County counterpart, it discusses an attorney's obligation to reveal improper juror conduct to the court.[137] But it addresses other issues, such as the potential for deception or misrepresentation when researching jurors on social networking sites.[138]

Noting Rule 8.4's prohibition on deception and misrepresentation, the opinion states that—in the jury research context—attorneys may not misrepresent their identities, associations, or memberships in order to access otherwise unavailable information about a juror.[139] So, for example, an attorney "may not claim to be an alumnus of a school that she did not attend in order to view a juror's personal webpage that is accessible only to members of a certain alumni network."[140]

With the proliferation of specialized subgroups on social networking sites (such as LinkedIn groups restricted to people in a particular specialty area or with a specific affiliation), this can be a valid concern. Similarly, the opinion observes that a lawyer is forbidden from using a third party to do what he or she could not otherwise do.[141] Accordingly, just as other ethics

---

[136] N.Y.C. Bar Ass'n Comm. Prof'l Ethics, Formal Op. 2012-2 (2012), http://www.nycbar.org/member-and-career-services/committees/reports-listing/reports/detail/formal-opinion-2012-2-jury-research-and-social-media [hereinafter N.Y.C. Op. 2012-2].

[137] *Id.* at *1.

[138] *Id.*

[139] *Id.*

[140] *Id.* at *6.

[141] *Id.*

opinions have held with regard to lawyers not being allowed to use those working under their supervision (such as a paralegal) to "friend" a witness or party under false pretenses, lawyers may not use third parties to surreptitiously gain access to a juror's profile.

The New York City Bar's Committee opinion also reflects some of the judges' concerns about the impact of social media research on those called to jury service. "It is conceivable that even jurors who understand that many of their social networking posts and pages are public may be discouraged from jury service by the knowledge that attorneys and judges can and will conduct active research on them or learn of their online—albeit public—social lives."[142] However, the committee notes that investigating online posts is analogous "to searching newspapers for letters or columns written by potential jurors because in both cases the author intends the writing to be for public consumption."[143] In other words, "[t]he potential juror is aware that her information and images are available for public consumption."[144]

While some potential jurors might be "unsophisticated in terms of setting their privacy modes or other website functionality . . . the Committee believes that jurors have a responsibility to take adequate precautions to protect any information they intend to be private."[145] However, the Committee concludes that the relative level of social media sophistication of a juror does not change the ethical posture for the researching attorney.[146]

New York State Bar Association

The prior two ethics opinions are not the only source of guidance from New York. In March 2014, the Commercial and Federal Litigation Section of the New York State Bar Association issued a comprehensive set of Social Media Ethics Guidelines.[147] These guidelines address a variety of issues impacting a practitioner's use of social media. Guidelines 6 A-E address various

---

[142] N.Y.C. Op. 2012-2, *supra* note 136.

[143] *Id.*

[144] *Id.*

[145] *Id.*

[146] *Id.*

[147] THE SOCIAL MEDIA COMM. OF THE COMMERCIAL & FED. LITIG. SECTION, N.Y. ST. BAR ASS'N SOCIAL MEDIA GUIDELINES OF THE COMMERCIAL AND FEDERAL LITIGATION SECTION OF THE NEW YORK STATE BAR ASSOCIATION 15 (2015), http://www.nysba.org/socialmediaguidelines/ [hereinafter N.Y. St. Bar Social Media Guidelines].

aspects of researching social media profiles or posts of prospective and sitting jurors and reporting juror misconduct.[148] Relying on and citing the New York County and City Bar ethics opinions, these guidelines reaffirm that (1) lawyers can conduct social media research; (2) lawyers may view a juror's social media website as long as there is no communication with the juror; (3) lawyers may not use deceit to view a juror's social media profile; (4) lawyers may view or monitor the social media profile or posts of a juror during trial, provided that there is no communication; and (5) lawyers must promptly inform the court of possible juror misconduct the lawyer discovers by viewing a sitting juror's online postings.[149]

These guidelines, with their citations to earlier ethics opinions, as well as specific provisions of the New York Rules of Professional Conduct, are quite useful. In addition, the guidelines provide handy, practical pointers for lawyers seeking not to be identified through LinkedIn when viewing a juror's public LinkedIn profile. They also raise an occasional unanswered question: "whether a lawyer may non-deceptively view a social media account that from a prospective or sitting juror's view is putatively private, which the lawyer has a right to view, such as an alumni social network where both the lawyer and juror are members."[150]

Oregon

Oregon joined the New York opinions and indicated that investigation of jurors on social media is permissible if appropriately conducted, meaning no direct online contact with a juror such as a friend request.[151]

ABA Formal Opinion 466

The American Bar Association has also opined in its Formal Opinion 14-466, "Lawyer Reviewing Jurors' Internet Presence," which agrees with the prior ethics opinions in part and attempts to more specifically outline categories

---

[148] *Id.* The Guidelines were updated in 2019, https://archive.nysba.org /2019guidelines/.

[149] *Id.*

[150] *Id.*

[151] Or. St. Bar, Formal Op. 2013-189 (2013), https://www.osbar.org/_docs /ethics/2013-189.pdf. Interestingly, the Oregon opinion also discusses the exception in its rules that permits pretexting in the context of investigations of the violations of civil and constitutional rights as well as criminal matters. It notes that under these limited circumstances, pretexting on social media may be permissible

of online review. The opinion identifies three levels of attorney review of a juror's Internet presence:

1. Passive lawyer review of a juror's website or electronic social media (ESM) that is available without making an access request where the juror is unaware that a website or ESM has been reviewed
2. Active lawyer review where the lawyer requests access to the juror's [profile]
3. Passive lawyer review where the juror becomes aware through a website or ESM feature of the identity of the viewer[.][152]

The opinion advises that passive review, which amounts to "[t]he mere act of observing that which is open to the public" is not communication.[153] On the other hand, active review, such as sending a friend request to obtain information that is not publicly available, constitutes impermissible communication with a juror.[154] The opinion analogizes the difference between passive and active review to the distinction between driving by a juror's street to see where he or she lives and "driving down the juror's street, stopping the car, getting out, and asking the juror for permission to look inside the juror's house because the lawyer cannot see enough when just driving past."[155]

The ABA Opinion parts ways with New York on the issue of auto-notifications, which the ABA concludes is not impermissible communication with a juror.[156] "[T]he fact that a juror or potential juror may become aware that the lawyer is reviewing his Internet presence when a network setting notifies the juror of such review does not constitute a communication from the lawyer in violation of Rule 3.5(b)."[157] The opinion defines auto-notifications as communications from the Internet site rather than from the lawyer.[158] Applying the drive-by analogy, the opinion explains that an auto-

---

[152] *Id.*

[153] *Id.*

[154] ABA Comm. on Ethics & Prof'l Responsibility, Formal Op. 14-466 (2014), http://www.americanbar.org/content/dam/aba/administrative /professional_responsibility/formal_opinion_466_final_04_23_14 .authcheckdam.pdf [hereinafter ABA Op.14-466].

[155] *Id.* at 5.

[156] *Id.*

[157] *Id.* at 1.

[158] *Id.*

notification "is akin to a neighbor's recognizing a lawyer's car driving down the juror's street and telling the juror that the lawyer ha[s] been seen driving down the street."[159]

One other area of Opinion 14-466 marked a departure from some of the other ethics opinions—the thorny issue of a lawyer's obligation to notify the court of information gleaned through his or her social media research that indicates juror misconduct. Model Rule 3.3, Candor to the Tribunal, provides in section (b) that a lawyer's obligation to act upon discovering "improper conduct" arises only when the juror or prospective juror engages in conduct that is "fraudulent or criminal."[160] Thus, Rule 3.3(b) does not prescribe what a lawyer must do in the event he or she discovers juror conduct that violates a court order, but that does not rise to the level of criminal or fraudulent activity (such as a juror doing online research about the case or discussing it on Twitter).

Opinion 14-466 nonetheless tries to provide guidance. It states that "applicable law might treat such juror activity as conduct that triggers a lawyer's duty to take remedial action including, if necessary, reporting the juror's conduct to the court under current Model Rule 3.3(b)."[161] As the opinion points out, "[t]he materiality of juror Internet communications to the integrity of the trial will likely be a consideration in determining whether the juror has acted criminally or fraudulently."[162] In other words, it is not the lawyer's call to decide whether the juror misconduct he or she discovers rises to the level of "criminal or fraudulent"; the lawyer's remedial duty, according to Opinion 14-466, is triggered by knowledge of the conduct itself, and "is not preempted by a lawyer's belief that the court will not choose to address the conduct as a crime or fraud."[163]

When it was issued, Formal Opinion 14-466 received national publicity and engendered some controversy, including criticism that it sanctioned the

---

[159] *Id.* at 5.

[160] *Id.* at 7. While the Ethics Commission that previously amended Rule 3.3 apparently intended that this subsection also include lesser wrongdoing—"improper conduct"—and thus impose a broader duty, this part was unfortunately never carried out.

[161] *Id.*

[162] ABA Op.14-466, *supra* note 154.

[163] *Id.* at 9.

wholesale invasion of juror privacy.[164] But the very next state to consider the issue of researching jurors using social media followed the ABA approach.

Pennsylvania Bar Association

The Pennsylvania Bar Association released Formal Opinion 2014-300 and agreed with the New York opinions and the ABA in permitting appropriate online investigation of jurors.[165] However, Pennsylvania sides with the ABA on the issue of auto-notification and found that "[t]here is no ex parte communication if the social networking website independently notifies users when the page has been viewed."[166] Pennsylvania is also in accord with the finding that "a lawyer may be required to notify the court of any evidence of juror misconduct the lawyer discovers on a social networking website."[167]

West Virginia

In 2015, the West Virginia Lawyer Disciplinary Board released Legal Ethics Opinion 2015-02, entitled "Social Media and Attorneys."[168] It was a sweeping opinion covering a host of attorney uses of, and behavior on, social networking websites—including such issues as "friending" judges and contacting witnesses on platforms like Facebook and LinkedIn. Subsection (9) of that ethics opinion stated that attorneys "may review the public sections of a juror's social networking websites," although it prohibited lawyers from attempting to access the private portions of a juror's social media page. Doing so, it observed, would violate Rule 3.5 of West Virginia's Rules of Professional Conduct and its prohibition against communicating with or attempting to influence a member of a jury. The opinion also noted that it could be improper for attorneys to use the assistance of a third party

---

[164] *See Editorial: A Troublesome Opinion Regarding Juror Internet Research,* The CONN. L. TRIBUNE (June 24, 2014), http://www.ctlawtribune.com/id=1202660686891/Editorial-A-Troublesome-Opinion-Regarding-Juror-Internet-Research?slreturn=20160829143447 ("The combination of allowing lawyers to do internet research on jurors and requiring the reporting of potential inconsistencies has the potential to make jury selection more adversarial and less pleasant for the citizens who are doing their civic duty.").

[165] Pa. Bar Ass'n Comm. On Legal Ethics & Prof'l Responsibility, Formal Op. 2014-300 (2014).

[166] *Id.*

[167] *Id.*

[168] W. Va. Law. Disciplinary Board, L.E.O. No. 2015-02 (2015), http://www.wvodc.org/pdf/LEO%202015%20-%2002.pdf.

(such as an investigator or jury consultant) in order to gain access to the private sections of a juror's social media page.

Colorado

Later in 2015, the Colorado Bar Association Ethics Commission added its voice to the chorus of bar ethics opinions that echoed the ABA's position on researching jurors on social media.[169] Like its counterparts, the Colorado ethics body opined that it was ethically permissible for lawyers to conduct a passive review of a juror's publicly viewable social media profile. And consistent with the ABA perspective, it disagreed with early New York opinions that felt a passive review that resulted in an auto-alert to users that their profile had been viewed constituted a "communication." Passive review of a social media profile, the Colorado opinion observed, was not "communicating" just because "a technical feature" of the site alerts users to hits on their profiles.[170]

Colorado's Ethics Opinion 127 would go on to discuss other issues, like review of a judge's profile, use of deception to gain access to the private portions of a witness's profile, and contact with a represented party. However, the Colorado opinion's analysis of lawyers reviewing jurors' social media profiles also raised an interesting ethical concern for lawyers: can you do *too* much passive review, to the point where it has negative repercussions?

The Colorado Committee noted that "a lawyer might take improper advantage of the fact that a particular individual will receive automatic notification that the lawyer or someone on the lawyer's behalf viewed the individual's social media profile."[171] In such a scenario, the committee said, the lawyer might risk violating another ethical rule—Colorado's Rule of Professional Conduct 4.4 (a), which bans a lawyer from using means "that have no substantial purpose other than to embarrass, delay or burden a third person." Repetitive view of an individual's social media profile, with the lawyer knowing that the other person would receive notice each time the lawyer viewed the profile, could rise "to the level of harassment or intimidation," the Committee said.[172] However, it's hard to conceive a situation in which a lawyer would be consciously engaging in such repetitive viewing of a profile

---

[169] Colo. Bar Ass'n, Formal Op. 127 (2015).

[170] *Id.*

[171] *Id.*

[172] *Id.*

hoping to have this harassing effect, and indeed the committee agreed it would have to be "an extreme situation."[173]

District of Columbia

In November 2016, the District of Columbia Bar released Opinion 371 and noted that, on the one hand, competent and zealous representation may require the social media investigation of jurors.[174] On the other hand, the opinion cautioned lawyers to be aware of the pitfalls of violating a judge's order prohibiting investigation of jurors on social media.[175] The opinion also agrees with the ABA position that automatic notification from a social media site indicating that an individual (lawyer) has viewed a juror's profile does not constitute impermissible communication with a juror.[176] Finally, the opinion noted that if a lawyer discovers online juror misconduct, the obligation to report the misconduct to the tribunal requires a legal analysis unless the misconduct constitutes fraud, in which case the misconduct should be reported in accordance with Rule 3.5.[177]

The Bottom Line

As recent cases remind us, lawyers continue to struggle with their ethical responsibilities when it comes to researching jurors online. In a 2020 employment law case in Hawaii, for example, one of the plaintiff's lawyers—on the sixth day of trial—sent Juror #1 an invitation to connect on LinkedIn. The juror properly reported the contact, and the judge investigated. The lawyer initially claimed that he neither used LinkedIn nor was familiar with it. The court didn't buy that excuse, particularly when it was revealed that the attorney had not one but two LinkedIn profiles! Then, the lawyer insisted that the contact had been unintentional, done inadvertently while scrolling through that juror's LinkedIn profile while in court, in preparation for closing argument. The judge wasn't impressed with that excuse either, and while she ultimately didn't

---

[173] *Id.*

[174] D.C. Bar Ethics Opinion 371 (2016).

[175] *Id.*

[176] *Id.*

[177] *Id.*

sanction counsel, she did express concern about his "reckless" and "less than professional" behavior.[178]

So what are some of the key takeaways for lawyers who wish to research prospective jurors online while remaining within the ethical boundaries? First, be aware of the ethics guidance already handed down by the ABA, state, and local ethics bodies, particularly any authority applicable to your jurisdiction.

Second, raise the issue with your trial judge if it has not already been addressed in a pre-trial order or local rule.[179] Getting a sense for the court's comfort level with this practice can prove vital.

Third, make sure you are comfortable with the features and functionality of the technology you'll be using, or make sure to obtain the assistance of someone who is (like a jury consultant or tech-savvy colleague). Social media offerings and a site's settings can change, and you want to avoid anything that could be construed as an impermissible communication, no matter how inadvertent.

Fourth, remember that such online research is just one tool in a trial lawyer's toolbox, and isn't intended as a complete substitute for your own insight from conducting voir dire. People may share a version of themselves online, and that version may not be consistent with the picture painted by your carefully constructed voir dire and the responses it elicited. Keep in mind that—spoiler alert!—not everything found on the Internet is true. Use any social media juror research as a supplement to, and not a substitute for, your own professional judgment.

And, finally, remember that the discussion of your ethical obligations merely begins with the practice of researching prospective jurors online; it does not end with it. If your research uncovers improper conduct by a juror, your ethical duty to notify the court of such misconduct is triggered.

---

[178] Reyes v. Tanaka, 2020 WL 1663341 (D. Haw. Apr. 3, 2020).

[179] *See, for example,* United States District Court for the Middle District of Florida Rule 5.02 (C) RESEARCH OF A PROSPECTIVE JUROR. During jury selection, no party may use an electronic device to gather or transmit information about a prospective juror. https://www.flmd.uscourts.gov/local-rules/rule-502-jury-selection-and-prohibition-communication-juror. Last visited July 18, 2022.

CHAPTER 7

Through the Prosecutorial Looking Glass: Prosecutors, Ethics, and Social Media

Media like Facebook and Twitter may provide a digital treasure trove of information for prosecutors, but they can also provide an environment rich in potential ethical missteps. No doubt, prosecutors have certain ethical obligations unique to their roles, which may implicate special concerns about the use of social media. Of course, some of the ethical implications for prosecutors arise out of the same type of digital concerns that have been discussed elsewhere in this book, such as the question of digital competency or the difficulty some lawyers have separating their professional and personal online personas.

Nonetheless, we pause here to highlight issues confronting prosecutors. Technology in various forms has bedeviled prosecutors over the years—as reflected in states like Florida and Texas where there have been high-profile cases of judges and prosecutors texting each other during trial.[1] We pose just one main question and provide the answer in the subparts noted below.

---

[1] *See, e.g.*, the troubled saga of former Broward County (Florida) Judge Ana Gardiner and former county prosecutor Howard Scheinberg: Tonya Alanez, *Texting ex-Broward Judge Faces Bar Inquiry*, Sun-Sentinel (Nov. 27, 2012); Rafael Olmeda, *Supreme Court Suspends Former Prosecutor over Relationship with Judge*, Sun-Sentinel (June 20, 2013). Or consider the cautionary tale of former Texas judge Elizabeth Coker and her texting during trial with former prosecutor Kaycee Jones: Martha Neil, *Judge Texted During Trial to Help State, Says Ex-Prosecutor*, ABA J.

QUESTION

1. **I'm an assistant district attorney, and our office uses social media quite a bit, including for researching incriminating posts by defendants. But are there any ethical danger areas of which we should be aware?**

The short answer is "yes." The ethical danger areas for prosecutors in the use of social media generally fall into one of four categories: (1) disregarding confidentiality; (2) disregarding court orders; (3) improper use of social media leading up to and during trial; and (4) allowing one's personal feelings or beliefs to impact one's professional persona.

Danger Area #1—Disregarding Confidentiality

Even something as fundamental as the duty of confidentiality can prove problematic in an environment where individuals rely on the illusory shield of anonymity online. Jim Letten, a 2001 appointee of President George W. Bush, was the US Attorney for the Eastern District of Louisiana (encompassing New Orleans) and in 2012 he was the country's longest-tenured US Attorney.[2] Yet, by December, he had resigned in the midst of investigations into two of his top deputies who had gone online to pseudonymously discuss cases pending in the US Attorney's office, comment on presiding judges, and attack the subjects of their office's investigations.[3]

Sal Perricone, the first top deputy, resigned in March 2012 after it was revealed that he had made hundreds of online posts on NOLA.com (the website of the New Orleans Times-Picayune).[4] The posts consisted primarily of critical comments about Fred Heebe, a local landfill owner whose company

---

(July 9, 2013, 11:00 AM), http://www.abajournal.com/news/article/judge _texted_during_trial_to_help_state_says_ex-prosecutor/.

[2] Sari Horwitz, *New Orleans U.S. Attorney Resigns amid Scandal over Anonymous Online Postings*, WASH. POST (Dec. 6, 2012), https://www .washingtonpost.com/world/national-security/new-orleans-us-attorney -resigns-amid-scandal-over-anonymous-online-postings/2012/12/06 /c95c0d4a-3ef1-11e2-bca3-aadc9b7e29c5_story.html.

[3] *Id.*

[4] *See* John Simerman, *Jan Mann Spread Vitriol Across Political Land-scape in Online Posts*, THE TIMES-PICAYUNE (Jan. 5, 2013, 9:23 AM), http://www.nola.com/crime/index.ssf/2013/01/jan_mann_spread_vitriol _across.html.

was the subject of an investigation by Letten's office. Perricone posted hundreds of times using the pseudonym "Henry L. Mencken1951."

Shortly after the revelation about Perricone, it was revealed that another top deputy of Letten's, First Assistant Attorney Jan Mann, had also posted numerous times on NOLA.com.[5] Her posts included not just comments about Heebe and the investigation into his activities, but also statements criticizing colleagues and discussing open cases. While she was apparently not as prolific as Perricone (the investigation into her online misconduct revealed approximately forty comments), federal authorities issued subpoenas seeking information on eleven aliases she was believed to have used.

Danger Area #2—Disregarding Court Orders

Another area where prosecutors have found themselves in ethical trouble concerns disregarding court orders when it comes to social media. In May 2011, Guadalupe County, Texas, Assistant District Attorney Larry Bloomquist was found in contempt and fined for violating a court's gag order by posting a Facebook status update about an ongoing felony trial.[6] Apparently, the gag order was entered at the start of the manslaughter trial. Judge Gary Steel was not amused when Bloomquist posted "Happy ending" on Facebook when the jury returned a guilty verdict. Those two words cost the assistant D.A. $400.[7]

Danger Area #3—Improper Use of Social Media Before, During, and After Trial

Perhaps the most egregious example of a prosecutor's social media–related ethical lapse before trial is the "false friending" perpetuated by former Cleveland, Ohio, assistant prosecutor Aaron Brockler in April 2013. While prosecuting the homicide case of *People v. Damon Dunn*, Brockler was faced with the challenge of shaking the testimony of the defense's two alibi witnesses

---

[5] Gordon Russell, *First Assistant U.S. Attorney Jan Mann Demoted After Admitting Online Commentary*, THE TIMES-PICAYUNE (Nov. 8, 2012, 10:20 AM), http://www.nola.com/crime/index.ssf/2012/11/first _assistant_us_attorney_ja.html.

[6] *See* Roy Bragg, *Guadalupe County Prosecutor Fined for Facebook Comments*, SAN ANTONIO EXPRESS-NEWS (May 11, 2011, 10:11 PM), http://www.mysanantonio.com/news/local_news/article/Guadalupe -County-prosecutor-fined-for-Facebook-1376185.php.

[7] *Id.*

(ex-girlfriends of Dunn's who could testify that, at the time of the murder Damon Dunn was actually miles away on the other side of Cleveland). His solution? Invent a fake "baby mama" of the defendant and use this fictitious online persona to communicate on Facebook with the two alibi witnesses.

And communicate he did—apparently, he upset both witnesses with the (fake) knowledge that Dunn had a "baby mama" on the side. Once he had their Facebook attention, he urged them to change their testimony.[8] Subsequently, Brockler, in his role as the prosecutor, met with the witnesses. Brockler claims that one of the witnesses exclaimed, "[t]his is bogus, I'm not going to lie for him."[9] The other alibi witness also decided that she "wasn't going to lie for him" and "wanted the truth to be known."[10]

Although Brockler asserted that he informed defense counsel Myron Watson (think Rule 3.8 responsibilities of a prosecutor) that Dunn's alibi was no longer viable, he also printed and filed the transcripts of the "baby mama's" Facebook chats with the alibi witnesses. Brockler later revealed the subterfuge when an attorney filling in for Brockler asked about the Facebook transcripts. After Brockler explained that he was the baby mama, the curious attorney informed his supervisors.

County Prosecutor Timothy J. McGinty immediately[11] recused his office and transferred the case to the Ohio Attorney General. Defense counsel and the Cuyahoga County Common Pleas Judge were also informed. Brockler was subjected to a disciplinary investigation that ultimately resulted in his termination. McGinty explained:

> This office does not condone and will not tolerate such unethical behavior. . . . He disgraced this office and everyone who works here. . . . By creating false evidence, lying to witnesses as well as another prosecutor, Aaron Brockler has damaged the prosecution's chances in a murder case where a totally innocent man was killed at his work.[12]

---

[8] James F. McCarty, *Cuyahoga County Prosecutor Fired after Posing as an Accused Killer's Girlfriend on Facebook to Try to Get Alibi Witnesses to Change Their Testimony*, CLEVELAND.COM (June 7, 2013, 10:35 AM), http://www.cleveland.com/metro/index.ssf/2013/06/cuyahoga_county _prosecutor_fir.html.

[9] *Id.*

[10] *Id.*

[11] *Id.*

[12] *Id.* (internal quotation marks omitted).

Incredibly, Brockler believed that his conduct was justified because justice was served. His unrepentant attitude was reflected in his comments to the media in which he shared his sympathy for the victim's mother, saying he "felt her pain over losing her son,"[13] and adding "I think the public is better off for what I did."[14]

Brockler's conduct violated the Ohio Disciplinary Rules of Professional Conduct that address acting with deception toward a third party.[15] However, it is important to note that if his conduct had taken place in another state like California or Texas with statutory prohibitions against "e-personation" (impersonating someone else online), Brockler could have faced criminal charges.[16]

Ultimately, Brockler received a suspension of his license for one year for his Facebook misconduct, after a finding that "his subterfuge prejudiced the administration of justice because it had the potential to induce false testimony, injected significant new issues into the case shortly before trial, and intentionally delayed the resolution of the case by requiring further investigation and the appointment of a special prosecutor."[17] However, the one-year suspension was stayed by a majority of the Ohio Supreme Court. In a sharply worded dissent, Chief Justice O'Connor vehemently disagreed, writing that Brockler's conduct, his efforts to hide his deceptive activities, and his refusal to admit wrongdoing militated in favor of serving the suspension.[18] The Chief Justice added that the court's failure to require any suspension time does nothing to "ensure the integrity of prosecutors and the ethical administration of justice."[19]

Brockler's case does not solely serve as an example of a case involving violations of the ethical rules against tampering with evidence, suborning perjury, becoming a necessary witness, and engaging in dishonest and deceptive conduct toward a third party. It also illustrates how, in the

---

[13] *Id.* (internal quotation marks omitted).

[14] *Id.* (internal quotation marks omitted).

[15] OH. RULES OF PROF'L CONDUCT r. 8.4(c) & cmt.2 (2013).

[16] CAL. PENAL CODE § 528.5(a)-(d) (West 2014); TEX. PENAL CODE ANN. § 33.07(a)-(c) (West 2014); *see generally* Rodolfo Ramirez, *Online Impersonation; A New Forum for Crime on the Internet*, 27 CRIM. JUST. 6, 7-8 (2012) (discussing the California and Texas online impersonation laws).

[17] Disciplinary Counsel v. Brockler, 48 N.E.3d 557, 560 (Oh. 2016).

[18] *Id.*

[19] *Id.*

prosecutorial context, it may be disarmingly tempting to rationalize such conduct as ends justifying the means. However, misconduct is nevertheless misconduct regardless of any "good cause" rationalization. As the New York City Bar ethics opinion on acting with deception toward witnesses during the online investigation of a case cautioned, such conduct is especially possible on social media. As that opinion pointed out, "[I]t may be easier to deceive an individual in the virtual world than in the real world."[20]

Another question that arises in this context is as follows: may a prosecutor ethically discuss a pending case on a social media platform? The answer is that it depends on what is said. A prosecutor may ethically make statements to inform the public about the prosecutor's role and actions or otherwise serve a legitimate law enforcement purpose. But prosecutors may not make extrajudicial statements that have a substantial likelihood of heightening public condemnation of the accused or jeopardizing the accused's right to a fair trial. Ultimately, the issue will turn on not only what the comments were and when they were made, but also on whether or not they had any demonstrable prejudicial effect. Consider three cases that illustrate the potential for social media commentary by a prosecutor to have such a prejudicial effect: *People v. Usee*, *People v. Armstrong*, and *State of Missouri v. Polk*.

State v. Usee

A Somali immigrant, Usee, was convicted of three counts of murder in a Minnesota court.[21] He challenged his conviction based, in part, on prosecutorial misconduct resulting from the prosecutor's publicly available Facebook posts.

The prosecutor posted that she was "comfortable" about her case given one juror's college affiliation.[22] She also explained that she was "keep[ing] the streets of Minneapolis safe from the Somalias [sic]."[23] Even though the posts appeared before the case was submitted to the jury, the appellate court concluded that "[a]bsent evidence of juror exposure, appellant did not

---

[20] Ass'n of the Bar of the City of N.Y. Comm. on Prof'l Ethics, Formal Op. 2010-2 (2010).

[21] State v. Usee, 800 N.W.2d 192, 195 (Minn. Ct. App. 2011).

[22] Rochelle Olson, *Hennepin County (MN) Prosecutor Accused of Posting AntiSomali Comment on Facebook*, STAR TRIBUNE (Dec. 16, 2010), http://freerepublic.com/focus/f-news/2452919/posts.

[23] *Usee*, 800 N.W.2d at 200 (alteration in original) (internal quotation marks omitted).

establish a prima facie case of juror misconduct."[24] The court also noted that the jurors had been instructed "not to research the case, the issues, or anyone involved in the case on the Internet." It stated that the defendant had not provided any evidence that any of the jurors had read the posts.[25]

People v. Armstrong

In 2014, a California appellate court also confronted the dangers of extra-judicial statements made by prosecutors via social media. In *People v. Armstrong*,[26] a domestic violence case, the defendant sought to reverse his conviction based on various acts of prosecutorial misconduct. The alleged misconduct included alleged witness intimidation and threats to arrest his wife (the alleged victim who refused to testify).[27] Included in the list of acts of prosecutorial misconduct was the prosecutor's Facebook postings from the week before voir dire.

On the day that the prosecutor was ordered to produce the defendant's thirteen-year-old daughter for an interview with defense counsel, she posted: "[a]fter I spent the day trying to prevent my 13-year-old star witness from being kidnapped, I found out I am getting the Prosecutor of the Year Award from the Victims Service Center. I almost cried when they called and told me."[28]

The Court of Appeals referred to the comment as "an incredible display of poor judgment," and added that the suggestion of a plot to kidnap the minor child "would appear to violate Rule 5-120 of [California's] Rules of Professional Conduct, which prohibits members of the bar from making extrajudicial statements when the member knows or reasonably should know that [the statement] will have a substantial likelihood of materially prejudicing an adjudicative proceeding in the matter."[29]

The court further observed that the prosecutor's Facebook post also had "the potential of creating a mistrial and thus wasting valuable government resources."[30] The court noted that the Internet is "available to anyone with access to a computer," and that "a posting on the internet is available to

---

[24] Id. at 201 (citing State v. Martin, 614 N.W.2d 214, 226 (Minn. 2000); State v. Beier, 263 N.W.2d 622, 626-27 (Minn. 1978)).

[25] *Usee*, 800 N.W.2d at 201.

[26] People v. Armstrong, No. F064006, 2014 WL 125939, at *2 (Cal. Ct. App. 2014), review denied (Apr. 9, 2014).

[27] *Id.* at *1.

[28] *Id.* at *40.

[29] *Id.* at *40-41 (quoting CAL. RULES OF PROF'L CONDUCT r. 5-120).

[30] *Id.* at *41.

more people than a local newspaper in a magnitude impossible to comprehend." Therefore, the court cautioned that "[a]ll that is required is for one juror to learn of such comments, either directly or indirectly, to sabotage the entire trial."[31] However, despite the court's concerns and cautions, it concluded that based on the record the prosecutor's "foolishness" did not rise to the level of prosecutorial misconduct warranting a new trial.[32] The defendant did not offer any evidence that the prosecutor intended to influence the jury. Moreover, there was no evidence that any juror became aware of the comments.

State of Missouri v. Polk

A 1992 St. Louis "cold case" involving multiple counts of sexual assault of an eleven-year-old child made the news in 2011 when DNA identified the defendant, David Polk.[33] He was prosecuted, convicted, and sentenced to concurrent fifteen-year terms.[34] He appealed and alleged that the trial court had erred by failing to either dismiss the case with prejudice or strike the jury panel due to the prosecutor's "inappropriate public comments about the case on Twitter."[35]

Before jury selection began, the prosecutor, Joyce, tweeted: "David Polk trial next week. DNA hit linked him to 1992 rape of 11 yr old girl. 20 yrs later, victim now same age as prosecutor."[36]

During the trial Joyce tweeted: "Watching closing arguments in David Polk 'cold case' trial. He's charged with raping 11 yr old girl 20 years ago." Also, "I have respect for attys who defend child rapists. Our system of justice demands it, but I couldn't do it. No way, no how."[37]

Joyce tweeted during jury deliberations with comments such as: "Jury now has David Polk case. I hope the victim gets justice, even though 20 years late."[38]

Joyce continued her observations on Twitter after the verdict, when she tweeted: "Finally, justice. David Polk guilty of the 1992 rape of 11 yr old

---

[31] *Id.* at *41-42.

[32] *Id.* at *41.

[33] State v. Polk, 415 S.W.3d 692, 695 (Mo. Ct. App. 2013).

[34] *Id.*

[35] *Id.* at *1,*4.

[36] *Id.* (internal quotation marks omitted).

[37] *Id.*

[38] *Id.* (internal quotation marks omitted).

girl. DNA cold case. Brave victim now the same age as prosecutor."[39] And, "[a]side from DNA, David Polk's victim could identify him 20 years later. Couldn't forget the face of the man who terrorized her."[40]

On appeal, the defendant alleged that the prosecutor's tweets violated the professional conduct rules, noting Rule 4-3.8(f). The rule provides in pertinent part that "except for statements that are necessary to inform the public of the nature and extent of the prosecutor's action and that serve a legitimate law enforcement purpose, [prosecutors should] refrain from making extrajudicial comments that have a substantial likelihood of heightening public condemnation of the accused."[41]

Similar to the cases discussed above, the appellate court did not find grounds for a new trial because when reviewing the record, the court could not conclude that the trial had been unfair or that the jury was even aware of the prosecutor's ongoing tweets.[42] In other words, to rise to the level of "substantial prejudice," there has to be evidence that "the misconduct substantially swayed the judgment."[43] Thus, lacking any evidence that the jury had been tainted, the appellate court concluded, "the trial court did not abuse its discretion in denying Polk's motion to dismiss and to strike the jury panel."[44]

However, the appellate court noted that "extraneous statements on Twitter or other forms of social media, particularly during the time frame of the trial, can taint the jury and result in reversal of the verdict."[45] The court's opinion expressed "doubt that using social media to highlight the evidence against the accused and publicly dramatize the plight of the victim serves any legitimate law enforcement purpose or is necessary to inform the public of the nature and extent of the prosecutor's actions."[46] The court also cautioned about the danger of tainting a jury:

> Likewise, we are concerned that broadcasting that the accused is a 'child rapist' is likely to arouse heightened public condemnation.

---

[39] *Id.* at 4-5 (internal quotation marks omitted).

[40] *Id.* at 5 (internal quotation marks omitted).

[41] *Id.* (alteration in original) (quoting Mo. Sup. Ct. r. 4-3.8(f) (2013)).

[42] *Polk*, 415 S.W.3d at 695.

[43] *Id.* at *6-7 (quoting State v. Forest, 183 S.W.3d 218, 227 (Mo. 2006) (en banc)).

[44] *Id.*

[45] *Id.*

[46] *Id.*

We are especially troubled by the timing of Joyce's Twitter posts, because broadcasting such statements immediately before and during trial greatly magnifies the risk that a jury will be tainted by undue extrajudicial influences.[47]

Of course, the depth of the court's faith in admonishments and instructions by the trial judge is debatable, as is its belief that just because none of the jurors admitted to following the circuit attorney on Twitter, no harm could result. Even without being Twitter followers of a given individual, people can be exposed to a tweet through a variety of different means, including retweets, mentions, and links to those tweets by others. Tweets can spread in as viral a manner as other forms of social media content, regardless of the number of followers of the original tweeter. And while admonishments against venturing online to research a case are well intended, such instructions exist primarily because of the widespread problem of mistrials and overturned verdicts resulting from the online misconduct of jurors.

In most instances, the court and counsel only become aware of the influence of outside tweets or other online activities involving jurors when one juror comes forward and implicates another. It is rarely discovered through the court's investigation of the attorneys involved in the case. It would be naive of any court to assert that if it is not aware of any effect on the jury of extrajudicial statements posted on social networking platforms, then no such effect occurred. Moreover, despite the fact that the appellate courts did not find the prosecutorial social media conduct to warrant reversals in the above three cases, the court's deep concern about the potential for social media posts to taint the jury, create a mistrial, and waste government resources along with one court's characterization of the prosecutor's social media post as "an incredible display of poor judgment," should serve as a warning to prosecutorial offices throughout the country.

Danger Area #4—Letting Your Personal Life Impact Your Professional Life Online

In chapter 12, "Selfie Sabotage: Lawyers Are Human, Too!" we present a social media rogue's gallery of lawyers breaking bad in cyberspace; prosecutors are unfortunately just as susceptible to allowing their personal opinions or predilections to overshadow their professional selves online. The example of the Florida prosecutor who was fired after making inflammatory

---

[47] *Id.*

comments following the Orlando mass shootings is but one of numerous such instances. Consider the following:

- In July 2012, a former Norfolk, Virginia, Assistant Prosecutor Clifton C. Hicks used Facebook as a forum for airing his grievances against his former boss.[48] When the prosecutor's Facebook grievances allegedly became threats, Hicks was charged with the felony of making "a written threat to kill or do bodily injury."
- In July 2012, Brooklyn Assistant District Attorney Justin Marrus garnered national attention when a media outlet published his Facebook page that contained photographs of Marrus in blackface, displaying a Confederate flag, and engaging in a simulation of prison rape.[49] The D.A.'s office responded: "We think the [photos] are abhorrent, stupid, and childish. We're asking Mr. Marrus for [a] full explanation of his conduct, which is totally unacceptable. And we will take appropriate action."[50]
- In August 2013, US Assistant Attorney John Craft posted a graphic that read "Obama: Why Stupid People Shouldn't Vote."[51] Craft also characterized President Obama as "the Dalibama."[52] Craft created another controversy when he posted thoughts about the Trayvon Martin case. Craft wrote:

How are you fixed for Skittles and Arizona watermelon fruitcocktail (and maybe a bottle of Robitussin, too) in your neighborhood? I am fresh out of "purple drank." So, I may come by for a visit. In a

---

[48] *See* Louis Hansen, *Ex-Norfolk Prosecutor Charged after Facebook Post*, The Virginian-Pilot (July 27, 2012).

[49] *See* Garth Johnston, *Should Brooklyn ADAs Wear Blackface, Simulate Prison Rape on Facebook?*, Gothamist (July 9, 2012, 2:41 PM), http://gothamist.com/2012/07/09/should_brooklyn_adas_put_blackface.php#photo-1.

[50] *Id.* (internal quotation marks omitted).

[51] *See* Brooke Crum, *Assistant U.S. Attorney's Facebook Posts Probed*, Beaumont Enterprise (Aug. 14, 2013, 11:33 AM), http://www.beaumontenterprise.com/news/article/Assistant-U-S-attorney-s-Facebook-posts-probed-4730814.php.

[52] *Id.*

rainstorm. In the middle of the night. In a hoodie. Don't get upset or anything if you see me looking in your window . . . kay?[53]

- The US Attorney for the Eastern District of Texas, John Malcolm Bales, responded by declaring Craft's comments to be "reprehensible"[54] and not a reflection of the US Attorney's office.[55]
- In May 2015, Teana Walsh, a prosecutor with the Wayne County (Michigan) Prosecutor's office, reacted to the news about people rioting in Baltimore in response to the death of an African American man in police custody with a Facebook post. It read: "So I am watching the news in Baltimore and see large swarms of people throwing bricks, etc. at police who are fleeing from their assaults . . . 15 in the hospital already. Solution. Simple. Shoot em. Period. End of discussion. I don't care what causes the protestors to turn violent . . . what the 'they did it because' reason is . . . no way is this acceptable. Flipping disgusting." In response, the prosecutor's office noted that Ms. Walsh's Facebook post was "completely out of character," and that it was taken down immediately.

Bottom Line

The potential for attorneys' misuse of technologies like social media can result in any number of ethical issues, as we have seen. But social media misuse by prosecutors adds a new dimension of ethical concerns, in part because of the power of the state to deprive an individual of liberty and life, the resources that prosecutors enjoy, and the resulting unique ethical obligations incumbent upon them. Just like attorneys in any other practice area, prosecutors must remember that the same ethical rules that govern every other mode of communication are equally applicable when engaging on social

---

[53] *Id.* (internal quotation marks omitted). The post refers to the fact that Martin, who was wearing a hoodie when he was fatally shot on February 26, 2012, in Sanford, Florida, had been to a nearby store for a package of Skittles and an Arizona Iced Tea. *Id.*

[54] *Id.* (internal quotation marks omitted).

[55] See Brooke Crum, *Beaumont Prosecutor's Comments Draw Attention from D.C., Opposing Counsel,* BEAUMONT ENTERPRISE (Aug. 15, 2013, 9:07 AM), http://www.beaumontenterprise.com/news/article/Beaumont -prosecutor-s-comments-draw-attention-4733372.php (internal quotation marks omitted).

networking platforms. Prosecutorial misconduct can translate to a digital dimension—whether one is blogging or posting about a pending case in the perceived (if illusory) anonymity of the Internet, or whether one is using Facebook or Twitter as a digital bully pulpit to condemn the accused and arouse public opinion.

CHAPTER 8

"Friends" with No Benefits? Judges, Legal Ethics, and Social Media

With the incredibly wired world in which we live, and with courts themselves embracing technological innovations like electronic filing, it should come as no surprise that social media use among judges has increased much like it has among society as a whole. A national survey of judges by the Conference of Court Public Information Officers (CCPIO) showed that social media use among the judiciary grew from 40 percent in 2010 to 86 percent in 2013—an illustration that the judiciary is finally joining the public it serves where the public has chosen to congregate. Yet according to the CCPIO's 2014 survey, less than half (44.5 percent) of the judges responding agree that judges can use Facebook without ethical concerns.[1]

Judges have long been criticized for being inaccessible and a source of mystery to the public they serve. One reason for the increased use of social media by judges may be the growing importance of these platforms in political races. With thirty-nine jurisdictions in the United States using some form of partisan election

---

[1] 2014 CCPIO NEW MEDIA SURVEY, A REPORT OF THE CONFERENCE OF COURT PUBLIC INFORMATION OFFICERS, CCPIO 23RD ANNUAL MEETING (AUG. 6, 2014), http://ccpio.org/wp-content/uploads/2014/08/CCPIO-New-Media-survey -report_2014.pdf.

to select their judges, use of social networking platforms as a political tool has become necessary to professional survival. In fact, a number of state judicial ethics opinions pointedly address social media use in campaigns. In addition, as learned observers like Texas Supreme Court Justice Don Willett (the "Tweeter Laureate" of Texas) have noted, harnessing technology is "indispensable to openness" and "another fruitful way for the judiciary to engage citizens."[2]

Yes, judicial attitudes toward social media use may be changing, thanks in part to its utility as a political tool. Yet even as more and more judges assume the role of "digital citizens," there is a persistent need for guidance for judges on the ethical boundary lines of social media use. At least eighteen states have either issued formal judicial ethics opinions or decided cases on this topic, and the number continues to grow—as does the number of judges facing disciplinary issues over social media use. Most jurisdictions are quick to remind us that interactions involving judges via social media must be evaluated in the same way as other interactions employing more traditional avenues of communications. Avoiding ex parte communications, the appearance of impropriety, or the implications of special influence are just as critical in cyberspace as they were on the golf course, at a restaurant, or in any other setting.

So, let's begin with a look at those jurisdictions that have analyzed the question of judicial use of social media and the ethical restrictions governing such use. Afterward, we examine some of the types of activity on social media that have resulted in judicial disciplinary actions (such as posting about cases or litigants, and communicating ex parte). This chapter will also look at some other questions that can arise (like what happens when the judge is Facebook friends with a witness or with a family member of a crime victim or litigant). And we examine how, just like lawyers, judges sometimes find themselves on shaky ethical ground on social media when their personal lives spill over online and tarnish their professional personas.

---

[2] Justice Don Willett, *The Tweeter Laureate of Texas Discusses Judge's Use of Social Media*, WASH. TIMES (July 22, 2015), http://www.washingtontimes.com/news/2015/jul/22/celebrate-liberty-month-the-tweeter-laureate-of-te/.

QUESTIONS

1. **I have an important hearing coming up and when I looked up opposing counsel's Facebook page, I saw that among her "friends" is the judge in our case. Is this ethically permissible? Should I file a motion to recuse?**

   The short answer is that most states that have examined the issue of judges and lawyers being Facebook "friends" have said there's nothing unethical about such a connection—provided that there is no additional conduct that would constitute an ethical breach, such as ex parte communications about the case between that lawyer and the judge. However, there are a few states such as Florida, Oklahoma, and Massachusetts that consider a Facebook friendship between a judge and a lawyer who may appear before the judge to be impermissible, thereby potentially warranting the disqualification of a judge.

   ABA Formal Opinion 462, entitled "Judges' Use of Electronic Social Networking Media," was issued on February 21, 2013, by the ABA Standing Committee on Ethics and Professional Responsibility and generally reflects the views of the majority of states that have issued opinions. (A detailed discussion of state opinions is provided at the end of this chapter.) It reminds judges to heed the ABA Model Code of Judicial Conduct when using electronic social media (ESM).[3] This opinion is a detailed look at the issue that serves as a useful guide.

   The ABA Opinion begins by acknowledging that "[j]udicious use" of such sites can be a valuable means of reaching out to and remaining accessible to the public.[4] The opinion points out, "[w]hen used with proper care, judges' use of ESM does not necessarily compromise their duties under the Model Code any more than use of traditional and less public forums of social connection such as US Mail, telephone, email, or texting."[5] It also notes the value of social media in political campaigns in jurisdictions where judges are elected,[6] but it warns judges (and judicial candidates) to be mindful of how common features of social networking sites can be ethical traps

---

[3] ABA Comm. on Ethics & Prof'l Responsibility, Formal Op. 462 (2013).

[4] *Id.* at 4.

[5] *Id.*

[6] *Id.* at 3.

for the unwary. For example, the opinion says, under Model Rule 4.1(A)(3), "[s]itting judges and judicial candidates are expressly prohibited from 'publicly endorsing or opposing a candidate for any public office.'"[7] By clicking a "like" button to photos, shared messages, et cetera, on the political campaign sites of others, a judge could be viewed as having improperly endorsed such a candidate. In addition, the opinion reminds judges who might *privately* express their views about candidates to make sure that these expressions are actually kept private "by restricting the circle of those having access to the judge's ESM page, limiting the ability of some connections to see others, limiting who can see the contact list, or blocking a connection altogether."[8]

Formal Opinion 462 also reminds judges that they must "maintain the dignity of the judicial office at all times, and avoid both impropriety and the appearance of impropriety in their professional and personal lives," especially with regard to whom they connect with and what they share via social media.[9] Circulation of embarrassing comments or images, the opinion warns, can potentially "compromise or appear to compromise the independence, integrity, and impartiality of the judge, as well as to undermine public confidence in the judiciary."[10]

Besides such commonsense reminders about social networking interactions in general, the opinion also reminds judges that concerns about ex parte communications, independent research, and the impression that others may be in a position to influence the judge are just as valid in cyberspace as they are with more traditional modes of communication. It cautions that

> judge[s] should not form relationships with persons or organizations that may . . . convey[] an impression that these persons or organizations are in a position to influence the judge. A judge must also take care to avoid comments and interactions that may be interpreted as ex parte communications concerning pending or impending matters . . . and avoid using any ESM site to obtain information regarding a matter before the judge in violation of [ABA Model Code of Judicial Conduct] Rule 2.9(C). Indeed, a judge should avoid comment about a pending or impending matter in any court.[11]

---

[7] Id. at 4 (quoting ABA MODEL CODE OF JUDICIAL CONDUCT r. 4.1(A)(3) (2011)).

[8] ABA Comm. On Ethics & Prof'l Responsibility, Formal Op. 462, at 4 (2013).

[9] *Id.* at 1 (quoting ABA MODEL CODE OF JUDICIAL CONDUCT pmbl. 2 (2011)).

[10] *Id.* at 1-2.

[11] *Id.* at 2.

In addition, the opinion lends guidance on disclosure or disqualification concerns for judges using the same social media sites used by lawyers and others who may appear before a judge. Judges may be Facebook "friends" with lawyers or parties who appear before them, but when it comes to disclosure, "context is significant."[12] The opinion states that "[b]ecause of the open and casual nature of ESM communication, a judge will seldom have an affirmative duty to disclose an ESM connection. If that connection includes current and frequent communication, the judge must very carefully consider whether that connection must be disclosed."[13]

The opinion also observes that whenever a judge shares a social networking connection with someone—whether lawyer, witness, or party—"the judge must be mindful that such connection may give rise to the level of social relationship or the perception of such a relationship that requires disclosure or recusal."[14] In this regard, the opinion notes, a "judge should conduct the same analysis that must be made whenever matters before the court involve persons the judge knows or has a connection with professionally or personally."[15] This would include officially disclosing any information that parties "might reasonably consider relevant to a possible motion for disqualification even if the judge himself believes there is no basis for the disqualification."[16]

But judges need not review all Facebook "friends," LinkedIn connections, et cetera, "if a judge does not have specific knowledge of an ESM connection" that may potentially or actually be problematic.[17] In such circumstances, the number of "friends" that a judge has, whether the judge has a practice of simply accepting all "friend" requests, and other factors may help demonstrate that there is no meaningful connection between the judge and a given individual.

Formal Opinion 462 recognizes that judges are not expected to lead isolated existences, and that in fact they benefit from remaining connected and accessible via social media. But the opinion simultaneously urges caution in

---

[12] *Id.* (citations omitted).

[13] *Id.* at 3.

[14] *Id.* (citations omitted).

[15] *Id.* (citing Jeremy M. Miller, *Judicial Recusal and Disqualification: The Need for a Per Se Rule on Friendship (Not Acquaintance)*, 33 Pepp. L. Rev. 575, 578 (2006)).

[16] *Id.* (citing ABA Model Code of Judicial Conduct r. 2.11 cmt. 5 (2011)).

[17] *Id.*

using these sites and reminds judges that traditional ethical standards will still apply to newer technologies.

On the other end of the permissibility spectrum were the five separate ethics advisory opinions that had been issued in Florida to caution judges about being friends with lawyers who may appear before them. The Florida opinions, which are discussed in detail in the chapter appendix, have specifically addressed Facebook, LinkedIn, and Twitter. In each opinion, Florida concluded that judges should not be connected on social media with lawyers who may appear before them.

Florida's main concern was the appearance that someone connected to the judge on social media may be in a position to specially influence the judge, which violates the judicial canons. Thus, Florida also rejected an inquiring judge's proposed solution to friend all attorneys and posting a disclaimer as to limited definition of a social media friend was rejected. Florida did carve out exceptions for the use of a Facebook fan page and a Twitter account for judicial campaigning, but cautioned that there could be no restrictions on who might become a Facebook fan. Additionally, Florida noted that Twitter potentially creates an ethical land mine in that a judge's retweet might also be perceived to have originated with someone who has special influence over the judge.

Thus, given Florida's attention to the judges on social media issue, it was not surprising that a Florida appellate court found that a Facebook friendship between a prosecutor and a judge was grounds for the judge's recusal in the case.[18] Florida's Fourth District Court of Appeal found that the Facebook friendship violated the judicial canon requiring judges to avoid the appearance of impropriety and that because "Domville ha[d] alleged facts that would create in a reasonably prudent person a well-founded fear of not receiving a fair and impartial trial"[19] that he had met his burden for reversing the denial of the disqualification motion.

Interestingly, in a subsequent case, although Florida's Fifth District Court of Appeal upheld the disqualification of a judge who had initiated an ex parte contact with one of the parties in a divorce case, the court took the opportunity to disagree with its neighboring district.[20]

> We have serious reservations about the court's rationale in *Domville*. The word 'friend' on Facebook is a term of art. A number of

---

[18] Domville v. State of Florida, No. 4D12-556 (Fla. 4th DCA 2012).
[19] *Id.*
[20] Chace v. Loisel Jr. No. 5D13-4449 (Fla. 5th DCA 2014).

words or phrases could more aptly describe the concept, including acquaintance and, sometimes, virtual stranger. A Facebook friendship does not necessarily signify the existence of a close relationship. Other than the public nature of the Internet, there is no difference between a Facebook 'friend' and any other friendship a judge might have. *Domville*'s logic would require disqualification in cases involving an acquaintance of a judge. Particularly in smaller counties, where everyone in the legal community knows each other, this requirement is unworkable and unnecessary. Requiring disqualification in such cases does not reflect the true nature of a Facebook friendship and casts a large net in an effort to catch a minnow.[21]

Finally, Florida's Third District Court of Appeal created the definitive split in the circuits that caused the Florida Supreme Court to address the issue. In *Law Offices of Herssein & Herssein, P.A. v. United Servs. Auto. Ass'n*, the Plaintiff's filed a motion to disqualify the judge because an attorney who was representing one of the witnesses was a former judge and listed as a Facebook friend on the judge's Facebook page.[22] The judge refused to recuse herself, and the Third District Court of Appeal affirmed. The Plaintiffs appealed to the Florida Supreme Court and 2018 it that held that a Facebook friendship alone does not warrant disqualification.[23] However, the opinion did not have a record from which to analyze the friendship and thus the holding has been viewed as an extremely narrow one that provides little guidance.[24] In fact, the concurrence reads somewhat like a dissent as it warns judges to refrain from social media use.[25] Nonetheless, Florida has come into the mainstream, or at least dipped its toe into the stream, and left its infamous Judicial Ethics Advisory Committee opinions behind.

---

[21] *Id.*

[22] *Law Offices of Herssein & Herssein, P.A. v. United Servs. Auto. Ass'n*, Case No. SC17-1848, 2018 Fla. LEXIS 2209 (Fla. Nov. 15, 2018).

[23] *Id.*

[24] Ralph Artigliere, William F. Hamilton, David Hazouri, Jan L. Jacobowitz, and Meenu Sasser, *Face-Off On Facebook: Judges And Lawyers As Social Media "Friends" In A Post-Herssein World*, *The Florida Bar Journal, p 18*, Vol. 93, No. 4 July/August 2019.

[25] *Law Offices of Herssein & Herssein, P.A. v. United Servs. Auto. Ass'n*, Case No. SC17-1848, 2018 Fla. LEXIS 2209 (Fla. Nov. 15, 2018).

2. I found out that the judge in one of my cases is a Facebook friend of a family member of one of the parties. Is this grounds for recusal?

With over 2.6 billion people on Facebook, the issue of whether more attenuated "friendships" on social media justify the recusal of a judge is likely to crop up time and time again. However, most courts have rejected such disqualification bids, so they are probably doomed to be viewed as a desperate measure by the moving party.

For example, in one Georgia child custody case, the father appealed three different trial court orders from three different judges, ultimately arguing that one judge should have been removed due to the mother's Facebook post implying a meeting between the judge and the father.[26] The appellate court was not persuaded that such an accusation had any merit, and both sides were ultimately enjoined from posting social media comments about each other.

A similar challenge was made during a contentious divorce case in Alabama.[27] Unhappy with the division of marital assets, a disgruntled ex-wife sought recusal of the trial judge on the grounds of the judge's Facebook status with the couple's adult daughter. The trial judge denied the motion, pointing out that Facebook "friendship" did not translate to a personal relationship. The appellate court agreed, noting that a showing of something more than "the bare status of the parties' daughter as a 'friend' of the judge" would be necessary before any recusal would be granted.[28]

In *Illinois v. Schiller*, defendant Ryan Schiller appealed his first-degree murder conviction in part because "the trial judge's daughter was a Facebook friend of the victim's sister."[29] The appellate court rejected the argument, observing that judges are presumed to be impartial and that defendant "did nothing more than allege the possible appearance of impropriety on the judge's behalf, which is not a basis to force the removal of a judge."[30]

And in a May 2013 ethics opinion, New York's Committee on Judicial Ethics addressed the question of whether a judge must recuse in a criminal matter because he is Facebook friends with the parents or guardians of minors allegedly affected by the defendant's conduct. Referring to an earlier

---

[26] Lacy v. Lacy, 740 S.E.2d 695 (Ga. Ct. App. 2013).

[27] Clore v. Clore, 2013 WL 3242824 (Ala. Civ. App. 2013).

[28] *Id.*

[29] Order, Illinois v. Schiller, No. 09-CF-2815 (Ill. App. Ct. Dec. 19, 2012).

[30] *Id.*

ethics opinion about lawyers and social media, the committee held "the mere status of being a 'Facebook friend,' without more, is an insufficient basis to require recusal."[31] As long as the parents of the purported victims were only acquaintances, the committee wrote, there was no appearance of impropriety.[32] The committee did, however, "recommend[ ] that [the judge] make a record, such as a memorandum to the [court's] file, of the basis for [his] conclusion," should a challenge to the decision surface.[33]

The bottom line for judges (except for those in Florida, of course) is that social media use can be, when used cautiously, a highly useful tool for public outreach that can demystify the judiciary and remove the distance between judges and the public they serve. However, ethical pitfalls abound, and jurists are well-advised to review the guidance provided by their particular jurisdiction and/or the ABA. Judges should familiarize themselves with the privacy settings and other features of the platforms they intend to use, and they should keep in mind that a statement on Facebook or Twitter is subject to the same ethical rules as any other communication or judicial conduct. After all, whether crafting a 140-page opinion or a 280-character tweet, judges must always be judicious.

3. What are some of the primary concerns about judicial misuse of social media?

As many of these judicial ethics opinions have counseled, there is a wide-ranging array of ways in which judges can find themselves in trouble for using—or, perhaps more accurately misusing—social media. Some of the main areas in which judges make social media missteps, that were apparent in our first edition, are areas that would cause just as much concern if the conduct occurred offline: engaging in ex parte communications; commenting on cases, parties, or issues before the court; and engaging in conduct that brings the court or the administration of justice into disrepute. Many of the judges who have crossed these ethical lines did so under the mistaken belief that the online forum in question offered them a measure of privacy for their comments or conduct. Here are illustrative examples in each of these categories.

---

[31] N.Y. Advisory Comm. on Jud. Ethics, Op. 13-39 (2013).

[32] *Id.*

[33] *Id.*

Communicating Ex Parte

North Carolina Judge B. Carlton Terry is often cited as an example of "what not to do" on social media if you're a judge. In April 2009, the North Carolina Judicial Standards Commission publicly reprimanded Judge Terry for the activities of a Facebook "friendship" between himself and an attorney appearing before him.[34] Just before a child custody and support proceeding that lasted from September 9 to September 12, 2008, Judge Terry was in chambers with Charles Schieck, counsel for Mr. Whitley, and Jessie Conley, attorney for Mrs. Whitley. When the conversation turned to Facebook, Ms. Conley said she was not familiar with it and, in any event, did not have time for it. However, the judge and Mr. Schieck were Facebook "friends." The next day, during another in-chambers meeting, the judge and attorneys discussed testimony that raised the possibility of Mr. Whitley having had an affair, at which point Schieck commented on having to "prove a negative."[35] That evening, Schieck posted on Facebook, "how do I prove a negative. [sic]"[36] Judge Terry responded with a comment about having "two good parents to choose from," as well as a comment about the case continuing.[37] Schieck posted, "I have a wise Judge."[38] Then, on September 11, 2008, Terry and Schieck exchanged Facebook comments about whether or not the case was in its last day of trial, with Terry responding, "[Y]ou are in your last day of trial."[39] Judge Terry also ventured online to view a website that Mrs. Whitley maintained for her photography business, looking at photos and poetry she posted. On September 12, 2008, in announcing his ruling, Judge Terry even quoted from one of her poems.[40]

Although Judge Terry disclosed to Ms. Conley the Facebook exchanges between himself and Mr. Schieck the day before he ruled, he waited until after ruling to disclose the independent Internet research he had done. Shortly after the trial, Ms. Conley filed a motion asking that Judge Terry's

---

[34] Public Reprimand: B. Carlton Terry, Inquiry No. 08-234, at 1 (N.C. Jud. Standards Comm'n Apr. 1, 2009); *see also* Gena Slaughter & John G. Browning, *Social Networking Dos and Don'ts for Lawyers and Judges*, 73 Tex. B.J. 192, 194 (2010).

[35] *Id.*

[36] *Id.*

[37] *Id.*

[38] *Id.*

[39] *Id.*

[40] *Id.* at 2-3.

order be vacated, that he be disqualified, and that a new trial be granted. On October 14, 2008, Judge Terry disqualified himself; his order was vacated, and a new trial was granted on October 22, 2008. The Judicial Standards Commission determined that he "was influenced by information he independently gathered," as well as by his ex parte communications with Mr. Schieck.[41] Furthermore, his behavior demonstrated "a disregard of the principles embodied in the North Carolina Code of Judicial Conduct" and "constitute[d] conduct prejudicial to the administration of justice that brings the judicial office into disrepute."[42]

Alternatively, a Texas appellate case provides an example of an appropriate judicial response to an ex parte Facebook communication. Texas has not provided ethical guidance to judges in the form of a judicial ethics opinion. Instead, guidance comes via an appellate opinion in a criminal case, *Youkers v. State*.

Youkers appealed the revocation of his eight-year prison sentence and community supervision following his conviction for assaulting his pregnant girlfriend.[43] Among the grounds was his contention that he did not receive a fair trial because of a Facebook "friendship" between the judge and his girlfriend's father and an alleged ex parte communication between the two. At the motion for new trial, the trial judge testified that he knew the father from having run for elected office at the same time, and that while they were Facebook "friends," that was "the extent of their relationship."[44] Their only communication through Facebook began just before to the defendant's original plea when the father messaged the judge to seek leniency for Youkers.

As the court pointed out, the trial judge's actions were a model of how to respond to any ex parte communication, whether received through Facebook or more traditional media:

> The judge responded online formally[,] advising the father [that] the communication was in violation of rules precluding ex parte communications . . . [and] that any further communications from the father about the case or any other pending legal matter would result in the father being removed as one of the judge's Facebook 'friends.' The judge's online response also advised that the judge

---

[41] *Id.*

[42] *Id.* at 3-4 (citations omitted).

[43] Youkers v. State, 400 S.W.3d 300 (Tex. App. Ct. 2013).

[44] *Id.* at 204.

was placing a copy of the communications in the court's file, disclosing the incident to the lawyers, and contacting the judicial conduct commission to determine if further steps were required.[45]

The father responded and apologized "for breaking any 'rules or laws' and promised not to . . . make comments 'related to criminal cases' in the future." According to the testimony offered at the hearing on the motion for new trial, the trial judge followed through with all of the steps that he indicated he would be taking.

In its opinion, the Dallas Fifth District Court of Appeals first pointed out that this was a case of first impression in Texas: "No Texas court appear[ed] to have addressed the propriety of a judge's use of social media websites such as Facebook. Nor [wa]s there a rule, canon of ethics, or judicial ethics opinion in Texas proscribing such use." The court went on to cite ABA Judicial Ethics Opinion 462 approvingly, both for the beneficial aspects of allowing judges to use Facebook (i.e., remaining active in the community) and for the proposition that the status of Facebook "friends" is not necessarily representative of "the degree or intensity of a judge's relationship with that person.'"[46] As the court pointed out, "the designation, standing alone, provides no insight into the nature of the relationship."[47] And in examining the record for further context, the court noted that there was nothing to indicate that the "Facebook friendship" between the judge and the girlfriend's father—who was actually asking for leniency—was anything but a fleeting acquaintance.

Most importantly, the court pointed out, the judge fully complied with the appropriate protocol for dealing with ex parte communications.[48] And while the court noted that judges should, in using social media, remain mindful of their responsibilities under applicable judicial codes of conduct, everything about this judge's actions was consistent with promoting public confidence in the integrity and impartiality of the judiciary.[49] Significantly, the court observed that while new technology may have ushered in new ways to communicate and share information, the same ethical rules apply: "[W]hile the [I]nternet and social media websites create new venues for communications,

---

[45] *Id.*

[46] *Id.* at 205-6 (quoting ABA Comm. on Ethics & Prof'l Responsibility, Formal Op. 462, at 3 (2013)).

[47] *Id.* at 206 (citation omitted).

[48] *Id.* at 207.

[49] *Id.*

our analysis should not change because an ex parte communication occurs online or offline."[50]

Commenting on the Case

Although Senior Judge Edward Bearse had served on the bench for thirty-two years and continued to serve, even after his retirement in 2006, by statewide appointment, his foray into Facebook was as a novice. His Facebook foibles included posts in which he deemed the Hennepin County District Court "a zoo"[51] and one in which he expressed frustration about the repercussions of a defense counsel being escorted by ambulance from the middle of a trial. He posted and noted that the defense counsel's unavailability is likely to result "in chaos because the defendant has to hire a new lawyer who will most likely want to start over and a very vulnerable woman will have to spend another day on the witness stand. . . ."[52] And during a sex trafficking trial Judge Bearse posted the following:

> Some things I guess will never change. I just love doing the stress of jury trials. In a Felony trial now State prosecuting a pimp. Cases are always difficult because the women (as in this case also) will not cooperate. We will see what the 12 citizens in the jury box do.

This post came to light when the prosecutor, having obtained a guilty verdict, happened upon the post and shared it with the defense who succeeded in obtaining a new trial based on a lack of impartiality as demonstrated in the Facebook post.

Judge Bearse explained to the Minnesota Board of Judicial Standards that he was a Facebook novice and did not realize that his posts were available for viewing by the public. Nonetheless, the findings of the board that publicly reprimanded Judge Bearse included the conclusion that he had placed his "personal communication preferences above his judicial responsibilities," and had engaged in "conduct prejudicial to the administration of justice that brings the judicial office into disrepute."[53]

In 2015, Kentucky Circuit Court Judge Olu Stevens used Facebook to express his frustration about a victim statement from a mother who claimed that after witnessing a home invasion by two black men, her white child

---

[50] *Id.* at 206.

[51] *Id.*

[52] *Id.*

[53] *Id.*

was now "in constant fear of black men." He ignited a firestorm of controversy with his Facebook posts. Stevens—who is African American—created tremendous controversy when he posted what amounted to a condemnation of the mother's statements, suggesting that "Perhaps the mother had attributed her own views to her child as a manner of sanitizing them."[54] Judge Stevens also became embroiled in a dispute with the Commonwealth's Attorney over allegedly racially biased jury selection, and he began posting on this topic as well. In 2016, Judge Stevens agreed to a ninety-day suspension, without pay, for his Facebook commentary.

Later in 2016, a remorseful judge in South Carolina agreed to a six-month suspension because of his Facebook activity. Judge Kenneth E. Jones Jr. expressed great regret after he commented on the settlement of a high-profile wrongful death claim against the local police force in an estate case that was pending in his probate court.[55] The police force settled with the family for over $2 million. The judge's Facebook post stated, "'In the end it's all about the money. Always. Unfortunately, I see it EVERYDAY.' . . . [And he] later added: 'Once ck is in hand, they'll disappear.'"[56]

Apparently, the judge had also used his Facebook page to endorse a presidential candidate and engage in fundraising for a local church. In agreeing to the suspension, the judge submitted "that he is deeply embarrassed about the matter and seeks to assure the Court that, in the future, he will not make reference to anything involving his court and will refrain from making political posts or posting fundraising information on Facebook or any other social media."[57]

Commenting on a Case to Educate the Public

Unlike the cases mentioned above in which judges are voicing their frustrations about a case, in *In re Honorable Michelle Slaughter*, the controversy stemmed from Facebook posts that Judge Slaughter had made on the court's public Facebook page in her proclaimed effort to educate the public.[58]

---

[54] Andrew Wolfson, *Judge Slams Victims for Tot's 'Black Men' Fear*, COURIER-JOURNAL (Apr. 15, 2015), http://www.courier-journal.com/story/news/local/2015/04/10/judge-slams-victims-tots-black-men-fear/25581605/.

[55] In the Matter of Kenneth E. Johns Jr., Supreme Court of South Carolina, Case No. 2016-001996, Op. No. 27677 (filed Nov. 16, 2016).

[56] *Id.*

[57] *Id.*

[58] In re Honorable Michelle Slaughter, Special Court of Review (Texas), 480 S.W.3d 842 (2015).

On April 26, 2014, Judge Slaughter posted the following about a high-profile criminal jury trial that was scheduled to begin on April 28, 2014. "We have a big criminal trial starting Monday! Jury selection Monday and opening statements Tuesday morning."[59]

Shortly after the trial started, the judge posted the following on April 29, 2014: "Opening statements this morning at 9:30 a.m. in the trial called by the press 'the boy in the box' case;" "After we finished Day 1 of the case called the 'Boy in the Box' case, trustees from the jail came in and assembled the actual 6 foot × 8 foot 'box' inside the courtroom!" and "This is the case currently in the 405th!" One of those posts included a link to a *Reuters* article entitled, "Texas father on trial for putting son in a box as punishment."[60]

On April 30, 2014, defense counsel filed a motion to recuse Judge Slaughter from the case, along with a motion for mistrial, claiming that Judge Slaughter had improperly commented about the trial on her Facebook page and had improperly posted the link to the *Reuters* article. A visiting judge hearing the recusal motion granted it and removed Judge Slaughter from the case. Following the recusal, the case was transferred to another court. That new judge granted the defense's motion, and consequently, the case had to be retried. (The defendant was later acquitted.)[61]

The two defense attorneys then brought a judicial conduct complaint against Judge Slaughter. She was accused of violating Canon 3B of the Texas Code of Judicial Conduct, which states, in pertinent part:

A judge shall abstain from public comment about a pending or impending proceeding, which may come before the judge's court in a manner which suggests to a reasonable person the judge's probable decision on any particular case. . . . This section does not prohibit judges from making public statements in the course of their official duties or from explaining for public information the procedures of the court.[62]

---

[59] Charging Document, Inquiry Concerning Judge, Hon. Michelle Slaughter, Docket No. 15-0001, Before the Special Court of Review Appointed by the Supreme Court of Texas (June 4, 2015).

[60] *Id.*

[61] *Id.*

[62] TEXAS CODE OF JUDICIAL CONDUCT, CANON 3B (2002).

She was also charged with violating Canon 4A of the Code, which states that "A judge shall conduct all of the judge's extra-judicial activities so that they do not: (1) cast reasonable doubt on the judge's capacity to act impartially as a judge; or (2) interfere with the proper performance of judicial duties."[63]

In addition to the Facebook statements regarding the "boy in the box" trial, the State Commission on Judicial Conduct also cited Facebook statements made in connection with two other matters. The first involved the following comment from a February 2014 trial: "We have a jury deliberating on punishment for two counts of possession of child pornography. It is probably one of the most difficult types of cases for jurors (and the judge and anyone else) to sit through because of the evidence they have to see. Bless the jury for their service and especially bless the poor child victims." The second statement was a Facebook post by the judge from a May 2014 trial, saying, "We finished up sentencing today with a very challenging defendant."[64]

The Commission on Judicial Conduct issued a public admonishment of Judge Slaughter in April 2015 and ordered her to obtain additional training in social media ethics. Slaughter appealed the sanction and received a new trial before a Special Court of Review composed of three appellate justices appointed by the Supreme Court of Texas. The Special Court of Review of Texas issued a per curiam opinion September 30, 2015, which dismissed the public admonition.

The court found that "no rule, canon of ethics, or judicial ethics opinion in Texas prohibits Texas judges from using social media outlets like Facebook." It also noted "technology's transformative effect on society" and concluded that there was not any evidence indicating that Slaughter's online comments "would suggest to a reasonable person the judge's probable decision on any particular case or that would cause reasonable doubt on the judge's capacity to act impartially as judge."

Although the court cautioned that "comments made by judges about pending proceedings" may "detract from the public trust and confidence in the administration of justice," it did not find that the postings or Judge Slaughter's recusal constituted a misuse of her office or any violation of the Canons of the Code of Judicial Conduct. The court further observed that Judge Slaughter's goal of educating the public about the events occurring

---

[63] TEXAS CODE OF JUDICIAL CONDUCT, CANON 4A (2002).

[64] Charging Document, Inquiry Concerning Judge, Hon. Michelle Slaughter, Docket No. 15-0001, Before the Special Court of Review Appointed by the Supreme Court of Texas (Tex. Sup. Ct. June 4, 2015).

in her court was consistent with the Preamble to the Code of Judicial Conduct, which calls for judges to "strive to enhance and maintain confidence in our legal system."[65] Among other observations, the court noted that Judge Slaughter's Facebook posts regarding the "boy in the box" case consisted of mere factual statements that did not go beyond what any visitor to her courtroom could have witnessed firsthand.

The Hybrid Commenting on the Case—Personal and Educational?

Another look at the ethical concerns for judges commenting about cases on social media occurred in late June 2016 in the New Mexico Supreme Court's decision in *State v. Thomas*.[66] In this case, the court reversed a murder conviction because an expert witness for the prosecution testified via Skype, and the court held that this violated the defendant's Sixth Amendment rights under the Confrontation Clause. Because the court decided the case on the Confrontation Clause issue, they didn't need to reach the other grounds for appeal—that the trial court judge had made certain comments on Facebook about the case, and that these comments demonstrated judicial bias.[67]

Nonetheless, what about the postings by the trial judge that were the source of controversy? The first, made during trial, stated "I am on the third day of presiding over my 'first' first-degree murder trial as a judge."[68] The second, posted after the jury's verdict of guilty, but prior to the sentencing, said, "In the trial I presided over, the jury returned guilty verdicts for first-degree murder and kidnapping just after lunch. Justice was served. Thank you for your prayers."[69]

---

[65] *Id.*

[66] State v. Thomas, 376 P.3d 184 (N.M. 2016). The court also took advantage of the opportunity to opine about judicial use of social media in the context of judicial election campaigns. While the court found nothing wrong with judicial use of social media overall, it did warn that certain conduct and activity "can easily be misconstrued and create an appearance of impropriety." The court warned that judges who are candidates should "post no personal messages" other than a statement of qualifications, "should allow no posting of public comments," and "should engage in no dialogue." It also cautioned judges to regard all social media postings as public communications, and not to be lulled into complacency by reliance on privacy settings.

[67] *Id.*

[68] *Id.*

[69] *Id.*

As the Code of Judicial Conduct cautions, it is the appearance of impropriety and the perception of bias or impartiality that must also be avoided, not just actual impropriety or actual bias. The New Mexico Supreme Court recognized this, warning that "'friending,' online postings, and other activity can easily be misconstrued and create an appearance of impropriety."[70]

Thus, evaluating the statements in accordance with the court's cautionary message, the first statement, with its matter-of-fact reporting of the judge's day seems to be like Judge Slaughter's postings, which did not ultimately result in an ethical violation. However, the second post is more problematic. Besides a strictly factual statement about the trial's outcome, it includes an opinion—"Justice was served," which more closely resembles Judge Stevens's comments that resulted in his ninety-day suspension. Moreover, given that the timing of the New Mexico judge's post was pre-sentencing, it is concerning from an ethical standpoint to have the judge sharing his thoughts or feelings on the verdict, particularly when he must still preside over the sentencing phase and potential post-trial motions as well.

Personal Conduct

Sometimes, personal issues that lead to questionable behavior on social networking platforms can spell professional trouble for judges. An example of such an unfortunate overlap between personal lives and professional personas is Dianna Bennington, a former city court judge in Indiana. Her personal Facebook posts during an acrimonious child support dispute with her children's father led to a finding of "injudicious behavior."[71] In 2016, a Facebook relationship led to a six-month suspension for Judge Leon Archer, a probate judge for Tallapoosa County, Alabama.[72] Judge Archer met a woman (a former litigant) in his capacity as probate judge, and an online relationship ensued in which the parties engaged in sexually explicit messages and exchanges of graphic photos via Facebook. The exchanges became public when the woman copied and shared them with a local news reporter. The Alabama Judicial Inquiry Commission and Judge Archer entered into a final judgment in which the judge was found guilty of violating several of the Alabama Canons of Judicial Ethics, including failing to avoid impropriety and the appearance of impropriety in all of his activities, and engaging in conduct

---

[70] *Id.*

[71] *In re* Bennington, 24 N.E.3d 958, 961 (Ind. 2015).

[72] In the Matter of Leon Archer, Case No. 47 (Ala. Ct. of the Judiciary 2016).

prejudicial to the administration of justice that brings the judicial office into disrepute.[73]

Judges and the Ethical Risks of "Benign" Social Media Activity

Since the first edition, another area that we refer to as "benign activity" has become a growing concern. Looming even larger than Canon 2.12(A)'s mandate that judges require their staff to act in a manner consistent with the judges' ethical obligations—the "guilt for the sins of others" standard, if you will—is Canon 1.2's admonition for judges to act at all times in a manner that promotes public confidence in the impartiality of the judiciary and to avoid not only impropriety but also the appearance of impropriety. This broad but vital standard encompasses a judge's "active" misconduct on social media, including such things as ex parte communications with counsel, inappropriate sexual overtures to parties, and discussing a case on social media.[74] Understandably, this "active" misconduct attracts the lion's share of attention when judicial misuse of social media is discussed. However, the arguably more "benign" types of activities on social media—"liking" or sharing the posts or tweets of a party or someone associated with a party to a case pending before the judge, "following" a party or someone associated with a party, and so forth—can be no less concerning. In a way, it is more troubling *because* it is not as overt, as blatant, as more "active" misconduct on social media. If commenting on a case on Facebook or ex parte communication with a party is an ethical iceberg, the "benign" acts, like a judge following one of the parties or counsel appearing before her and liking their tweets or posts, is that portion of the iceberg unseen below the water: invisible, but no less dangerous for the unwary.

One reason why judges get into ethically compromising situations arising out of such benign conduct on social media is that they may view it as harmless, rather than as behavior that can raise questions about their impartiality or create at least the appearance of impropriety. Likes on social media platforms signify validation, approval, agreement, support, and even endorsement of the post or tweet itself. Likes and follows have commercial significance, as indicated by the billions of dollars spent annually by brands on establishing and maintaining a social media presence.[75] The business

---

[73] *Id.*

[74] *See, e.g.,* John G. Browning, *Why Can't We Be Friends? Judges' Use of Social Media*, 68 Miami L. Rev. 487 (2014).

[75] Leslie K. John, Daniel Mochon, Oliver Emrich, & Janet Schwartz, *What's the Value of a Like?*, Harv. Bus. Rev. (Mar./Apr. 2017), https://hbr.org/2017/03/whats-the-value-of-a-like.

valuation of an entity's Twitter followers and similar social media metrics has become a recurring issue in digital age litigation.[76] In addition, a number of studies have documented the psychological value of garnering likes and followers, and the impact such "engagement metrics" can have on an individual's well-being.[77]

"Likes" on social media have significance. In fact, as a US Circuit Court of Appeals decision has recognized, clicking "like" on a social media page is a form of speech protected by the First Amendment.[78] "Liking" a political campaign page, for example, can constitute an endorsement in clear violation of ABA Model Rule of Judicial Conduct 4.1(A)(3)'s prohibition on judges' "publicly endorsing or opposing a candidate for any public office."[79] Some judges have learned this the hard way and been disciplined for casually "liking" another individual's campaign Facebook page. For example, Butler County, Kansas District Judge Jan Satterfield caused a controversy in 2012 when she was among several dozen people who clicked "like" on a Facebook post by the campaign of Sheriff Kelly Herzet.[80] A supporter of Herzet's opponent filed a complaint against Judge Satterfield with the Kansas Commission of Judicial Qualifications, noting that "[w]ith the growth of social media, the court system needs to define how its rules for judges apply in cyberspace."[81] Judge Satterfield, for her part, did not seem to understand how her "like" could be viewed as an endorsement.[82]

Clearly, a judge engaging on social media with one party, or someone associated with that party (such as counsel), in some way to the exclusion of the other side calls into question that judge's impartiality and can undermine public confidence in the integrity of the judiciary. Even when the social

---

[76] *See, e.g.*, Phonedog v. Kravitz, 2011 WL 5415612 (N.D. Cal. Nov. 8, 2011); *see also e.g.*, Michael Furlong, *Putting a Price on Friendship: Examining the Ownership Battle between a Business' Social Media Networks, and the Humans That Operate Them*, 47 J. MARSHALL L. REV. 745 (2013).

[77] For a general discussion, *see The Psychology of Being 'Liked' on Social Media*, MEDIUM.COM (Nov. 28, 2017); https://medium.com/swlh /likes-on-social-media-87bfff679602.

[78] Bland v. Roberts, 730 F.3d 368 (4th Cir. 2013).

[79] MODEL RULE OF JUD. CONDUCT r. 4.1(A)(3) (Am. B. Ass'n 2020).

[80] *Kansas Judge Causes Stir with Facebook 'Like'*, RealClearPolitics (July 29, 2012).

[81] *Id.*

[82] *Id.*

engagement seems benign or innocuous, such as following someone on Twitter and liking or retweeting a tweet, that "heart" icon can send a message of approval or affiliation. While it may be unintended, it can also convey to observers the impression that one side or viewpoint enjoys a special or favored position with the judge. And while many judges might be followers of certain media outlets or specific journalists—a fact that, in isolation, is harmless enough—a judge's liking, sharing, or retweeting an article that is written about a case pending before that judge can be ethically problematic, particularly if that article takes an editorial stance regarding a party or key issue involved in the case. Is subjecting a judge to recusal or even disciplinary sanction an appropriate response to concerns over the integrity of the judiciary and the appearance of impropriety? Or is such a "guilt by association" standard unduly harsh? To answer these questions, let's look at a handful of cautionary tales: one that reached the Wisconsin Supreme Court, another that reached the Ninth Circuit, and a trio of recusal cases from Texas.

1. *Judge Michael Bitney*

Our first example is Barron County Circuit Court Judge Michael Bitney of Wisconsin. In 2017, Judge Bitney presided over a contested hearing in a custody dispute between mother Angela Carroll and father Timothy Miller.[83] After the hearing, but before rendering a decision, Judge Bitney accepted a Facebook "friend" request from Carroll. Over the course of the next 25 days, Carroll "liked" sixteen of the judge's Facebook posts, "loved" two more, commented on two of his posts, and shared and "liked" several third-party posts that related to a contested issue at the hearing (domestic violence).[84] Judge Bitney did not "like" or comment on any of Carroll's posts, nor did he reply to any of her comments on his posts. However, the judge never disclosed the Facebook friendship or Ms. Carroll's communications, and he ultimately ruled entirely in the mother's favor.[85]

On the same day as his decision, Ms. Carroll posted "the Honorable judge has granted everything we requested."[86] Miller, the husband, discovered the Facebook connection and moved for reconsideration of the ruling and for Judge Bitney's disqualification. While Judge Bitney

---

[83] *In re* Paternity of B.J.M., 392 Wis. 2d 49, 944 N.W.2d 542 (Wis. 2020).

[84] *Id.*

[85] *Id.*

[86] *Id.*

admitted to the Facebook interactions, he maintained that he was impartial. The appellate court reversed and remanded the case, with directions to have it heard before a different judge. On appeal to the Wisconsin Supreme Court, the high court affirmed the appellate decision, concluding that "the extreme facts of this case rebut the presumption of judicial impartiality and establish a due process violation."[87]

The Wisconsin Supreme Court based its conclusion that "a serious risk of actual bias" had been shown on the totality of the circumstances.[88] These included the timing of the Facebook friendship (it was sent after evidence and briefing were submitted, implying Carroll's desire to influence Judge Bitney's decision, and Judge Bitney accepted it, gaining access to off-the-record facts relevant to the dispute); the volume of Carroll's posts and the likelihood Judge Bitney viewed these posts and comments; the content of the Facebook activity as it related to the nature of the pending proceeding (Carroll had essentially 25 more days to portray herself in the best possible light, through her Facebook access to the judge); and Judge Bitney's lack of disclosure (which deprived Miller of an opportunity to refute what Carroll was posting and sharing).[89]

The court observed that while it was not determining the "general propriety" of judicial use of social media, it did caution that "judges should recognize that online interactions, like real-world interactions, must be treated with a degree of care."[90] In her concurring opinion, Justice Ziegler urged even more vigilance, reminding judges that their social media use "may expose both the judge and the judiciary as a whole to an appearance of bias or impropriety."[91]

2. *Judge William Shubb*

In a case that nearly reached the US Supreme Court, a federal judge was almost recused because of his Twitter activity. In the 2017 case of *United States v. Sierra Pacific Industries, Inc.*, US District Court Judge William B. Shubb was presiding over a case arising out of a 2007 wildfire that had devastated nearly 65,000 acres in California.[92] The federal government, which blamed lumber producer Sierra Pacific, reached a

---

[87] *Id.*

[88] *Id.*

[89] *Id.*

[90] *Id.*

[91] *Id.*

[92] United States v. Sierra Pac. Indus., 862 F.3d 1157 (9th Cir. 2017).

settlement that the lumber company sought to vacate. Judge Shubb denied Sierra Pacific's motion. It appealed, pointing out that not only was Judge Shubb a Twitter follower of the federal prosecutors on the case—and so had received tweets about the merits of the case from the prosecutors' Twitter account—but also that he himself had tweeted about the case from his then-public Twitter account (@Nostalgist1).[93]

On the same day that Judge Shubb denied Sierra Pacific's motion to set aside the settlement, the U.S Attorney's Office for the Eastern District of California posted multiple tweets about the case. In addition, Judge Shubb tweeted a link to a news article about his ruling, bearing the headline Sierra Pacific Still Liable for Moonlight Fire Damage.[94] This irked the lumber giant, which had expressly denied liability as part of the settlement. The defendants appealed, arguing (among other grounds) that the judge had violated multiple Canons of the Code of Conduct for US Judges. These included Canon 2, calling for judges "to avoid impropriety and the appearance of impropriety in all activities"; Canon 3A(4), prohibiting *ex parte* communications or any "communications concerning a pending or impending matter that are made outside the presence of the parties or their lawyers"; and Canon 3A(6), mandating that a judge "should not make public comment on the merits of a matter pending or impending in any court."[95] Sierra Pacific also argued that, under Canon 3C, Judge Shubb was required to disqualify himself "in any proceeding in which his impartiality might reasonably be questioned."[96]

While the case was on appeal, the federal prosecutors notified Judge Shubb that his Twitter activity had become an issue. Shortly thereafter, the judge changed his Twitter account from "public" to "protected," a privacy setting permitting only certain authorized followers to view his tweets.

In July 2017, the US Court of Appeals for the Ninth Circuit affirmed the trial court's ruling and declined to require Judge Shubb's recusal on procedural grounds.[97] However, the Court recognized the significance of the issue arising out of Judge Shubb's Twitter activity, saying, "[T]his case is a cautionary tale about the possible pitfalls of judges engaging in social media activity relating to pending cases, and we reiterate the

---

[93] *Id.*

[94] *Id.*

[95] *Id.*

[96] *Id.*

[97] *Id.*

importance of maintaining the appearance of propriety both on and off the bench."[98]

Undaunted, Sierra Pacific filed a petition for writ of certiorari to the US Supreme Court. The question presented asked whether a district court judge's impartiality might reasonably be questioned "when he not only follows the prosecution on social media, but also, just hours after denying relief to the opposing party, tweets a headline and link to a news article concerning the proceedings pending before him." Despite the questions raised, however, in June 2018, the US Supreme Court denied the petition for writ of certiorari.

3. *Judge Steve Burgess*

To date, there have been only two appellate cases in Texas dealing with judicial use of social media. In *Youkers v. State*, while the Fifth Court of Appeals rejected the notion that a judge's Facebook friendship alone was disqualifying, it did note that social media use by judges presents concerns "unique to the role of the judiciary in our justice system," and that in using such platforms, "judges must be mindful of their responsibilities under applicable judicial codes of conduct."[99] And in *In re Honorable Michelle Slaughter*, a Special Court of Review appointed by the Texas Supreme Court observed that while social media activity of the judge at issue (who had been recused in connection with Facebook posts about the case before her) did not warrant judicial discipline, judges should nevertheless be aware that their conduct on social media is subject to existing rules of judicial conduct and that such online behavior by judges about their own proceedings "create the very real possibility of a recusal (or even a mistrial) and may detract from the public trust and confidence in the administration of justice."[100]

But instead of a retweet or a "like," what about a judge who follows one of the parties on Twitter? That was the question posed in a 2015 Texas case, *Texas Ethics Commission v. Michael Quinn Sullivan*.[101] In that case, the Texas Ethics Commission (TEC) (a state agency charged with administering and enforcing statutes governing elections and related governmental processes) filed an action against Sullivan (a conservative

---

[98] *Id.*

[99] Youkers v. State, 400 S.W.3d 200–05 (Tex. App.—Dallas 2013, pet. ref'd).

[100] *In re* Hon. Michelle Slaughter, 480 S.W.3d 842 (Tex. Spec. Ct. of Rev. 2015).

[101] 2015 WL 6759306 (Tex. App.—Fort Worth 2015, pet. denied).

activist and president of an influential conservative-leaning organization) for failure to register as a political lobbyist. Sullivan appealed the TEC's decision in that case by filing suit in Denton County, Texas, his alleged county of residence. The TEC disputed his residency and filed a motion to transfer venue; Sullivan responded by filing a motion to dismiss the TEC's claims under Texas's anti-SLAPP law. On February 18, 2015, the case was heard by Judge Steve Burgess of the 158th Judicial District Court, and he denied the motion to transfer venue and granted Sullivan's motion to dismiss.

That same day, however, a reporter for the *Fort Worth Star-Telegram* tweeted about the hearing, noting that Judge Burgess was a Twitter follower of Sullivan. The next day, the same reporter posted on Twitter that "1 day after ruling in [Sullivan's] favor without disclosing he's a Twitter follower, judge deletes account." On February 23, the TEC filed a motion to recuse Judge Burgess, arguing that the jurist's following of Sullivan on Twitter not only called into question Burgess's impartiality but also made it likely that Burgess and Sullivan had ex parte communications using the platform. The later accusation had no foundation; for two Twitter users to communicate privately, both must follow each other—and there was no indication that Sullivan likewise followed Judge Burgess. Moreover, it was hardly unusual that an elected Republican judge like Steve Burgess, in a decidedly Republican county and state, might choose to follow the Twitter account of the leader of an influential conservative organization known for its endorsements of Republican political candidates—including judges. Certainly, there was no indication that, out of the nearly 15 thousand of Sullivan's Twitter followers, Judge Burgess and Sullivan enjoyed any real relationship.

Despite all of this, another judge was appointed to hear the recusal motion, and that judge granted it.[102] Should following a party automatically warrant recusal? Courts and judicial ethics opinions in multiple jurisdictions have already addressed the question of a judge's Facebook friendships with parties, counsel, and even expert witnesses, with most noting that such a tenuous connection is not disqualifying—absent other indications of a special relationship or position of influence, or the potential for bias. In Judge Burgess's case, the appearance of impropriety was

---

[102] John Reynolds, *A Twitter Follow Leads to a Recusal*, Tex. Tribune (Mar. 5, 2015); https://www.texastribune.org/2015/03/05/twitter-follow-leads-recusal/.

likely not helped by either his failure to disclose the connection or by his deletion of his Twitter account after the journalist's revelation.

4. *Judge Staci Williams*

In 2016, Judge Staci Williams of Dallas County's 101st Judicial District Court was presiding over *State Fair of Texas v. Riggs & Ray, P.C.*[103] The lawsuit had been brought by the ostensibly nonprofit corporation that oversees the annual State Fair of Texas against an Austin law firm that had filed an open records request seeking extensive financial records, contracts, and correspondence between fair executives and various Dallas government officials. The litigation was closely followed and covered by certain local journalists, including on Twitter. Beginning in the summer of 2016, Judge Williams's activity on her official Twitter account began to attract the plaintiff's attention.[104] In July, she retweeted, without comment, a tweet by a local radio host and political commentator referencing the case, linking to an article sympathetic to the defendant's position, and praising the judge. On another date, Judge Williams had "liked" a tweet by a Dallas City Council member that linked to another news article by a different journalist that was again sharply critical of the plaintiff and its position.[105]

In Twitter parlance, retweeting without comment or indication of disagreement is commonly understood to signify approval, while "likes" are usually understood to show appreciation for a tweet. Reacting to the judge's retweet and "like"—publicly posted approval by Judge Williams of tweets linked to reporting that was highly critical of one party's position in the case—the plaintiff filed a motion to recuse on

---

[103] Plaintiff's Motion for Recusal, Cause No. DC-15-04484, State Fair of Tex. v. Riggs & Ray, P.C. (Dall. Dist. Ct. [101st Dist.] Nov. 29, 2016).

[104] *Id.*

[105] The articles in question included two pieces by Jim Schutze in the *Dallas Observer*. Both articles, along with screenshots from Judge Williams' Twitter account, were exhibits to the motion. *See* Jim Schutze, *Take an Embarrassing Peek into the Love between the State Fair of Texas and Fair Park*, DALL. OBSERVER (June 9, 2016); https://www .dallasobserver.com/news/take-an-embarrassing-peek-into-the-love -between-the-state-fair-of-texas-and-fair-park-8374766; Jim Schutze, *Transparency Isn't Just Important in Fair Park Debate. It's the Whole Enchilada*, DALL. OBSERVER (July 20, 2016), https://www.dallasobserver .com/news/transparency-isnt-just-important-in-fair-park-debate-its -the-whole-enchilada-8504231.

November 29, 2016.[106] In December, Judge Williams voluntarily recused herself and asked for a new judge to be assigned to the case.[107] Regardless of whether this Twitter activity truly reflected a lack of impartiality, one can certainly understand why one party might question the judge's impartiality; at the very least, such activity created the appearance of bias or impropriety.

5. *Judge Glen Harrison*

In 2015, Judge Glen Harrison of west Texas' 32nd Judicial District presided over a complex breach of contract case against attorney and businessman Kerwin Stephens by several individuals and entities over a speculative project to buy (and later sell) oil and gas leases in Fisher County, Texas. The case resulted in a verdict of over $97 million. In addition to making a number of rulings adverse to the defense during the trial itself, later in 2015 and well into 2016, Judge Harrison denied a variety of defendants' motions for post-trial relief, including a motion for new trial, a motion for judgment notwithstanding the verdict (JNOV), motions regarding the entry of judgment, and a motion pertaining to the defendants' ability to supersede the judgment. Baffled by rulings they felt were inconsistent with Texas law, the defendants took the case up on appeal.[108] On appeal, the Eastland Court of Appeals embraced most of the JNOV arguments that Judge Harrison had rejected, and also allowed Stephens the supersedeas that Harrison had denied not once, but three times. Although Stephens was compelled to file for bankruptcy protection regardless, the appellate court's rulings greatly diminished a verdict that had been hailed in 2015 as one of the largest of that year not only in Texas, but nationally as well. The appellate rulings constituted a sharp rebuke of the trial court.

During the bankruptcy proceeding, as the court contemplated a remand to the state trial court on several issues, Stephens alerted his legal team to some disturbing revelations he had recently learned about,

---

[106] Plaintiff's Motion for Recusal, Cause No. DC-15-04484, State Fair of Tex. v. Riggs & Ray, P.C. (Dall. Dist. Ct. [101st Dist.] Nov. 29, 2016).

[107] Signed Order of Referral on Motion to Recuse, Cause No. DC-15-04484, State Fair of Tex. v. Riggs & Ray, P.C. (Dall. Dist. Ct. [101st Dist.] Nov. 29, 2016) (on file with author).

[108] Stephens v. Three Finger Black Shale P'ship, 580 S.W.3d 687 (Tex. App.—Eastland 2019, pet. denied).

discoveries that led them to point out reasons for Judge Harrison's recusal.

An examination of Judge Harrison's activity on Twitter during and after the trial (using the Twitter handle @gharrison32nd) revealed some interesting things. Judge Harrison had apparently begun following at least one of the plaintiffs' lawyers, Jordyn Gingras, and on August 20, 2015—just one day after the trial's conclusion—Judge Harrison "liked" a tweet by Gingras. The tweet in question said "The truth doesn't cost you anything but a lie could cost you everything," an apparent reference to the trial; it was accompanied by the hashtags "#proudlawyermoment," "#rumbleinroby," and "#sweetwaterproud" (references to the trial's location).[109] The same day, Judge Harrison "liked" Gingras' tweet about the "new friends" she'd made in Sweetwater and Roby, a tweet that contained a hyperlink to an Instagram post with the Stephens trial–related hashtags "#wefilledthebucket," "#sweetwaterproud," "#rumbleinroby," and "#proudlawyermoment."[110] Just two days later, on April 22, 2015, Judge Harrison "liked" yet another tweet by Gingras, this time thanking her paralegal, Amber Schrandt.[111]

Later on, there would be more "likes" coming from Judge Harrison in response to tweets by Ms. Gingras. On November 16, 2015, before the hearing on Stephen's JNOV motion, Judge Harrison "liked" Gingras' tweet about a CLE presentation she gave to the Dallas Bar Association about the subject matter of the trial entitled "Landman or Lawyer? $70MM+ Reasons Why You Should Care."[112] Not long after entering judgment against defendant Stephens on March 30, 2016, Judge Harrison "liked" a tweet by another member of the team suing Stephens, Christina Mullen, boasting about obtaining the #15 verdict in the nation.[113] Days later, on May 24, 2016, Harrison "liked" yet another tweet by attorney Gingras, this time retweeting a positive article about two more of the plaintiffs' attorneys, Frank and Debbie Branson.[114] And on June 29, 2016, not long before denying Stephens' efforts at

---

[109] *See* **Brief in Support of Debtor Kerwin Stephens' Motion to Remand Certain Claims (and Exhibits thereto), Adversary Proceeding No. 21-04040-elm,** *In re* **Kerwin Stephens et al., U.S. Bankruptcy Court for the Northern District of Texas (Fort Worth Division) (copy on file with author).**

[110] *Id.*

[111] *Id.*

[112] *Id.*

[113] *Id.*

[114] *Id.*

supersedeas, Judge Harrison liked yet another of Gingras' trial-related tweets—this time one about receiving "top billing" on the 2015 Top Texas Verdicts and Settlement Report.[115]

Indeed, Judge Harrison continued to follow Twitter accounts associated with Ms. Gingras and other members of the trial team suing Kerwin Stephens. What's more, his Twitter interactions, including likes of tweets by Ms. Gingras, continued as well. Collectively, all of this Twitter activity—particularly the fact that Judge Harrison followed and commented (in the form of likes) on tweets by one side of the litigants in a matter before him—is indicative at the very least of the appearance of partiality and prejudgment against Kerwin Stephens and his related entities.

And while judicial rulings are rarely enough by themselves to demonstrate bias sufficient to warrant recusal, the fact that a presiding judge made rulings that were incorrect[116] and in favor of the side of the case he followed and commented on via Twitter would tend to reinforce concerns about impartiality. Following, liking the tweets of, and referencing lawyers on only one side of what was a high-stakes and contentious piece of litigation (including tweets that referenced the size and newsworthiness of the verdict) cannot help but foster objectively reasonable doubts as to Judge Harrison's impartiality.

The fact that this Twitter engagement apparently did not occur during the trial itself is of no consequence; it occurred during a period of time in which Judge Harrison maintained jurisdiction over pending post-trial matters. In *State v. Thomas*, a case in which a relatively new trial judge posted on Facebook about how "[j]ustice was served" after a murder trial but before sentencing, the New Mexico Supreme Court was not amused by the judge's "Facebook page discussions of his role in the case and his opinion of the outcome."[117]

After reversing the conviction on other grounds, the court cautioned that judges must avoid not only actual impropriety but also its appearance, and judges must "act at all times in a manner that promotes public confidence in the independence, integrity, and impartiality of the judiciary." These limitations apply with equal force to virtual actions and online comments and must be kept in mind if and when a judge decides to participate in electronic social media.[118]

---

[115] *Id.*

[116] At least three times out of five, according to the Eastland Court of Appeals.

[117] State v. Thomas, 376 P.3d 184 (N.M. 2016).

[118] *Id.*

Does it matter whether Judge Harrison's Twitter activity demonstrated actual bias or prejudice? No, because, under Texas law, that is not the standard. Texas Rule of Civil Procedure 18b(b)(1) provides that a trial judge "must recuse" when "the judge's impartiality might reasonably be questioned." The test for recusal under such circumstances is "whether a reasonable member of the public at large, knowing all the facts in the public domain concerning the judge's conduct, would have a reasonable doubt that the judge is actually impartial."[119] Under well-settled Texas law, it is not a showing of actual bias or prejudice that matters so much as the appearance of partiality, bias, or prejudice. As the Texas Supreme Court noted decades ago—more than forty years before the advent of social media:

> [t]he judiciary must not only attempt to give all parties a fair trial, but it must also try to maintain the trust and confidence of the public at a high level [and] it is of great importance that the courts should be free from reproach or the suspicion of unfairness.[120]

Given such legitimate concerns about the appearance of partiality or bias stemming from Judge Harrison's following and likes of one side's tweets referencing the case before him, it is not surprising that the bankruptcy judge agreed with Stephen's concerns.[121] Nor is it surprising that after being informed of this ruling and of the basis for Stephens' seeking his recusal, Judge Glen Harrison entered a voluntary order recusing himself and requesting that another judge be appointed to preside over all matters in this case.[122]

Conclusion

The privilege of the judicial robe comes with the obligation to follow the judicial canons—canons that were enacted long before social media yet nonetheless continue to apply to every post, tweet, like, and comment that a judge may post in cyberspace.

---

[119] Drake v. Walker, 529 S.W.3d 516, 528 (Tex. App.—Dallas 2017, no pet.).

[120] Indemnity Ins. Co. v. McGee, 356 S.W.2d 666, 668 (Tex. 1962).

[121] Adversary Case No. 21-04021-elm, *In re* Kerwin Stephens et al., Order Granting Motion to Remand (Nov. 19, 2021), Doc. No. 70.

[122] Cause No. DC2016-0027, Voluntary Order of Recusal (Dec. 23, 2021) (copy on file with author).

Appendix
Guide of Ethics Advisory Opinions
Regarding Judges on Social Media

Arizona

Arizona is also a member of the majority of jurisdictions cautiously approving judges' use of social media. In 2014, the Arizona Supreme Court Judicial Ethics Advisory Committee issued Advisory Opinion 14-01.[123] Like Utah, it tackled a wide-ranging list of issues, including not just judicial use of sites like Facebook, Twitter, and LinkedIn, but also judges' participation in blogs and websites. It held that a judge could be active on social media sites like Facebook or LinkedIn, but "should avoid participating in or being associated with discussions about matters falling within the jurisdiction of his or her court."[124] And like the majority of states, the Arizona committee held that while Facebook "friend" or Twitter "follower" status didn't warrant automatic disqualification of a judge, a judge should be guided by whether or not his or her "friend" status with a given attorney might lead to the judge's impartiality being reasonably questioned. In addition, the committee reminded judges about the dangers of ex parte communications, public discussion of pending cases, and conducting independent investigations online.

California

With its California Judges Association Judicial Ethics Committee Opinion 66 in November 2010, this jurisdiction announced distinct concerns about judges being connected via social networking sites to lawyers appearing before them.[125] While the California Committee gave "a very qualified yes" to the questions of

---

[123] Ariz. Sup. Ct. Jud. Ethics Advisory Comm., Advisory Op. 14-01 (2014), https://www.azcourts.gov/LinkClick.aspx?fileticket=zNRP1_l8sck%3D &portalid=137 ("Use of Social and Electronic Media by Judges and Judicial Employees").

[124] *Id.*

[125] *See* Cal Judges Ass'n Ethics Comm., Op. 66 (2010).

whether a judge may be a member of an "online social networking community" and whether a judge may be Facebook "friends" with lawyers who may appear before him, the answer was "no" when it came to judges "friending" lawyers who actually appear before them.[126] The California opinion examines some of the ethical risks that can be posed by using social media, including posting information about cases currently before the judge on "friends'" "walls"; expressing views or not deleting posts by others that may call into question a judge's impartiality; posting inappropriate comments or pictures that demean the judicial office; endorsing candidates for nonjudicial office by "liking" their candidate pages; and "lending the prestige of the judicial office" to improperly advance the personal interests of the judge or others.[127]

The opinion also carefully analyzes the factors that should be considered by a judge before participating in social media and determining if there are any appearance issues with attorney "friends" appearing before that judge. These factors include the following:

1. The nature of the site: Bottom line, a site that has more unique and personal details available to the public is more likely to create at least the perception that the attorney has inappropriate influence over the judge. Conversely, social media pages for an organization like an alumni group or bar association are less likely to create such an impression.

2. The number of persons "friended" by the judge: Simply put, "the greater number of 'friends' on the judge's page, the less likely it is . . . that any one individual participant is in a position to influence the judge."[128]

3. How the judge determines whom to "friend": A judge who accepts all "friend" requests is less likely to create the impression that a certain lawyer or group of lawyers holds any influence over the judge.[129] But, a more selective practice of "friending" only lawyers from the plaintiff's bar, or excluding lawyers from a particular firm, is more likely to lead to the appearance of bias, either for parties with whom the judge is "friends" or against those who lack such a Facebook "friendship" with the judge.[130]

---

[126] *Id.* at 1.

[127] *Id.* at 4-5.

[128] *Id.*

[129] *Id.*

[130] *Id.*

4. How regularly an attorney appears before a judge: Essentially, the more frequently an attorney actually appears before a judge, the less likely it is that being Facebook "friends" would be permissible. On the other hand, online relationships pose less of a risk of creating the appearance of having a special position of influence when the attorney rarely appears before his "friend" the judge. By way of illustration, a civil litigator who happens to have a "friend" relationship with a criminal court judge is less likely to prompt cries of "foul."

The California ethics opinion also provides several useful hypothetical scenarios of where social media interaction would and would not be permissible. With regard to its position that a judge should *not* be Facebook "friends" with an attorney who has a case pending before him, the California Ethics Committee is blunt. And,

[i]f the online interaction were permitted, a judge would have to disclose not only the fact that interaction took place in the first instance, but also that it is going to continue. This continuing contact could create the impression that the attorney is in a special position to influence the judge simply by virtue of the ready access afforded by the social networking site.[131]

Connecticut

In Connecticut Committee on Judicial Ethics Opinion 2013-06, the committee joined the majority of jurisdictions holding that judges were ethically permitted to participate in "internet-based social networking sites" such as Facebook. However, the committee also cautioned that such participation is "fraught with peril" because "of the risks of inappropriate contact with litigants, attorneys, and other persons unknown to the Judicial Officials."[132] It made judicial participation subject to twelve conditions, consisting of references to existing judicial canons of ethics—including prohibitions against practicing law, on maintaining the dignity of the office, and on avoiding impropriety.[133] It also warns the judge to be more aware of

---

[131] *Id.* at 11.

[132] Conn. Comm. on Jud. Ethics, Op. 2013-06 (2013), http://jud.ct.gov /Committees/ethics/sum/2013-06.htm.

[133] *Id.*

the contents of his or her social networking profile, to be familiar with site policies and privacy controls, and to stay abreast of new features and changes.[134]

District of Columbia

The District of Columbia is the most recent jurisdiction to opine on judges on social media. In its November 2016 Opinion 371 that pertains to ethics and social media in the provision of legal services, D.C. includes a few paragraphs, which indicate that judges may freely participate in social media in accordance with the judicial canons.[135] The opinion warns that during the pendency of a proceeding not only must ex parte communication be avoided, but also that a lawyer may want to consider "de-friending" the decision maker during the proceeding.[136]

Florida

Florida, without a doubt, had been the most restrictive jurisdiction when it comes to judicial use of social media until 2018 and the Florida Supreme Court's ruling in the Herssein case discussed above. Although the Florida Supreme Court ruling overshadows the prior ethics opinions, we leave them in the appendix as reflective of the slow, deliberative process that often occurs with regard to any social media issue and the practice of law.

Florida issued five ethics opinions between 2009 and 2013 on the topic, and a dispute over how narrowly to interpret its prohibition on judges and social networking went all the way to the Florida Supreme Court.

The first (and most widely criticized) ethics opinion from the Florida Supreme Court Judicial Ethics Advisory Committee was Opinion No. 2009-20, issued in November 2009.[137] It presented several questions: (1) whether judges could be "friends" on a social

---

[134] *Id.*

[135] D.C. Bar Ethics Opinion 371 (2016). Interestingly, D.C. notes that it may be a matter of competence for a lawyer to investigate a decision maker on social media prior to a hearing.

[136] *Id.*

[137] Fla. Jud. Ethics Advisory Comm., Op. 2009-20 (2009), http://www.jud6.org/LegalCommunity/LegalPractice/opinions/jeacopinions/2009/2009-20.html.

networking site with lawyers; (2) whether a judge's campaign committee could post material related to a judge's candidacy on a social networking site; and (3) whether lawyers and other supporters may list themselves as "fans" on a judge's campaign social networking site. The answers to the second and third inquiries, perhaps acknowledging the realities of political campaigning in the digital age, were yes—as long as the judge or his or her campaign committee does not control who is permitted to list him- or herself as a "fan" or supporter.

The first inquiry has the most reference to our discussion. The majority believed that allowing a judge to accept or reject contacts or "friends" on his or her social networking profile would violate Canon 2B of the Code of Judicial Conduct, because "this selection and communication process . . . [may] convey[] or permit[] others to convey the impression that [such friends] are in a special position to influence the judge." According to the committee, there is something special about being classified as a judge's "friend" because that status is viewable not only to the judge's other "friends," but to all of their "friends" as well.[138] While the majority conceded that "friend" status doesn't automatically mean that such individuals are in a special position of favor or influence, it was more concerned with the appearance of such status. As a result, the committee concluded, "[S]uch identification in a public forum of a lawyer who may appear before the judge does convey this impression and therefore is not permitted."[139] However, the opinion did discuss the position of a minority of the committee, which felt that the majority was attributing an importance to the status of being "friends" on Facebook that bears no resemblance to the term's actual meaning in an online context.[140]

The second opinion, Judicial Ethics Advisory Committee Opinion No. 2010-04, issued in March 2010, posed the same inquiry about "friending" lawyers with regard to a judge's judicial assistants or clerks.[141] Here, the committee recognized that keeping a judicial assistant from "friending" a lawyer presented First Amendment concerns. Moreover, the same fear of creating a public perception

---

[138] *Id.*

[139] *Id.*

[140] *Id.*

[141] Fla. Jud. Ethics Advisory Comm., Op. 2010-04 (2010), http://www .jud6.org/legalcommunity/legalpractice/opinions/jeacopinions /2010/2010-04.html.

that such a lawyer "friend" would be in a position to influence the judge was absent, in the eyes of the committee. As the committee concluded,

> [a]s long as a judicial assistant utilizes the social networking site outside of the judicial assistant's administrative responsibilities and independent of the judge, thereby making no reference to the judge or the judge's office, this Committee believes that there is no prohibition for a judicial assistant to add lawyers who may appear before the judge as 'friends' on a social networking site.[142]

The third opinion, Judicial Ethics Advisory Committee Opinion No. 2010-06, also issued in 2010, addressed a scenario where a judge had taken certain steps to minimize, if not eliminate, public perception that being a "friend" of the judge carried with it implications of a special relationship or position of influence.[143] In the fact pattern before the committee, the judge offered to communicate with all "friends" who were attorneys and "post a permanent, prominent disclaimer on the judge's Facebook profile" explaining that the Facebook "friend" status meant that the judge and the friend were merely acquaintances, not necessarily a "friend" in the "traditional sense." The committee was not convinced, however; even with such caveats, a judge still would not be permitted to "friend" an attorney who might appear before her. Even if it was the judge's custom to "friend" all the lawyers who sent such a request, or all those whose names she recognizes or who have "friends" in common with her, the committee held it would still not be permissible to have as a Facebook "friend" a lawyer who appeared before the judge.[144]

The fourth opinion, Florida Judicial Ethics Advisory Committee Opinion No. 2012-12, issued in May 2012, examined the question of "[w]hether a judge may add lawyers who may appear before the judge as 'connections' on the professional networking site, LinkedIn [sic], or permit such lawyers to add the judge as their 'connection' on that site." The answer again was a curt "[n]o." While the committee took note of the inquiring judge's distinction

---

[142] *Id.*

[143] *See* Fla. Jud. Ethics Advisory Comm., Op. 2010-06 (2010), http://www .jud6.org/legalcommunity/legalpractice/opinions/jeacopinions /2010/2010-06.html [hereinafter Fla. Op. 2010-06]

[144] *Id.*

between sites like Facebook and the more professional LinkedIn, it based its ruling on the unwieldiness of requiring "each judge who had accepted a lawyer as a friend or connection to constantly scan the cases assigned to the judge, and the lawyers appearing in each case, and 'defriend'" or delist each lawyer upon a friend or connection making an appearance in a case assigned to the judge."[145]

In the fifth opinion, the Florida Supreme Court Judicial Ethics Advisory Committee addressed judicial activities on yet another social networking platform, Twitter. In this opinion, the narrow questions confronted by the committee were whether a judge seeking re-election would be allowed to "create a Twitter account with a privacy setting open so that anyone—including lawyers—would be able to follow" the judge and whether the campaign manager would be permitted to "create and maintain the Twitter account, instead of the judge" directly.[146] The committee's answer to both questions was "yes," noting the utility of Twitter for political campaigning as the Twitter account could share "tweets" about a candidate's "judicial philosophy, campaign slogans, and blurbs about the candidate's background," as well as update followers about upcoming events.

However, the Florida Judicial Ethics Advisory Committee echoed its earlier opinions restricting judicial use of social media, noting that certain dimensions of Twitter could violate Canon 2B's prohibition against conveying or permitting others "to convey the impression that [they are] in a special position to influence the judge."[147] The committee observed that a Twitter user could block specific followers, mark certain tweets as "favorites," create lists of followers, and subscribe to lists created by another user. These features, the committee observed, posed the potential of violating Canon 2B:

> If a user posts a tweet that is complimentary or flattering to the . . . judge, the judge could re-tweet it or mark it as a "favorite." No matter how innocuous the tweet, this could convey or permit the tweeter to convey the impression that the tweeter is in a special position to influence the judge . . . [Twitter followers] could be perceived to be in a special position to influence the judicial candidate.

---

[145] *Id.*

[146] *Id.*

[147] *Id.*

The committee also expressed concern that "[a] judge's Twitter account [could] create[] an avenue of opportunity for ex parte communication."[148]

However, such concerns reflect a limited grasp of how Twitter actually works. The risk of ex parte contact by virtue of having a Twitter account is no greater than the risk created by having a direct dial telephone number, a publicly known email address, or a known physical address at the courthouse.

Kentucky

Kentucky's approach, like that of nearly every other state, cautiously approves of judges being active on social networking sites. Its ethics opinion holds that a judge may "participate in an [I]nternet-based social networking site, such as Facebook, LinkedIn, MySpace, or Twitter, and be 'friends' with . . . persons who appear before the judge in court, such as attorneys, social workers, and/or law enforcement officials."[149] However, this is a "qualified yes" from the committee that comes with a note of caution for "judges [to] be mindful of 'whether online connections alone or in combination with other facts rise to the level of a 'close social relationship' which should be disclosed and/or require recusal"[150] and how to be careful that their social media activities do not lead to violations of the Kentucky Code of Judicial Conduct.[151] Alerting the unwary, the Kentucky opinion notes, "[S]ocial networking sites are fraught with perils for judges," warning them that the committee's approval of social media use "should not be construed as an explicit or implicit statement that judges may participate in such sites in the same manner as members of the general public."[152] The opinion also warns judges of the illusory feeling of privacy that may accompany social media use; although these sites "may have an aura of private, one-on-one conversation, they are much more public than

---

[148] *Id.*

[149] Ethics Comm. of the Ky. Judiciary, Formal Ethics Op. JE-119, at 1 (2010).

[150] *Id.* at 3 (quoting N.Y. Advisory Comm. on Judicial Ethics, Op. 08-176).

[151] *Id.* at 5.

[152] *Id.* at 4.

off-line conversations, and statements once made in that medium may never go away."[153]

Kentucky's Opinion noted the fact that its judges run in partisan elections, an important reality in the age of social media. Moreover, like the New York Opinion that it cites so approvingly, the Kentucky opinion also pointed out that in reality, a "friend" designation on Facebook was nothing more than a term of art for the site, and that it did not actually convey to others the impression that such "friends" were in a special position to influence the judge.

Maryland

Maryland issued its opinion in June 2012.[154] The Maryland Judicial Ethics Committee addressed two main questions—the first of which was whether "the mere fact of a social [media] connection creates a conflict" for a judge. The committee found that it does not. Analogizing an online connection to friendships outside of cyberspace, the committee observed that the mere fact of a friendship between a judge and an attorney does not automatically warrant disqualification from cases involving the attorney, and with regard to online relationships, the committee "sees no reason to view or treat 'Facebook friends' differently."[155]

The committee also asked more broadly, "What are the restrictions on the use of social networking by judges?" Like its counterparts in other states, the Maryland Committee urged caution, "admonish[ing] members of the Judiciary to 'avoid conduct that would create in reasonable minds a perception of impropriety.'" The opinion approvingly references ethics opinions from other states, including New York and California, ultimately concluding that a judge may participate in social media as long as he or she does so in a manner that complies with the existing rules of judicial conduct.[156] Like other ethics committees, it advises judges to proceed with caution.[157]

---

[153] *Id.* at 5.

[154] Md. Jud. Ethics Comm., Published Op. 2012-07 (2012), http://www.courts.state.md.us/ethics/pdfs/2012-07.pdf.

[155] *Id.*

[156] *Id.* at 2-3.

[157] *Id.* at 3.

Massachusetts

Massachusetts, like other states examining this issue, holds that judges can be members of social networking sites.[158] However, it provided more specific guidance, rather than just sounding a general note of caution. Referencing specific activities proscribed by the Code of Judicial Conduct, it urges judges to refrain from the following activities on social media:

> comment[ing] on or permit[ting] others to comment on cases currently pending before [the judge] . . . join[ing] "Facebook groups" that would constitute membership in an organization in violation of Section 2C [of the Code of Judicial Conduct]; . . . [making] political endorsements . . . [or] identify[ing] [oneself] as a judge or permit[ting] others to do so . . . [so as to avoid] lend[ing] the prestige of judicial office to advance the private interests of the Judge or others[159]

Significantly, Massachusetts' stance on "friending" of attorneys is stricter than most states, putting it closer to Florida's restrictive approach. The opinion states, "[T]he Code prohibits Judges from associating in any way on social networking web sites [sic] with attorneys who may appear before them. Stated another way, in terms of a bright-line test, judges may only 'friend' attorneys as to whom they would recuse themselves when those attorneys appeared before them."[160] Here, the Massachusetts authorities cited with approval the most draconian of the states to examine this issue, Florida, agreeing that such relationships "create[ ] a class of special lawyers who have requested this status" and that such lawyers would at least "appear to the public to be in a special relationship with the judge."[161] Significantly, Massachusetts does not focus on the number of "friends" a judge may have, his or her practice with regard to "friend" requests (i.e., accept them all or be more selective), or even the nature of the relationship.[162] For the Massachusetts Committee, the most important element is apparent

---

[158] Mass. Comm. on Jud. Ethics, Op. 2011-06 (2011).

[159] *Id.*

[160] *Id.*

[161] *Id.* (quoting Fla. Op. 2010-06, *supra* note 90).

[162] *Id.*

impropriety, and Massachusetts justifies such a limitation on judges with the fact that it is part and parcel of being a jurist—judges must "accept restrictions on . . . the judge's conduct that might be viewed as burdensome by the ordinary citizen."[163]

Massachusetts later addressed the subject of whether a judge could accept a LinkedIn connection request from an attorney practicing before that judge.[164] The committee maintained that the same reasoning in its previous opinion was equally applicable to LinkedIn, stating that "the same overarching principles and concerns stated in Op. 2016-01 apply to all forms of social media that are currently available."[165] The committee concluded that "a judge who uses LinkedIn may not be connected with any attorney who is reasonably likely to appear before that judge," a conclusion that "requires a judge to reject requests to connect with and to disconnect from lawyers who are reasonably likely to appear before the judge."[166] Such disconnection and disclosure, the committee reasoned, were "necessary to protect the independence, integrity, and impartiality of the judiciary."[167] The committee concluded with a sobering reminder to judges to exercise restraint when using social media and to "carefully weigh the risks and benefits" while keeping in mind that "each judge who uses social media must take steps to minimize the likelihood that the manner in which that judge uses social media would lead a reasonable person to question the judge's impartiality."[168]

Missouri

In 2015, Missouri's judicial ethics body weighed in on judicial use of social media as well.[169] Like the majority of its counterparts, it held that there was nothing per se unethical about a judge being active on social media, and it pronounced that social media involvement would be scrutinized "under the same ethical requirements

---

[163] *Id.* (quoting Mass. Code of Judicial Conduct r. 2A cmt. (2003)).

[164] Mass. Comm. on Jud. Ethics, Op. No. 2016-08 (2016), ("LinkedIn: Using Social Networking Site").

[165] *Id.*

[166] *Id.*

[167] *Id.*

[168] *Id.*

[169] Mo. Comm'n on Retirement, Removal & Discipline, Op. 186 (April 24, 2015).

as any other public statements."[170] Consequently, avoiding impropriety or the appearance of impropriety, making statements "that would impair fairness of pending or impending matters," and avoiding statements indicating bias or prejudice were paramount concerns. As with several other jurisdictions, it held that as far as terms like "friending" or "liking" were concerned, the context rather than the mere label was of primary importance in gauging a judge's relationship with an attorney, party, or witness. Missouri's Commission cautioned judges to review third-party posts as well, where such posts would place the judge in the position of appearing to endorse forbidden conduct. And while the commission found nothing wrong with social media being part of a judge's election campaign, it recommended that the judge keep such a public social media site separate. Finally, it warned that "in order to limit the potential of ethical violations and the number of cases in which the judge might be required to recuse, the judge should take care to adjust the 'privacy' setting" so that the judge's social media profile would not be accessible to the public.

New York

With its 2009 Advisory Opinion 08-176, New York was one of the first jurisdictions to address judicial use of social media.[171] In concluding that it is perfectly appropriate for a judge to embrace social networking, it points out the many reasons for a judge to do so, including "reconnecting with law school, college, or even high school classmates; increased interaction with distant family members; staying in touch with former colleagues; or even monitoring the usage of that same social network by minor children in the judge's immediate family."[172] Like the ABA opinion, it urges caution, reminding judges to "employ an appropriate level of prudence, discretion and decorum in how they make use of this technology."[173] It also warns judges that social networks and technology in general are subject to change and that accordingly judges "should stay abreast of new features of, and changes to, any social networks they use," lest new developments of social media cause judges to run afoul of the principles of the Rules of Judicial Conduct. Finally,

---

[170] *Id.*

[171] N.Y. Advisory Comm. on Jud. Ethics, Op. 08-176 (2009).

[172] *Id.*

[173] *Id.*

New York's Advisory Opinion also includes the now-familiar—but still important—reminders to judges: Avoid impropriety and the appearance of it when using social networking and be mindful of the appearance that might be created by virtue of establishing a Facebook "friendship" with a lawyer or anyone else appearing in the judge's court.

North Carolina

North Carolina addressed judicial use of social media in 2014 Formal Ethics Opinion 8.[174] At issue was whether lawyers and judges with LinkedIn profiles could connect with each other, and whether judges and lawyers could endorse or recommend each other on that site. Noting that social media interactions between judges and lawyers should be treated differently than offline interactions, the committee held that, generally, lawyers and judges could connect with each other on LinkedIn. However, ethical prohibitions against ex parte communications, conduct prejudicial to the administration of justice, and stating or implying an ability to influence the judge remain.[175] While lawyers may recommend or endorse judges, a judge may not endorse or recommend a lawyer (and a lawyer should not accept such an endorsement) because it could "create the appearance of judicial partiality."[176] Finally, the committee noted that its guidance was not just limited to LinkedIn, but to all other social media sites as well.

Ohio

Ohio gave its cautious blessing for judges to be active on social media in an opinion by the Supreme Court of Ohio's Board of Commissioners on Grievances and Discipline in December 2010.[177] However, doing so, said the board, "require[s] a judge's constant vigil."[178] Acknowledging a basic reality of the Facebook era—that "[a] social network 'friend' may or may not be a friend in the

---

[174] N.C. St. Bar, 2014 Formal Ethics Op. 8 (2015), https://www.ncbar .gov/for-lawyers/ethics/adopted-opinions/2014-formal-ethics-opinion-8/ ("Accepting an Invitation from a Judge to Connect on LinkedIn").

[175] *Id.*

[176] *Id.*

[177] *See* Ohio Bd. of Comm'rs on Grievances & Disputes, Op. 2010-07 (2010).

[178] *Id.* at 7.

traditional sense of the word"—the Ohio Board stated that there was nothing wrong with a judge being Facebook "friends" with lawyers, including lawyers who appear before the judge. The Ohio opinion goes into considerable detail, discussing not only ethics opinions from other states, but also the Judge B. Carlton Terry disciplinary proceeding from North Carolina (discussed *infra*).

The Ohio Board does not merely content itself with making generalizations or generic warnings urging jurists to be careful. Instead, it goes through a detailed litany of specific rules of judicial conduct that might be impacted by social networking, including several that have eluded commentary by other states' judicial ethics authorities, including the following specific admonitions:

> A judge must maintain dignity in every comment, photograph, and other information shared on the social network. . . .

> A judge must not foster social networking interactions with individuals or organizations if such communications will erode confidence in the independence of judicial decision making. . . .

> A judge should not make comments on a social networking site about any matters pending before the judge. . . .

> A judge should not view a party's or witness' page on a social networking site and should not use social networking sites to obtain information regarding the matter before the judge. . . .

> . . . .

> A judge should disqualify himself or herself from a proceeding when the judge's social networking relationship with a lawyer creates bias or prejudice concerning the lawyer for a party. . . .

> A judge may not give legal advice to others on a social networking site.[179]

---

[179] *Id.* at 7-8.

Like other counterparts, the Ohio Board's opinion also urges judges to be cautious posting content to their social networking profiles and to keep abreast of specific site policies and privacy controls.

Oklahoma

Like nearly every jurisdiction, Oklahoma answers the question of whether judges may have a presence on social media with a cautious "yes."[180] However, in answering the question of whether a judge may add "court staff, law enforcement officers, social workers, attorneys and others who may appear in his or her court as 'friends,'" Oklahoma's Judicial Ethics Advisory Panel provide a distinct "no" (except for court staff). Agreeing with the observation that "social networking sites are fraught with peril for judges," Oklahoma's Panel opines that whether or not being a Facebook "friend" of the judge actually puts that individual in a special position is immaterial.[181] What matters, as far as the Panel is concerned, is whether or not the designation of "friend" could convey the impression of inappropriate influence over the judge to others. Stating "public trust in the impartiality and fairness of the judicial system is so important that it is imperative to err on the side of caution," Oklahoma held that judges should not be Facebook "friends" with "social workers, law enforcement officers, or others who regularly appear in court in an adversarial role."[182]

South Carolina

Opinion Number 17-2009 from South Carolina's Advisory Committee on Standards of Judicial Conduct is brief and limited in scope.[183] It concludes, "A judge may be a member of Facebook and be friends with law enforcement officers and employees of the Magistrate as long as they do not discuss anything related to the judge's position as magistrate."[184] The opinion is silent as to any other issues,

---

[180] Okla. Jud. Ethics Advisory Panel, No. 2011-3, at ¶ 3 (2011), http://www.oscn.net/applications/oscn/DeliverDocument.asp?CiteID=464147.

[181] *See Id.* at ¶ 7.

[182] *Id.* at ¶ 8.

[183] S.C. Jud. Dep't Advisory Comm. on Standards of Judicial Conduct, Op. 17-2009 (2009).

[184] *Id.*

such as whether a judge would be subject to disclosure or possible disqualification if he or she were Facebook "friends" with a lawyer or party who appeared before the court. However, the opinion did note the positive side of judges being on Facebook or other social networking sites, observing, "[A] judge should not become isolated from the community in which the judge lives," and that permitting a judge to use social media "allows the community to see how the judge communicates and gives the community a better understanding of the judge."[185]

Tennessee

In an October 2012 advisory opinion, Tennessee aligned itself with the majority of states in allowing judges to use social networking sites, albeit cautiously.[186] Citing other states that have previously addressed this issue, with particular emphasis on California's analysis, Tennessee warns judges that their use of social networking "will be scrutinized [for] various reasons by others."[187] The committee declined to provide specific details on permissible or prohibited activity by judges "[b]ecause of constant changes in social media." Instead, it urges judges to "be constantly aware of ethical implications as they participate in social media," and to decide "whether the benefit and utility of participating in social media justify the attendant risks."[188]

Utah

Utah joined the majority view of judicial use of social media with its 2012 Informal Opinion 12-01 from the Judicial Ethics Advisory Committee.[189] Noting the need to "provide guidance in a landscape that is constantly changing," the committee approvingly cited Kentucky's opinion on the subject in answering a host of questions involving judicial activity on Facebook, Twitter, and LinkedIn. As the committee observed, while there are many issues and rules in

---

[185] *Id.*

[186] *See* Tenn. Jud. Ethics Comm., Op. 12-01, at 1 (2012), http://www .Tncourts.gov/sites/default/files/docs/advisory_opinion_12-01.pdf.

[187] *Id.* at 3-4

[188] *Id.*

[189] Utah Courts, Utah Informal Op. 12-01 (2012), https://www.utcourts .gov/resources/ethadv/ethics_opinions/2012/12-1.pdf.

Utah's Code of Judicial Conduct implicated by use of social media, "the problems presented by social media are simply the same problems that have existed in other social and public settings."[190] The committee discussed the pertinent rules, particularly those prohibiting a judge's participation "in activities that would appear to a reasonable person to undermine the judge's independence, integrity, or impartiality," and those requiring a judge to avoid impropriety or the appearance of impropriety. The committee held that judges may be "friends" with lawyers on Facebook, but that under certain circumstances such a friendship status may require recusal. It also held that a judge may identify himself as a judge on Facebook, appear in judicial robes on the site, "like" entities or activities, and post content and comment on personal pursuits and interests. It also held that judges may participate in sites like LinkedIn and Twitter and may follow individuals or join groups on such sites.

---

[190] *Id.*

CHAPTER 9

Cover Your Digital Assets! Social Media's Impact on the Transactional Lawyer

. . . .

While the intersection of social media and legal ethics often appears in the headlines in the context of litigation or inappropriate comments by an outspoken lawyer, the integration of social media and attendant ethical obligations throughout the practice of law should not be overlooked. The rules of professional conduct mandate that lawyers stay abreast of changes in their practice areas, and the digital age has affected lawyers in most areas of the law.

This chapter highlights just a few of the practice areas in which lawyers function as advisors and facilitate transactions rather than engage in litigation. Hopefully, the facts and ideas below will prompt discussion and thought about how social media may be impacting your practice area and the next client matter that comes your way. We pose only one question . . .

QUESTION

1. How has social media impacted the fundamental ethical obligations of competence, diligence, communication, and confidentiality across various practice areas?

Trust and Estate Law

Trust and estate lawyers are accustomed to communicating with clients about their assets and other confidential matters so as to draft wills, draft trusts, and diligently engage in estate planning.[1] However, the digital age has given rise to digital assets that have not traditionally been a part of a lawyer's asset inventory checklist. A failure to inventory a client's digital assets may result in an incompetent representation of the client.

A digital asset is "any asset that 'exists only as a numeric encoding expressed in binary form.'"[2] Thus, any "information created, generated, sent, communicated, received, or stored by electronic means on a system for the delivery of digital information or on a digital device" is considered to be a digital asset.[3] Simply stated, digital assets involve content that an individual maintains on the Internet such as photographs, videos, bank account and credit card information, software, emails, and electronic documents.[4] The financial value of digital assets varies, but it has been estimated that the average individual's digital assets are worth approximately $35,000[5] and sometimes increase in value when measured in emotional or aesthetic worth.[6] Additionally, "[e]ach internet user has an average of twenty-six different online accounts and uses roughly ten different passwords or pin numbers in a day."[7]

---

[1] Jamie P. Hopkins, *Afterlife in the Cloud: Managing a Digital Estate*, HASTINGS SCI. & TECH. L. J. 209, 210 (2013).

[2] *Id.* at 211 (citing Delia Babeanu et al., *Strategic Outlines: Between Value and Digital Assets Management*, 11 ANNALES UNIVERSITATIS APULENSIS SERIES OECONOMICA 318, 319 (2009)).

[3] Sasha A. Klein & Mark R. Parthemer, *Plan Ahead: Protect Your #DigitalFootprint*, 89 THE FLA. B. J. 51 (2015) (citing Abena Hagen, *Secure Your Digital Legacy By Planning Ahead*, THE DIGITAL BEYOND (July 31, 2014), http://www.thedigitalbeyond.com/2014/07/secure-your -digital-legacy-by-planning-ahead/).

[4] Hopkins, *supra* note 1, at 211 (noting also that digital assets do not include tangible electronic devices, such as phones, computers, televisions, and tablets); *see also* Victoria Blachly, *Uniform Fiduciary Access to Digital Assets Act: What UFADAA Know*, PROBATE & PROPERTY MAGAZINE (last visited Sept. 24, 2015).

[5] Klein & Parthemer, *supra* note 3 (citing Evan Carroll, *How Much Are Your Digital Assets Worth? About $35,000*, THE DIGITAL BEYOND (July 24, 2014), http://www.thedigitalbeyond.com/2014/07/how-much -are-your-digital-assets-worth-about-35000/).

[6] *Id.*; *see also* Blachly, *supra* note 4.

[7] Hopkins, *supra* note 1, at 212.

Upon an individual's death, if his or her digital assets have not been inventoried and intentions made known, chaos may ensue because a fiduciary may not be able to gain access to the assets—even assuming the digital assets may be located to create an accurate listing.[8] For example, one recent case involved family members of a young woman who died after falling out of a twelfth story window. The family was unsuccessful in seeking access to her Facebook account to attempt to understand whether her death was a suicide. Facebook denied access based upon a lack of consent from the deceased and its terms of service, and subsequently the court ruled for Facebook.[9]

There are vehicles for providing authorization for a trustee or descendant to access various social media accounts. A competent lawyer must include a discussion of digital assets during estate planning with a client[10] and stay abreast of current changes to the law such as state statutory attempts to address digital assets. In fact, approximately nine states have enacted legislation to address digital assets. Moreover, the Uniform Law Commission drafted and approved the Uniform Fiduciary Access to Digital Assets Act (UFADAA) in 2014.[11]

Bottom line: A lawyer needs to check the law in his jurisdiction and be aware that social media accounts are among a client's digital assets and need to be considered in estate planning.

---

[8] *See* David M. Lenz, *Afterlife on the Cloud: Creating a Heavenly Plan for Digital Assets*, AM. L. INST. (June 2015) (Federal laws have not kept pace with the advent of digital assets and therefore, both Stored Communications Act and the Computer Fraud and Abuse Act may constrain fiduciaries from accessing digital assets, especially when there is no written authorization and the passwords are unknown.)

[9] In re Request for Order Requiring Facebook, Inc. to Produce Documents and Things, No. C12-80171 LHK (PSG) (N.D. Ca. Sept. 20, 2012); *see also* Ajeman v. Yahoo! Inc., 83 Mass. App. Ct. 565 (2013).

[10] The literature reflects an ongoing debate as to whether digital assets should be listed in the will or placed in a trust, but that discussion is beyond the scope of this book although it does reflect the evolving definition of competence in the digital age. *See* Lenz, *supra* note 8; *see also* Klein & Parthemer, *supra* note 3.

[11] NATIONAL CONFERENCE OF STATE LEGISLATURES, ACCESS TO DIGITAL ASSETS OF DECEDENTS (March 31, 2016), http://ncsl.org/research/telecommunications-and-information-technology/access-to-digital-assets-of-decedents.aspx; BLACHLY, supra note 4.

Securities Law

Securities law is another area in which lawyers must stay abreast of the law, which is evolving due to the digital environment. For example, securities regulations regarding the fair disclosure of nonpublic information were revisited in 2008 to consider whether information posted on a company's website might comply with Regulation Fair Disclosure (Regulation FD), which requires that when a company releases material information to select investors, it must also make that information publicly available.[12] Regulation FD also defines the officers, directors, and employees who qualify as company spokespersons and who are therefore covered by the regulation. The Securities and Exchange Commission (SEC) issued guidance that allowed companies to determine whether their website postings were sufficient to comply with Regulation FD.[13]

In 2013, the Regulation FD definition of company spokespersons became more significant as social media had taken hold: the SEC issued a Report of Investigation in which it found that social media channels such as Twitter and Facebook could be employed to meet Regulation FD dissemination of information requirements.[14] The Report of Investigation refers companies to the 2008 website guidance, which indicates that the digital source of information must be a channel of which investors, the market, and the media are aware. Thus, lawyers advising corporations subject to Regulation FD must analyze whether the use of social media conforms with the regulation and whether the company should establish social media guidelines and monitor the release of material nonpublic information posted on social media.

Another category of regulated information is "forward looking statements," which relate to a company's future performance and are permitted in accordance with Section 27A of the Securities Act of 1933 (the "Securities Act") and the Exchange Act if the statements are properly identified and contain a disclaimer. Twitter's character limit prevents the inclusion of the disclaimer.

---

[12] Selective Disclosure and Insider Trading, 65 Fed. Reg. 51716 (Final Rule Aug. 24, 2000) (codified in 17 C.F.R. 240, 243, & 249), http://www.gpo.gov/fdsys/pkg/FR-2000-08-24/pdf/00-21156.pdf.

[13] Commission Guidance on the Use of Company Web Sites, 73 Fed. Reg. 45862 (Aug. 7, 2008) (soliciting comments), http://www.gpo.gov/fdsys/pkg/FR-2008-08-07/pdf/E8-18148.pdf.

[14] SECURITIES & EXCHANGE COMMISSION, REPORT OF INVESTIGATION PURSUANT TO SECTION 21(A) OF THE SECURITIES EXCHANGE ACT OF 1934: NETFLIX, INC., AND REED HASTINGS, RELEASE NO. 34-69279 (Apr. 2, 2013) [hereinafter 21(a) Report], https://www.sec.gov/litigation/investreport/34-69279.pdf.

Some companies have attempted to comply with the disclaimer requirement by linking the Tweet to the company website, but it remains unclear whether the SEC or a court would deem this approach to be sufficient.[15]

There are several other areas of securities law that have been impacted, and although an in-depth review of securities law is beyond the scope of the book,[16] one other area interesting to note is the impact of social media on investment advisors. In 2012, the SEC's Office of Compliance Inspections and Examinations (OCIE) published a National Examination Risk Alert to warn investment advisors about the inappropriate use of social media to solicit clients.[17]

Similar to the attorney advertising regulations, investment advisers are prohibited from social media posts that contain testimonials and certain references to past recommendations, and may be misleading. Moreover, the OCIE Alert expresses concern that investment firms have not specifically included social media in their compliance programs and urges them to do so. It also cautions against linking to third-party websites and social media accounts due to the changing nature of social media—a link may provide appropriate information today and be altered so that it is misleading tomorrow.

Bottom line: Competent lawyers advising public corporations and investment firms need to be aware of the SEC's published guidance on the use of social media and the compliance issues that it raises for companies who are thereby regulated.

Mergers and Acquisitions

Mergers and acquisitions (M&A) is another complex area of the law that has been invaded by social media. In particular, social media has become a necessary consideration in competently conducting M&A due diligence. When representing the buyer, a request for information concerning the target company's social media accounts, social media usage, employees who are authorized social media users, and any social media–related files not

---

[15] *See* JAY G. BARIS & DAVID M. LYNN, THE GUIDE TO SOCIAL MEDIA AND THE SECURITIES LAWS, 6 (2015).

[16] *Id.* Baris and Lynn's guide includes registration statements, FINRA guidelines for broker-dealers, and guidance for investment companies in addition to the areas mentioned above.

[17] OFFICE OF COMPLIANCE INSPECTIONS AND EXAMINATIONS, NATIONAL EXAMINATION RISK ALERT, INVESTMENT ADVISER USE OF SOCIAL MEDIA (2012), https://www.sec.gov/about/offices/ocie/riskalert-socialmedia.pdf.

only provides additional information, but also may reveal potential liabilities that may not otherwise be uncovered.[18]

Additionally, reviewing social media posts of employees may reveal potential liability created by employees' posts on their own public accounts that reveal confidential information or malign the company.[19] Finally, the prospective buyer should investigate third-party social media accounts to gain additional information about the target company and also to determine whether the target company's intellectual property appears to be compromised.[20]

Thus, a target company's social media presence must be evaluated from both "a value-added and risk management perspective."[21] Digital due diligence includes the company's social media presence, its process for creating and posting information, and its social media policy that governs its employees.[22]

Bottom line: A competent M&A lawyer must generally understand social media and specifically understand the significance of social media in the context of a particular M&A deal.

Bankruptcy

Social media accounts can be "property of the estate" in a bankruptcy case of a business, and thus belong to the business, even when the contents of the accounts are intermingled with personal content of managers and owners. This principle was recently confirmed by the Bankruptcy Court for the Southern District of Texas in *In re CTLI, LLC*,[23] which featured a battle among

---

[18] MYRIAM RASTAETTER & PETER FLÄGEL, USE OF SOCIAL MEDIA IN THE M&A DUE DILIGENCE PROCESS (2013), http://www.gibbonslaw.com/Files /Publication/6f0e9f05-7218-421f-a98d-0d515d61bef2/Presentation /PublicationAttachment/4da64848-8275-4b1f-b97a-1164bb9238aa /Social%20Media.pdf.

[19] *Id.*; *see also* Ernst & Young, *How Social Media Is Changing M&A, EY Capital Insights,* EY.COM.

[20] *Id.*

[21] CITIZENS COMMERCIAL BANKING, THE NEXT EDGE IN M&A: LEVERAGING SOCIAL MEDIA & BIG DATA (2014), https://www.citizensbank.com/assets /docs/pdf/Perspective_Leveraging_Social_Media_and_Big_Data_in _MandA.pdf.

[22] *Id.*

[23] In re: CTLI, LLC., 528 B.R. 359 (Bankr. S.D. Tex. 2015).

equity holders over Facebook and Twitter accounts promoting a business called Tactical Firearms.[24]

Tactical Firearms was a gun store and shooting range.[25] Prior to filing for bankruptcy, the business had used Facebook and Twitter accounts in its marketing.[26] The original majority shareholder and managing officer, Jeremy Alcede, had mixed his quasi-celebrity personal activities and personal politics with the promotion of the business; he frequently used Facebook and Twitter for both personal purposes and for the promotion of the business.[27] When the company filed for bankruptcy, Alcede ultimately lost ownership and control of the company to another investor through a Chapter 11 plan of reorganization.[28]

Despite the loss of the business, Alcede fought to retain control over the Facebook and Twitter accounts.[29] However, although he had changed the names of the accounts to reflect his personal name rather than that of the company, the bankruptcy court held that the accounts belonged to the business.[30] The court applied Bankruptcy Code 541, which provides that a bankruptcy estate included "all legal or equitable interest" of a debtor, in holding that the social media accounts belonged to the debtor and thus constituted property of the bankruptcy estate.[31]

As the court recognized, Alcede had originally created the Tactical Firearms business, and the accompanying social media accounts, as "an extension of his personality" and, "like many small business owners, closely associated his own identity with that of his business."[32] The court, however, rejected Alcede's definitions of "personal" versus "business related" media posts, finding that the best marketing for business through social media is "subtle" and can involve the use of celebrities to promote the business.[33]

---

[24] *Id.* at 361.

[25] *Id.* at 361.

[26] *Id.* at 362.

[27] *Id.* at 362-63.

[28] *Id.* at 363.

[29] *Id.*

[30] *Id.*

[31] *Id.* at 366.

[32] *Id.* at 368.

[33] *Id.* at 367.

Rejecting Alcede's property and privacy arguments, the court determined that the social media accounts were property of the bankruptcy estate, much like subscriber or customer lists, despite some intermingling with Alcede's personal social media rights.[34] The court then exercised various remedies and contempt powers to protect the successor-owned business from Alcede's further interference and to assure that the successor could take control of the assets, including requiring delivery of possession and control of passwords for the accounts.[35]

The court concluded that the "likes" that the Facebook page received belonged to the bankrupt entity, even though Alcede had registered as a Facebook user and page administrator with his personal Facebook profile.[36]

The court also held that the Twitter account belonged to the business, given that the Twitter handle was "@tacticalfirearm" and that the account description included a description of the business.[37]

The court rejected Alcede's privacy concerns by analogizing to cases finding that parties had waived the attorney-client privilege by sharing privileged information with nonclients, or to cases where an employee used the employer's computer system and thereby waived privacy rights as to personal emails.[38] Because the social media accounts were for the benefit of the business, Alcede lost any personal privacy right in his content and was forbidden to modify either the Facebook or Twitter account by adding or deleting any material.[39]

Thus, the court ordered Alcede to transfer control of the account to the new owner of the reorganized business.[40]

Bottom line: This decision is noteworthy because disputes regarding social media assets, like many other rights newly created in the digital age, have generally been addressed below the public radar in bankruptcy cases and other commercial settings. This case evidences a change as parties in bankruptcy cases and related proceedings are increasingly focused on capturing the value of these kinds of assets.

---

[34] *Id.* at 367-68.

[35] *Id.* at 367.

[36] *Id.* at 366.

[37] *Id.* at 371-72.

[38] *Id.* at 372.

[39] *Id.* at 372-73.

[40] *Id.* at 377-78.

Labor and Employment Law

Although employment lawyers may be involved in a significant amount of lit-igation, the lawyers who advise employers on labor and employment matters need to be aware of the importance of social media from a risk management standpoint. Today, employers are advised to develop social media policies; however, if an employer's policies or conduct infringes upon employee rights that are protected by the National Labor Relations Act (NLRA) then the employer may incur the cost and expense of litigation. The Office of the General Counsel of the National Labor Relations Board (NLRB) has issued a few reports that include a compilation of social media cases, which provide guidance.[41]

Many of the cases involve employees' NLRA section 7 rights to engage in "concerted activity," or the discussion of the terms and conditions of their employment. Often an employer, who is upset about being maligned on social media, terminates the offending employee only to learn that it is the employer who violated the law.

For example, two employees participated in a Facebook discussion in which they used profane language about their employer's ineptitude in deal-ing with the deduction of state income tax in their paychecks. The employer terminated the employees and defended the termination based upon the fact that the employees had posted malicious comments and evidenced a lack of loyalty. The NLRB sided with the employees, who claimed to be seek-ing mutual support in encouraging the employer to correct the paycheck inaccuracies.[42] Additionally, the NLRB concluded that the employer's social media policy violated the NLRA because it prohibited "inappropriate discus-sions about the company, management, and/or co-workers," which could be interpreted by employees to preclude statutorily protected discussions.[43] In fact, the NLRB has been extremely conservative in approving the language of employers' social media policies and has often ruled that an employ-er's restrictions on social media are impermissibly vague or lack the clarity required to establish a policy that does not violate employee rights.[44]

---

[41] National Labor Relations Board, *The NLRB and Social Media*, NLRB. GOV (last visited Sept. 18, 2016).

[42] Triple Play Sports Bar and Grille, No. 34-CA-012915 (N.L.R.B. 2014); Triple Play Sports Bar, No. 34-CA-012926 (N.L.R.B. 2014).

[43] *Id.*

[44] *See* Durham Sch. Servs.,L.P.,360N.L.R.B.85(N.L.R.B.2014);LilyTransp. Corp., 2014 WL 1620731 (N.L.R.B. Div. of Judges 2014); *see also* George Patterson, *NLRB Continues Aggressive Crackdown on Social Media*

Social media and concerted activity is only one of many areas of which employment lawyers need to be aware. Employers are also seeking legal guidance concerning monitoring employees' online activities, consideration of job applicants' social media presence, the duty to investigate an employee's comments on social media when another employee claims it impacts the workplace, and other social media situations.[45]

Bottom line: A competent labor and employment lawyer understands that social media has permeated the workplace and that he or she must consider social media implications in advising his or her clients.

Government Law

Lawyers who advise governmental entities and government officials who are subject to open meeting or sunshine laws and public records acts need to be aware that social media activity may be subject to public records requests. Additionally, communication among government officials on social media, such as a Facebook page, may not only be subject to production under a public records request, but also may constitute a meeting in violation of the sunshine laws.[46] Moreover, municipalities who maintain Facebook accounts must be careful in restricting public comments to avoid criticism or dissension among members of the public. While the jurisprudence is still in its infancy, the First Amendment implications of inappropriately limiting speech in a public forum are well established.[47]

Thus, government agencies and the lawyers who advise them must continue to create and modify social media policies to keep pace with innovative social media networks while remaining mindful of the First Amendment implications.[48] Government lawyers must also be aware of other considerations such as

---

Policies, THE NAT'L L. REV. (Sept. 3, 2014), http://www.natlawreview.com /article/nlrb-continues-aggressive-crackdown-social-media-policies.

[45] *See generally* Molly DiBianca, *The eWorkplace: Balancing Privacy and Information Security to Manage Risks,* YOUNG, CONAWAY STARGATT & TAYLOR, LLP. (2014).

[46] PATRICIA SALKEN & JULIE A. TAPPENDORF, SOCIAL MEDIA AND LOCAL GOVERNMENTS: NAVIGATING THE NEW PUBLIC SQUARE 60-65 (A.B.A. Book Publishing 2013).

[47] *Id.* at 47.

[48] *Id.* at 46 (Salken and Tappendorf provide a discussion of the public forum and government speech doctrines and indicate that the use of social media may implicate both doctrines depending on the conduct of the municipality).

advising municipalities to avoid social media activity that may give rise to copy-right issues, and incidental discrimination or other issues arising from a failure to consider the Americans with Disabilities Act and those citizens who may not be able to participate in accessing information or a government meeting conducted via a social media network.[49]

Additionally, government employees may be constrained from participation on social media when speaking in their capacities as government representatives; however, when speaking in an individual capacity, a government employee is entitled, in accordance with the First Amendment, to speak as a private citizen on a matter of public concern.[50] Thus, similar to the private-sector labor laws discussed above, a government employee may not be terminated based on a social media comment that he or she posted in his or her individual capacity as a private citizen. One court has found that clicking the "like" button for the candidate running for election to unseat the employee's supervisor does not constitute sufficient grounds for termination, as the "like" button constitutes protected speech.[51]

Lawyers advising government officials also need to be aware of the growing body of First Amendment authority that restricts an elected official's ability to block or silence critics on social media platforms. From Donald Trump to Alexandria Ocasio-Cortez, elected officials at all levels and at all points along the political spectrum have come under fire for their attempts at blocking or censoring critics on social media platforms. Courts all over the country have confronted the question of how sites run by a governmental entity or public official qualify as "limited public forums" protected by the First Amendment. Multiple federal circuit courts, as well as numerous district courts nationwide, have examined these issues and have generally ruled that such social media blocking constitutes viewpoint discrimination forbidden by the First Amendment.[52]

---

[49] *Id.* at 67-73.

[50] Bland v. Roberts, 750 F.3d 368, 387 (4th Cir. 2013) (citing Cf. Garcetti v. Ceballos, 547 U.S. 410, 421 (2006)).

[51] *Id.*

[52] *See, e.g.*, Davison v. Randall, 912 F.3d 666 (4th Cir. 2019); Knight First Amendment Institute et al. v. Trump, 928 F.3d 226 (2d Cir. 2019); Robinson v. Hunt Cty., 921 F.3d 440 (5th Cir. 2019); *see generally* John G. Browning & Reginald A. Hirsch, *Blocked in the Digital Age: Constitutional Dimensions of Elected Officials Silencing Critics on Social Media*, Tex. B.J. (May 2020).

Bottom line: A competent lawyer who represents government entities must understand social media as it relates to the myriad of statutory requirements and First Amendment jurisprudence that is pertinent to government officials as well as the state and municipal departments and agencies that they administer.

CHAPTER 10

Attorney Advertising in an Age of LinkedIn, Twitter, and Blogs

Attorney advertising has garnered more national attention since the advent of social media. Attorneys are able to advertise on firm websites and on social networking sites such as LinkedIn, Facebook, and YouTube. Moreover, a clever YouTube "commercial" may be produced and posted at virtually no cost. Unlike the days when attorney advertising was limited to print ads, television, radio, and billboards, which often required a significant financial investment, the low cost of the Internet has leveled the playing field.

Thus, many more attorneys are creatively providing information about their services. And while this phenomenon is touted as a positive development in providing greater information to the public, well . . . there is just no accounting for taste. One lawyer's exploding firestorm "special effects" commercial during the Super Bowl a few years ago created quite a controversy—it inspired another attorney to create an outrageous parody of the commercial and the state bars refrained from comment.[1]

However, in 2016 a bankruptcy attorney in Indiana was suspended for thirty days for his comments on his website that were interpreted as promising results and also included the statement,

---

[1] Bob Ray, *ADAM REPOSA: Lawyer, Patriot, Champion*, YOUTUBE (May 21, 2012), https://www.youtube.com/watch?v=tBLTW-KLdHA; *see also* Vince Mancini, *Insane Georgia Lawyer Commercial Gets an Even Insaner Rebuttal from the I! Am! A Lawyer! Guy*, UPROXX (Feb. 17, 2014), http://uproxx.com/filmdrunk/georgia-super-bowl-lawer-commercial-rebuttal-reposa/ (article discussing how Adam Reposa created a rebuttal video to Jamie Casino's "totally bonkers" commercial that aired during the Super Bowl).

"We have been screwing banks since 1992."[2] The attorney defended his use of "screwing banks" as a reference to the use of thumb-screws in debtors' prisons to torture people into paying debts. He said a prurient language interpretation missed the mark because there is no literal manner in which one could actually screw a bank. The American Civil Liberties Union (ACLU) was unsuccessful in its defense of the attorney on First Amendment grounds.[3]

Interestingly, the same Indiana attorney maintains a picture of a bulldog on his website with the slogan, "We love to take a bite out of a banker."[4] In Florida, the bulldog would likely be impermissible, as Florida has prohibited one law firm from using a pit bull dog logo deeming it to send the "wrong" message to the public.[5] And lest we think that the 2005 Pit Bull case is outdated, The Florida Bar assured lawyers that it remains impermissible to employ the pit bull when it reprimanded another attorney in 2021 for his use of a pit bull on his Facebook page, his website, and his boat. The Florida Bar found the use of the pit bull to violate the advertising rules as being potentially misleading and unduly manipulative or intrusive.[6]

On the other hand, a Rhode Island ethics opinion found that a lawyer could use the slogan "Win with ____," where the attorney's name rhymes with win to create a clever jingle.[7] Rhode Island uses a reasonable person standard in determining whether an adver-tisement would be substantially misleading.[8] In other states, the

---

[2] In re Welke, No. 49S00-1505-DI-293 (Ind. 2016).

[3] Debra Cassens Weiss, *Bankruptcy Lawyer Suspended for 'Screwing Banks' Ads*, A.B.A. JOURNAL (Jan. 13, 2016, 06:15 AM), http://www .abajournal.com/news/article/bankruptcy_lawyer_suspended_for _screwing_banks_ads.

[4] *Welke Law Firm*, WELKELAWFIRM.NET (last visited July 6, 2016), http:// welkelawfirm.net/.

[5] The Fla. Bar v. Pape, 918 So.2d 240, 243 (Fla. 2005).

[6] Debra Cassens Weiss, Top Florida court reprimands 'Pitbull Lawyer' for advertising campaign ABA Journal (August 6, 2021) https://www .abajournal.com/news/article/top-florida-court-reprimands-pitbull -lawyer

[7] R.I. Sup. Ct. Ethics Advisory Panel Op. 2015-03 (2015), https:// www.courts.ri.gov/AttorneyResources/ethicsadvisorypanel/Opinions /15-03.pdf.

[8] *Id.*

use of "win" in a slogan would no doubt be considered promising results and therefore be impermissible.[9]

The discrepancy among the state bar advertising regulations and varying interpretations of the same rules by different state bars has added to the confusion and motivated the Association of Professional Responsibility Lawyers (APRL) to study the situation. In 2015, APRL released a report that proposes that the advertising rules be virtually eliminated so that only fraudulent or misleading advertisements are prohibited.[10] A fraudulent and misleading standard both provides lawyers with greater flexibility and protects the public from the type of advertising abuse that occurred in South Carolina when a young attorney created a website on which he grossly overstated his experience, claimed expertise in fifty areas of the law, and guaranteed positive results. (The South Carolina Supreme Court reprimanded him and required him to attend legal ethics and advertising classes.)[11] Also captured by the fraudulent standard would be the California attorney who was suspended because she Photoshopped herself into pictures with celebrities and then posted the pictures on her law firm's website to attract clients.[12]

APRL's report has been reviewed and debated by various states and the American Bar Association. In fact, the American Bar Association amended the Model Rules in 2018 to adopt a more streamlined version of the advertising rules. Several states have amended their advertising rules based upon the APRL report and the ABA's amendments. Nonetheless, the advertising rules continue to be debated in the legal community as the state bars struggle to determine the appropriate application of the traditional advertising rules to the digital age and the constantly evolving state of

---

[9] *See, e.g.,* FLA. BAR RULES OF PROFESSIONAL CONDUCT R. 4-7.13 (B), which states, "Deceptive or inherently misleading advertisements include, but are not limited to advertisements that contain: (1) statements or information that can reasonably be interpreted by a prospective client as a prediction or guaranty of success or specific results;" FLA. BAR RULES OF PROFESSIONAL CONDUCT R. 4-7.13(B) (Fla. Bar 2013).

[10] ASS'N OF PROF. RESP. LAWYERS, 2015 REPORT OF THE REGULATION OF LAWYER ADVERTISING COMMITTEE 5 (2015).

[11] *In the Matter of Dannitte Mays Dickey,* SC., No. 27090, Feb. 1, 2012, http://www.sccourts.org/opinions/displayOpinion.cfm?caseNo=27090.

[12] *See* Decision, In the Matter of Svitlana Sangary, 13-O-13838-DFM (St. Bar Ct. of Cal. 2014).

technology and social media. In some cases, the state bars seem to be attempting to govern professionalism in the guise of protecting the public and thereby are running smack into the protective wall of the First Amendment.[13]

A brief look at the history of attorney advertising provides context for the current controversy over appropriate advertising. In fact, *all* advertising was deemed to be inappropriate and unprofessional until the US Supreme Court sided with the lawyers in *Bates v. Arizona* in 1977 and declared advertising to be a First Amendment right in accordance with the commercial speech doctrine, which also provides for reasonable state regulation.[14] After *Bates*, attorney advertising evolved relatively slowly with the *Central Hudson* test eventually predominating.[15] In other words, if a state has a compelling interest (think protecting the public) and narrowly tailors its regulations to achieve its goal (think prohibiting fraud or misrepresentation), then all is well.

Sounds clear enough; however, with the emergence of the digital age and a more informed public, the test has become more difficult to apply. In fact, several federal courts have deemed unconstitutional some of the attorney regulations promulgated by the state bars in Louisiana, New York, and Florida.[16]

The Fifth and Second Circuits have found the complete prohibition of client testimonials to be unconstitutional.[17] The Second Circuit similarly struck down an "irrelevant techniques" rule, which was designed to minimize the use of special effects that have nothing to do with the practice of law.[18] Both circuits noted that the public is not so naïve as to think that a verifiable

---

[13] *See, e.g.*, Rubenstein v. Fla. Bar, 72 F. Supp.3d 1298, 1308 (S.D. Fla. 2014).

[14] *See* APRL REPORT, *supra* note 9, at 6 (discussion of regulation prior to *Bates*).

[15] *Id*. at 9 (outlining *Central Hudson* standard).

[16] *Id*. at 13. ("Five notable cases have been brought in the last decade: Alexander v. Cahill, Public Citizen v. La. Att'y Disciplinary Board, Harrell v. The Fla. Bar, Searcy et al. v. The Fla. Bar, and Rubenstein v. The Fla. Bar.")

[17] *See* Pub. Citizen Inc. v. Louisiana Att'y Disciplinary Bd., 632 F.3d 212, 223 (5th Cir. 2011); *see also* Alexander v. Cahill, 598 F.3d 79, 92 (2d Cir. 2010).

[18] *Id*. at 94.

testimonial from one client assures the same results in the next case. The Second Circuit also commented that the public is sophisticated to the point of understanding that the parody of a lawyer as superhero is a contemporary advertising technique.[19]

The Eleventh Circuit deemed unconstitutional Florida's determination that advertising past results on billboards, radio, and television is inherently misleading and therefore impermissible.[20] Also rendered unconstitutional was Florida's rule that required a lawyer to be board certified to be able to advertise as an expert or specialist.[21]

In 2014–15, state bar associations in New York, Pennsylvania, California, and West Virginia, along with bar associations in Philadelphia, New York City, and New York County, issued advisory opinions with social media and advertising guidelines that provide additional insight to attorneys.[22] Florida maintains social

---

[19] *Id.* at 92; *Pub. Citizen Inc.*, 632 F.3d at 222.

[20] *Rubenstein*, 72 F. Supp.3d at 1317.

[21] Searcy v. Fla. Bar, 140 F. Supp.3d 1290, 1299 (N.D. Fla. 2015).

[22] W. Va. Office of Disciplinary Couns., L.E.O. No. 2015-02: Social Media and Attorneys (Sept. 22, 2015), http://www.wvodc.org/pdf/LEO%20 2015%20-%2002.pdf [hereinafter W. Va. Op. 2015-02]; N.Y. State Bar Ass'n, Com. and Fed. Litig. Sec., Social Media Ethics Guidelines (June 9, 2015), http://www.nysba.org/socialmediaguidelines/; Pa. Bar Ass'n, Formal Op. 2014-300: Ethical Obligations for Attorneys Using Social Media (2014); Phila. Bar Ass'n Prof. Guidance Committee, Op. 2014-5 (July 2014), http://www.philadelphiabar.org/WebObjects/PBAReadOnly .woa/Contents/WebServerResources/CMSResources/Opinion2014 -5Final.pdf; State Bar of Cal., Standing Committee on Prof. Resp. and Conduct, Formal Op. No. 2012-186 (2012), [hereinafter Cal. Op. No. 2012-186]; N.C. State Bar, 2014 Formal Ethics Op. 5: Advising a Civil Litigation Client about Social Media (July 17, 2015), https:// www.ncbar.gov/for-lawyers/ethics/adopted-opinions/2014-formal -ethics-opinion-5/; The Ass'n of the Bar of the City of New York: Committee on Professional Ethics, Formal Op. 2015-7: Application of Attorney Advertising Rules to LinkedIn (Dec. 30, 2015), http://www.nycbar .org/member-and-career-services/committees/reports-listing/reports /detail/formal-opinion-2015-7-application-of-attorney-advertising -rules-to-linkedin (references N.Y. County Lawyer's Ass'n, Ethics Op. 748 (2015)).

media advertising guidelines on its state bar website.[23] These opinions, along with the prior advisory opinions, federal court cases, and disciplinary cases, provide an overview for best practices for advertising in the digital age.

So, what are some best practices?

QUESTIONS

1. Is my law firm website compliant?

The answer to the question depends in part on where you are located and whether you are engaged in a local or national practice. If you have a national practice, it is often suggested that you adhere to the strictest states' guidelines. If you maintain a local practice then your answer lies in your state's attorney advertising rules. While some states, notably Florida, have extremely detailed rules, there are general guidelines that should apply in nearly all of the states.

Your website should list the name of the firm, at least one of the attorneys, and the office address or location.[24] It is generally permissible to list the firm attorneys with biographical information and areas of practice. Most states require board certification or its equivalent to list an attorney as an expert or specialist.[25]

If you want to use client testimonials, make sure that you have the client's permission, that the client wrote the testimonial, and that it is not misleading as an atypical result.[26] If you want to include past success stories, obtain client consent for detailed examples, otherwise just assure that the

---

[23] The Fla. Bar Standing Committee on Advertising, *Guidelines for Networking Sites* (May 9, 2016).

[24] *See, e.g.,* MODEL RULES OF PROF'L CONDUCT R. 7.2 (Am. Bar Ass'n 2002); FLA. BAR RULES OF PROFESSIONAL CONDUCT R. 4-7.12 (2013); N.Y. RULES OF PROFESSIONAL CONDUCT R. 7.3 (N.Y. STATE BAR ASS'N 2015).

[25] *See* MODEL RULES OF PROF'L CONDUCT R. 7.4 (Am. Bar Ass'n 2016); N.Y. RULES OF PROFESSIONAL CONDUCT R. 7.4 (N.Y. STATE BAR ASS'N 2015); TEXAS DISCIPLINARY RULES OF PROFESSIONAL CONDUCT R. 7.04 (STATE BAR OF TEX. 2016). But Florida, for example, is one of the states where the court has struck down this requirement: *see* Searcy v. Florida Bar, 140 F. Supp. 3d 1290, 1299 (N.D. Fla. 2015)).

[26] MODEL RULES OF PROF'L CONDUCT R. 7.1 COMMENT (Am. Bar Ass'n 2016); *see also, e.g.,* N.Y. RULES OF PROFESSIONAL CONDUCT R. 7.1 (N.Y. State Bar Ass'n 2015).

description is verifiable and not subject to various interpretations so as to be misleading.[27] Depending on your practice area, you may want to include a disclaimer on the website indicating that both client testimonials and references to past results do not guarantee that another client will attain the same results. In some states a disclaimer is required.[28]

If you plan to provide a form through which a potential client may contact you, then you should ask for minimal information and have a disclaimer indicating that filling out the form does not constitute the establishment of an attorney-client relationship.[29]

Based on the introduction above, it is important to ensure that nothing appearing on your website may be overtly misleading or misleading due to omission of certain facts.[30] Information should be verifiable.[31] Just the facts . . . embellishments cause trouble.

2. What are some guidelines for blogging?

Attorneys' blogs run the gamut from photography and cooking to every imaginable area of the law. If the blog reflects an attorney's passion for cooking and does not reference the practice of law, then in accordance with guidance from California and Florida (and common sense), the blog is not subject to attorney advertising rules.[32]

---

[27] *Id.*

[28] *Id*; *see also* APRL REPORT, *supra* note 9, at 24-25.

[29] ABA Standing Committee on Ethics and Prof. Resp., Formal Op. 10-457 (Aug. 5, 2010), [hereinafter A.B.A. Op. 10-457]; *see also* Cal. Standing Committee on Prof. Resp. and Conduct, Formal Op. 2001-155 (2001), (attorney may avoid incurring duty of confidentiality to persons who seek legal services by visiting attorney's website and disclosing confidential information only if site contains clear disclaimer).

[30] *See* MODEL RULES OF PROF'L CONDUCT R. 7.1 (Am. Bar Ass'n 2016); SEE ALSO N.Y. RULES OF PROFESSIONAL CONDUCT R. 7.1 (N.Y. State Bar Ass'n 2015); ILL. RULES OF PROFESSIONAL CONDUCT R. 7.1 (S. Ct. Ill. 2010); CAL. RULES OF PROFESSIONAL CONDUCT R. 1-400 (State Bar of Cal. 2013).

[31] *See, e.g.,* FLA. BAR RULES OF PROFESSIONAL CONDUCT R. 4-7.13(B)(2) (Fla. Bar 2013).

[32] The Fla. Bar Standing Committee on Advert., Guidelines for Networking Sites (May 9, 2016); *see also* The State Bar of Cal. Standing Committee on Prof. Resp. and Conduct, Formal Op. Interim No. 12-0006 (Feb. 4, 2016), http://www.calbar.ca.gov/Portals/0/documents/public Comment/2016/2016_12-0006AttyBlogging020416.pdf [hereinafter Cal. Op. No. 12-0006].

A California opinion explains that if an attorney is blogging about an area of the law in which she practices, even if she does not overtly suggest that her followers retain her, then the attorney should adhere to the advertising rules in the same manner as discussed above for websites.[33] California's view is similar to Florida's guidelines, which explain that if social media content is purely personal and not related to the practice of law, then it is not subject to the rules; however, once the content crosses the line into information about legal services, then it becomes subject to the rules.[34]

Assuming that a blog is subject to the advertising rules, it should contain basic information about the attorney or the attorneys who are blogging and assure that facts stated about cases are accurate and not misleading. Moreover, a recent District of Columbia opinion advises "that social media posts regarding a lawyer's own cases should contain a prominent disclaimer making clear that past results are not a guarantee that similar results can be obtained for others."[35]

If the blog permits or encourages comments and questions, be careful not to provide specific advice based on an individual's specific facts, or you are likely creating an attorney-client relationship (at least of the prospective client type).[36] In fact, the D.C. opinion also advises "that all social media postings for law firms or lawyers, including blogs, should contain disclaimers and privacy statements sufficient to convey to prospective clients and visitors that the social media posts are not intended to convey legal advice and do not create an attorney-client relationship."[37]

Protect client confidentiality and curb your enthusiasm for uttering derogatory language when describing a judge. Several lawyers have been reprimanded or settled cases with their state bars after breaching client confidentiality or maligning a judge through the use of personal attacks.[38]

---

[33] *Id.* at 3.

[34] *Id.* at 1-8.

[35] D.C. Bar Ethics Opinion 370 (2016).

[36] Judy M. Cornett, *The Ethics of Blawging: A Genre Analysis*, Loy. U. Chi. L. J. 221, 249 (2009); *see also* Katy Ellen Deady, *Cyberadvice: The Ethical Implications of Giving Professional Advice Over the Internet*, 14 Geo. J. Legal Ethics 891 (2001).

[37] D.C. Bar Ethics Opinion 370 (2016).

[38] *See* In re Disciplinary Proc. Against Peshek, 798 N.W.2d 879, 879 (Wis. 2011) ("The public blog contained confidential information about her clients and derogatory comments about judges. The blog had

A public defender suffered suspensions in both Illinois and Wisconsin and was terminated as a result of blogging about her clients and a judge.[39] An attorney in Florida agreed to a public reprimand after he was prosecuted for referring to a judge as an "evil, unfair witch" and other derogatory terms when blogging about her questionable courtroom procedures.[40]

(Note: the Virginia Supreme Court disagreed with its own state bar and sided with an attorney who was blogging about his cases and identifying clients without their consent.[41] He asserted a First Amendment right to use information that had become a part of the public record.[42] Virginia uses an older version of the confidentiality rule, which refers to maintaining confidentiality over confidences and secrets identified by the client.[43] Regardless, the opinion is generally viewed as an outlier and therefore does not comport with general best practice advice.[44])

---

information sufficient to identify those clients and judges using public sources."); The D.C Bar Ethics Opinion 370 also emphasizes client confidentiality and consent. "It is advisable that the attorney share a draft of the proposed post or blog entry with the client, so there can be no miscommunication regarding the nature of the content that the attorney wishes to make public. It is also advisable, should the client agree that the content may be made public, that the attorney obtain that client consent in a written form."

[39] *Id.*

[40] The Fla. Bar v. Conway, 996 So.2d 213 (Fla. 2008); *see also* Brielynne Neumann, *The 21st Century Online Carnival Atmosphere: Ethical Issues Raised by Attorneys' Usage of Social Media*, 27 Geo. J. Legal Ethics 747, 755 (2014) ("The Florida Supreme Court found that Mr. Conway's statements 'were false or posted with reckless disregard as to their truth or falsity' in violation of Model Rule 8.2 and recommended that Conway be found 'guilty of misconduct justifying bar discipline.'").

[41] Hunter v. Virginia State Bar ex rel. Third Dist. Comm., 744 S.E.2d 611, 619 (Va. 2013).

[42] *Id.* at 616.

[43] *See* Jan L. Jacobowitz and Kelly Jesson, *Fidelity Diluted: Client Confidentiality Gives Way to the First Amendment & Social Media In Virginia State Bar, ex rel. v. Horace Frazier Hunter*, 36 Campbell L. Rev. 75, 84 (2014).

[44] *Id.* at 97.

3. Any problem with linking my blog to my law firm website?

There is no problem linking a blog to a law firm website as long as both the website and the blog comply with the attorney advertising regulations, even if the blog contains information that is not necessarily about the practice of law.[45] In other words, once the blog becomes an adjunct to the website, the blog must also comply with the advertising rules.[46]

4. Any problem with advertising on Facebook?

Many law firms and individual lawyers maintain Facebook accounts for professional use. These accounts must comply with the advertising regulations.[47]

Problems generally arise when a lawyer is using his personal account to comment on his cases or clients. Once a personal account becomes blended with a professional use, then the account must comply with the advertising regulations. A California opinion contrasted the following two posts:

1. "Case finally over. Unanimous verdict! Celebrating tonight."[48]
2. "Another great victory in court today! My client is delighted. Who wants to be next?"[49]

The opinion found that the first comment was not a message or communication that offered legal services, regardless of the subjective intent of the lawyer.[50] On the other hand, the second comment was defined as advertising because of the sentence, "Who wants to be next?"[51] Once the post was defined as advertising it became noncompliant under the California rules, because the post is not designated as advertising, it promises results, and it contains a testimonial without the required disclaimer.[52] Thus, mixing business with pleasure on a Facebook account may be a formula for disaster.

---

[45] *See* Cal. Op. No. 12-0006, *supra* note 31, at 1 (remember California rules, for example, say that blogs are not subject to advertising rules simply because they linked to the firm website, but if "extensive and/or detailed professional identification information announcing the attorney's availability for professional employment will itself be a communication subject to the rules and statutes.").

[46] *Id.*

[47] Cal. Op. No. 2012-186, *supra* note 21, at 6.

[48] *Id.* at 1.

[49] *Id.*

[50] *Id.* at 4.

[51] *Id.*

[52] *Id.*

Moreover, lawyers who comment on their personal accounts, thinking that they are just "chatting" with "friends" about pending clients or cases, may not only be making comments that may be construed as advertising; they also may risk their positions and breach confidentiality or other professional responsibility rules pertaining to misconduct and the fair administration of justice. For example, a Miami public defender was terminated after she posted and commented on a picture of leopard underwear that was delivered by her client's family with his other clothing for trial.[53] A North Florida prosecutor posted Mother's Day greetings to "all you crack hoes out there" and was sent straight to sensitivity training.[54]

5. What about YouTube or TikTok?

If you search YouTube, you will find no shortage of lawyer commercials. Once again, video sharing sites are subject to the advertising rules.[55] Depending on your jurisdiction, there may be restrictions on what a lawyer may depict, sound effects, who may appear in the video, and disclaimers that may be required. Another area where the controversy often swirls around differences of opinion is whether restrictions should be made where lawyers'

---

[53] Martha Neil, *Lawyer Puts Photo of Client's Leopard-Print Undies on Facebook; Murder Mistrial, Loss of Job Result*, A.B.A. J. (Sept. 13, 2012), http://www.abajournal.com/news/article/lawyer_puts_photo_of _clients_leopard-print_undies_on_facebook_murder_mistri/.

[54] Joe Kemp, *'Happy Mother's Day to All the Crack Hoes Out There': Florida Prosecutor Sparks Outrage over Rude Facebook Rants*, N.Y. DAILY NEWS, May 22, 2014, http://www.nydailynews.com/news/national /florida-prosecutor-sparks-outrage-rude-facebook-rants-article-1 .1801757. The same prosecutor was recently terminated after violating the social media policy that his office established after his Mother's Day message. The termination was for inappropriate comments that he posted after the tragic massacre at an Orlando nightclub. *See* Andrew Blake, *Kenneth Lewis, Florida Prosecutor, Fired over Orlando Shooting Comments*, THE WASHINGTON TIMES, June 24, 2016, http:// www.washingtontimes.com/news/2016/jun/24/kenneth-lewis -florida-prosecutor-fired-over-orland/

[55] *See* MODEL RULES OF PROF'L CONDUCT R. 7.3 COMMENT (Am. Bar Ass'n 2002); *see also* The Fla. Bar Standing Committee on Advert., Guidelines for Video Sharing Sites (May 9, 2016); DEBRA L. BRUCE AND D. TODD SMITH, COMPLYING WITH THE ADVERTISING RULES WHEN PROMOTING YOUR PRACTICE ON THE INTERNET, STATE BAR OF TEXAS, 24TH ANNUAL ADVANCED ADMINISTRATIVE LAW COURSE: CHAPTER 11 (JUNE 7, 2011), http://www .texasbarcle.com/Materials/Events/11311/143365_01.pdf.

videos violate "good taste" or professionalism, but the First Amendment often prevails as to the right of the lawyer to post.[56]

Interestingly, a cadre of young lawyers have flocked to TikTok to share "a day in the life" type of videos. A sign of the evolving embrace of social media by BigLaw is apparent in Bloomberg interviews with some of these young lawyers. Rather than being frowned upon by their BigLaw employers, the law firm media folks are collaborating with their TikTok "stars" so that the firm may benefit from exposure and provide appropriate guidance.[57]

6. I have been asked to be an expert on a website where members of the public may pose questions. Any ethical issues I need to consider?

South Carolina provided guidance in an opinion that discourages involvement with websites that promote an attorney as an expert, require that an attorney answer individuals' specific fact-based legal questions, and that pay an attorney for his service.[58] The conclusion was based upon the generally impermissible designation of expert, the inevitable formation of the attorney-client relationship arising from answering individualized questions, and fee issues resulting from the attorney receiving payment from a third party rather than the client.[59]

The South Carolina opinion did, however, agree with other opinions such as those rendered by New York and the ABA that explain that an attorney may offer general legal advice online with the disclaimer that folks should not solely rely on general Internet advice, but rather seek counsel as to the specific facts of their situations.[60]

---

[56] Penn. Bar Ass'n, Report of the Pennsylvania Bar Association Task Force on Lawyer Advertising (May 2007); *see also* Anna Massoglia, *Lawyer Videos That Push the Boundaries of Dignity and Good Taste*, Lawyerist.com (Sept. 30, 2015).

[57] Tiana Headley, *Big Law's TikTok Stars Embrace Industry's New Social Media Norms* (July 12, 2021) https://news.bloomberglaw.com /business-and-practice/big-laws-tiktok-stars-embrace-industrys-new -social-media-norms?context=search&index=0; Amanda Robert, *Three BigLaw attorneys share stories about their TikTok personas* (July 16, 2021) https://www.abajournal.com/news/article/three-big-law-attorneys -share-stories-about-their-tiktok-personas

[58] S.C. Bar, Ethics Advisory Op. 12-03 (Feb. 21, 2012).

[59] *Id*.

[60] *Id*; *see also* A.B.A. Op. 10-457, *supra* note 28, at 3; Ass'n of the Bar of the City of New York Committee on Prof. and Jud. Eth. Formal Op. 1998-2 (1998).

7. Should I claim my Avvo page?

Whether to claim your Avvo page is a matter of personal preference and marketing strategy. However, in the event that you do claim your page, keep in mind that it is controlled by Avvo and provides clients with the opportunity to both favorably comment and criticize. It is a natural human instinct to want to respond to criticism and defend your reputation, but on Avvo, as on any other website, that can pose an ethical dilemma for an attorney. In fact, two attorneys, one in Illinois and one in Georgia, have been reprimanded for breaching confidentiality when responding to a client's criticism on Avvo.[61] While there is an exception to the confidentiality rule when a lawyer is defending himself or herself in response to client allegations, that exception has generally been interpreted as applying in the context of a tribunal rather than in an online forum.[62] (See chapter 11 for a discussion of how to respond to online client reviews.)

8. Any issues with using pay-per-lead or pay-per-click advertising?

During the 2012 ABA Annual Meeting, the ABA ratified the following change to the comments to Model Rule 7.2 governing lawyer advertising, which renders pay-per-lead advertising permissible under the Model Rules and provides guidance as to the circumstances in which it may be used:

> [A] lawyer may pay others for generating client leads, such as Internet-based client leads, as long as the lead generator does not recommend the lawyer, any payment to the lead generator is consistent with Rules 1.5(e) (division of fees) and 5.4 (professional

---

[61] Debra Cassens Weiss, *Lawyer's Response to Client's Bad Avvo Review Leads to Disciplinary Complaint*, A.B.A. JOURNAL: LEGAL ETHICS BLOG (Sept. 12, 2013), http://www.abajournal.com/news/article/lawyers_alleged _response_to_bad_avvo_review_leads_to_disciplinary_complaint/ ("Illinois employment lawyer is accused of revealing confidential information about a former client when the lawyer responded online to a negative review on Avvo."); *see also* Samson Habte, *Reprimand is Not Enough When Lawyer Uses Private Info to Counter Client's Barbs*, BLOOMBERG DNA (Mar. 27, 2013), ("A sanction stronger than a reprimand is called for when a lawyer revealed confidential information about a former client in response to 'negative reviews' the client posted about the lawyer on the internet, the Georgia Supreme Court concluded March 18 in a case of first impression (*In re Skinner*, Ga., No. S13Y0105, 3/18/13)").

[62] *See* MODEL RULES OF PROF'L CONDUCT R. 1.6 COMMENT (Am. Bar Ass'n 2003).

independence of the lawyer), and the lead generator's communications are consistent with Rule 7.1 (communications concerning
a lawyer's services). To comply with Rule 7.1, a lawyer must not
pay a lead generator that states, implies, or creates a reasonable
impression that it is recommending the lawyer, is making the referral without payment from the lawyer, or has analyzed a person's
legal problems when determining which lawyer should receive the
referral.[63]

Although the adopted ABA comment clearly permits an attorney to pay a
lead generator for generating leads, which in turn would constitute "reasonable costs" and "usual charges," these rules are not binding on any state.

Once again this becomes a state-specific question. Some of the states
have opined on pay-per-click or pay-per-lead advertising and provide additional guidance.[64] It is important to note that in many of these states a
lawyer referral service is impermissible, which renders the analysis as one
that seeks to determine whether a pay-per-click or pay-per-lead program is
permissible advertising or constitutes an impermissible referral service.[65]

These states generally apply criteria such as those listed throughout
the ABA comment above to distinguish valid advertising from an impermissible referral service. There are states, such as Florida, that authorize
and regulate attorney referral services, and thus require a different analysis

---

[63] *See* MODEL RULES OF PROF'L CONDUCT R. 7.2 COMMENT (Am. Bar Ass'n
2012); A.B.A., August 2012 Amendments to ABA Model Rules of Professional Conduct 19 (Aug. 2012), http://www.americanbar.org/content
/dam/aba/administrative/ethics_2020/20120808_house_action
_compilation_redline_105a-f.authcheckdam.pdf.

[64] *See* Ky. State Ethics Op. E-429 (2008), [hereinafter Ky. Op. E-429];
Or. Formal Op. No. 2007-180 (2007), https://www.osbar.org/_docs
/ethics/2007-180.pdf [hereinafter Or. Op. No. 2007-180]; Ariz. St. Ethics Op. 11-02 (2011), [hereinafter Ariz. Op. 11-02]; S. Ct. of N.J. Comm.
on Attorney Adver. Op. 43 (2011), https://www.judiciary.state.nj.us
/notices/2011/n110629a.pdf [hereinafter N.J Op. 43] ("New Jersey recognized the distinction between pay-per-click and pay-per-lead and
determined that both constitute advertising as opposed to impermissible referral service arrangements and thus are not flatly prohibited if
the payment is based on actual leads or clicks and not the prospective
client hiring the lawyer.").

[65] In Kentucky, Maine, Massachusetts, North Carolina, Oklahoma, and
South Carolina, a for-profit lawyer referral service is impermissible.

consistent with that state's lawyer referral service regulations.[66] Regardless, there is guidance to be found in some of the commentary about the validity of the payment arrangements in these advertising programs.

Generally, the pay-per-click analysis, where an attorney pays based on the number of times an Internet advertisement for his or her law firm is clicked upon by anyone, is considered to be less direct contact between the lead generator and a potential client than a pay-per-lead arrangement (which generally involves the lead generator collecting and submitting a potential client's information directly to a law firm).[67]

Therefore, pay-per-click is often compared to the yellow pages where potential clients look for information and do not necessarily retain a law firm simply because they have looked in a paper directory or clicked on an Internet advertisement. In these instances, states usually find payper-click to be permissible advertising for which a lawyer may pay a reasonable cost based upon the number of clicks he receives as a result of the advertisement.

For example, upon reviewing various iterations of a pay-per-click arrangement, Kentucky concluded that it is permissible for lawyers to participate in a group marketing program via a toll-free number or a website. Lawyers may pay the service based on the number of hits using a pay-per-click analysis but may not pay based upon a specific referral. Additionally, a lawyer may not pay the group marketing program based on a percentage of the fee generated by a case in which the lawyer was retained by a consumer via the toll-free number or via the website.[68]

Similarly, Oregon determined that "a charge to the Lawyer based on the number of hits or clicks on [the] Lawyer's advertising, which is not based on actual referrals or retained clients, would also be permissible."[69] The opinion further states that although attorneys may not compensate a third party based on "the number of referrals, retained clients, or revenue received from

---

[66] A.B.A. Standing Committee on Law. Referral and Info. Serv., The Regulation of Lawyer Referral Services: a Preliminary State-by-State Review, (last visited June 26, 2016). Note: Florida is currently in the process of revamping its referral service rules in an attempt to be more inclusive of the for-profit companies that have arisen as a result of the Internet. *See* The Florida Bar, Lawyer Referral Service Rule Proposed Amendments (Revised Aug. 12, 2016), http://www.floridabar.org /proposedlrsamend.

[67] *See, e.g.,* N.J Op. 43, *supra* note 62, at 11.

[68] Ky. Op. E-429, *supra* note 62, at 6.

[69] Or. Op. No. 2007-180, *supra* note 62, at 533.

the advertisements," attorneys may pay a fee based on "a fixed annual or other set periodic fee not related to particular work generated from a directory listing."[70] The opinion does not elaborate on whether a lead constitutes a referral for purposes of structuring a permissible payment arrangement.[71]

Arizona has also concluded that "a lawyer also may ethically participate in Internet advertising on a pay-per-click basis in which the advertising charge is based on the number of consumers who request information or otherwise respond to the lawyer's advertisement, provided that the advertising charge is not based on the amount of fees ultimately paid by any clients who actually engage the lawyer."[72]

New Jersey recognized the distinction between pay-per-click and pay-per-lead and determined that both constitute advertising as opposed to impermissible referral service arrangements and are not flatly prohibited if the payment is based on actual leads or clicks and not on the prospective client hiring the lawyer. However, the opinion emphasizes that the advertising offering the legal services must not be inherently deceptive or misleading.[73]

Thus, the analysis conducted by some of the states that have issued ethics opinions suggests that pay-per-lead fee arrangements are permissible if the lawyers' payment is based solely on leads (i.e., potential clients) rather than based on the number of retained clients or the revenue generated.[74]

---

[70] *Id.* at 532-533.

[71] *Id.* at 530-534.

[72] Ariz. Op. 11-02, *supra* note 62.

[73] N.J Op. 43, *supra* note 62, at 12.

[74] Avvo recently launched a legal services matching program, which has billing procedures that are more complex than typical pay-per-lead advertising. The consultation fee is paid to the attorney from Avvo, and the ultimate marketing fee may depend upon the type of case and fee involved. *See* http://sociallyawkwardlaw.com/wp-content/uploads /Avvo-Legal-Services-and-the-RPC-with-supporting-details-2016-2-11 .pdf. Avvo's program has been found problematic by three states because its marketing fee has been deemed either an impermissible referral fee or an impermissible splitting of attorney fees. *See* South Carolina, Ethics Advisory Op. 16-06 (2016); Pa. Bar Ass'n Comm. On Legal ethics & Prof'l Responsibility, Formal Op. 2016-200 (2016); NYSBA Ethics Opinion No. 1081 (2016). Avvo's program is worthy of mention as one of the most recent innovations in the delivery of legal services; however, as the debate over this type of program continues to evolve it is premature to speculate as to whether or in what form these programs will find acceptance with the state bars.

9. May I offer a Groupon or other daily deal coupon for my services?

The ABA and several states have opined on whether a lawyer's use of a marketing firm that offers coupons that entitle the buyer to discounted legal services or prepaid services may be structured so as to comply with the legal ethics rules.[75] A threshold issue is the requirement that the advertising of the coupon does not violate any attorney advertising regulations. Assuming compliance, there are various issues that arise as to potential conflicts of interest, assuring that the buyer is aware that the purchase of a coupon does not create an attorney-client relationship, collection and deposit of prepaid fees, the payment of a fee from the lawyer to the marketing firm, and the issue of return of fees if the client does not use the coupon.[76]

The ABA opinion concluded with confidence that a coupon that entitles the buyer to a discount on the price of services may be structured to comply

---

[75] A.B.A. Standing Committee on Ethics and Prof. Resp., Formal Op. 465 (Oct. 21, 2013), http://www.americanbar.org/content/dam/aba /administrative/professional_responsibility/formal_opinion_465 .authcheckdam.pdf. *Citing* Maryland State Bar Ass'n Comm. on Ethics, Op. 2012-07 (2012) (where website collects fees upfront and retains percentage of purchase price, arrangement is cost of advertising and not legal fee-splitting arrangement); North Carolina State Bar, Formal Op. 10 (2011) (portion of fee retained by website is merely advertising cost because "it is paid regardless of whether the purchaser actually claims the discounted service and the lawyer earns the fee . . . "); South Carolina Bar Ethics Advisory Comm., Advisory Op. 11-05 (2011) (website's share of fee paid by purchaser was an "advertising cost" and not sharing of legal fee with nonlawyer). *But see Advertising on Groupon and Similar Deal of the Day Websites,* Alabama State Bar, Formal Op. 2012-01 (2012) (percentage taken by site is not tied in any manner to "reasonable cost" of advertisement, and thus use of such sites to sell legal services is violation of Rule 5.4 because legal fees are shared with a nonlawyer); Indiana State Bar Ass'n Legal Ethics Comm., Advisory Op. 1, *supra* note 3 (online providers are being paid to channel buyers of legal work to specific lawyers in violation of advertising and fee sharing rules); Pennsylvania Bar Ass'n, Advisory Op. 2011-27 (2011) (use of deal-of-the-day website is impermissible fee splitting under Rule 5.4); State Bar of Arizona, Formal Op.13-01 (2013) (even if portion retained is reasonable, it constitutes illegal fee sharing because the consumer pays all the money directly to the website versus the lawyer paying fees for advertising out of already earned fees).

[76] *Id*. at 1-7.

with the legal ethics rules.[77] (For example, a $25 coupon entitles the buyer to five hours of legal services at a rate of one hundred dollars per hour instead of the usual rate of two hundred dollars per hour).

The ABA opinion was skeptical about fashioning a coupon that entitles the buyer to prepaid legal services at a reduced fee.[78] (For example, a coupon for which the buyer pays five hundred dollars for five hours of legal services that would cost one thousand dollars without the coupon.) The skepticism was born of the complication of collecting fees in advance, the requirement to hold unearned fees in trust, and the potential of having to return the fees if the coupon holder did not use the coupon.[79] It is interesting to note that the ABA opinion did not have a problem with the marketing company retaining a percentage of the coupon payment as the reasonable cost of the advertisement (rather than deeming it to be the impermissible splitting of a fee with a nonlawyer).[80]

If you are interested in this type of advertising, it is important to check on whether your state has opined on the daily deal scenario either through an advisory opinion or a disciplinary proceeding, as the ABA opinion noted that there are varying opinions in the states that have provided guidance in this area.[81]

10. Is it okay to purchase Google AdWords to increase my business?

Google AdWords are not apparent on a website but are embedded in the site and designed to drive traffic to the site. AdWords are a permissible form of attorney advertising as long as the advertisement is otherwise compliant, and the keywords are not purchased with the intent to mislead the public or engage in other prohibited misconduct.[82] The question in this area is generally whether the use of a competitor's name as an ad word is tantamount to misconduct.

---

[77] *Id.* at 6.

[78] *Id.*

[79] *Id.* at 5-7.

[80] *Id.* at 3.

[81] ABA Op. 465, *supra* note 73 at 835.

[82] Kyle J. Russell, *Google Adwords for Law Firms*, THE NAT'L L. REV. (May 13, 2013), http://www.natlawreview.com/article/google-adwords -law-firms; *see also* Sarah Andropolous, *Should Attorneys Use the Names of Rival Attorneys or Law Firms in Advertising?*, JUSTIA: LEGAL MARKETING & TECH. BLOG (Dec. 16, 2015), https://onward.justia.com/2015/12/16 /competitive-keyword-advertising-a-good-idea-for-lawyers/.

In 2010, the North Carolina Bar responded in the affirmative when it issued an advisory opinion concluding that the purchase of a competitor's name for use as an embedded ad word is impermissible as it violates North Carolina's misconduct rules that require honesty and straightforwardness.[83]

Subsequently, the South Carolina Supreme Court also opined that attorneys cross the line by purchasing their competitors' names or other keywords. A South Carolina attorney was reprimanded when he purchased keywords that contained the names of a timeshare company and attorneys representing that company so that when an individual searched for those names or related keywords, the individual might land on the attorney's advertisement, which read:

Timeshare Attorney in SC—Ripped off? Lied to? Scammed?

Hilton Head Island, SC Free Consult[84]

The South Carolina Supreme Court found that not only was the advertisement noncompliant with the advertising rules, which required the name and office address of one attorney responsible for the advertisement, but also it violated South Carolina's Lawyer's Oath.[85] The Oath pledges integrity and civility in communications with opposing counsel and opposing parties, and pledges to perform conduct that is consistent with trust, honor, and principles of professionalism.[86]

However, Texas issued an opinion finding that it is permissible to use a competitor's name as a keyword in advertising that otherwise complies with the Texas attorney advertising rules.[87] Texas explained:

. . . [A] person familiar enough with the internet to use a search engine to seek a lawyer should be aware that there are advertisements presented on web pages showing search results, it appears highly unlikely that a reasonable person using an internet search engine would be misled into thinking that every search result

---

[83] North Carolina State Bar 2010 Formal Ethics Opinion 14 (Adopted April 27, 2012).

[84] In re Naert, 414 S.C. 181, 183, 777 S.E.2d 823, 824 (2015).

[85] *Id.* at 184.

[86] *Id.*

[87] Texas State Bar Professional Ethics Committee Opinion No. 661 (July 2016).

indicates that a lawyer shown in the list of search results has some type of relationship with the lawyer whose name was used in the search.[88]

Texas noted that it had considered and rejected North Carolina's analysis.[89] Once again, the importance of checking your own state bar becomes apparent as state bars struggle to interpret and apply traditional advertising standards to today's technology.

11. May I use LinkedIn for advertising? How should I list my skills? What about accepting endorsements and recommendations?

LinkedIn is a popular social network among attorneys and other profession-als. It has created much confusion and inquiry within the legal profession initially stemming from its section in which account owners were origi-nally asked to list their specialties. Other LinkedIn features that have been problematic are those that permit others to endorse and recommend an individual on his or her LinkedIn profile.

The categories of "specialties" and "skills and expertise" prompted both Florida and New York to clarify that those lawyers who did not otherwise qualify as "experts" under the legal ethics rules could not use these LinkedIn features.[90] Likewise, law firms with LinkedIn pages could not complete the "specialties" section.[91] LinkedIn, aware of these legal ethics issues, has more recently modified its terminology so that the feature that previously contained the offending language is now referred to as "skills."[92] However, when an individual edits his or her account, the question that he or she is asked is "do you have any of these skills or areas of expertise?"[93] Although

---

[88] *Id.* at 2.

[89] *Id.* at 3.

[90] APRL REPORT, *supra* note 9, at 23.

[91] *Id.*

[92] Sheenika Shah, *Lawyers: Remove "Specialties" from your LinkedIn Profile . . . Now*, LINKEDIN: PULSE (June 24, 2014), https://www.linkedin .com/pulse/20140624151137-48608874-lawyers-remove-specialities -from-your-linkedin-profile-now.

[93] Michelle Braun, *How to Get Endorsements & Recommendations on Your LinkedIn Profile*, LINKEDIN: PULSE (Oct. 21, 2014), https:// www.linkedin.com/pulse/20141022020108-4907991-how-to-get -endorsements-recommendations-on-your-linkedin-profile-more-tips -to-optimize-your-online-presence.

the public does not see this question, other LinkedIn users know that an individual is listing skills in response to a question about expertise, so query whether we have seen the end of this "expertise" discussion.

A more recent LinkedIn debate stems from its feature that permits users to post endorsements and recommendations that they receive from others. Pennsylvania, New York, West Virginia, and the District of Columbia have all issued guidelines that permit attorneys to accept recommendations and endorsements as long as the content is true and not misleading.[94] (For example, if a criminal defense lawyer receives an endorsement for commercial litigation, he should not accept or post the endorsement.) The more complicated question becomes how to comply with state bar advertising guidelines that may deem an endorsement or recommendation to be a testimonial and therefore require a disclaimer.

The District of Columbia opinion also cautions lawyers about the feature that is also available on some social media sites that permits the site to import all of the user's email contacts, which are often a blend of personal and professional contacts.[95] The opinion warns that the import may later cause the lawyer to inadvertently send inappropriate or embarrassing communications to some of his contacts.[96] For example, a lawyer who allows LinkedIn to import all of his contacts may find that he posts information that constitutes attorney advertising and it is automatically sent to someone who is not a family member, another lawyer, or a former or current client in violation of the solicitation rules. Thus, the D.C. opinion suggests that "great caution should be exercised whenever a social networking site requests permission to access e-mail contacts or to send e-mail to the people in the lawyer's address book or contact list and care should be taken to avoid inadvertently agreeing to allow a third-party service access to a lawyer's address book or contacts."[97]

Interestingly, all of the discussion about attorneys on LinkedIn has presumed that LinkedIn, a professional networking site, is by definition a vehicle for attorney advertising. In fact, a New York County Bar Association opinion

---

[94] Penn. Bar Ass'n, Formal Op. 2014-300 12 (2014), http://www.pabar .org/members/catalogs/Ethics%20Opinions/formal/f2014-300.pdf; N.Y. County Law. Ass'n Prof. Ethics Committee, Formal Op. 748 4 (March 10, 2015), http://www.nycla.org/siteFiles/Publications/Publications 1748_0.pdf [hereinafter N.Y. County LinkedIn Opinion]; W. Va. Op. 2015-02, *supra* note 21, at 15. D.C. Bar Ethics Opinion 370 (2016).

[95] *Id.*

[96] *Id.*

[97] *Id.*

clarified that if an attorney listed more on his profile than basic biographical data, then his LinkedIn profile became advertising.[98] In December 2015, the New York City Bar (NYC) released an opinion that attempts to shift the paradigm in thinking about LinkedIn. The NYC opinion begins with the premise that a LinkedIn profile is not attorney advertising unless it meets the following five criteria:

a. it is a communication made by or on behalf of the lawyer;
b. the primary purpose of the LinkedIn content is to attract new clients to retain the lawyer for pecuniary gain;
c. the LinkedIn content relates to the legal services offered by the lawyer;
d. the LinkedIn content is intended to be viewed by potential new clients; and
e. the LinkedIn content does not fall within any recognized exception to the definition of attorney advertising.[99]

The opinion emphasizes that if the primary purpose of a lawyer's LinkedIn profile is not to attract paying clients, then the profile should not be considered advertising.[100] If a lawyer is not aggressively attempting to expand his or her contacts; connects primarily with friends, family, colleagues, and current or former clients; and posts information of a branding or educational value, then the mere listing of skills, employment, and areas of practice are not enough to presume that the LinkedIn profile is advertising and thus subject to the attorney advertising rules.[101] The New York City opinion is new as of the time of writing of this chapter, so it remains to be seen whether the state bars will embrace NYC's novel analysis. Thus, check your state bar to determine whether you should err on the side of caution when accepting endorsements and recommendations that may be considered advertising, and stay tuned for the evolving perspective on lawyers on LinkedIn.

---

[98] N.Y. County LinkedIn Opinion, *supra* note 92, at 5.

[99] The Ass'n of the Bar of the City of New York: Committee on Professional Ethics, Formal Op. 2015-7: Application of Attorney Advertising Rules to LinkedIn (Dec. 30, 2015).

[100] *Id.*

[101] *Id.*

Conclusion

D.C. Bar Ethics Opinion 370, *Social Media I: Marketing and Personal Use,* offers valuable concluding thoughts on social media and advertising:

> Social media is a constantly changing area of technology. Social media can be an effective tool for providing information to the public, for networking and for communications. However, using such tools requires that the lawyer maintain and update his or her social media pages or profiles in order to ensure that information is accurate and adequately protected.
>
> . . . [A] lawyer who chooses to maintain a presence on social media, for personal or professional reasons, must take affirmative steps to remain competent regarding the technology being used and to ensure compliance with the applicable Rules of Professional Conduct.
>
> The world of social media is a nascent area that continues to change as new technology is introduced into the marketplace. Best practices and ethical guidelines will, as a result, continue to evolve to keep pace with such developments.[102]

In other words, be attentive to the "now" and stay tuned for the evolving ethical guidelines to come.

---

[102] D.C. Bar Ethics Opinion 370 (2016).

CHAPTER 11

They Said *What* about Me? Ethically Filtering Your Response to a Negative Online Review

The sobering reality is that lawyers have to care about their online reputations more than ever before, because the Internet has supplemented word-of-mouth referrals from family and friends as the most popular resource for people in need of legal representation. What does this mean for lawyers? It means the "good old days" are gone, when dealing with an unhappy client meant fielding a few angry phone calls or responding to a curt letter informing you that your services were no longer needed. In today's digital age, where everyone is just a few clicks away from the opportunity to air grievances to the world, comments posted on lawyer rating sites like Avvo.com and LawyerRatingz.com or consumer complaint sites like Yelp.com and RipoffReport.com can live online forever and pop up in response to Internet searches for your name.

According to Clio's 2017 legal trends report "62 percent of clients get a lawyer referral from friends or family members, 37 percent of clients find a lawyer with an online search engine, 31 percent of clients get a referral from another lawyer, [and] 28 percent of clients look in a lawyer directory."[1]

---

[1] Willie Peacock, *How Do Clients Find Their Lawyers?* (May 14, 2021) https://www.clio.com/blog/how-do-clients-find-their-lawyers/#section-2

In a 2019 survey it appears that perhaps the margin between personal referrals and online searches to find a lawyer is diminishing. *Hiring an Attorney 2019*, reports that Martindale-Avvo's survey of 6,300 people revealed that 43 percent of respondents began their search for a lawyer by asking friends and family for a referral while an equal percentage listed Google searches as their method. Additionally, 46.5 percent indicated that they used online review sites and online directories.[2]

With the Internet assuming ever-increasing marketing importance for lawyers, legal analysts have been paying increased attention to lawyers' options and risks in addressing online reviews.[3] Some commentators have pointed to cautionary examples from the medical profession, in which physicians' attempts to restrict patients from posting online reviews through the use of nondisclosure agreements have led to litigation, bad publicity, and accusations of everything from censorship to unconscionability to violations of medical ethics guidelines.[4]

---

[2] Celia Colista, *How Do Clients Research and Find Their Attorneys?* (January 9, 2020) https://www.martindale-avvo.com/blog/how-do-clients -research-and-find-their-attorneys/

[3] *See, e.g.*, Jan L. Jacobowitz Ms., *Negative Commentary—Negative Consequences: Legal Ethics, Social Media, and the Impact of Explosive Commentary*, 11 ST. MARY'S JOURNAL ON LEGAL MALPRACTICE & ETHICS 312,345 (2021). Available at: https://commons .stmarytx.edu/lmej/vol11/iss2/3; David Hudson, *Lawyers Must Use Caution When Responding to Negative Online Reviews, New Ethics Opinion Says,* ABA Journal (January 13,2021) https://www.abajournal .com/news/article/lawyers-must-use-caution-responding-to-negative -online-reviews; Frederick Hermann,*4 Examples of Attorneys Responding to Negative Reviews,* (Dec 13, 2021) https://birdeye.com/blog /attorneys-responding-to-negative-reviews/; https://www.furiarubel.com /news-resources/should-lawyers-respond-to-negative-online-reviews -law-firm-marketing/; Debra L. Bruce, *How Lawyers Can Handle Bad Reviews and Complaints on Social Media*, 75 TEX. B.J. 402, 403 (May 2012); Josh King, *Your Business: Someone Online Hates You,* THE RECORDER (Aug. 16, 2013), http://www.therecorder.com/id =1202614786352/Your-Business-Someone-Online-Hates-You?slreturn =20160828100040; Laurel Rigertas, *How Do You Rate Your Lawyer? Lawyers' Responses to Online Reviews of Their Services*, 4 ST. MARY'S J. LEGAL MAL. & ETHICS 242 (2014).

[4] *See, e.g.*, Sean D. Lee, *"I Hate My Doctor": Reputation, Defamation, and Physician-Review Websites*, 23 HEALTH MATRIX: J. L.-MED. 573 (2013).

In the first edition of the book, we noted that surprisingly little guidance on the issue had come from bar ethics authorities around the country. However, since the book's initial 2017 publication and the growing incidences of negative online reviews, the ABA Standing Committee on Professional Responsibility and Ethics released Opinion 496 Responding to Online Criticism on January 13, 2021.[5] Opinion 496 not only provides guidance, but also contains cites to the various state bars that have provided advice.[6]

The Florida Bar released two Ethics Advisory Opinions. In October 2020, Opinion 20-1 addresses responding to a client's negative online review, and in June 2021, Opinion 21-1, which advises on responding to a negative online review posted by someone who is not a client.[7] The Florida Bar also has pending proposed amendment to the confidentiality rule that would permit a lawyer to respond to a negative online review that inaccurately alleges conduct that is a prosecutable criminal offense.[8]

So, given the additional, but not definitive guidance . . .what can a lawyer do when a client or former client attacks the lawyer's professional reputation online? The following questions are designed to provide insight into both the potential disciplinary consequences and the legal options for a lawyer maligned online.

QUESTIONS

1. **An unhappy former client of mine has slammed me on Facebook and on online consumer sites like Yelp! My reputation is being trashed, and I want to defend myself. May I go online and set the record straight by telling my side of the story?**

   As with any criticism, there's a right way and a wrong way to respond— and the wrong way can land you in front of the disciplinary board. Rule 1.6 mandates that a lawyer maintain a client's confidentiality. Although the

---

[5] https://www.americanbar.org/content/dam/aba/administrative/professional_responsibility/aba-formal-opinion-496.pdf

[6] *Id.*

[7] https://www.floridabar.org/etopinions/opinion-20-1/; https://www.floridabar.org/etopinions/opinion-20-1/

[8] Mark D. Killian, *Ethics Opinion Addresses Responding to Online Criticism From Nonclients* Florida Bar News, (January 31,2022) https://www.floridabar.org/the-florida-bar-news/ethics-opinion-addresses-responding-to-online-criticism-from-nonclients/

confidentiality rule provides an exception that authorizes a lawyer to disclose confidential information "to establish a claim or defense on behalf of the lawyer in a controversy between the lawyer and the client,"[9] the exception has not been found applicable to online negative reviews. Thus, the current guidance provided by the early disciplinary cases and ethics advisory opinions discussed below indicates that a lawyer may respond, but not with any detailed information that is tantamount to a breach of his duty of client confidentiality.

Disciplinary Cases

One of the first cases occurred in Georgia after a client not only terminated his attorney, but also subjected the attorney to negative online reviews. The Georgia Bar found that the attorney, Margaret Skinner, responded to the negative reviews by posting "personal and confidential information about the client that Ms. Skinner had gained in her professional relationship with the client."[10] Although the Georgia disciplinary opinion noted that the record didn't show any "actual or potential harm to the client as a result of the disclosures,"[11] it nonetheless disciplined Skinner, who had admittedly suffered additional ethical lapses having nothing to do with online activity.[12]

Approximately one year later, Illinois reprimanded attorney Betty Tsamis for similar online activity.[13] Tsamis's client, a former flight attendant, was seeking unemployment benefits after being terminated for an alleged assault on another flight attendant. The client, Rinehart, not only fired Tsamis, but also expressed his dissatisfaction on Avvo where he claimed that Tsamis "only wants your money," utters "a huge lie" when she assures clients that she is on their side, and accepted his money when she knew "full well a certain law in Illinois would not let me collect unemployment."[14] Tsamis contacted Rinehart by email and asked him to remove the post, but Rinehart refused to do so unless Tsamis provided him with a copy of his file and a full refund of his $1,500 payment.

---

[9] MODEL RULES OF PROF'L CONDUCT R. 1.6 (B)(5) (AM. BAR ASS'N, 2016)

[10] *In re Skinner*, 740 S.E.2d 171, 172 (Ga. 2013); *see also* John G. Browning, *Digital Detractor: A New Ethical Trap for Lawyers*, 77 Tex. B. J. 611, 611 (2014).

[11] *Skinner*, 740 S.E.2d at 173 n. 6; *see also* Browning, *supra* note 6, at 612.

[12] *Id*.

[13] In the Matter of Tsamis, 2013 PR 95 (Ill. Hearing Board Reprimand, Jan. 15, 2014); *see also* Browning, *supra* note 6, at 611.

[14] *Tsamis*, 2013 PR 95; *see also* Browning, *supra* note 6, at 611.

After Avvo removed the post, Rinehart posted another negative review of Tsamis. This time, Tsamis posted a reply. She noted that Rinehart's allegations were "simply false," and wrote, "I feel badly for him, but his own actions in beating up a female coworker are what caused the consequences he is now so upset about."[15] Ultimately, Tsamis stipulated to a reprimand for breaching client confidentiality and for other issues not pertaining to the Rinehart case.[16]

And from Colorado comes another cautionary tale of how not to respond to a negative online review. Colorado attorney James C. Underhill Jr. was retained by a married couple to help with the husband's ongoing post-divorce decree issues with his ex-wife. When the clients had problems paying Underhill's full fee, Underhill threatened to withdraw unless he was paid in full in two business days. When the clients terminated the representation, Underhill failed to refund the "filing fee" (nothing had been filed).

The clients posted complaints about Underhill on two websites. He responded with postings of his own that, according to Colorado disciplinary authorities, "publicly shamed the couple by disclosing highly sensitive and confidential information gleaned from attorney-client discussions."[17] As if that wasn't bad enough, Underhill then sued the couple for defamation, and even though he was aware that they had retained counsel, he continued to communicate with them ex parte despite being instructed not to by their lawyers.

Underhill's lawsuit was dismissed, but he then brought a *second* defamation suit in a different court, alleging an unfounded tale of further Internet postings by his former clients that Colorado authorities found to be frivolous. Among the myriad of disciplinary breaches by Underhill, he was also found to have violated Colorado Rule of Professional Conduct 8.4 (d) ("a lawyer shall not engage in conduct that prejudices the administration of justice"). As a result of his misconduct, Underhill received an 18-month suspension effective October 1, 2015.[18]

In July 2016, the District of Columbia Office of Disciplinary Counsel joined the above-mentioned states when it issued an informal admonition to a lawyer who reacted to his client's posting "highly critical" comments about his representation on a website by responding and revealing "specific information about her case, her emotional state, and what transpired during

---

[15] *Tsamis*, 2013 PR 95; *see also* Browning, *supra* note 6, at 611.

[16] *Id.*

[17] People v. Underhill, No. 15PDJ040, 2015 WL 4944102, at *1 (Colo. O.P.D.J. 2015).

[18] *Id.*

[the] attorney-client relationship."[19] Like its counterparts, the D.C. disciplinary authority found that the lawyer's online response violated Rule 1.6, and did not come within the self-defense exception applicable to formal charges.

Finally, in May 2020, the Supreme Court of New Jersey's Disciplinary Review Board suspended a lawyer for one year for various violations of the legal ethics rules. One of the highlighted instances was the attorney's response to a negative online review.[20] The attorney did not respond directly to the review, but instead found the former client's massage business on Yelp and posted these comments:

"Well, [client] is a convicted felon for fleeing the state with children. A wonderful parent. Additionally, she has been convicted of shoplifting from a supermarket. Hide your wallets well during a massage. Oops, almost forgot about the DWI conviction. Well, maybe a couple of beers during the massage would be nice."[21]

The attorney's response to the disciplinary action likely did not better his situation:

"As to the Yelp rating about [client's] massage therapy business, I admit to same. I was very upset by [her] Yelp rating of my practice. This rating was

---

[19] Informal Admonition by the D.C. Office of Disciplinary Couns., In re: John P. Mahoney, Bar Docket No. 2015-D 141 (June 9, 2016). It is interesting to note that the D.C. Bar's Social Media Opinion 370 issued in November 2016 notes that the D.C. confidentiality rule contains exception that allows an attorney to reveal confidences to respond to *specific* allegations. The opinion also notes that attorneys may respond to online reviews, but adds that the confidentiality rule does provide a specific exception for online responses, which leaves the reader wondering whether a measured online response to a specific allegation that reveals a confidence is permissible.

[20] Charles Toutant, New Jersey Lawyer Suspended for 2 Years After String of Disciplinary Scrapes, LAW.COM (Oct. 08, 2020, 6:26 PM), https://www.law.com/njlawjournal/2020/10/08/new-jersey-lawyer -suspended-for-2-years-after-string-of-disciplinary-scrapes/ [https://perma .cc/65Z8-ANW3].

[21] In re Calpin, IIIB-2018-0011E, IIIB-2018-0012E, IIIB-2018-0014E, IIIB-2018-0031E (No. DRB 19-172), at *13–14 (N.J. Disciplinary Rev. Bd. Dec. 17, 2019), http://drblookupportal.judiciary.state.nj.us/Document Handler.ashx?document_id=1124239 [https://perma.cc/XBJ6-5ST5], aff'd, 229 A.3d 1270 (N.J. May 7, 2020).

made more than a year and a half after the conclusion of my representation. My disclosures, i.e. her arrests, were public information and I did not violate attorney[-]client privilege. My position was that what was good for the goose was good for the gander. I do concede that I do not believe that the rating was my finest moment. However, it was not unethical. That posting has subsequently been taken down."[22]

The so-called "good for the goose, good for the gander" defense failed to persuade the New Jersey Review Board that found a violation of client confidentiality. It is important to note that the Review Board also specifically distinguished publicly available information from generally known information. Information may be publicly available (e.g., in court records) but that does not necessarily mean that it is generally known and, if not generally known, then the attorney's duty of confidentiality is not waived under Rule 1.9, Duties to Former Clients.[23]

Ethics Advisory Opinions

Since the initial publication of this book in 2017, additional ethics opinions have joined the original "handful" of advisory opinions that had emerged to deal squarely with the question of whether an attorney may respond to a client's negative online review.

American Bar Association Opinion 496

On January 13, 2021, the ABA Standing Committee on Professional Responsibility and Ethics released Opinion 496, which was an acknowledgment of that lawyers are frequently the targets of criticism in the form of negative online reviews. While not binding or even a safe harbor in any state, Opinion 496 captures both the prevalence of the issue and the need for advice. The Opinion highlights a lawyer's duty of confidentiality and explains that a negative online review does not give rise to an exception to a lawyer's responsibility to maintain confidentiality of all information relating to the representation of a client. The Opinion also notes that any information that may lead a third party to the client's confidential information is also off limits. The Opinion suggests contacting the website to have the review removed; sending a message to contact the comment poster privately; or considering the Streisand effect and declining to respond thereby avoiding calling more attention to the matter. The Opinion further advises that if a

---

[22] *Id.* at *13–14

[23] *Id.* at *25.

response is posted that the lawyer use extreme caution to avoid disclosing any confidential information.

State Opinions

Florida

As discussed above, Florida issued two Ethics Advisory Opinions. Opinion 20-1 advises that a lawyer may not respond with confidential information but may indicate that the lawyer is constrained to fully respond and that the review is not fair or accurate. Opinion 21-1 focuses on responding to a negative online review from a third party who is not a client. The advice is consistent with the ABA Opinion 496 in cautioning lawyers to avoid the disclosure of confidential information but does allow a lawyer to indicate that the poster is not a client, and that the information is not accurate. Florida also has a confidentiality rule amendment awaiting approval from the Florida Supreme Court. The amendment would create another exception to the confidentiality rule to permit a limited response to a negative online review that alleges a prosecutable criminal offense.

New Jersey

New Jersey's Advisory Committee on Professional Ethics released Opinion 738 in 2020, and it specifies that a lawyer may respond to indicate disagreement with the facts contained in the review but cautions to avoid disclosure of confidential information unless it meets New Jersey's "generally known" standard.

Missouri

The Missouri Bar issued Opinion 2018-08[24] that aligns with the other states in advising that a negative online review does not give rise to an exception to the confidentiality rule, but the Opinion notes that a response may include a comment or acknowledgment of a lawyer's professional obligations.

Texas

The State Bar of Texas Professional Ethics Committee issued Opinion 662 in 2016.[25] The Opinion contains similar analysis regarding confidentiality, but notes that a lawyer may post a response if it complies with the professional conduct rules and is done in a "proportional and restrained" manner.

---

[24] Mo. Bar Informal Op. 2018-08 (2018)
[25] State Bar of Tex. Prof'l Ethics Comm. Op. 662 (2016)

District of Columbia

The D.C. Bar issued D.C. Bar Op. 370[26] in November 2016. The advice is a bit of an outlier based upon permission in its confidentiality rule to disclose a client's confidences or secrets to "the extent reasonably necessary to respond to specific allegations by the client concerning the lawyer's representation of the client." The Opinion cautions that the rule does not mention or provide a general safe harbor for responses to negative online reviews and notes that general allegations about a lawyer's conduct or representation fall outside of the "specific allegation" requirement that justifies a permissible but limited response.

West Virginia

West Virginia Ethics Committee Advisory Opinion 2015-02[27] also aligns with other states in noting that a lawyer may respond to both positive and negative reviews if the response does not disclose confidential information.

New York and Pennsylvania

New York and Pennsylvania were relatively early opinions that followed on the heels of the early Los Angeles and San Francisco Bar Associations opinions described below. In October 2014, the New York State Bar issued Ethics Opinion 1032, in which it stated that "[a] lawyer may not disclose client confidential information solely to respond to a former client's criticism of the lawyer posted on a website that includes client reviews of lawyers." The Pennsylvania Bar agreed and held that the "self-defense" exception to preserving client confidentiality did not apply where online reviews were concerned. In Opinion 2014-200 (2014), the Pennsylvania state bar ethics committee opined that an online disagreement about the quality of a lawyer's services is not a "controversy" and that no "proceeding" is pending or imminent just because a client impugns his lawyer in an online review. It did, however, propose the following generic response to a negative online review:

> A lawyer's duty to keep client confidences has few exceptions and in an abundance of caution I do not feel at liberty to respond in a point-by-point fashion in this forum. Suffice it to say that I do not believe that the post presents a fair and accurate picture of the events.

---

[26] D.C. Bar Op. 370 (2016)
[27] W. Va. Ethics Comm. Advisory Op. 2015-02 (2015)

County Bar Associations

NASSAU COUNTY

In May 2016, responding to an inquiry from a lawyer embroiled in a fee dispute with a client, the Nassau County (N.Y.) Bar Association Committee on Professional Ethics urged restraint.[28] The lawyer in question had been described as a "thief" in comments posted to a lawyer review website by someone claiming to be the client's brother, and the inquiring attorney wanted guidance on how detailed he could be in telling "his side." Distinguishing between formal complaints that do raise the "self-defense exception," which insulates a lawyer from discipline for disclosing confidential information, and "informal complaints such as posting criticisms on the Internet," Nassau County's Committee held that only the context of formal charges, not "casual ranting," would justify the inclusion of confidential client data. Being subject to the slings and arrows of the Internet, the Committee ruled, was "an inevitable incident of the practice of a public profession and may even contribute to the body of knowledge available about lawyers for prospective clients seeking legal advice."

BAR ASSOCIATION OF SAN FRANCISCO

In January 2014, the Bar Association of San Francisco weighed in on this subject as well.[29] Like its Los Angeles counterpart, it addressed a scenario with "a free public online forum that rates attorneys," in which the negative review by the ex-client did not disclose any confidential information.[30] And like its fellow association, the San Francisco Bar reasoned that while an attorney "is not ethically barred from responding generally" to such an online review, the ongoing duty of confidentiality would prohibit the lawyer from disclosing any confidential information. In addition, it concluded, if the matter previously handled for the client was not over, "it may be inappropriate under the circumstances for [the] attorney to provide any substantive response in the online forum, even one that does not disclose confidential information."[31]

---

[28] Bar Ass'n of Nassau Cty. Comm. on Prof'l. Ethics, Op. No. 2016-01 (2016).

[29] Bar Assoc. of S.F., Ethics Op. 2014-1 (2014).

[30] *Id.*

[31] *Id.*

LOS ANGELES COUNTY BAR ASSOCIATION

In December 2012, the Los Angeles County Bar Association issued Formal Opinion No. 525, which dealt with the Ethical Duties of Lawyers in Connection with Adverse Comments Published by a Former Client.[32] In the scenario discussed in this opinion, the adverse comments posted by the client did not disclose any confidential information, nor was there any pending litigation or arbitration between the lawyer and the former client. (If there had been, so-called "self-defense" exceptions to discussing a client's confidential information, analogous to those in legal malpractice or grievance context, might apply.) The Los Angeles Bar Association committee concluded that an attorney may publicly respond as long as he or she does not disclose any confidential information, does not injure the client with respect to the subject of the prior representation, and the response is "proportionate and restrained."[33]

2. **Why can't I bring a defamation lawsuit? After all, this client is trashing me by making false statements about my handling of the case.**

A defamation suit may be an option. In fact, some lawyers have chosen to go the route of filing a defamation lawsuit, and in some instances that has proven to be successful. In one recent Georgia decision, *Pampattiwar v. Hinson et al.*, the appellate court upheld a $405,000 trial verdict in favor of divorce lawyer Jan V. Hinson, who sued her former client Vivek A. Pampattiwar over negative reviews he allegedly posted online.[34]

Hinson withdrew from Pampattiwar's case after a series of disagreements concerning both the representation and the billing. Approximately six weeks later, Pampattiwar posted on Kudzu.com, a professional services review site, and allegedly described Hinson as "a CROOK lawyer" who "inflates her bills by 10 times" and is a an "Extremely Fraudulent Lady" who "duped 12 people i[n] the last couple of years."[35] Notably, the statements were posted by "STAREA," but Hinson investigated and learned that

---

[32] L.A. Cnty. Bar Ass'n. Prof'l. Responsibility & Ethics Comm., Formal Op. No. 525 (2012), http://www.lacba.org/docs/default-source/ethics-opinions/archived-ethics-opinions/ethics-opinion-525.pdf.

[33] *Id.*

[34] Pampattiwar v. Hinson, 756 S.E.2d 246, 249 (Ga. Ct. App. 2014), cert. denied (June 2, 2014); *see also* Browning, *supra* note 6, at 612.

[35] *Pampattiwar*, 756 S.E.2d at 249; *see also* Browning, *supra* note 6, at 611.

STAREA's IP address matched the IP address from which Pampattiwar had previously contacted Hinson via email.[36]

After discovering a second review on Kudzu.com that accused Hinson of using her office staff to post "bogus" reviews, Hinson filed suit against Pampattiwar.[37] Hinson alleged breach of contract over unpaid legal bills, but also included counts for fraud, libel per se, invasion of privacy, and false light. Georgia tort law allows recovery for "wounded feelings," a form of personal injury to reputation, thus, rendering unsuccessful Pampattiwar's assertion that Hinson needed to prove actual monetary damages.

And in a Florida appellate decision, attorney Ann-Marie Giustibelli's $350,000 defamation verdict over a former client was affirmed.[38] The former client had posted negative reviews of the lawyer on Avvo.com and other sites that included what both the trial judge and the appellate court deemed "demonstrably false allegations" that claimed Giustibelli had falsified a contract.[39] The verdict, incidentally, consisted entirely of punitive damages.

More recently, a Chicago lawyer, David Freydin, was unsuccessful in his defamation suit against third-party posters who had not been his clients.[40] The dispute began when Freydin posted an offensive comment about Ukrainians on his Facebook page. When challenged by commentors, Freydin posted additional negative comments such as:

"My business with Ukrainians will be done when they stop declaring bankruptcies. If this offends your national pride, I suggest you look for underlying causes of why 9 out of 10 cleaning ladies we've had were Ukrainian and 9 out of 10 of my law school professors were not. Until then, if you don't have a recommendation for a cleaning lady, feel free to take your comments somewhere else."[41]

---

[36] *Id.*

[37] *Pampattiwar*, 756 S.E.2d at 250; *see also* Browning, *supra* note 6, at 611.

[38] Blake v. Giustibelli, 182 So.3d 881, 885 (Fla. 4th DCA 2016).

[39] *Id.* at 884.

[40] Law Offices of David Freydin v. Victoria Chamara, No. 18-3216 (7th Cir. 2022) *See also, Debra Cassens Weiss, Lawyer can't pursue suit over negative online reviews by nonclients, 7th Circuit rules,* ABA Journal (February 1, 2022) https://www.abajournal.com/news/article/chicago-lawyer-cant-pursue-suit-over-negative-online-reviews-7th-circuit-rules; https://news.justia.com/7th-circuit-upholds-dismissal-of-lawyers-lawsuit-over-negative-online-reviews/.

[41] *Id.*

Subsequently, various individuals began leaving negative online reviews on Freydin's law firm Facebook, Yelp, and Google pages. One of the posters, Victoria Chamara, who had not used Freydin's legal services, commented and referred to Freydin as an "embarrassment and a disgrace to the US judicial system," categorized his comments as "unethical and derogatory," and deemed him to be a "hypocrite," "chauvinist," and "racist" who "has no right to practice law." [42]

Freydin sued Ms. Chamara, and others based on claims of libel, false light, tortious interference, and civil conspiracy. His case was dismissed by the District Court.[43]

The Seventh Circuit upheld the District Court's dismissal, finding the comments were opinions and therefore not actionable. The Court noted that the defendants did not have any direct consumer relationship with Freydin and also commented, "We trust that readers of online reviews are skeptical about what they read, both positive and negative. But it is enough in this case that these short reviews did not purport to provide any factual foundation and were clearly meant to express the opinions of the defendants in response to Freydin's insults to Ukrainians generally."[44]

The case has received national coverage so one may wonder if it stands as another illustration of the "Streisand effect."

3. How does *anonymous* online criticism impact the viability of a defamation suit?

Courts may be hesitant to unmask anonymous commenters, and websites like Avvo.com, Yelp.com, and others enjoy broad protections under the law. Tampa attorney Deborah Thomson found this out firsthand when she filed a defamation suit against an anonymous reviewer on Avvo.com and asked courts in Seattle (where Avvo is based) to enforce a subpoena for information unmasking her critic. Both the trial court and the appellate court denied her motions.[45]

4. Do anti-SLAPP statutes limit defamation suits against clients for negative online criticism?

Filing a defamation lawsuit in response to a negative online review or comment by a former client may be met with an anti-SLAPP motion to dismiss.

---

[42] *Id.*

[43] *Id.*

[44] *Id.*

[45] Thomson v. Doe, 356 P.3d 727, 736 (Wash. Ct. App. 2015).

In states that have adopted anti-SLAPP (Strategic Lawsuit Against Public Participation) statutes as in California and Texas, the purpose of such laws is to prevent free speech and opinion or commentary on an issue of public concern from being stifled. Not only can a successful anti-SLAPP motion lead to dismissal of the defamation lawsuit, it can also result in an award of attorney's fees against the party who brought the lawsuit. Consequently, lawyers should think twice before bringing a defamation lawsuit against a former client.

As an example of how this played out, look at the unpublished 2013 California case of *Gwire v. Bloomberg*, where an aggrieved former client anonymously posted comments about attorney William Gwire on ComplaintsBoard.com. The client accused Gwire of committing "a horrific fraud" and wrote a "partial summary of Gwire's incredibly unethical history." Gwire responded by posting that the client was "unreliable," "a proven liar," and "mentally unbalanced," making references to the client's divorce file and "previous business failures."[46] Gwire sued the client for defamation and trade libel, but the client responded by filing a motion to dismiss under California's Anti-SLAPP statute.[47]

5. Is there a best practice for dealing with negative online reviews?

So just what is the best approach for dealing with negative online reviews, where posting a rebuttal that's too specific and betrays attorney-client privilege may lead to a trip to the disciplinary board and filing a defamation suit may lead to more trouble or, at best, a paper judgment? First, take a deep breath before lashing out. Then, if you feel you must respond online, keep in mind that your reading audience is not just your disgruntled ex-client, but also an online readership of countless potential clients. (In other words, you want to avoid the "Streisand effect," in which your online response draws even more attention to the commenter's claims than the original post.) Choose your words accordingly. Do not under any circumstances reveal confidential information about the client or the matter you handled for that client.

Consider addressing your former client's comment with a gracious apology or expression of regret for his or her dissatisfaction. You might even go further by conveying your appreciation for the feedback, along with an invitation to address the matter personally (offline) with the complainant. Josh

---

[46] Gwire v. Bloomberg, 2013 WL 549339 (Col. Ct. App. 2013) (unpublished opinion); *see also* Browning, *supra* note 6, at 611.

[47] *Gwire*, 2013 WL 549339; *see also* Browning, *supra* note 6, at 611.

King, the general counsel at Avvo, views negative commentary as "a golden opportunity." King says:

> By posting a professional, meaningful response to negative commentary, an attorney sends a powerful message to any readers of that review. Done correctly, such a message communicates responsiveness, attention to feedback, and strength of character. The trick is to not act defensive, petty, or feel the need to directly refute what you perceive is wrong with the review.[48]

Above all, besides the obvious ethical concerns and disciplinary consequences that have been discussed in this chapter, bear in mind that ours is a service profession and that how you respond to client complaints about the services you rendered speaks volumes about who you are professionally. Comments made online can go viral and reach an incredibly wide audience. Take the high road.

---

[48] Browning, *supra* note 6, at 611.

CHAPTER 12

Selfie Sabotage? Lawyers Are Human, Too!

A veteran state prosecutor in Orange County, Florida, decided to post the following 2014 Facebook Mother's Day greeting: "Happy Mother's Day to all the crack hoes out there. It'[s] never too late to turn around, tie your tubes, clean up your life and make [a] difference to someone out there [who] deserves a better mother."[1] The message was not about a particular person or case in the State Attorney's Office, but nonetheless created quite a controversy.[2]

The prosecutor, who was generally well regarded for his legal acumen, initially did not apologize, but rather explained that it was meant as an aspirational message.[3] The State Attorney explained that the prosecutor would not be terminated because he had exercised his First Amendment rights and had not violated the nonexistent social media policy in the office. Instead, the prosecutor was required to attend sensitivity training.[4] Thereafter the state attorney's office adopted a social media policy.[5]

---

[1] Joe Kemp, *'Happy Mother's Day to All the Crack Hoes Out There':* *Florida Prosecutor Sparks Outrage over Rude Facebook Rants*, N.Y. DAILY NEWS (May 22, 2014, 9:53 AM), http://www.nydailynews.com /news/national/florida-prosecutor-sparks-outrage-rude-facebook -rants-article-1.1801757.

[2] *Id.*

[3] *Id.*

[4] *Id.*

[5] Tobias Salinger, *Florida Prosecutor Fired over Facebook Post Following Pulse Massacre Calling Downtown Orlando 'A Melting Pot of 3rd World Miscreants And Ghetto Thugs,'* N.Y. DAILY NEWS (June 23, 2016,

Fast-forward to June 12, 2016, and the horrendous terrorist attack on an Orlando gay nightclub, during which one individual armed with a machine gun and a pistol murdered forty-nine people and injured fifty-three people in a three-hour assault.[6] On the morning of the attack, the same prosecutor posted the following on Facebook:

> Downtown Orlando has no bottom. The entire city should be leveled. It is void of a single redeeming quality. It is a melting pot of 3rd world miscreants and ghetto thugs. It is void of culture. If you live down there, you do it at your own risk and at your own peril. If you go down there after dark there is seriously something wrong with you.

This time the prosecutor was greeted with a suspension, which quickly led to a termination of employment. In response to the suspension, the prosecutor asserted his First Amendment rights and his belief that his feelings about Orlando had nothing to do with his ability to do his job. He further stated that his comment was not work-related and only posted on his personal account.[7] The State Attorney, who was now armed with a social media policy that had been violated, more importantly explained in a letter to the prosecutor:

> Apparently, your first response to the massacre of dozens of your fellow citizens was to suggest the entire city of Orlando be leveled. Your Facebook rant, taken as a whole, could be perceived by some as suggesting an act of domestic terrorism. . . . Based upon your most recent comments that are the subject of this discipline and your history in this regard, I can no longer defend you as a prosecutor free of bias.[8]

6:41 PM), http://www.nydailynews.com/news/national/prosecutor-fired-facebook-post-orlando-massacre-article-1.2685858.

[6] Christal Hayes & Emilee Speck, *Deputies Searched through Bodies for Life Inside Pulse, Records Show*, ORLANDO SENTINEL (July 22, 2016, 12:49 PM), http://www.orlandosentinel.com/news/pulse-orlando-nightclub-shooting/os-deputies-searched-bodies-for-life-inside-pulse-records-show-20160721-story.html.

[7] Salinger, *supra* note 5.

[8] *Id.*

The prosecutor responded on Twitter: "I just got fired for a Facebook post after 20 years as a prosecutor. The founding fathers would turn in their graves. God help this country!"[9]

While the Orange County prosecutor example may seem extreme, it is not an isolated occurrence. In fact, other attorneys have posted comments on social media that were not related to their cases, but resulted in termination of employment based upon the impact on their offices and public perception. For example, an Indiana prosecutor was terminated after tweeting: "use live ammunition" in connection with the fact that riot police had been summoned to deal with protestors in Madison, Wisconsin.[10]

Two Broward County, Florida, public defenders were also terminated after a derogatory post about Palestinians in the aftermath of the killing of three Israeli teenagers. The Broward County Public Defender was quoted in the local newspaper as saying that the "time for us to learn and grow and draw the line in the sand firmly that as public defenders we have a higher calling and we cannot engage in hate speech that interferes with the mission of this office which is equal justice for all."[11]

Despite these instances often being reported in the national news and becoming frequently used slides in CLE presentations across the country, the trend continues and perhaps has become even more dramatic, given the tenor of the current events in our country over the past several years.

As the pandemic locked down the world, and the death of George Floyd captured on video was posted repeatedly throughout the world, frequent protests occurred. From the Black Lives Matter movement to the COVID-19 shutdown and mask mandate protests, tempers flared. Moreover, people began expressing adamant support or opposition regarding candidates in the upcoming presidential election. Social media platforms were filled with the expression of passionate points of view on many of these events

---

[9] *Prosecutor Fired over Facebook Post Sounds Off on Twitter,* WFLA.COM: NEWS CHANNEL 8 (June 24, 2016, 10:28 AM), http://wfla.com/2016/06/24 /prosecutor-fired-over-facebook-post-sounds-off-on-twitter/.

[10] CNN Wire Staff, *Indiana State Prosecutor Fired over Remarks about Wisconsin Protests,* CNN (Feb. 23, 2011, 9:57 PM), http://www.cnn.com /2011/US/02/23/indiana.ammo.tweet/.

[11] Martha Neil, *Two Public Defenders Fired over 'Hate Speech' in Facebook Comments,* A.B.A. J. (July 8, 2014, 04:40 PM), http://www .abajournal.com/news/article/two_public_defenders_fired_over_hate _speech_in_facebook_comments.

and issues. Unfortunately, there were lawyers who joined in the social media discussions who ultimately suffered damage to their reputations and their careers.

One such example arose in Broward County, Florida, during the George Floyd protests. An Assistant State Attorney posted on Facebook: "When will people learn that their criminal acts and obnoxious protesting actually gets you nowhere? . . . Act civilized and maybe things will change. I've never seen such animals except at the zoo."[12] The Broward County State Attorney's Office's response was swift and final:

"Following our review of the Facebook posting by [the Assistant State Attorney], we have made the decision to terminate her effective immediately," the statement read. "The views expressed in that posting are entirely inconsistent with the ideals and principles of the Broward State Attorney's Office and the duties and responsibilities of an assistant state attorney.[13]

The Assistant State Attorney posted a clarification:

"I made a post and realized that it could be misinterpreted, so I *deleted it within seconds*," she wrote. "I believe in justice for all and that ALL lives matter. I don't look at anybody by their color shape or size . . . My post specifically referenced the people who took advantage of the opportunity to protest. I respect the people who have a mission and wanted to accomplish it. It is hard to respect those who are taking it away with violence and destruction. (Emphasis added.)[14]

Seconds—And an eight-year career at the State Attorney's Office came to an end due to the emotional environment in which she posted an inflammatory opinion.

The District Attorney's Office in Harris County, Texas, also witnessed the end of a prosecutor's career. In this case the attorney reposted someone else's post without realizing its provocative nature. The original post included a photo of wedding rings shot in black and white. The problem was a caption stating that the rings had been "removed from Holocaust victims prior to being executed . . . Never forget, Nazis tore down statues . . . Banned free

---

[12] Bob D'Angelo, *South Florida Prosecutor Fired over Facebook Post Comparing Protesters to 'animals,'* WSOCTV, (Jun. 2, 2020), https://www.wsoctv.com/news/trending/south-florida-prosecutor-fired-over-facebook-post-comparing-protesters-animals/AELGXJWOXZBMHAH5TCBUA2YVGA/.

[13] *Id.*

[14] *Id.*

speech. Blamed economic hardships on one group of people. Instituted gun control. Sound familiar?"[15]

The prosecutor who reposted the entry was not aware until the following day that the post was being seen as racist, at which point, she deleted it. She was quoted in the *New York Times* as saying that a racist message was never her intention and that she had spent her life defending the rights of both wrongfully accused and victims.

Her remorse did not prevent the circulation of a petition calling for her resignation. The Harris County District Attorney explained, "this organization and my administration has zero tolerance for racism in any shape or form." She added that it is "not our intent to involve ourselves in employees' personal lives," but that the law allowed her to "implement graduated sanctions ranging from education and counseling up to termination" when an employee's social media posts "publicly contradict and violate this office's policies . . ." She added, "When speech made in the privacy of one's home or on social media contradicts our core values, . . . we take action."[16]

The prosecutor, who was the trial bureau chief, resigned from her position and thereby became another example of a career destroyed in relative moments.

Social media posts that damage careers are not unique to prosecutors. Public defenders, judges, and lawyers in private practice also experience the negative repercussions of explosive commentary. For example, summer 2020 also gave rise to a post that depicted people being assaulted by water cannons and the caption read, "The next riot at the Market House,"—an apparent reference to an incident at which there was an attempt to burn down the property where there had been a peaceful protest in the aftermath of George Floyd's death. The Cumberland County's Chief Public Defender had authored it; he ultimately deleted it and resigned with remorse.[17]

---

[15] Jacey Fortini, *Texas Prosecutor Resigns over Facebook Post about Nazi Germany*, The NY Times, (Jun. 29, 2020), https://www.nytimes.com/2020/06/29/us/kaylynn-williford-harris-county-prosecutor-resign.html.

[16] *Id.*

[17] Michael Futch, *Public Defender Resigns after Social Media Post*, The Fayette Observer, (Jun, 10, 2020), https://www.fayobserver.com/story/news/courts/2020/06/10/public-defender-resigns-after-social-media-post/41730835/.

And to provide some global context, negative repercussions are not unique to lawyers and law offices in the United States. In Alberta, Canada during the summer of 2020 a lawyer's Facebook post resulted in his resignation from his appointment to a judicial nominating committee. His post included a "comparison of a future COVID-19 vaccine to Auschwitz tattoos and posting of a video that called Black Lives Matter a "leftist lie" controlled by a Jewish philanthropist."[18]

Another example comes from Hong Kong, where a French investment bank's in-house counsel resigned from his position after his posts controversially commented on protestors in China. His termination was demanded followed by the bank's statement that encouraged people to avoid social division and also stated, "We deeply apologise for the offence caused by a social media post that was expressed on one of our employees' personal accounts."[19]

Back to the United States . . . it is worth noting that although most of these examples concern high-profile current events, other missteps may be of a more personal nature. In Tampa, Florida, a lawyer found trouble after his video post went viral. The video contains footage in which he is uttering profanities as he knocks a stowaway raccoon off of his boat and leaves it to drown.[20] The Florida Bar took notice and after a seven-month investigation ultimately recommended a diversion program that included the completion a $750.00 professionalism workshop as a requirement to remain in good standing.[21]

Also, in the United States, there have been additional challenges for judges who feel compelled to comment on the events of the day. For example, the 2017 Charlottesville protests over confederate statues prompted a Gwinett County, Georgia judge to express his views in Facebook posts that referred to the protestors

---

[18] Rachel Ward, *Lawyer Who Posted Black Lives Matter Video Resigns from Alberta Judicial Vetting Committee*, CBC, (Jun. 19, 2020), https://www.cbc.ca/news/canada/edmonton/pcnc-member-alberta-1.5618816.

[19] Alvin Lum & Chris Lau, *Hong Kong Lawyer Quits BNP Paribas after Facebook Post Supporting Anti-government Protests and Ridiculing Pro-Beijing Activists*, South China Morning Post, (Sep 27, 2019), https://www.scmp.com/news/hong-kong/article/3030581/hong-kong-lawyer-quits-bnp-paribas-after-facebook-post-supporting.

[20] Colin Wolf, *Florida Lawyer Who Filmed Himself Leaving a Raccoon to Die 20 Miles Offshore Told to Take a Workshop*, Orlando Weekly, (Dec. 17, 2019).

[21] *Id.*

as "snowflakes [who had] no concept of history;" and "the nut cases tearing down Confederate monuments are equivalent to ISIS destroying history."[22] The Chief Magistrate suspended the judge and explained:

"As the Chief Magistrate Judge, I have made it clear to all of our Judges that the Judicial Canons, as well as our internal policies, require Judges to conduct themselves in a manner that promotes public confidence in the integrity, impartiality, and fairness of the judiciary . . . I consider any violation of those principles and policies to be a matter of utmost concern, and will certainly take any action necessary to enforce compliance and to maintain the integrity of this Court."[23]

In 2019 the Tennessee Board of Judicial Conduct reprimanded another judge for his Facebook posts despite finding no evidence of the judge acting with actual bias, prejudice, or partiality in the courtroom. The letter of reprimand explained that the judge's Facebook posts were "partisan in nature . . . [and a] clear violation of the code of judicial conduct."[24] The judge was required to set his Facebook page to private and to enroll in a course in the use of social media and judicial ethics. The letter explained:

"Specifically, those images you 'shared' on your Facebook account reflects among other things a concern for credibility of certain federal agencies, a strong position on professional athletes kneeling during the national anthem, the effect of illegal aliens on the economy, opposition to certain democrat platform principles, opposing support for then presidential candidate Hillary Clinton, a position on black lives matter and the double standard of the news media."[25]

If the trouble for lawyers on social media stemmed solely from comments about current events posted after working hours and on personal accounts, then perhaps we could have a debate as to the First Amendment tension inherent in the restrictions that are

---

[22] Mollie Cahillane, *Georgia Judge is Suspended after Calling Anti-racist Protesters in Charlottesville 'Nutcases' and 'Snowflakes' and Comparing them to ISIS for Tearing Down Confederate Monuments*, Daily Mail (Aug. 15, 2017), https://www.dailymail.co.uk/news/article-4793686/Georgia-judge-suspended-posts-Charlottesville.html.

[23] *Id.*

[24] Yolanda Jones, *Judge Jim Lammey Reprimanded for Social Media Posts*, Daily Memphian, (Nov. 18, 2019), https://dailymemphian.com/article/8953/judge-jim-lammey-reprimanded-for-social-media.

[25] *Id.*

placed on lawyers in exchange for the privilege of practicing law.[26] Some of the lawyers terminated may be mounting a constitutional challenge to their losses of employment. These situations are worthy of mention because whatever a lawyer may conclude about social media and a lawyer's right to free speech, a lawyer should also pause to decide before posting whether that is a battle that he or she wants to wage from a position of unemployment.

However, this is a legal ethics handbook, and an extensive First Amendment analysis involving comments that were posted on social media concerning events outside of a lawyer's work life would be a diversion from the task at hand.[27] Returning to the idea that lawyers get into legal ethics trouble on social media when their posts are related to their cases, one finds that there is no shortage of examples.[28]

One case garnered national attention because it involved an attorney's blog comments about a judge in whose courtroom the attorney routinely appeared.[29] Sean Conway expressed his concern about a South Florida judge's courtroom procedures and characterized the judge as an "evil unfair witch," a "malcontent," and unfit to be a judge. Among the ethics violations alleged by the Florida Bar was Florida Rule of Professional Conduct 4-8.2, which is similar to ABA Model Rule 8.2 Judicial and Legal Officials; Rule 8.2 provides that a "lawyer shall not make a statement that the lawyer knows to be false or with reckless disregard as to its truth or falsity concerning the qualifications or integrity of a judge. . . ."[30] Sean

---

[26] *See* Jan L. Jacobowitz & Kelly Rains Jesson, *Fidelity Diluted: Client Confidentiality Gives Way to the First Amendment & Social Media in Virginia State Bar, ex rel. Third District Committee v. Horace Frazier Hunter*, 36 Campbell L. Rev. 75, 95 (2013).

[27] The First Amendment reference is not meant to preclude the possibility that a lawyer could be disciplined under Model Rules of Prof'l Conduct R.8.4 (Misconduct) for acting in a discriminatory manner or striking at the heart of the fair administration of justice, but the cases mentioned usually involve swift punishment in an employment context.

[28] Jan L. Jacobowitz, *Lawyers Beware! You Are What You Post—The Case for Integrating Cultural Competency, Legal Ethics and Social Media*, 17 SMU Sci. & Tech. L. Rev. 541, 568-71 (2014).

[29] The Fla. Bar v. Conway, 996 So.2d 213 (Fla. 2008); *see also* John Schwartz, *A Legal Battle: Online Attitude vs. Rules of the Bar*, N.Y. Times (Sept. 12, 2009), http://www.nytimes.com/2009/09/13/us/13lawyers.html.

[30] Model Rules of Prof'l Conduct r. 8.2 (Am. Bar Ass'n, 2016).

Conway invoked the First Amendment, but ultimately settled with the Florida Bar by accepting a public reprimand and paying a fine.[31]

Judges have also suffered the consequences of ill-advised social media posts. One Arkansas state court judge posted comments about his cases on a University of Louisiana online message board under the pseudonym "geauxjudge." Some of his comments evidenced bias against minorities, women, and the gay community. He also inappropriately commented on the confidential adoption of a child by a celebrity. He was removed from the bench and banned from seeking office again.[32]

Lawyers who have lost sight of the confidentiality required by Model Rule 1.6[33] when posting on social media have suffered suspensions or reprimands. One of the first reported disciplinary cases involved a public defender in Illinois who blogged about her clients using their first names or prison numbers. She not only was terminated but also was suspended by both the Illinois and Wisconsin Bars.[34]

As discussed in the chapter about negative online research, a Georgia lawyer was reprimanded for breaching client confidentiality when she attempted to refute a negative review on Avvo.com, a third-party lawyer rating service.[35]

A Florida public defender was terminated after posting and commenting on the leopard underwear that her client's family had provided with his trial attire. Miami-Dade Public Defender Carlos Martinez explained that the repercussions of posting the picture of the underwear went beyond a breach of confidentiality. He stated,

---

[31] *Conway*, 996 So.2d at 213.

[32] See Debra Cassens Weiss, *Controversial 'Geauxjudge' Commenter Admits He Is a Judge, Drops Out of Appellate Race*, A.B.A. J. (Mar. 7, 2014, 1:13 PM), http://www.abajournal.com/news/article/controversial _gauxjudge_commenter_admits_he_is_a_judge_drops_out_of_appella; Martha Neil, *Judge Banned from Bench Due to Online Comments, Disclosing Confidential Info on Celebrity's Adoption*, A.B.A. J. (Sept. 11, 2014, 2:20 PM), http://www.abajournal.com/news/article/judge_who _talked_about_adoption_by_actress_charlize_theron_in_online_posts/ ?utm_source=internal&utm_medium=navigation&utm_campaign =most_read.

[33] MODEL RULES OF PROF'L CONDUCT R. 1.6 (Am. Bar Ass'n, 2016).

[34] In re Kristine Ann Peshek, Disciplinary Comm'n, M.R. 23712 (Ill. 2010); In re Disciplinary Proceedings Against Peshek, 334 Wis. 2d 373, 376-77 (Wis. 2011).

[35] In re Skinner, 740 S.E.2d 171, 173 (Ga. 2013).

"[w]hen a lawyer broadcasts disparaging and humiliating words and pictures, it undermines the basic client relationship, and it gives the appearance that [the client] is not receiving a fair trial."[36]

There have also been cases in which lawyers have been found to be inappropriately tweeting about a proceeding as putative reporters. A Kansas court of appeals research lawyer was terminated after tweeting about a disciplinary proceeding that she was observing. She predicted the attorney would be disbarred and offered derogatory commentary. She later apologized and explained that she was tweeting to her friends and "forgot" that she was also speaking to the public and reflecting poorly on the Kansas judicial system.[37]

A more seasoned Chicago BigLaw attorney tweeted pictures and comments from a trial that he was observing, despite the four-foot sign outside the courthouse door that prohibited the use of cell phones and the taking of photographs in the courtroom. The presiding judge sanctioned the attorney by ordering him to: attend a CLE on social media and legal ethics, donate at least 50 hours to the pro se assistance desk at the Chicago Federal Courthouse, and pay $5,000 to the Chicago Bar Foundation. The attorney apologized and explained that he had not noticed the sign, was "caught up in the moment," and unaccustomed to being a spectator.[38]

From Sean Conway's blogging in 2009 to the BigLaw attorney's tweets in 2015, there have been plenty of cases that serve

---

[36] Martha Neil, *Lawyer Puts Photo of Client's Leopard-Print Undies on Facebook; Murder Mistrial, Loss of Job Result*, A.B.A. J. (Sept. 13, 2012), http://www.abajournal.com/news/article/lawyer_puts_photo_of _clients_leopard-print_undies_on_facebook_murder_mistri/.

[37] Debra Cassens Weiss, *Research Lawyer Is Fired for Tweeting about 'Naughty Boy' Ex-AG during Ethics Hearing*, A.B.A. J. (Nov. 19, 2012), http://www.abajournal.com/news/article/research_lawyer_is_suspended _after_tweeting_during_ethics_hearing_of_naught/.

[38] Jason Meisner, *Tweeted Photos from 'Spoofing' Trial Get Chicago Lawyer in Trouble*, CHICAGO TRIBUNE (Nov. 9, 2015, 12:55 PM); Debra Cassens Weiss, *Biglaw Partner Is Ordered to Donate $5,000 for Tweeting Photos during Federal Trial*, A.B.A. J. (Dec. 15, 2015, 12:35 PM), http://www.abajournal.com/news/article/biglaw_partner_is_ordered _to_donate_5000_sanction_for_tweeting_photos_durin; *see also* Ronald D. Rotunda, *Judges Coercing Lawyers to Donate to Charities*, VERDICT (Mar. 28, 2016), https://verdict.justia.com/2016/03/28/judges-coercing -lawyers-to-donate-to-charities (discussing the propriety of the court sanctioning attorney with fine of $5,000 donation to charity).

as a warning to attorneys to avoid discussing their cases on social media, but all have not taken heed. More recently, in November 2019, the Massachusetts Bar reprimanded an attorney after he discussed a juvenile case on his public, personal Facebook page. He represented a grandmother who was seeking custody of her grandson who had been removed from his mother's home. The public reprimand explained:

> On September 22, 2015, the respondent appeared at a hearing in Juvenile Court. The judge gave the respondent until October 2015 to present his client's guardianship petition. The day after the hearing, September 23, 2015, the respondent posted the following on his personal Facebook page, which was public and had no privacy setting:
> I am back in the Boston office after appearing in Berkshire Juvenile Court in Pittsfield on behalf of a grandmother who was seeking guardianship of her six-year-old grandson and was opposed by DCF yesterday. Next date-10/23.

Two people responded to the respondent's public Facebook post. The first (a lawyer in Massachusetts who is a Facebook friend of the respondent) asked, "What were the grounds for opposing"? To which the respondent replied: "GM [grandmother] will not be able to 'control' her daughter, the biological mother, and DCF has 'concerns.' Unspecific." The friend responded (with apparent sarcasm), "DCF does have a sterling record of controlling children and questionable mothers, after all." The respondent similarly replied, "Indeed."

A second Facebook friend of the respondent (who is not an attorney) wrote, "So, what's the preference . . . Foster care? What am I missing here"? The respondent answered, "The grandson is in his fourth placement in foster care since his removal from GM [grandmother]'s residence in late July. I will discover what DCF is doing or not doing as to why DCF opposes the GM [grandmother] as guardian. More to come."[39]

The child's mother saw the posts and informed the grandmother who filed a disciplinary complaint. The attorney argued that his posts were not confidentiality violations because he never disclosed the identity of his client. The Massachusetts Board of Bar Overseers of the Judicial Supreme Court did not find the defense

---

[39] Bar Counsel v. Frank Arthur Smith, Pub. Reprimand No. 2019-16 (Mass. 2016); https://bbopublic.blob.core.windows.net/web/f/pr19-16.pdf.

compelling. Instead, the Board concluded that the attorney had not only violated the confidentiality rule, but also advised that "[t]here is no requirement that a third party actually connect the dots. If it would be reasonably likely that a third party could do so, the disclosure runs afoul of the rule."[40]

A variation on the commenting on cases theme is found in the Ashley Krapacs case in Florida. Because Ms. Krapacs represented herself in a domestic violence petition for an injunction, which she ultimately dismissed, she spoke on social media about opposing counsel and the judge as both attorney and client.

In fact, her attack on her opposing counsel Russell Williams was so vicious that he hired his own attorney, Nisha Baccus, to file a defamation suit against Krapacs. Krapacs then increased her social media attack to include both Williams and Baccus. The social media vitriol reached a level that caused Baccus to file for an anti-stalking injunction. The Florida Bar filed a thirty-two-page Petition for an Emergency Suspension that included twenty-three exhibits detailing the social media posts.[41] The body of the petition included the following excerpt from Krapacs' YouTube video.[42]

- I have been laughing a lot. I can't stop laughing since I read this complaint that has been filed against me on me [sic] behalf of Russell J. Williams. . . . Twenty-five pages of garbage, lies, fake news . . . riddled with lies and other non-truths . . . obscene.
- . . .lying on the record is just what Mr. Williams does best . . . I have the court recording and the official court transcript of that hearing that confirms his lies.
- More lies. This guy just—he cannot get enough of lying in formal proceedings. I mean, man, like, it's just, it's a lie.
- . . .he also whines that I call him a moron and a sexist and a bully. Well, sorry—I'm not sorry, but you are all of those things.

---

[40] *Id.*

[41] *The Fla. Bar Pet. for Emergency Suspension*, Feb. 20, 2019, Case No.'s 2018-50,829(17I),FES 2018-50,851(17I), 2019-50,081(17I) https://lsg .floridabar.org/dasset/DIVADM/ME/MPDisAct.nsf/DISACTVIEW /E3EBEFB5728CF546852583B00010320E/$FILE/_19.PDF

[42] *Id.* at 12-13.

- Um, you know, and there is—there is another option here. There is a really easy option. You could, you know, just stop being a dick. Like, that's a really simple solution, just don't be a dick. Um, but men like Russell J. Williams want to have their cake and eat it too. Listen, when you have been having your cake and eating it too for three decades and it worked and it has made you a lot of money, I guess it would piss you off when someone comes along and makes it clear that that just isn't going to work anymore.

- You know, it pisses him off that he can't just keep acting a fool and then pretending to be a good guy. He wants to act like a baby, bully people around, lie and cheat his way through cases and then pretend like he's a decent human being. Sorry, that's just not an option anymore. It's just not.

- If you want to take cases where you're going after a domestic violence survivor in a completely frivolous bullshit lawsuit, you cannot also claim to support women's rights. You just can't. I mean, you can do whatever you want, but the math just doesn't add up. And I'm going to call you out. So, Nisha Bacchus, you're a backstabbing traitor. I almost feel bad for you, almost. Almost. Because he's playing her. He is playing her like a fucking fiddle. He knew he was going to have a hard time finding any attorney who was actually going to file this piece of garbage. He knew it. So, what did he do? He found someone desperate for work, someone so hard up for cases that she would do anything for a quick buck. And this much is obvious to me. It's really clear from her website.

- So, I almost feel bad for her but not quite. At the end of the day no matter how convincing and manipulative he is, it is still her choice to represent him and it's a choice that she'll live with for the rest of her life. Um, the choice to file this utter bullshit complaint. The choice to go after a rape survivor when you claim to be pro women's rights. Are you fucking kidding me? The choice to sell out to make a quick buck. It's her choice. Her actions have spoken volumes about the kind of person she really is. And that is a woman who does not like women very much. So, sorry, honey, you're exposed.

- Everyone has a price and Russell J. Williams figured out Nisha's. But, girl, it's going to cost you. It's going to cost you, girl. You made your bed, so lay in it. Hope you're comfortable.

- So, you get to choose your branding. And your choice of branding is representing misogynist pigs, misogynist bullies like Russell J. Williams, that's not good branding.[43]
- Krapacs also posted an image of a boy holding a gun up to the face of a man looking in through a dog door (from the 20th Century Studios film, *Home Alone*), along with the following caption: "When opposing counsel tries to use the exact same trick you saw in your last case."

It was highly unusual for The Florida Bar to file an emergency motion for suspension when there were no allegations of financial fraud; however, the Bar's petition alleged that Krapacs' behavior "strike[s] [at] the heart of conduct prejudicial to the administration of justice" because her attacks were solely based upon the fact that attorneys Williams and Bacchus represent or represented individuals adverse to Krapacs.[44] The Florida Bar's petition further stated that

"[b]y waging a personal and public war on social media against attorneys representing clients, Ms. Krapacs has resorted to terrorist legal tactics. The practice of law, for attorneys Williams and Bacchus, should not subject them to guerilla warfare, and such behavior is the essence of conduct prejudicial to the administration of justice and great public harm. Additionally, Respondent's outrageous conduct only serves to perpetuate the public's perception that lawyers are uncivilized.[45]

The Florida Supreme Court granted the emergency suspension and ultimately disbarred Ms. Krapacs.[46] While the Krapacs case stands as an extreme example of a social media career demolition, it nonetheless provides a cautionary tale for the legal profession.

Indeed, while not every example of such outrageous social media misconduct rises (or sinks) to the level of the *Krapacs* case, there are simply too many to ignore. In 2014, Indiana attorney James Hanson wrote a Facebook post to the ex-husband of the client he was representing in both a divorce and a misdemeanor domestic battery case, saying "You pissed off the wrong attorney . . . I'm

---

[43] *Id.* at 15.

[44] *Id.* at 3.

[45] *Id.* at 6.

[46] *The Fla. Bar v. Krapacs*, SC19-277 (Fla. 2020); https://efactssc-public .flcourts.org/casedocuments/2019/277/2019-277_disposition_149706 _d33b.pdf.

going to gather all of the relevant evidence and then I'm going to anal rape you so hard your teeth come loose . . . Watch your ass, you little (expletive deleted), I've got you in my sights now." That online tirade resulted in Hanson being arrested and charged with felony intimidation; his law license was also suspended for thirty days.[47]

In 2014, the Kansas Supreme Court imposed a six-month suspension on a lawyer for his "egregious" and "over the top" messages on Facebook to an unrepresented mother while representing the baby's biological father during an adoption proceeding. The court felt that the lawyer's communications, trying to make the mother feel guilty about consenting to give the child up, violated both Rule 8.4(d) (Conduct Prejudicial to the Justice System) and Rule 8.4(g) (Conduct Reflecting Adversely on the Lawyer's Fitness to Practice).[48]

Even more recently, in what it called "a cautionary tale on the ethical problems that can befall lawyers on social media," the Tennessee Supreme Court imposed a four-year suspension on a lawyer for his Facebook posts advising a person on how to set up and conceal a possible killing.[49] The lawyer posted comments in response to a female Facebook friend's inquiry about carrying a gun in her car during a tumultuous relationship. Emphasizing that his advice was given "as a lawyer," the attorney recommended that if she wanted "to kill" her ex-boyfriend, she should "lure" him into her home, "claim" that he broke in and that she feared for her life before shooting. He also advised her to "keep mum" and delete the thread because it could be used against her to show premeditation.[50]

In addition, some lawyers forget that while they are certainly entitled to their political leanings, outrageous social media conduct related to these leanings can result in job loss, reputational damage, and disciplinary consequences. After live-streaming videos to his Instagram account detailing his presence at the January 6, 2021, US Capitol riot, Texas attorney Paul Davis was fired from his job as associate general counsel at Goosehead Insurance. He

---

[47] Martha Neil, *Lawyer Charged with Felony Intimidation over Facebook Message to Client's Ex-Husband*, ABA J. (May 23, 2014), https://www.abajournal.com/news/article/divorce_lawyer_charged_with_intimidation_over_facebook_message_to_clients.

[48] *In re* Gamble, 301 Kan. 13, 338 P.3d 576 (Kan. 2014).

[49] *In re* Winston Bradshaw Sitton, S.Ct. TN, BPR #018440 (Jan. 22, 2021).

[50] *Id.*

also lost his fiancée, friends, and his house.[51] In October 2017, a senior in-house counsel at CBS posted insensitive comments on Facebook in the aftermath of the Las Vegas mass shooting during a country music festival at the Mandalay Bay Hotel. Vice president and senior counsel Hayley Geftman-Gold proclaimed that she was "actually not even sympathetic" to the victims because "country music fans often are Republican gun toters." She also referred to them as "Repugs" who "wouldn't do anything when children were murdered." The response from CBS was quick and decisive: Geftman-Gold was fired, and the network issued a statement saying that she had "violated the standards of our company" and that "[h]er views as expressed on social media are deeply unacceptable to all of us at CBS."[52]

Thus, if there was ever any doubt, there is no question that lawyers are human, too. Human nature sometimes compels a person toward language or conduct that is born out of emotional reactivity rather than thoughtful decision making. Unfortunately, when a lawyer posts on social media, he or she is posting not only as a human, but also as lawyer—a role that has a 24/7 connotation where legal ethics are concerned. Moreover, lawyers may be particularly susceptible to ethical errors on social media because the cultures of social media and the legal profession possess inherently clashing values—social media is an environment of instantaneous sharing and connecting, while the legal profession prides itself on confidentiality and careful, analytical thinking.[53] Moreover, recent studies have concluded that social media is a forum particularly conducive to emotional discourse.[54]

---

[51] Debra Cassens Weiss, *Lawyer Lost His Job, His Fiancée, and His Friends after Presence Outside Capitol Riot*, ABA J. (Feb. 17, 2022), https://www.abajournal.com/news/article/lawyer-lost-his-job-his -fiancee-and-his-friends-after-presence-outside-capitol-riot.

[52] Debra Cassens Weiss, *CBS Fires Lawyer over Facebook Posts Calling Vegas Shooting Victims Likely 'Republican Gun Toters,'* ABA J. (Oct. 2, 2017), https://www.abajournal.com/news/article/cbs_fires_lawyer_over _facebook_comments_calling_vegas_victims_likely_republ.

[53] Jacobowitz, *supra* note 14, at 560

[54] Jan L. Jacobowitz, Negative Commentary—*Negative Consequences: Legal Ethics, Social Media, and the Impact of Explosive Commentary*, 11 St. Mary's Journal On Legal Malpractice & Ethics 312. 352 (2021).

As we have seen above, the emotional discourse often becomes problematic for lawyers and judges, especially when posting implicates candor to tribunal, client confidentiality, and inappropriate bias. The questions and answers that follow first focus on circumstances, rules, and opinions that address candor, confidentiality, and bias and then move to those designed to shed both awareness and insight about the ethical land mines awaiting lawyers in cyberspace. Creating awareness and enhancing insight not only benefit the individual lawyer but also assists in creating social media policies and training to ensure that lawyers in public, private, and nonprofit legal organizations have the tools to avoid joining the rogue's gallery of lawyers who have tripped on social media land mines.

QUESTIONS

1. **I might have "stretched the truth" a bit in telling the judge why I wanted a recent continuance. But it's not like the judge is going to be checking up on me on Facebook and see the photos from my beach getaway weekend—is she?**

   The short answer is that if the judge doesn't, your opposing counsel likely will. Just as social media content can cause a litigant's lies to unravel, lawyers who lie or misrepresent something to the court can be undone by their own posts or tweets. Rule 3.3 of the Model Rules of Professional Conduct states that a lawyer shall not knowingly "make a false statement of fact or law to a tribunal or fail to correct a false statement of material fact or law previously made to the tribunal by the lawyers."

   Being truthful to the court was a lesson learned the hard way by New York labor and employment lawyer Lina Franco. While representing a group of restaurant workers in a wage-and-hour violations case in New Jersey federal court (*Ha v. Baumgart Café*), Franco missed a deadline to file a motion for certification of a collective action under the Fair Labor Standards Act. Sixteen days after the motion was due, Franco filed a motion along with a request for an extension of time. As good cause for the extension, Franco represented to the court that she had missed her deadline due to a family medical emergency in Mexico City. She even attached what purported to be a travel website itinerary showing her flight from New York to Mexico City on Thursday, November 21, 2016, and a December 8 return flight.

   Unfortunately for Franco, her opposing counsel owned a calendar (November 21 was a Monday, not a Thursday), and was social media savvy.

Defense counsel responded with exhibits consisting of screenshots from Franco's own Instagram account. During the period of time she was supposedly in Mexico City caring for her ailing mother, Instagram photos posted by Franco herself showed her enjoying a Thanksgiving dinner in New York City, a Museum of Modern Art exhibit on December 1, visiting a bar in Miami, and sitting poolside in Miami as well (pro tip: enjoying a poolside margarita does not count as "visiting Mexico"). Even the itinerary was revealed to be a forgery.

Caught red-handed, Franco admitted her lack of candor to the court, saying she was "not honest" and claiming that she had experienced so much emotional distress from caring for her mother at an earlier juncture that it caused her to miss the filing deadline and provide the fake itinerary. Further falling on her sword, Franco withdrew as counsel for the three restaurant worker plaintiffs. However, lawyers for the restaurant owners sought sanctions against Franco. The judge agreed with the defense, finding that Franco's "misrepresentations to the court clearly constitute bad faith and were unreasonable and vexatious, not simply a misunderstanding or well-intentioned zeal." Although a total of $44,283 in attorney fees were sought by the defense firms, the judge only imposed sanctions of $10,000.[55]

Lawyers have to be careful about what they post about a case and when, and not just because of their duty of candor to the tribunal. Attorneys have been rebuked by courts for posts on the eve of trial that seemed calculated to taint the jury pool.

In January 2018, a Philadelphia judge punished two lawyers who had represented the plaintiff in a December 2017 product liability trial over the drug Xarelto. The two lawyers, Ned McWilliams of Pensacola, Florida and Emily Jeffcoat of New Orleans, had posted a number of photographs of the courtroom to Instagram with the hashtag "#killinnazis" (a reference to both the Quentin Tarantino movie *Inglorious Basterds* and German-based Bayer, the developer of Xarelto).[56]

Post-trial motions by the defense had argued that the plaintiff's attorneys' social media posts were intended to create a link in the minds of the jurors between the German pharmaceutical giant and Nazi Germany, calling it a "xenophobic" strategy. The court issued a judgment notwithstanding the

---

[55] Charles Toutant, *Late-Filing Lawyer's Excuse Undone by Vacation Photos on Instagram*, N. JERSEY L.J. (Apr. 27, 2018).

[56] John G. Browning, *Taking Heat for Tweets: Legal Ethics and Social Media Use*, FOR THE DEFENSE (Oct. 2021), http://digitaleditions.walsworthprintgroup.com/publication/?i=725009&article_id=4134245&view=articleBrowser&ver=html5.

verdict and set aside the $27.8 million verdict (on evidentiary grounds unrelated to the social media posts).

It also revoked the pro hac vice admission of McWilliams, and sanctioned Westcott $2,500 and ordered her to perform twenty-five hours of community service. The judge noted that the Instagram posts in question and the #killinnazis hashtag (which Westcott's law firm used in promotional materials) were "well beneath the dignity of the legal profession."

Lawyers have to be careful about what they post on social media, and not just because their lack of candor or professionalism might be revealed. As we've discussed earlier, lawyers run the risk of revealing client confidential information or discussing the character, credibility, reputation, and guilt or innocence of a client.

In November 2018, Iowa criminal defense attorney Chad Frese courted controversy when he made a number of Facebook posts referring to a client he was defending on federal drug and weapons charges. Frese called the client an "idiot" and a "terrible criminal," and added "You wonder why we need jails, huh?" Even though the client wasn't identified by name, enough information was shared that the man's name could be easily determined through court records.

In 2018, the ABA provided more guidance to lawyers on the subject of what can and cannot be said by lawyers communicating online about their cases or clients in the form of Formal Opinion 480, titled "Confidentiality Obligations for Lawyers Blogging and Other Public Commentary," issued on March 6, 2018. In a nutshell, this opinion imposes a heightened duty of confidentiality for lawyers who communicate publicly on the Internet, holding that lawyers may not reveal information relating to a representation, including information contained in a public record, unless authorized by a provision of the Model Rules.

In other words, for lawyers considering commenting about their cases in blogs, Facebook posts, tweets, listservs, website news, videos, webinars, podcasts, and of course more traditional avenues of communication, the ABA views confidentiality as so fundamental to the lawyer-client relationship that it will apply even to information that may be publicly available and easily obtained. In this regard, Formal Opinion 480 is more restrictive than certain state counterparts that don't apply to information that is a matter of public record.[57]

---

[57] *See, e.g.*, Texas and its Professional Ethics Committee Opinion No. 683, issued in March 2019, which exempts information that is contained in a public record. For a more detailed discussion of this issue, see John G. Browning, *Cyber Ethics: Ethical Restrictions on Commenting About a Case*, J.L. & TECH. AT TEX. (Dec. 2019).

Indeed, the foundation of this Formal Opinion is Model Rule of Professional Conduct 1.6(a), which states that "A lawyer shall not reveal information relating to the representation of a client unless the client gives informed consent, the disclosure is impliedly authorized in order to carry out the representation, or the disclosure is permitted by paragraph (b)." If you think this is a sweeping prohibition—with a scope arguably broader than the attorney-client privilege or the attorney-work product doctrine— you are correct. This covers everything related to the representation—not just information learned directly from the client but even details that are a matter of public record. As the opinion explains, "the duty of confidentiality extends generally to information related to a representation, whatever its source and without regard to the fact that others may be aware of or have access to such knowledge."

Accordingly, in the wake of Formal Opinion 480, lawyers need to be careful about violating Rule 1.6 when posting on social media about a case without client consent, regardless of the nature and source of information. Moreover, as the opinion points out, a lawyer's public commentary about a case may impact other Model Rules as well, including Model Rule 3.5 (Impartiality and Decorum of the Tribunal) and of course Rule 3.6 (Trial Publicity). The opinion acknowledges that new online platforms provide "a way to share knowledge, opinions, experiences, and news." However, it is careful to point out that while "technological advances have altered how lawyers communicate, and therefore may raise unexpected practical questions, they do not alter lawyers' fundamental ethical obligations when engaging in public commentary."

2. **For people from all walks of life, social media platforms have become a digital watercooler or town hall, in which individuals express their thoughts and opinions on all kinds of issues in a largely unfiltered manner. In the process, people often reveal "the good, the bad, and the ugly." Is it a legal ethics issue if I am simply revealing my authentic feelings on issues like racial relations, gender equality, religious beliefs, and immigration reform?**

For most people, a post or tweet perceived as prejudiced might result in embarrassment, reputational damage, and public shaming, or even job loss. But for lawyers, in addition to these potential consequences there are ethical implications as well.

In 2016, the ABA amended Rule 8.4 to add paragraph (g), making it professional misconduct to "engage in conduct that the lawyer knows or reasonably should know is harassment or discrimination on the basis of race, sex, religion, national origin, ethnicity, disability, age, sexual orientation, gender identity, marital status, or socioeconomic status in conduct related to the practice of law."[58] The Comments to this Model Rule make it clear that paragraph (g) can be violated by either verbal or physical conduct, and in fact broadly extends to any conduct related to the practice of law, including bar association, business, or even social activities in connection with the practice of law.

Not surprisingly, Model Rule 8.4(g) has been met with widespread criticism, largely based on First Amendment concerns, and most states have declined to adopt its language.[59] As of the end of 2021, only Vermont, Maine, Pennsylvania, Connecticut, the US Virgin Islands, American Samoa, and the Northern Mariana Islands had adopted some version of Rule 8.4(g).[60] A≈handful of federal district courts, such as the Northern District of Illinois, have adopted it as well. More than thirteen states have rejected Rule 8.4(g), including Texas, South Dakota, Illinois, Arizona, Tennessee, Montana, and Nevada.[61] Several states, such as New York and New Jersey, still have the Rule under consideration.[62]

The debate over Rule 8.4(g) was so intense that, in July 2020, the ABA Standing Committee on Ethics and Professional Responsibility issued Formal Opinion 493 clarifying the purpose, scope, and application of the Rule.[63] Part of the Opinion is devoted to addressing First Amendment concerns, and it insists that 8.4(g) "promotes a well-established state interest by prohibiting conduct that reflects adversely on the profession and diminishes the public's confidence in the legal system and its trust in lawyers."[64] Yet not long after this Opinion was released, the US District Court for the Eastern District of Pennsylvania issued an injunction blocking enforcement of the amendments to Pennsylvania's Rules of Professional Conduct, including 8.4(g), finding

---

[58] MODEL RULE OF PROF'L CONDUCT 8.4(g) (AM. BAR ASS'N 2020).

[59] Josh Blackman, *ABA Model Rule 8.4(g) in the States*, 68:4 CATH. U.L. REV. 629 (2019).

[60] Nellie Q. Barnard & Christopher Heredia, *Efforts toward Improved Diversity and Inclusion through the Anti-Bias Rule*, FED. BAR ASS'N (Dec. 15, 2021); https://www.fedbar.org/blog/efforts-toward-improved -diversity-and-inclusion-through-the-anti-bias-rule/.

[61] *Id.*

[62] *Id.*

[63] ABA Comm. on Ethics & Prof'l Responsibility, Formal Op. 493 (2020).

[64] *Id.*

that the amendments constituted viewpoint discrimination and were therefore unconstitutional.[65] The court noted:

> There is no doubt that the government is acting with beneficent intentions. However, in doing so, the government has created a rule that promotes a government-favored viewpoint monologue and creates a pathway for its handpicked arbiters to determine, without any concrete standards, who and what offends. This leaves the door wide open for them to decide what is bias and prejudice based on whether the viewpoint expressed is socially and politically acceptable and within the bounds of permissible cultural parlance.[66]

In an effort to address these concerns, in July 2021, the Pennsylvania Supreme Court approved revisions to the rule; the new version of 8.4(g) prohibits "knowingly engaging in conduct constituting harassment or discrimination."[67] However, the challenge to Pennsylvania's rule continues as the United States District Court for the Eastern District of Pennsylvania recently granted summary judgment to the plaintiff who challenged the rule with its revisions. The Court found that the rule is an unconstitutional as a violation of the First Amendment right of free speech and impermissibly vague under the Fourteenth Amendment.[68]

Even without the explicit application of Rule 8.4(g), lawyers whose biased statements or conduct are memorialized in the viral maelstrom of social media have found themselves under ethics scrutiny. In May 2018, New York lawyer Aaron Schlossberg was in a Manhattan delicatessen ordering a sandwich. Hearing one of the counter workers speaking in Spanish with another customer, Schlossberg unleashed a verbal tirade against the two men. Among other statements, he told one of them to "get the [expletive deleted] out of my country," "get a [expletive deleted] dictionary and assimilate," and asked why he didn't speak English. Turning his attention to the

---

[65] Greenberg v. Haggerty, 491 F. Supp. 3d 12 (E.D. Pa. 2020).

[66] *Id.* at 30.

[67] Pa. Rule of Prof'l Conduct 8.4(g) (2021).

[68] Greenberg v. Goodrich Civil Action No. 20-03822 (Slip opinion filed March 24, 2022) (E.D. Pa. 2022); Interestingly, one of the few states that joined Pennsylvania in passing a version of Rule 8.4(g), Connecticut, explicitly includes a provision addressing First Amendment concerns. *See* Conn. Rule of Prof'l Conduct 8.4(7) (2021).

counter worker, Schlossberg berated him for speaking Spanish and threatened to "call ICE" and have "each one of you [expletive deleted] deported."

Schlossberg's rant devolved into engaging disparagingly with other customers and the deli's manager, and a video recording of the encounter soon went viral online. Schlossberg's identity and profession became known. Clients denounced him, his commercial landlord evicted him, his associate quit, and a crowd-funded mariachi band played outside his private residence. Despite an online apology, Schlossberg also soon found himself facing a disciplinary charge under New York Rule of Professional Conduct 8.4(h), engaging in conduct that adversely reflects on his fitness as a lawyer. Schlossberg ultimately entered into a consent agreement and received a public censure for his misconduct.[69]

The following year, South Carolina attorney David Traywick received a six-month suspension in connection with biased posts on his personal Facebook account.[70] Traywick's Facebook profile identified him as a lawyer and referenced his law firm. South Carolina's Office of Disciplinary Counsel received complaints from forty-six separate individuals about inflammatory and biased posts that Traywick had posted, posts that the Office of Disciplinary Counsel (and eventually the South Carolina Supreme Court) maintained violated South Carolina's Rule 7(a)(5) (conduct tending to bring the courts or the legal profession into disrepute) as well as the South Carolina Lawyer's Oath (which requires that lawyers "maintain the dignity of the legal system"). In addition to statements about women, Traywick posted profane, racially charged statements about the murder of George Floyd.

The South Carolina Supreme Court, while mindful of First Amendment concerns, found that Traywick's "expressly incendiary" Facebook comments "were intended to incite, and had the effect of inciting, gender and race-based conflict beyond the scope of the conversation [Traywick] would otherwise have with his Facebook 'friends,'" an effect exacerbated by Traywick's status as a lawyer.[71] The court also found that Traywick's statement about George Floyd in particular "tended to bring the legal profession into disrepute" and "violated the letter and spirit of the Lawyer's Oath."[72]

Beyond the ethical implications of a lawyer's biased conduct on social media, there may be client representation dimensions as well. In February

---

[69] Matter of Schlossberg, 2020 NY Slip Op. 07712 (Dec. 22, 2020).

[70] *In re* Traywick, 860 S.E.2s 358, 433 S.C. 484 (S.C. 2021).

[71] *Id.*

[72] *Id.*

2022, two convicted men in Massachusetts, Anthony Dew and James Gaines, sought new trials after it was revealed that their now-deceased lawyer made racist and offensive Facebook posts while representing them.[73]

Between 2014 and 2017, the late attorney, Richard Doyle, allegedly made numerous posts denigrating Black people, Muslims, immigrants, and members of the LBGTQ community. At the same time, he was the appointed defense counsel for Dew on assault and drug distribution charges. Previously, Doyle had represented Gaines, who was convicted of armed assault with intent to murder. Both Dew and Gaines are Black and Muslim. Before Doyle's death in 2021, the Committee for Public Counsel Services suspended him from its cases when it learned of the posts. In motions filed after Doyle's death, Dew and Gaines contend they are entitled to new trials because of their representation being tainted by Doyle's public demonstrations on social media of his "virulent bigotry toward African Americans and Muslims, among others."[74]

These motions raise an interesting question: beyond reflecting on an attorney's fitness to practice or bringing the administration of justice into disrepute, can a lawyer's biased social media posts cast doubt on whether that lawyer has complied with his duty under Model Rule of Professional Conduct 1.3 to diligently represent a client? Can a lawyer, who is charged under this Rule with the responsibility to "act with commitment and dedication to the interests of the client and with zeal in advocacy upon the client's behalf," have that commitment and zeal called into question by social media posts that demean and disparage a racial, ethnic, national, religious, or gender-based community to which the client belongs? As lawyers continue to show an uglier, biased side of themselves online, these questions will persist.

3. What is the culture of social media?

Culture may be generally defined as "the language, values, beliefs, traditions, and customs people share and learn."[75] The culture of social media

---

[73] Debra Cassens Weiss, *Defendants Want New Trials Because of Racist Facebook Posts Said to be Written by Their Lawyer*, AM. BAR ASS'N J. (Feb. 24, 2022), https://www.abajournal.com/news/article/defendants-want-new-trials-due-to-racist-facebook-posts-said-to-be-written-by-their-lawyer.

[74] *Id.*

[75] RONALD B. ADLER ET AL., INTERPLAY: THE PROCESS OF INTERPERSONAL COMMUNICATION 31 (2012) (internal citations omitted). There is an enormous body of work focused on the definition and study culture. The brief

is one of instantaneous sharing and connection. Transparency is valued. Perhaps the culture is most readily apparent in original Facebook's statement of principles:

> We are building Facebook to make the world more open and transparent, which we believe will create greater understanding and connection. Facebook promotes openness and transparency by giving individuals greater power to share and connect, and certain principles guide Facebook in pursuing these goals. Achieving these principles should be constrained only by limitations of law, technology, and evolving social norms. We therefore establish these Principles as the foundation of the rights and responsibilities of those within the Facebook service.[76]

Moreover, some authors suggest that social media is merely the latest iteration that facilitates the inherent need of human beings to share information and connect with others; stated otherwise, social media "is merely the most recent and most efficient way that humans have found to scratch a prehistoric itch."[77]

4. What are the differences between the culture of social media and the culture of the legal profession, and how do these differences contribute to ethical missteps in the legal profession?

Defining and obtaining consensus on the definition of the culture of the legal profession is an arduous task; however, the legal ethics rules provide some guidance.[78] The core values of trust, loyalty, respect, and integrity are reflected in the rules that require a lawyer to maintain confidentiality, exhibit candor to the tribunal, respect others, and avoid conduct that

---

mention of it in this section is not an attempt to capture the essence of the vast amount of literature available, but rather to note that considering competing values in a cultural context that may contribute to an understanding of some lawyers' troubled social media conduct.

[76] *See Facebook Principles*, FACEBOOK, Jose Van Djeck, The Culture of Connectivity: A Critical History of Social Media 59–60. Oxford University Press, January 2013 (emphasis added).

[77] TOM STANDAGE, WRITING ON THE WALL: SOCIAL MEDIA—THE FIRST 2,000 YEARS 7–8 (2013).

[78] *See* Jacobowitz, *supra* note 14, at 555.

evidences misrepresentation or fraud.[79] Lawyers are also known for engaging in thoughtful, analytical thinking and decision making.[80]

Comparing the core values of the legal profession with social media's values of instantaneous sharing, transparency, and connection reveals a culture clash that may contribute to lawyers' ethical lapses on social media. In other words, since lawyers are human, too . . . they get lost in the moment and default to their basic human hard wiring that encourages them to impulsively share rather than thoughtfully consider the legal ethics rules, their lawyer roles, and the repercussions of their actions.[81]

On its face, the cultural comparison may appear to be a mere academic exercise; however, the practical reality is that a basic understanding of the cultural incongruities between the legal profession and social media provides a foundation upon which to develop tools, policies, and training to assist the legal profession in avoiding ethical misconduct on social media.

5. What have we learned about an individual's motivations for posting on social media?

Interestingly, social media has now existed for approximately eighteen years—long enough not only to be nearing adulthood, but also to have been subject of sociological or psychological study. So, beyond the culture clash theory, there is some data that sheds light on emotional posting and ethical minefields.

In fact, one 2013 study concluded that "venting negative feelings, including discontent and anger and fighting back against perceived unfairness, are all important gratifications sought through social media use."[82] Another study in 2018 concluded that a primary motivation for posting on Twitter and Reddit was to express anger about a particular event.[83] Anger begets incivility and hostility—a person who is angry is more likely to employ stereotypes and use less critical judgment, which aligns with studies that demonstrate that anger may impede cognitive effort.[84]

---

[79] *See* MODEL RULES OF PROF'L CONDUCT r. 1.6, 3.3, 4.1, & 8.4 (Am. Bar Ass'n, 2016).

[80] WILLIAM M. SULLIVAN ET AL., EDUCATING LAWYERS: PREPARATION FOR THE PROFESSION OF LAW 185–87 (2007).

[81] *See* Jacobowitz, *supra* note 14, at 572.

[82] See Dag Wollebæk et al., Anger, Fear, and Echo Chambers: The Emotional Basis for Online Behavior, 5 SOC. MEDIA + SOC'Y 1, 1 (2019) ("Based on survey data, we show that anger and fear are connected to distinct behaviors online.").

[83] *Id.*

[84] *Id.*

Additionally, yet another study found that increased sharing occurs when a message is emotionally charged. And so it follows that a Facebook experiment demonstrated that the expression of emotions—both positive and negative—appears to be contagious in social media communication.[85] It seems logical that vitriolic posting is more likely to be shared and to inspire others toward negative posting. Thus, beyond the posited culture clash is the primary observation that lawyers are human but must not necessarily give in to the human instincts to share or vent on social media.

6. What have we learned about the impact of technology on lawyer well-being?

In addition to the recent studies on the nature of human motivation to post on social media, it is also worth noting that there has been a growing movement to recognize the importance of lawyer well-being. One aspect of well-being, especially since the pandemic began, is the negative impact of technology on lawyers . . . Yes, negative. While the positive aspects are many and likely rescued the legal profession from potential ruin during the pandemic's lockdown, the downside of technology should not be denied.[86]

Technology's impact on attorney wellness is hardly a new phenomenon; while virtual lawyering during the pandemic certainly accelerated reliance on technology, it's a concern that has been around for a while. For example, a 2013 LexisNexis whitepaper explored the "paradox of technology" and noted that information overload may "actually be hindering [lawyers'] decision making capabilities, causing stress and leading to suboptimal outcomes."[87] The article observed:

> The emergence of mobile technologies [has] meant that practitioners now attempt to triage and respond to the daily mountain of emails, industry news, judgments and legislative updates from the time they get out of bed (or even while still in it) until they turn out the light last thing at night. They are "always on" and even then, key information is often missed in the deluge of data.[88]

---

[85] *Id.*

[86] John G. Browning and Jan L. Jacobowitz, *Wellness Unplugged: Technology's Impact on Attorney Mental Health*, THE BENCHER, (AMERICAN INNS OF COURT, MARCH/APRIL 2022).

[87] Frank McKenna, *In the Zone: Is Technology Helping or Hindering Lawyers' Decision Making?*, LEXISNEXIS (Sept. 2013).

[88] *Id.*

Another pre-pandemic warning about legal technology's potential for negative impact on lawyers' well-being was sounded by Dan Reed, UnitedLex founder and CEO. In his October 2019 op-ed penned for World Mental Health Day, Reed cautioned that lawyers' "risk of feeling under strain and developing mental health issues has not necessarily been reduced in a meaningful way by the evolution of legal technology, just changed." Reed suggested that "we should be encouraging those entering the profession to switch off and digitally detox as well as work hard."

An issue that looms over lawyers' increased reliance on technology and its impact on wellness is technology's overall impact on society—more specifically the use of social media—on mental health and well-being. Over a decade ago in 2010, studies established a firm relationship between depression and text messaging and emailing.[89] Most studies have documented the harmful effects of social media use among adolescents, noting such findings as social media intensifying feelings of anxiety, depression, or loneliness.[90]

In fact, tech companies own internal surveys indicate the existence of detrimental effects. For example, in 2021, Facebook researchers determined that 1 in 8 of its users reported engaging in compulsive use of social media that impacted their sleep patterns, work, parenting, or relationships. Moreover, Instagram found itself making headlines when it decided to suppress "likes" in its attempt to minimize comparisons and the wounded feelings associated when popularity is attached to shared content.

Of course, social media's general impact on lawyers' well-being, and the specific use of lawyers' social media during the anxiety and "doomscrolling" of the pandemic, have yet to be fully explored.[91] Yet, we have noticed an uptick in lawyers' and judges' use of social media in an ethically problematic manner since the pandemic began. It may be that feelings of isolation and uncertainty that lawyers experienced while working remotely have increased

---

[89] Mohamed Farouk Allam, *Excessive Internet Use and Depression: Cause-Effect Bias?*, 43:5 PSYCHOPATHOLOGY 334 (2010)

[90] *See, e.g.*, Zia Sherrell, *What to Know about Social Media and Mental Health*, MEDIA NEWS TODAY (Sept. 15, 2021), https://www.medicalnews today.com/articles/social-media-and-mental-health; Fazida Karim, Azeezat A Oyewande, Lamis F Abdalla, Reem Chaudhry Ehsanullah, and Safeera Khan, *Social Media Use and Its Connection to Mental Health: A Systematic Review*, CUREUS (Aug. 15, 2020), https://www .ncbi.nlm.nih.gov/pmc/articles/PMC7364393/.

[91] *See, e.g.*, Krista Howard, Merab Gomez, Stephanie Dailey, and Natalie Ceballos, *Social Media, Mental Health, and Lawyers' Well-Being*, 36:6 GPSOLO MAG. (Nov./Dec. 2019).

the need that many feel to comment on current events and controversial issues.

For example, in March 2020, a fifty-six-year-old lawyer was subjected to a viral backlash—including death threats—after tweeting about "tanking the entire economy" to save 2.5 percent of the population and expressing that it was "expensive to maintain" and "not productive." Like other lawyers that we have included in the book, the lawyer ultimately regretted the tweet, reflecting that "had I been a little bit more thoughtful of the situation people were going through, I wouldn't have said it."

Perhaps "a little bit more thoughtful" captures the compelling value of enhanced self-awareness in the midst of a digital world. A critical component of both performance and mental health is self-reflection; meta awareness or thinking about your thinking is explained in Daniel Kahneman's popular 2011 book, *Thinking, Fast and Slow.* Kahneman explores cognitive overload and explains that "[p]eople who are cognitively busy are . . . more likely to make selfish choices, use sexist language, and make superficial judgements in social situations."[92]

So, yes, we are back to lawyers are human, but humans who will benefit from more knowledge both about social media and themselves.

7. What policies may law firms establish to limit firm exposure to liability created by firm lawyers and other firm employees who engage in social media?

The supervisory lawyers in any type of law office have an ethical responsibility to create procedures that assure that junior lawyers and support staff conduct themselves in accordance with the rules of professional conduct.[93] Direct supervision over every individual's use of social media is a virtual impossibility; however, providing guidelines for social media use and training for employees is a cost-efficient approach to minimize exposure and maximize a positive online firm image.

Some law offices have established social media policies, which not only communicate the firm's rules for social media use, but also establish the basis for termination of employment. The policies generally address the following legal ethics areas: maintaining confidentiality of client information, avoiding online interaction that may create an attorney-client relationship, prohibition of crude and derogatory language or posts that are misleading or

---

[92] Daniel Kahneman, THINKING, FAST AND SLOW 20–21 (2011)

[93] MODEL RULES OF PROF'L CONDUCT r. 5.1, 5.2, & 5.3 (Am. Bar Ass'n, 1980).

that contain misrepresentations, respect for the rights of others, restraint in responding to angry messages or negative criticism posted by a client, and overarching adherence to all of the relevant legal ethics rules.[94] The detail to which a policy may instruct an employee with regard to a particular social media network such as Facebook, Twitter, or LinkedIn depends in part on the size and demographics of the membership of a particular law office or legal organization.[95]

Additionally, social media policies should be revisited from time to time as social media constantly evolves and sometimes creates new issues in its wake. Employee training is also important; associates, paralegals, and other staff are more likely to understand, appreciate, and remember the importance of the policy if the organization dedicates time and resources to integrate the policy into the fiber of the organization or law firm's culture.[96]

8. What are some suggestions to assist individual lawyers in avoiding the ethical land mines on social media?

Regardless of whether you are in search of strategies to incorporate into a social media workshop or you are just looking for some personal "self-help" tools to assist you in avoiding the pitfalls of social media, the following methods are often beneficial.

Phone a Friend: The proverbial "phone a friend" lifeline is a good method to employ before you post if you find yourself in an emotional state, whether it be anger resulting from a personal encounter or passion about a current event. Talk about the absurd ruling of the judge or the outrageous behavior of opposing counsel to privately vent your feelings and then consider whether you really want to blog about it.

Write Your Post on a Word Document: Similar to "phone a friend," but more therapeutic and a better reality check for some. Express all of your emotion on a Word document (thereby avoiding the inadvertent tapping of

---

[94] Marisa A. Trasatti & Jhanelle A. Graham, *The Top Ten "Do's" of a Law Firm Social Media Policy*, MARYLAND DEFENSE COUNSEL, INC.: THE DEFENSE LINE (Mar. 2014), http://www.mddefensecounsel.org/newsletter-spring2014/index.html.

[95] Kevin O'Keefe, *NY Times Social Media Policy a Good Model for Law Firms*, REAL LAWYERS HAVE BLOGS (Oct. 18, 2012), http://kevin.lexblog.com/2012/10/18/ny-times-social-media-policy-a-good-model-for-law-firms/.

[96] Greg Hamblin, *Five Steps in Creating a Social Media Policy for Your Law Firm*, FILEVINE (Sept. 3, 2015).

the send or post button). Have a colleague read the document or leave the document and come back to it several hours later and consider whether you want to post it.

Explore the Impact of Cognitive Psychology: Cognitive psychology, with its impact on decision making, has entered the mainstream discussion in the legal profession. Following books such as Daniel Kahneman's best seller, *Thinking, Fast and Slow*, in which he discusses the idea of "thinking about our thinking" or meta-awareness as a vehicle to recognize cognitive minefields,[97] there has been a growing body of literature in the legal profession focused on the benefits of understanding the psychology of decision making.[98]

Jennifer Robbennolt and Jean Sternlight suggest that "[l]awyers who can harness the insights of psychology" will not only be more effective practitioners, but also will be able to "better identify and avoid ethical problems."[99] Their book is quite long and filled with insights and suggestions. One of the overarching messages is to maintain awareness of the ethics rules and engage in prior planning for stressful situations. One method they suggest that may be especially beneficial for lawyers engaged in social media is to employ an implementation intention.

Robbennolt and Sternlight explain:

[a]n implementation intention is an if-then statement that specifies how we will behave in a future situation. In particular the statement anticipates and articulates a specific triggering circumstance or

---

[97] DANIEL KAHNEMAN, THINKING, FAST AND SLOW 417 (2011).

[98] *See generally* JENNIFER K. ROBBENNOLT & JEAN R. STERNLIGHT, PSYCHOLOGY FOR LAWYERS: UNDERSTANDING THE HUMAN FACTORS IN NEGOTIATION, LITIGATION, AND DECISION MAKING (A.B.A. 2012); *see also* Alan M. Lerner, *Using Our Brains: What Cognitive Science and Social Psychology Teach Us about Teaching Law Students to Make Ethical, Professionally Responsible, Choices*, 23 Q.L.R. 643 (2004); PAUL BREST & LINDA HAMILTON KRIEGER, PROBLEM SOLVING, DECISION MAKING, AND PROFESSIONAL JUDGMENT—A GUIDE FOR LAWYERS AND POLICY MAKERS 481 (2010); Kristen Holmquist, *Challenging Carnegie*, 61 J. LEGAL EDUC. 353 (2012); Andrew Perlman, *A Behavioral Theory of Legal Ethics*, 90 IND. L.J. 1639 (2015); Susan Swaim Daicoff, *Expanding the Lawyer's Toolkit of Skills and Competencies: Synthesizing Leadership, Professionalism, Emotional Intelligence, Conflict Resolution, and Comprehensive Law*, 52 SANTA CLARA L. REV. 795 (2012).

[99] *Id.* at 1.

feeling followed by a detailed statement of what we will do on that occasion. . . . [W]e might say, when I feel myself under pressure to make a concession, I will tell Joe that I need to make a phone call and take a five-minute break. When the trigger occurs the response is automatic. Specifying the trigger as well as the specifics of the behavioral response in this way has been shown to be effective in furthering the desired goal-directed behavior.[100]

Perhaps the creation of the Word document discussed above or just a ten-minute walk away from available social media technology would have spared some of the lawyers from the ethical mishaps that were described at the beginning of the chapter.

Mindfulness Meditation

From relative obscurity in our country, mindfulness has burst into the popular consciousness over the past several years and the legal community has taken notice. There is mindfulness in law legal organizations, mindfulness CLE seminars, and mindfulness courses being taught in a number of law schools.[101] While some lawyers develop mindfulness practices to reduce stress and enhance overall well-being, mindfulness is also being taught to enhance effective decision making.[102]

---

[100] *Id.* at 111-12.

[101] Scott Rogers & Jan L. Jacobowitz, *Mindful Ethics and the Cultivation of Concentration,* 15 Nev. L.J. 730 (2015).

[102] Jan L. Jacobowitz, *The Benefits of Mindfulness for Litigators,* 39 A.B.A. Litig. J. 2 (2013); *see also* Jan L. Jacobowitz, *Mindfulness and Professionalism, in* The Essential Qualities of a Professional Lawyer (Am. Bar Ass'n Ctr. Prof'l Responsibility ed., 2013) [hereinafter Jacobowitz Mindfulness chapter]; Jan L. Jacobowitz & Scott Rogers, *Mindful Ethics—A Pedagogical and Practical Approach to Teaching Legal Ethics, Developing Professional Identity, and Encouraging Civility,* 4 St. Mary's J. on Legal Malpractice & Ethics 198 (2014); Scott Rogers & Jan L. Jacobowitz, Mindfulness and Professional Responsibility: A Guide Book for Integrating Mindfulness into the Law School Curriculum 13 (2012); Nicole E. Ruedy & Maurice E. Schweitzer, *In the Moment: The Effect of Mindfulness on Ethical Decision Making,* 95 J. Bus. Ethics 73 (2010) [all sources in this note hereinafter Mindfulness Sources].

So, what is mindfulness? It is often defined as nonjudgmental awareness in the moment.[103] In other words, an awareness of your thoughts, feelings, and bodily sensations as an event is occurring—a meta-awareness. This type of awareness may be developed through a meditation practice, which in turn may take many different forms.[104]

While a full discussion of mindfulness meditation is beyond the scope of this book, it is worth noting that the meta-awareness that one may develop often allows for the critical understanding that between every action and reaction there is a pause.[105] However subtle that pause may be, it nonetheless exists and allows for an individual to consider a thoughtful response rather than one that is born of emotional reactivity.[106] For a lawyer who may be caught in a spiral of reactivity, the pause may make all the difference in the selection of the pathway that avoids the ethical land mines in the cyberspace terrain.[107]

---

[103] Leonard L. Riskin, *The Place of Mindfulness, in* HEALING AND THE LAW IN SHIFTING THE FIELD OF LAW & JUSTICE 99–120, CENTER FOR LAW AND RENEWAL (Linda Hager, Bonnie Allen & Renee Floyd Meyers, eds. 2007).

[104] Jan L. Jacobowitz, *The Benefits of Mindfulness for Litigators*, 39 A.B.A. LITIG. J. 2 (2013); Peter H. Huang, *Meta-Mindfulness: A New Hope*, RICHMOND J.L. & PUB. INTEREST (forthcoming), http://ssrn.com /abstract=2782930.

[105] Jacobowitz Mindfulness chapter, *supra* note 42; Leonard L. Riskin, *Awareness and Ethics in Dispute Resolution and Law: Why Mindfulness Tends to Foster Ethical Behavior*, 50 S. TEX. L. REV. 493, 478 (2009).

[106] *Id; See also* JON KABAT-ZINN, MINDFULNESS FOR BEGINNERS 1 (2012); *see also* MARK WILLIAMS & DANNY PENMAN, MINDFULNESS: AN EIGHT-WEEK PLAN FOR FINDING PEACE IN A FRANTIC WORLD 35 (2011).

[107] *See* Mindfulness Sources, *supra* note 42.

CHAPTER 13

Are We Our Digital Brother's Keeper? Exposure for the Social Media Activity of Third Parties

As we have seen, being active on social media platforms is rife with ethical pitfalls as well as potential disciplinary and employment consequences for lawyers and judges. But what about when the posts or tweets in question are made by someone else? Can a lawyer or judge get in trouble over what a third party does on social media? Are we becoming our "brother's keeper" at least in a digital sense?

Liability for the Online Comments of Third Parties

Generally speaking, the Anglo-American legal tradition has been sparing when it comes to imposing civil liability on a party for the conduct of another actor beyond that party's control, or right to control. Obviously, there are situations arising out of a contractual (indemnity) or employment relationship (witness the doctrine of *respondeat superior*) in which such responsibility is well recognized. For the most part, though, imposing civil liability for the wrongs of another is disfavored. But when it comes to conduct on social media, however, cracks have begun to appear in this edifice. In several recent cases in the United States and Australia, parties have been held accountable for the social media postings of third parties.

In December 2019, the North Carolina Court of Appeals considered a criminal contempt case, *In the Matter of Eldridge*.[1] On November 29, 2018, Davin Eldridge—a "citizen journalist" who published a Facebook page called "Trappalachia," went to the Macon County Courthouse.[2] Despite posted signs banning the use of cell phones, cameras, or any other recording devices, Eldridge proceeded to live-stream a criminal court hearing until he was caught. At a show cause hearing on why he shouldn't be held in contempt, Eldridge was found guilty, given a suspended jail sentence of 30 days, and placed on probation with several conditions. One of the conditions was to write a 3,000-word essay about respect for the court system and (following approval by the court) to post it on "all social media or internet accounts that defendant owns or controls . . . without negative comment or other criticism by the defendant *or others*."[3]

The court of appeals upheld the trial judge's order, but one justice dissented in part over the court-imposed obligation to monitor and delete the negative comments that might be made by third parties. Justice Brook felt that obligating the defendant to engage in "censoring the viewpoints of others expressed in response to speech compelled by the court raised serious First Amendment concerns."[4] As he put it, "it holds Defendant responsible for what is essentially the behavior of others; and while there is some truth to the adage that we are only as good as the company we keep, the relevant community in this context is incredibly diffuse, extending through cyberspace."[5] Yet despite the "deeply troubling constitutional problems with this condition of probation" raised by Justice Brook, on March 12, 2021, the Supreme Court of North Carolina affirmed the lower court.[6]

North Carolina is not a lone outlier. In December 2019, Houston's First Court of Appeals upheld a similar court order requiring a party to delete the comments of others on a Facebook post. In *Thang Bui and Bach Hac Nguyen v. Maya Dangelas*, an online defamation case brought under the Texas Citizens Participation Act, a

---

[1] In the Matter of Eldridge, 268 N.C. App. 491, 836 S.E.2d 859 (2019).

[2] *Id.*

[3] *Id.* (emphasis added).

[4] *Id.*

[5] *Id.*

[6] Order per curiam in 2021-NCSC-10, No. 478A19, In the Matter of Davin Eldridge (S. Ct. N.C. Mar. 11, 2021).

Harris County trial court ordered Bui and Nguyen to delete threatening comments by third parties on Facebook.[7] Bui and Nguyen's Facebook posts had been found to be defamatory (allegedly accusing Dangelas of being a Viet Cong operative who funneled communist money into the United States), and comments made by third parties in response to the posts made the plaintiff fear for her physical safety.[8]

Bui and Nguyen maintained that their own posts were not threatening and argued that they should not be compelled to police and delete the comments of others made in response to their posts. The First Court of Appeals rejected that argument, finding that Facebook made such deletion possible by an account holder and pointing to the absence of any "legal authority regarding how the First Amendment protects against deletion of someone else's threatening posts made in reply to one's own post."[9] On May 8, 2020, the Supreme Court of Texas denied Bui and Nguyen's petition for review, allowing the troubling ruling to stand.[10]

Should individuals be considered their "brother's digital keeper"? May someone be compelled to censor anyone in cyberspace who might comment on her Facebook post or tweet? If a sympathetic relative, friend, or business associate posts a comment that disparages or even threatens a party's adversary, can that party be held responsible? Under the reasoning of the *Eldridge* and *Bui* courts, new legal duties might be imposed, including duties to monitor and delete the comments of others. This very notion of imposing a duty to oversee the First Amendment–protected speech of third parties is concerning, indeed.

Lawyers' and Judges' Responsibility for the Social Media Conduct of Others

While the concept of bearing some measure of blame or responsibility for the social media conduct of others may seem jarring to the average person, it's actually not a particularly foreign concept for lawyers and judges. After all, ABA Model Rule of Professional

---

[7] Thang Bui and Bach Hac Nguyen v. Maya Dangelas, No. 01-18-00790-CV (Tex. App.—Houston [1st Dist.] 2019).

[8] *Id.*

[9] *Id.*

[10] The Supreme Court of Texas, Order Denying Petition for Review (May 8, 2020).

Conduct 5.3 provides that lawyers with direct supervisory authority over nonlawyers must make "reasonable efforts to ensure that the person's conduct is compatible with the professional obligations of the lawyer," and partners must make reasonable efforts to ensure that the firm has policies and procedures in place to assure the same.[11] Rule 5.3(c) mandates that a lawyer shall be responsible for conduct of a nonlawyer employee that would be a violation of the Rules of Conduct if engaged in by a lawyer, if the lawyer orders or ratifies the conduct involved, or if the supervising lawyer or the partner knows of conduct at the time when its consequences can be avoided or mitigated but fails to take reasonable remedial action.[12] For judges, the operative rules in such situations include Canon 1.2 of the ABA Model Code of Judicial Conduct. This Canon states that "A judge shall act at all times in a manner that promotes public confidence in the independence, integrity, and impartiality of the judiciary, and shall avoid impropriety and the appearance of impropriety."[13] In addition, Canon 2.12(A) of this Code stipulates that "A judge shall require court staff, court officials, and others subject to the judge's direction and control to act in a manner consistent with the judge's obligations under this Code."[14]

For lawyers, unfortunately, there has been no shortage of reminders that they are their "digital brother's keeper" when it comes to nonlawyer staff. For example, as discussed earlier, in early May 2020, lawyers at Dallas-based Thompson & Knight learned that the firm's document services manager, Kevin Bain, had made disturbing comments on Facebook related to his anger at retail businesses requiring shoppers to wear face masks during the pandemic. Referring to a local grocery store's policy, Bain posted that any business insisting that he wear a mask "will get told to kiss my Corona ass and will lose my business forever."[15] Following a series of threatening comments involving his handgun proficiency, Bain

---

[11] MODEL RULES OF PROF'L CONDUCT r. 5.3(a) and (b) (Am. B. Ass'n 2020).

[12] *Id.* at r. 5.3(c).

[13] MODEL CODE OF JUD. CONDUCT r. 1.2 (Am. B. Ass'n 2020).

[14] *Id.* at r. 2.12(A) (Supervisory Duties).

[15] Aebra Coe, *Thompson & Knight Fires Manager for COVID-19 Mask Post*, LAW360 (May 9, 2020, 6:41 PM), https://www.law360.com /articles/1272075/thompson-knight-fires-manager-for-covid-19 -mask-post.

went on to say, "They have reached the limit. I have more power than they do . . . they just don't know it yet."[16]

Thompson & Knight reacted swiftly to their employee's social media outburst, firing Bain for the "threatening and offensive" post.[17] The firm also released a statement, saying, "This post is a complete violation of the values of our firm, including our commitment to the health and safety of the communities we serve. We have terminated this individual's employment and notified the proper authorities about the post as a precaution."[18]

And if a staff member posting threatening comments online isn't troubling enough for lawyers, how about online conduct by a paralegal who threatens and "outs" witnesses or informants as "snitches," exposing them to intimidation, reprisals, or even death? That was the case with Tawanna Hilliard, a paralegal working at the US Attorney's Office in New Jersey.[19] Although prosecutors did not reveal how they discovered the misconduct[20] or whether their office has since instituted any social media and Internet protocol changes, the episode stands as an example of supervision gone terribly awry.

In August 2019, Hilliard was indicted on witness tampering, obstruction of justice, and conspiracy charges in Brooklyn federal court.[21] The paralegal allegedly used her position and official work computer at the US Attorney's Office to help her son Tyquan, a member of the Bronx 5-9 Brims branch of the notorious Bloods street gang who was serving a 10-year prison sentence for robbery.[22]

According to federal authorities, in 2016, Ms. Hilliard, a nine-year employee, used her work computer to help her son's gang find cooperating witnesses, as well as to obtain the personal information

---

[16] *Id.*

[17] *Id.*

[18] *Id.*

[19] Debra Cassens Weiss, *Former Paralegal at U.S. Attorney's Office Accused of Using Prosecutor Info to Expose Informants*, ABA J. (Aug. 16, 2019, 2:29 PM), https://www.abajournal.com/news/article/former-paralegal-at-us-attorneys-office-is-accused-of-using-prosecutor-info-to-expose-informants.

[20] Infra at 135

[21] *Id.*

[22] *Id.*

of a rival gang member whom she thought was "trying to jam [her] son up."[23]

And in 2018, during the then-pending robbery case against her son, Hilliard allegedly posted a video on YouTube showing a post-arrest statement given by her son's co-defendant about the robbery in order to prove he was "snitching."[24] She allegedly titled the video "NYC Brim Gang Member Snitching Pt. 1," and the video's circulation led to the witness and his family receiving death threats from fellow Bloods gang members.[25]

That video clip had been obtained by the US Attorney's Office as discovery material in Tyquan Hilliard's case.[26] A search of the paralegal's home led to video interviews with the co-defendant and another accomplice being found on Hilliard's computer.[27] IT investigators also recovered text messages from Ms. Hilliard in which she complained that the co-defendant was "giving up murders, victims, shooters, and all" and that her son "has no line of defense because his co-d told everything."[28] Hilliard pleaded not guilty, and was ordered to wear an ankle monitor, stay off social media, and refrain from contact with her son and other gang members.[29]

Judges also have to be wary when it comes to the online behavior of their staff. For example, in June 2020, the Stanislaus County (California) Superior Court was compelled to launch an internal investigation after a political tweet was posted to the court's official Twitter account.[30] The post was a retweet of a tweet originally made by One America News personality Alex Salvi, regarding a news item about a protester being injured during the removal of a Confederate statue in Portsmouth, Virginia.[31] The retweet

---

[23] *Id.*

[24] *Id.*

[25] *Id.*; Antonia Noori Farzan, *A Gang Member's Mother Worked in the U.S. Attorney's Office. Now She's Accused of Outing "Snitches,"* WASH. POST (Aug. 14, 2019), https://www.washingtonpost.com/nation/2019/08/14/tawanna-hilliard-paralegal-snitches-bloods-gang/.

[26] Farzan, *supra* note 40.

[27] *Id.*

[28] *Id.*

[29] *Id.*

[30] Sabra Stafford, *Stanislaus County Court Investigating Political Comments on Official Twitter Account,* CERES COURIER (June 17, 2020, 9:31 AM), https://www.cerescourier.com/news/local/stanislaus-county-court-investigating-political-comments-official-twitter-account/.

[31] *Id.*

attributed to the court's account featured the comment, "Some like their Karma instantly. I'll take mine in November. #Trump2020."[32] The court's account also included a "like" of a retweet by Fox News host Jeanine Pirro as well.[33]

The court reacted quickly by deleting the post and posting an apology, along with a terse statement that the official account had been "compromised."[34] The following day, the court's Twitter account displayed a more detailed tweet, reading "Yesterday's tweet about race and partisan politics was unauthorized and completely contrary to the Court's mission to provide equal access to justice and serve the needs of our community with integrity, quality, and fairness. The Court sincerely apologizes for the post."[35] Later, the court's executive officer provided a statement indicating that an unnamed employee was responsible for the political tweet, and that an internal personnel investigation was ongoing.[36] The statement promised "appropriate action consistent with its personnel rules and applicable laws," and added that as a preventative measure, the court "imposed additional restrictions on access to its social media accounts."[37]

As the risks of the social media conduct of court staff members have become more evident in the past two years, some guidance for judges has emerged. In October 2020, the California Supreme Court Committee on Judicial Ethics Opinions (CJEO) issued its CJEO Oral Advice Summary 2020-037, entitled "Judicial Obligations Relating to Social Media Comments by Appellate Court Staff."[38] In this opinion, the Committee mandates not only vigilance on the part of an appellate justice regarding staff members' online conduct, but action as well when a justice becomes aware of posts or comments that violate judicial canons.[39] The opinion advises a justice to "immediately take steps to remedy the ethical violation, including at a minimum requiring the staff member to take all

---

[32] *Id.*

[33] *Id.*

[34] *Id.*

[35] *Id.*

[36] *Id.*

[37] *Id.*

[38] Cal. Sup. Ct. Comm. on Jud. Ethics Ops., CJEO Oral Advice Summary 2020-037 (2020), https://www.judicialethicsopinions.ca.gov/wp-content /uploads/CJEO-Oral-Advice-Summary-2020-037.pdf.

[39] *Id.* at 2.

reasonable steps to have the post taken down and removed from the public domain."[40]

The opinion begins by taking note of the realities of life and work in the digital age, observing that social media "has taken the place of both the proverbial office water cooler and the town square."[41] Appellate court staff, the Committee explains, are no different from other members of the general public, and it should come as no surprise that their posts will frequently refer to their employment at the court.[42] And while acknowledging that court employees are not prohibited from posting comments about the courts or their employment generally, the Committee reminds justices that, these same employees "are required to keep confidential the decision making process of a court with respect to any pending matter," and that the canons "constrain the content of any such comment."[43]

In particular, the Committee points to California's Canon 3B(9) and 3C(3).[44] Canon 3B(9) provides, in part, that

A judge shall not make any public comment about a pending or impending proceeding in any court, and shall not make any nonpublic comment that might substantially interfere with a fair trial or hearing. The judge shall require similar abstention on the part of staff and court personnel subject to the judge's direction and control.[45]

Canon 3C(3) states that

A judge shall require staff and court personnel under the judge's direction and control to observe appropriate standards of conduct and to refrain from (a) manifesting bias, prejudice, or harassment based upon race, sex, gender, gender identity, gender expression, religion, national origin, ethnicity, disability, age, sexual orientation, marital status, socioeconomic status, or political affiliation, or (b) sexual harassment in the performance of their official duties.[46]

---

[40] *Id.*

[41] *Id.*

[42] *Id.* at 2–3.

[43] *Id.*

[44] *Id.*

[45] CAL. CODE OF JUD. ETHICS Canon 3B(9) (Cal. Sup. Ct. 2020).

[46] CAL. CODE OF JUD. ETHICS Canon 3C(3) (Cal. Sup. Ct. 2020).

The opinion goes on to note that appellate justices face discipline if they fail to exercise such "reasonable control and direction" over their staff—and cites at least one California example.[47] But what action must a justice take? At a minimum, the Committee cautions the justices to "instruct the staff member to take all reasonable steps to delete or to have removed from public view any improper comment that violates the canons and then follow up with the staff member to ensure that they have done so."[48] Practically speaking, however, given the viral nature of the Internet, a controversial post or tweet can live on and be further disseminated thanks to a screenshot being preserved by an original recipient or other third party, and subsequent deletion or other efforts at obscuring the post will consequently be futile. In that event, the opinion states, the justice "may need to instruct the staff member to correct or repudiate the comment on social media, particularly if the comment is demeaning or offensive, or otherwise undermines the dignity of the court."[49]

Conclusion

In our current technology-driven world, we must be increasingly wary not only of our own digital personas, but of those commenting on our posts. The role of being our "digital brother's keeper" is one that is increasingly placed on average citizens, and for lawyers and judges, it is a familiar burden to bear some measure of responsibility for those under our supervision. In the digital age, with the potential for posts to go viral and destroy reputations with blinding speed, this ethical duty for lawyers and judges has assumed new meaning and importance. Not only are we our "digital brother's keeper," but we are also increasingly judged by the digital company we keep. For the religious conservative politician who inadvertently "likes" a tweet by a porn site or for the NFL team owner who mistakenly "likes" a tweet critical of his starting quarterback, such online faux pas can usually be laughed off as embarrassing one-offs. Lawyers and judges, however, need to remain vigilant about

---

[47] CJEO Oral Advice Summary 2020-037, *supra* note 53, at 3 (citing *Pubic Admonishment of Commissioner Mark Kliszewski* (a 2017 judicial disciplinary proceeding in which the commissioner's failure to take corrective action to halt court staff from making inappropriate comments was held to have violated Canons 3B(4) and 3C(3)).

[48] *Id.*

[49] *Id.*

their contacts in cyberspace, and not be lulled into a false sense of security or anonymity. They cannot afford the casual remark exhibited by most social media users. Every "like," every share, and every follow can have meaning and serve as a reflection on a legal professional.

CHAPTER 14

The Once and Future Lawyer: Digital Defender and Client's Keeper?

Legal and political theorist Bernard Harcourt posits the theory that with the advent of social media, humans are forsaking broader freedoms for the sake of small doses of social interaction that give us pleasure. A generation raised on reality TV now yearns to be "Internet famous" as we trade privacy for Facebook likes and shares, retweets, and other illusory connections. We live in what Harcourt calls an "expository society," where privacy is no longer a core value and "all the formerly coercive surveillance technology is now woven into the very fabric of our pleasure and fantasies."[1] We want to expose ourselves and to see others exposed; we want to see and be seen, and to reinvent ourselves online.

For lawyers, however, there are real-world consequences to this shift in societal attitude in which digital intimacy is becoming the new norm. In a world in which 78 percent of the adult population maintains at least one social networking profile, and in which 293,000 status updates are posted on Facebook every minute and roughly a billion tweets are processed every forty-eight hours, people are providing the very ammunition that lawyers will use to impeach their claims or defenses and impugn their credibility. Moreover, as a growing number of state ethics opinions call for attorneys to both be aware of what their clients are posting on social media and also to take an active role in advising what to take

---

[1] BERNARD E. HARCOURT, EXPOSED: DESIRE AND DISOBEDIENCE IN THE DIGITAL AGE (2015).

down (or not post in the first place), it's become more important than ever for lawyers to serve as a kind of digital "client's keeper." And if lawyers are to be competent digital gatekeepers, then they must not only understand today's social media language, but must also embrace the reality of the constantly changing methods of digital communication and the ethical land mines that lie in their wake. With an eye toward the future, we offer some examples of the recent impact of various methods of digital communication and the repercussions of the timing and duration of these social media posts.

Digital Client Commentary

Consider, for example, the potential impact on cases where the lawyer is unaware of such social media postings. In the *Gulliver Schools* case discussed earlier, a party who had settled an employment discrimination case forfeited the entire settlement because a Facebook post revealed that he had breached one of the key terms of the release: keeping the settlement confidential. It's unclear whether his counsel advised him that "confidential" includes "don't blab about this on Facebook," but lawyers practicing in the digital age have to anticipate that their clients' means of communicating now include the bewildering and ever-multiplying variety of social media platforms.

Clients now have even more opportunities to undermine their own cases and as a result lawyers have parallel ethical obligations: to ferret out what helpful social media content from other parties may be out there, and to be aware of and appropriately deal with their own clients' inadvertent digital sabotage. Taking the previously discussed example of rapper 50 Cent's Instagram posts of stacks of cash and boasts of wealth in the midst of his hotly contested bankruptcy proceeding, lawyers should be prepared to inquire and advise about social media posts from the very outset of the attorney-client relationship. Lawyers should also be prepared to provide an explanation or take remedial steps should a client's Facebook faux pas surface during the engagement.

Yes, while justice may be blind, the lawyer who is pursuing it can't afford to be blind as well to what his or her client has posted or to the fact that his or her client may have chosen a very public forum for doing so. Attorneys who ignore their duty of digital competence are risking outcomes like that in *Womack v. Yeoman,* a personal injury case involving a car wreck.[2] The defense counsel researched mentions of the accident and injuries on publicly viewable Facebook and MySpace pages belonging to the plaintiff and members of her family; the results yielded photos, postings, and other information damaging to Womack's case.

Womack's lawyer accused the defense of engaging in "unethical and illegal conduct by 'hacking into' the accounts" and violating "Plaintiff's and her families (sic) right to privacy."[3] Plaintiff's counsel filed a motion for sanctions. The court granted sanctions, but against Womack's counsel—after noting that the defense attorney had merely accessed information posted on "a public medium, and available to anyone with access to the Internet." Womack's lawyer's sanctions motion was frivolous, the court held after admonishing him of the realities of twenty-first-century practice, observing: "Social media and Internet searches are becoming a normal step in an attorney's matter of public information."[4]

The Digital Confessional

Thus, the future will only bring a heightened need for lawyers to play the role of digital "client's keeper." Yet even when clients are not posting on social media during pending legal proceedings, all too frequently individuals are providing the compelling evidence against them in the form of social media—despite an acute awareness of their wrongdoing. The compulsion to share everything has resulted in social media serving as a kind of "digital confessional," in which people confess, flaunt, or otherwise share their transgressions with an online audience of potentially millions (the Fifth Amendment right against self-incrimination flying out the window). Even as they control their own narrative, they destroy any chance of innocence as they fulfill Harcourt's predictions of an expository society.

Consider the case of twenty-two-year-old Matthew Cordle, who on September 3, 2013, uploaded a 3½ minute long video to YouTube that chillingly stated: "My name is Matthew Cordle, and on June 22, 2013, I hit and killed Vincent Canzani. This video will

---

[2] Womack v. Yeoman, 83 Va. Cir. 401 at *1 (Va. Cir. Ct. 2011).

[3] *Id.* at *1.

[4] *Id.* at *2.

act as my confession."[5] Cordle had driven drunk that day in June and following the accident was found to have a 0.19 blood alcohol level. Within days of posting the haunting confession, Cordle's video had gone viral with over 1.3 million people viewing it. Ultimately, Cordle pled guilty to aggravated vehicular homicide and received a 6½ year sentence. While Cordle insists that he wanted to send a message about the dangers of drunk driving, cynical commenters speculated that the YouTube confession was a ploy done with the hope of a lenient sentence.[6]

Good intentions were presumably absent when sixteen-year-old Maxwell Morton and thirty-three-year-old Derek Medina posted their respective crimes. In 2015, Morton shot his friend and class-mate Ryan Mangan in the face, and then posed with the corpse for a grisly selfie on Snapchat. He sent it to another friend (including the caption "Ryan was not the last one") who captured a screen-shot before it disappeared and showed it to his mother, who alerted authorities.[7] The Pennsylvania teenager ultimately confessed and was charged as an adult with first-degree murder.

---

[5] Christine Ng, *YouTube Drunk Driving Confession Sentenced to 6.5 Years Despite Daughter's Plea for Maximum*, ABC NEWS (Oct. 23, 2013), http://abcnews.go.com/US/youtube-drunk-driving-confessor-sentenced-65-years-daughters/story?id=20656028.

[6] Another tragic and recent case raises not only legal questions, but also sociological questions about sharing and digital confessionals. In May 2016, a nineteen-year-old French woman live-streamed her own suicide on Periscope. She engaged with viewers in a series of videos, promising a live stream of "importance" and stating "[t]he video I am doing right now is not made to create buzz, but rather to make peo-ple react, to open minds, and that's it." Having previously sent a text message to a friend in which she accuses an ex-boyfriend of rape and abuse, the young woman then proceeded to jump in front of oncom-ing train at a suburban Paris railway station. The suicide happened live before around 1,000 viewers. Although the footage is no longer available on Periscope, excerpts from the videos—with the suicide blacked out—have been widely circulated on YouTube. See Lilia Blaise & Benoit Morenne, *Suicide on Periscope Prompts French Offi-cials to Open Inquiry,* N.Y. TIMES (May 11, 2016), http://www.nytimes.com/2016/05/12/world/europe/periscope-suicide-france.html.

[7] *Pa Cops Say Teen Killed Another Teen, Posed with Body for a Sel-fie,* FOX NEWS (Feb. 7, 2015), http://www.foxnews.com/us/2015/02/07/pa-cops-say-teen-killed-another-teen-posed-with-body-for-selfie.html.

Similarly, in Florida, Derek Medina killed his wife Jennifer Alonso at their house, took a photo of the dead body, and uploaded it to Facebook with the status update "I'm going to prison or death sentence for killing my wife."[8] True to his Facebook prediction, in 2016 Medina was convicted of second-degree murder and sentenced to life in prison.

Digital Live-Streaming: Real-Time Wrongdoing

With new technologies, individuals have found new ways to share their wrongdoing. Live-streaming apps like Periscope, Meerkat, Twitch, and Facebook Live host untold hours of footage that provide a glimpse into users' personal lives for sharing with potentially huge audiences. On Periscope alone, people are viewing the equivalent of forty years' worth of live videos every single day. Snapchat introduced its "Live Stories" feature in 2015, and it already has 100 million daily active users with 8 billion video views each day. Facebook CEO Mark Zuckerberg has touted the visceral appeal of live-streaming apps. "Because it's live, there is no way it can be curated. And because of that it frees people up to be themselves. It's live; it can't possibly be perfectly planned out ahead of time," Zuckerberg says.[9]

Using Periscope, people have live-streamed their own drunk driving offenses, committing driving while intoxicated (DWI) crimes while a live audience—including law enforcement—watched and commented. In March 2016, thirty-three-year-old Ahmed Almalki of Long Island, New York, live-streamed his drunk driving. State police received multiple calls about Almalki's driving from Periscope viewers and logged in themselves. Identifying his surroundings from the live-streaming, they caught up with him and charged him with felony DWI.[10]

---

[8] Crimesider Staff, *Convicted Fla. "Facebook Killer" Sentenced to Life in Prison*, CBS NEWS: CRIMESIDER (Feb. 8, 2016, 8:03 AM), http://cbsnews .com/news/florida-facebook-killer-derek-medina-who-killed-his-wife -posted-photo-sentenced/.

[9] Rossalyn Warren, *When Rape Is Broadcast Live on the Internet*, BUZZFEED (Apr. 20, 2016, 10:40 AM), https://www.buzzfeed.com /rossalynwarren/when-rape-is-broadcast-live-on-the-internet.

[10] Patrick Lohmann, *Long Island Man Live-streamed His Drunk Driving, State Police Say*, SYRACUSE.COM (Mar. 14, 2016, 1:21 PM),

Similarly, in October 2015, twenty-four-year-old Whitney Beall of Lakeland, Florida, live-streamed her drunk driving on Periscope. Footage shows Beall driving through neighborhoods, hitting a curb, and flattening a tire on her Toyota Corolla, describing herself as "drunk beyond belief" and slurringly expressing her hope to avoid a DWI because it would hurt her chances of getting into a neurology department.[11]

A number of texts were sent to Beall's cellphone from people pleading with her to stop driving before she killed herself or someone else, and commenters posted throughout the live video, asking "how is she still driving?" Others alerted the police, who finally stopped her. While Periscope videos stay on the site for only twenty-four hours, a detective was able to capture and preserve the video as evidence. In February 2016, Beall pleaded no contest and received a standard sentence for a first-time offender; however, she also received an enhanced sentence (150 hours of community service and ten days of weekend work release) for "publicly flaunting her disregard for the safety of the community."

And in another episode that could have ended tragically, two Sacramento men Periscoped their armed hunt for another individual suspected of sleeping with one man's girlfriend.[12] Twenty-eight-year-old Damon Batson and twenty-five-year-old Carlos Gonzalez live-streamed their search, at one point responding to a viewer who asked if their gun was real by firing it. Other viewers egged the men on, "liking" the broadcast with heart emojis and comments. Police found out about the episode, viewed a recording, and subsequently arrested Batson and Gonzalez after identifying them from the video.

In one of the most disturbing cases yet, twenty-nine-year-old Raymond Gates and eighteen-year-old Marina Lonina were charged in the alleged rape of an intoxicated seventeen-year-old girl in February 2016 in Columbus, Ohio. What makes this case so unusual is that Lonina—a supposed friend of the victim—was in

---

http://www.syracuse.com/crime/index.ssf/2016/03/ny_state_police _long_island_man_live_streamed_his_drunk_driving.html.

[11] John Chambliss, *Lakeland Woman Who Went Live While DUI Sentenced*, THE LEDGER (Feb. 17, 2016, 7:58 PM), http://www.theledger.com /news/20160215/lakeland-woman-who-went-live-while-dui-sentenced.

[12] *Police: Men Hunted Victim in Midtown Sacramento on Periscope*, CBS SACRAMENTO (Aug. 28, 2015, 4:15 PM), http://sacramento.cbslocal .com/2015/08/28/police-men-hunted-victim-in-midtown-sacramento -on-periscope/.

the room at the time and live-streamed the alleged assault through Periscope to an online audience.[13] Lonina is depicted pulling on the victim's leg, and the girl can be seen struggling, screaming "no, it hurts so much," and "please stop" while Lonina giggles and laughs, according to prosecutors.

Police were notified of the alleged attack not by Periscope's monitoring team, but by a friend of Lonina's watching the livestream from another state. Both Gates and Lonina have been charged with kidnapping, rape, sexual battery, and pandering sexual matter involving a minor. Lonina's lawyer claims that his client made "substantial" efforts to thwart the assault and maintains that Lonina was "swept up by the gravity of the situation" and "was filming in order to preserve" evidence, "not to embarrass or to shame or to titillate anybody."

Understandably, Franklin County prosecutor Ron O'Brien has a very different viewpoint. Noting, "I have never seen a case such as this where you would actually live-stream a sexual assault." O'Brien believes that Lonina was enthralled by positive feedback online and that she "got caught up in the likes."[14]

Certainly, the live-streaming of such criminal activity raises a whole host of legal issues, including what obligations companies like Periscope might have regarding the monitoring and removal of such content. (Periscope, it should be noted, has rules banning pornographic and overtly sexual content, as well as explicitly graphic content or media intended to incite violent, illegal, or dangerous activities.) Could a viewer of one of the live-streams be called as a witness in court to testify to what he or she observed? If someone "likes" such activity, or live-streams criminal behavior in public, would he or she be subject to prosecution as an accessory?

Criminal activity is not the only conduct that people are choosing to share with an online audience. The urge to share every moment with an encouraging, if unseen, group of people can lead to civil implications, too. For example, the plaintiff in a recent auto accident case filed in April in Spalding County, Georgia, blamed not only the teenaged driver who collided with him, but Snapchat as

---

[13] Mike McPhate, *Teenager Is Accused of Live-Streaming a Friend's Rape on Periscope*, N.Y. TIMES (Apr. 18, 2016), http://www.nytimes.com/2016/04/19/us/periscope-rape-case-columbus-ohio-video-livestreaming.html.

[14] *Id.*

well.[15] In particular, the lawsuit holds Snapchat's "speed filter," a feature that tracks the speed of its users, responsible for the crash. The speed filter uses a phone's GPS system to calculate the speed at which a user is moving at the time the "snap" (the photo or short video that can be edited to include filters, effects, text, captions, and even drawings) is created. The speed-reading is then added to the photo or video from the editing screen with a simple swipe to the left.

According to the complaint filed by the plaintiffs Wentworth and Karen Maynard, on September 10, 2015, eighteen-year-old Christal McGee was using Snapchat while driving her Mercedes. It alleges that she was motivated to drive fast—in this instance 113 mph—due to the Snapchat speed filter, and that Snapchat incentivized users of different features of its app by giving "trophies," making it "more of a game." The suit maintains that one of the three passengers in McGee's vehicle urged her to slow down but that she refused, arguing that she was "just trying to get the car to 100 miles per hour to post it on Snapchat." McGee supposedly said, "I'm about to post it" when the impact with Maynard's car occurred.

This case was in the early stages when the first edition of this book was published, and we commented that there may be some merit to the claim of Ms. McGee's social media obsession. The teen took a selfie of herself on a stretcher after the accident and posted it to Snapchat with the caption, "Lucky to Be Alive." McGee had allegedly been driving home from work at a local restaurant with three co-workers. Plaintiffs' counsel justified suing Snapchat on product liability grounds, while Snapchat pointed out that the filter includes a warning that it should not be used while driving. The case has continued winding its way through the courts and a recent March 2022 Georgia Supreme Court opinion indicates that the issue will continue to be litigated. The Georgia Supreme Court reversed the Court of Appeals on the issue of potential product liability for Snapchat and remanded the case for further hearings, noting that a manufacturer has a duty to design products to avoid reasonably foreseeable harm and that the claim against Snapchat was properly pled and should be allowed to be fully litigated.

---

[15] Debra Cassens Weiss, *Suit Blames Snapchat's Speed Tracker for High-Speed Auto Accident*, ABA J. (Apr. 28, 2016, 11:38 AM), http://www.abajournal.com/news/article/suit_blames_snapchats _speed_tracker_for_high_speed_auto_accident.

Digital Communication Trends

Users of social media are sharing everything, including the most heinous of criminal acts, driven to sacrifice privacy by an overwhelming need for attention and reinforcement in the form of "likes," shares, and retweets. The risk of self-incrimination and civil liability, it would seem, takes a back seat to the fleeting, transient illusion of digital intimacy. As lawyers, we may be called upon to exploit it or defend against it, but first we have to be aware of this trend. And of course, it's not just about knowing how clients are sharing information, but also cognizance of what they are sharing, for lawyers to be able to provide effective representation.

As mentioned earlier, even data from activity fitness trackers like Fitbit can be evidence in civil or criminal cases. A growing body of law is emerging on whether hashtags can be trademarked. And given the prevalence of emojis, perhaps it's only inevitable that these "smiling face," "winkie face," and other symbols that convey emotional nuance to online statements are starting to be viewed in a different light—for the evidentiary value that they might have in all types of cases. Ninety-two percent of all people online use emojis now, with one-third of them doing so on a daily basis. On a site like Instagram, for example, nearly half the posts contain emojis.[16] Emojis can add context, clarify meaning, or even completely transform a sentence by turning what initially appeared to be a serious statement into a joke simply by adding a winking or smiling face indicating sarcasm or joking. That may make lawyers ☺ or ☹ of course.

For example, in the high-profile criminal trial of "Silk Road" online black-market bazaar operator Ross Ulbricht, US District Court Judge Katherine Forrest ordered that the jury be allowed to read the online communications that were at issue (as opposed to having the text read to them), so that the jury could comprehend the emojis as "aspects of the written form that cannot be reliably or adequately conveyed orally."[17] Emojis have already figured into

---

[16] Clive Thompson, *The Emoji Is the Birth of a New Type of Language*, WIRED (Apr. 19, 2016, 5:27 AM), http://www.wired.com/2016/04/the-science-of-emoji.

[17] Debra Cassens Weiss, *Emoticons Matter, Judge Rules in Silk Road Trial*, ABA J. (Jan. 28, 2015, 5:45 AM), http://www.abajournal.com/news/article/emoticons_matter_judge_rules_in_silk_road_trial/; *see also* John G. Browning & Gwendolyn Seale, *More Than Words: The Evidentiary Value of Emoji*, 57 NO.10 DRI FOR DEF. 34 (2015).

criminal cases all over the country, and are also playing a greater role in civil cases involving such issues as breach of contract, libel, employment discrimination, and trade secrets.[18] In one case involving whether an actual agreement and binding contract had been formed, a skeptical judge took note of the casual nature of the communications between the parties and the use of the "smiley face" emoji in the initial communication from one side's president before concluding that no contract had been formed.[19]

Lawyers are in the business of communicating, and because of that we cannot ignore how our clients are choosing to communicate and share information. Since that range of communication has expanded to include everything from texts with emojis to Instagram photos and Vine videos, to Facebook and Snapchat posts to tweets to live-streaming on Periscope, lawyers have an ethical duty to know the benefits and risks associated with such platforms and other technologies. As we have seen, ethical concerns associated with social media permeate virtually every aspect of the attorney-client relationship, from the initial client interview all the way to selection of a jury and ultimately a trial. And much like the advances in technology that relegated the scrivener to the pages of history, the ubiquitous use of social media and the proliferation of new platforms represent just one more step in the inexorable march of innovation.

Social media in all its forms, with both the excitement and the trepidation it brings, is here to stay. Our profession will always be faced with the challenges posed by emerging technologies; the current debate over whether lawyerly functions will be replaced by artificial intelligence is just one example. Because social networking sites and social media content will continue to impact substantive areas of law as well as the legal system itself for the foreseeable future, now more than ever lawyers must appreciate where the ethical boundary lines are drawn and must seek help navigating this uncertain landscape.

---

[18] *Id.*

[19] Parcel Mgmt. Auditing & Consulting, Inc. v. Dooney & Bourke, Inc., No. 3:13-CV-00665 JAM, 2015 WL 796851 (D. Conn. 2015).

Final Thoughts

....

We are living in an incredible time of innovation and change. Indeed, just as most of us learned in history classes about how the industrial revolution dramatically altered the lives of those who witnessed it, so too is the digital age permanently changing the landscape of our daily lives. The speed at which the entire world may simultaneously receive the news of the day is impressive; the speed with which human beings may communicate with one another and share vast amounts of information is mind altering— especially for those of us who were raised before the invention of the computer and the cell phone.

Technology has permeated our culture—thermostats can adjust to our sleeping habits, Fitbits track our physical activity, digital pacemakers can run our hearts, cars can drive themselves, smartphones can deposit checks—the list goes on and on. In the midst of all this change sits the legal profession. A profession that is traditional in nature and that thrives on established rules and regulations. So, it is no wonder that lawyers were challenged by the digital age before the pandemic and thrust immediately into the challenges of surviving on technology during the pandemic: challenged to keep pace; cautioned to avoid the ethical land mines that lie in wait for the ill-informed lawyer.

We have moved from a profession that employed scriveners for efficiency to one in which the digital options available to maximize productivity are overwhelming to many. Social media, ubiquitous in our culture, has become a significant aspect of the practice of law. Both technology and social media have created havoc in the legal profession.

Yet, despite how disconcerting change may be, it brings with it opportunity and the promise of the future. Thus, during change, the legal profession has no choice but to continue to embrace innovation and move forward with society. This book is an effort to facilitate forward motion for the lawyers who are leading the charge.

Thank you for traveling with us on the social media–legal ethics highway!

Table of Cases

....

Index

....